CHAPTER 55

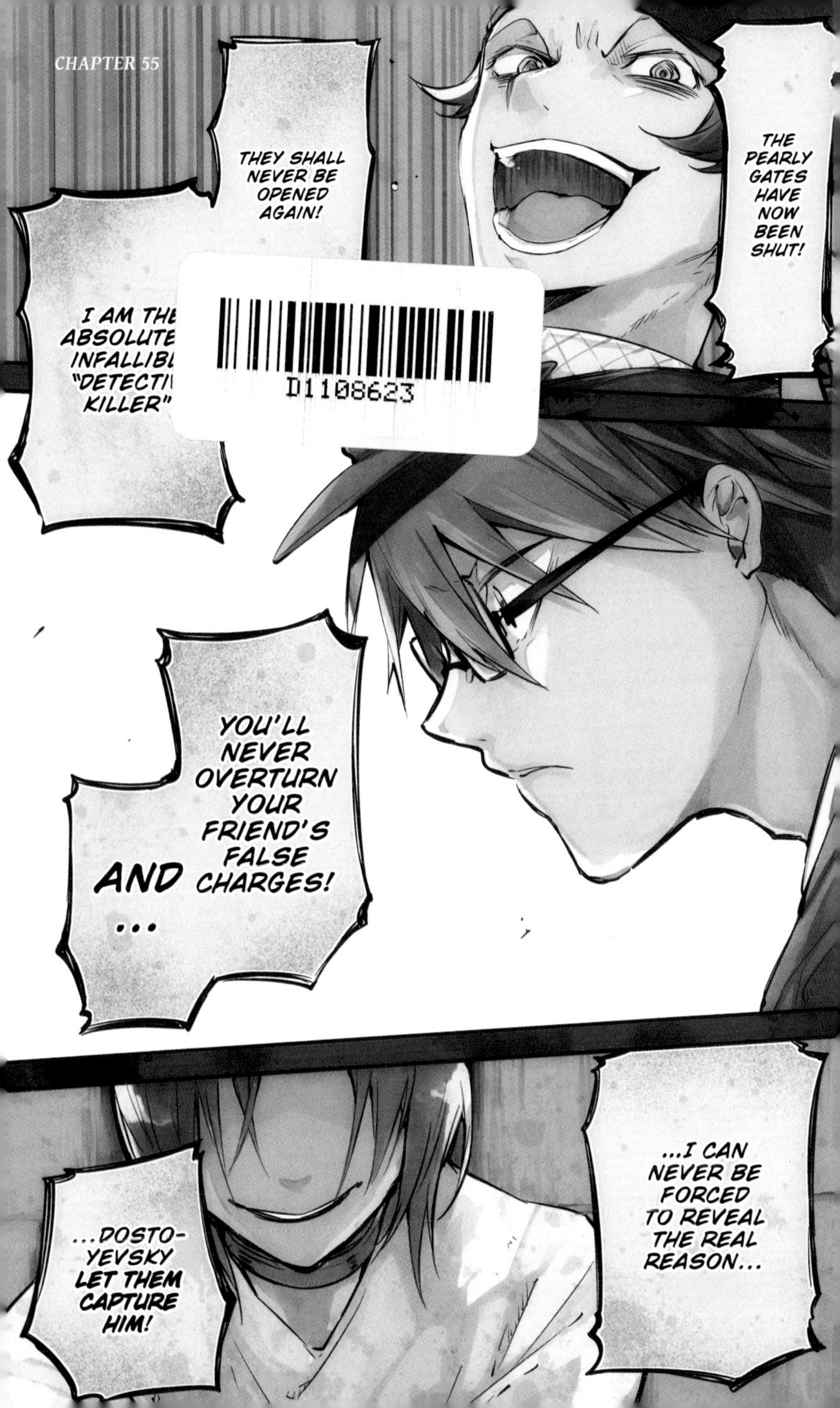
THE PEARLY GATES HAVE NOW BEEN SHUT!
THEY SHALL NEVER BE OPENED AGAIN!
I AM THE ABSOLUTE INFALLIBL "DETECTI KILLER"
YOU'LL NEVER OVERTURN YOUR FRIEND'S FALSE CHARGES!
AND ...
...I CAN NEVER BE FORCED TO REVEAL THE REAL REASON...
...DOSTO-YEVSKY LET THEM CAPTURE HIM!

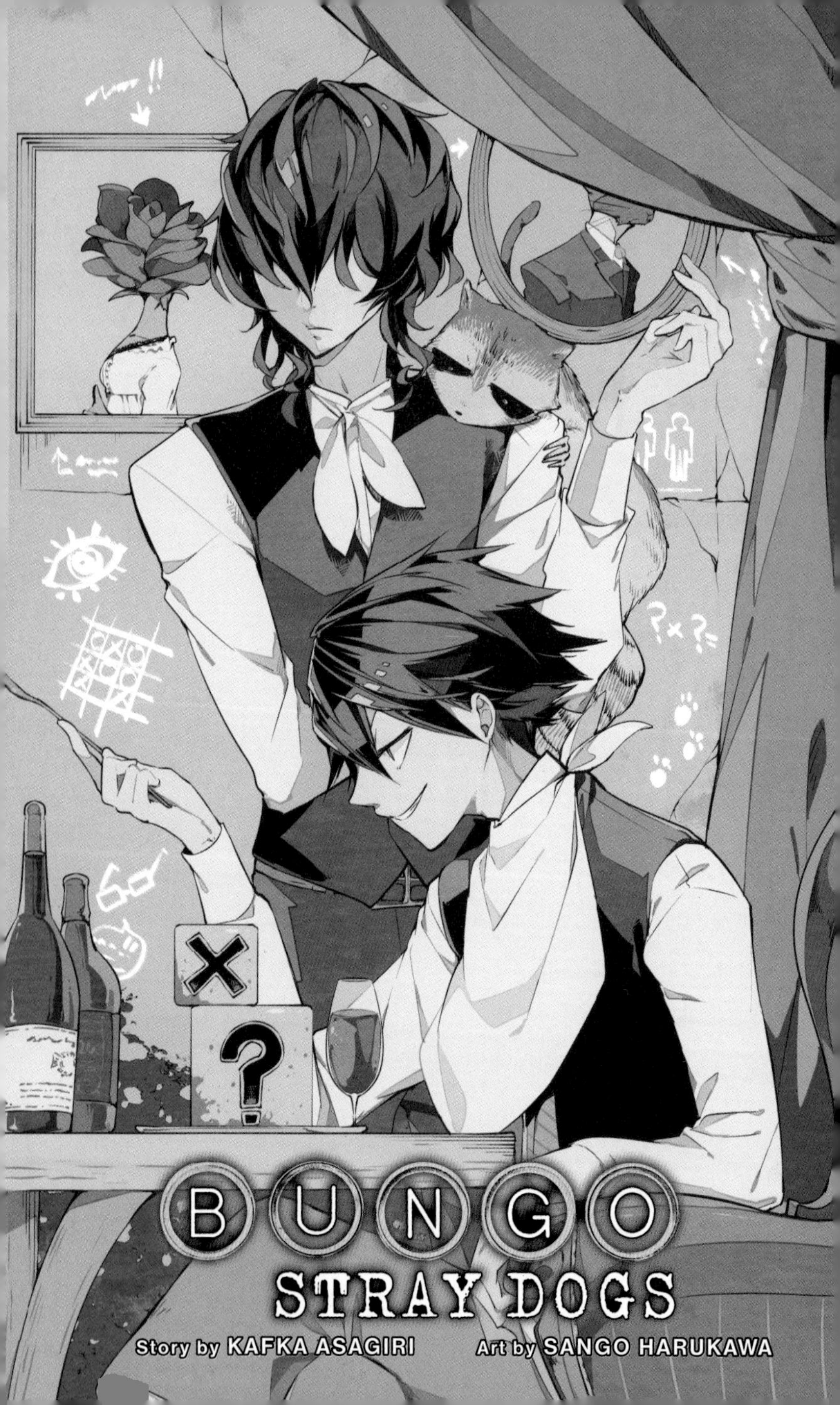
BUNGO
STRAY DOGS
Story by KAFKA ASAGIRI
Art by SANGO HARUKAWA

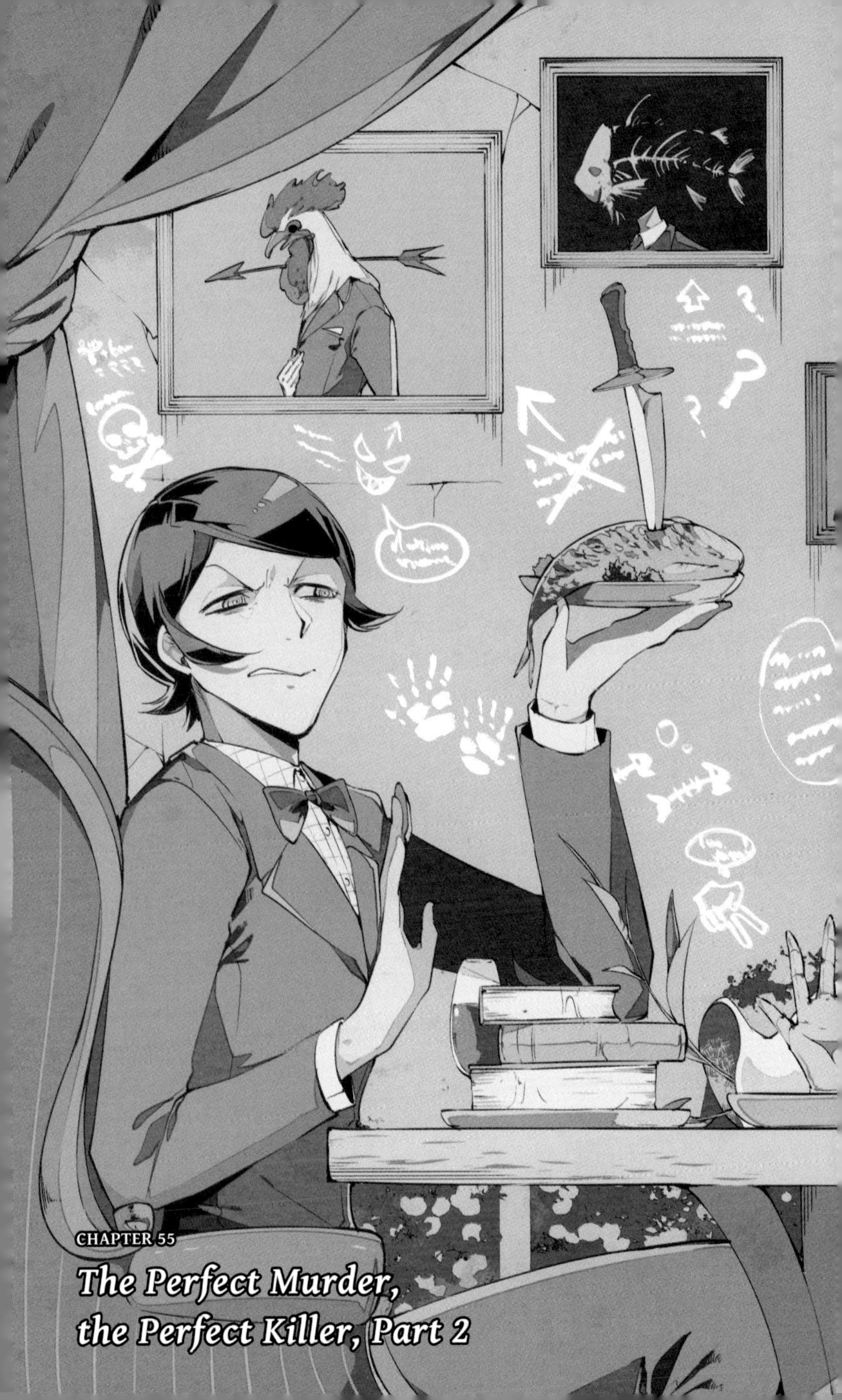

CHAPTER 55

The Perfect Murder, the Perfect Killer, Part 2

TABLE of CONTENTS

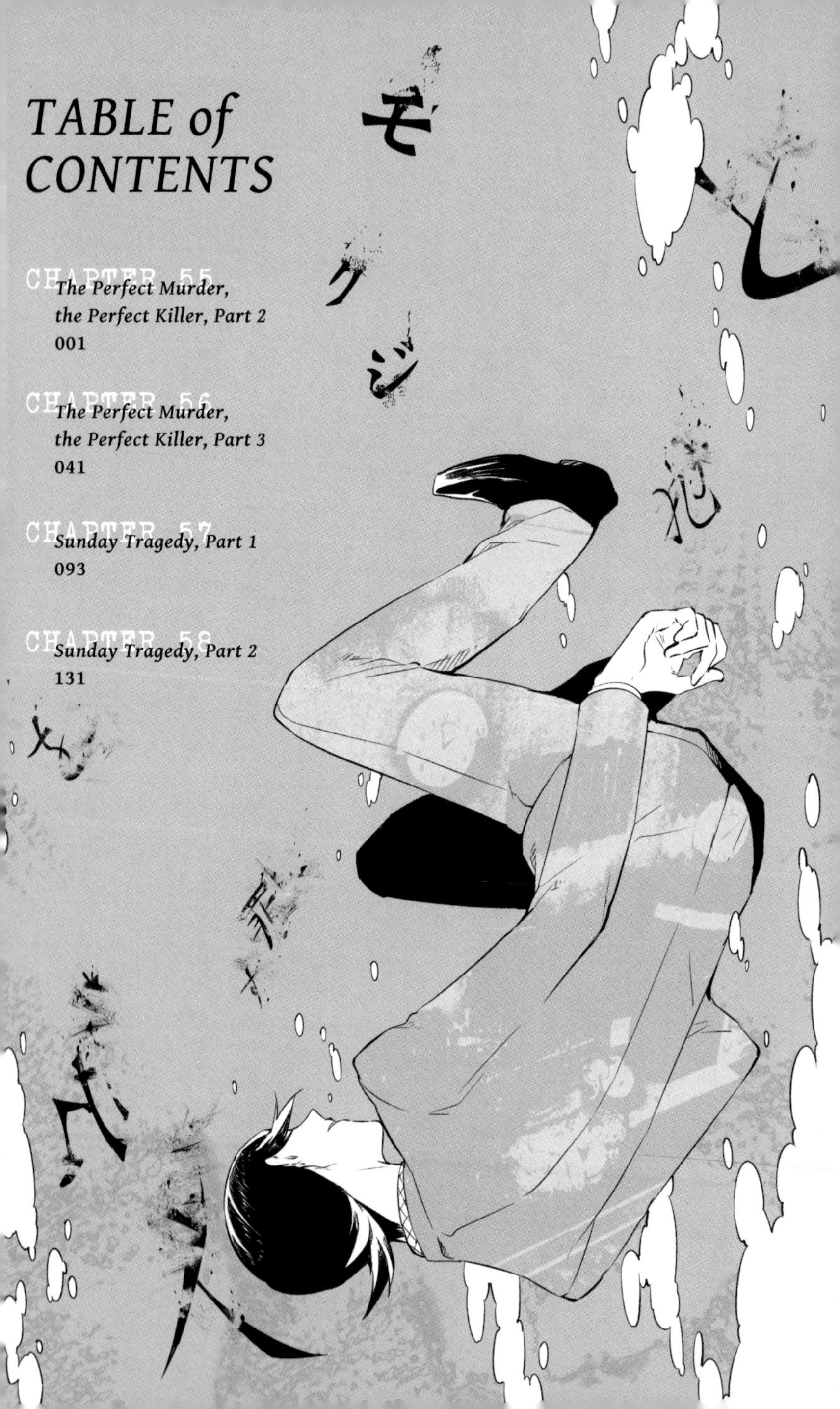

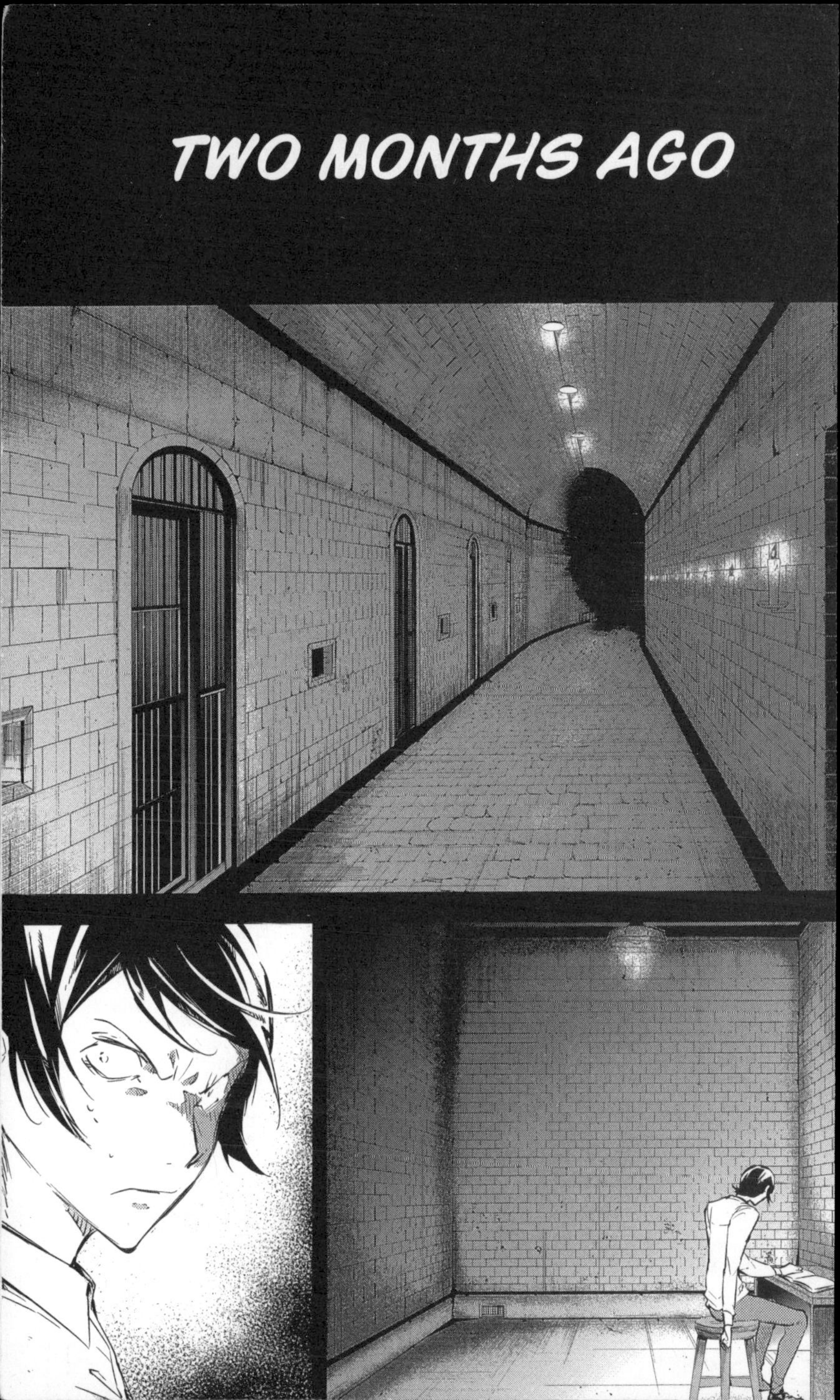
TWO MONTHS AGO

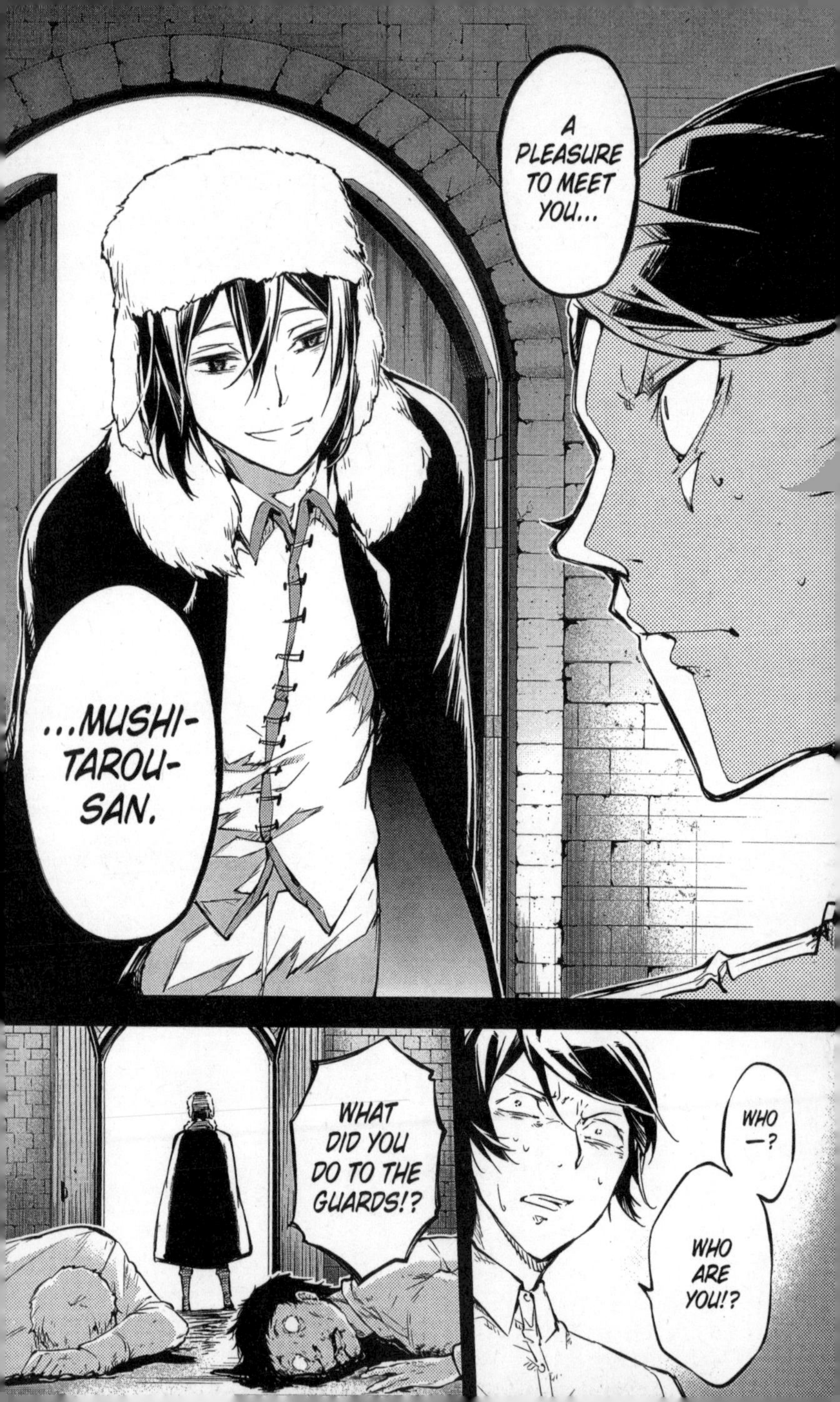
A PLEASURE TO MEET YOU...
...MUSHI-TAROU-SAN.
WHO —?
WHO ARE YOU!?
WHAT DID YOU DO TO THE GUARDS!?

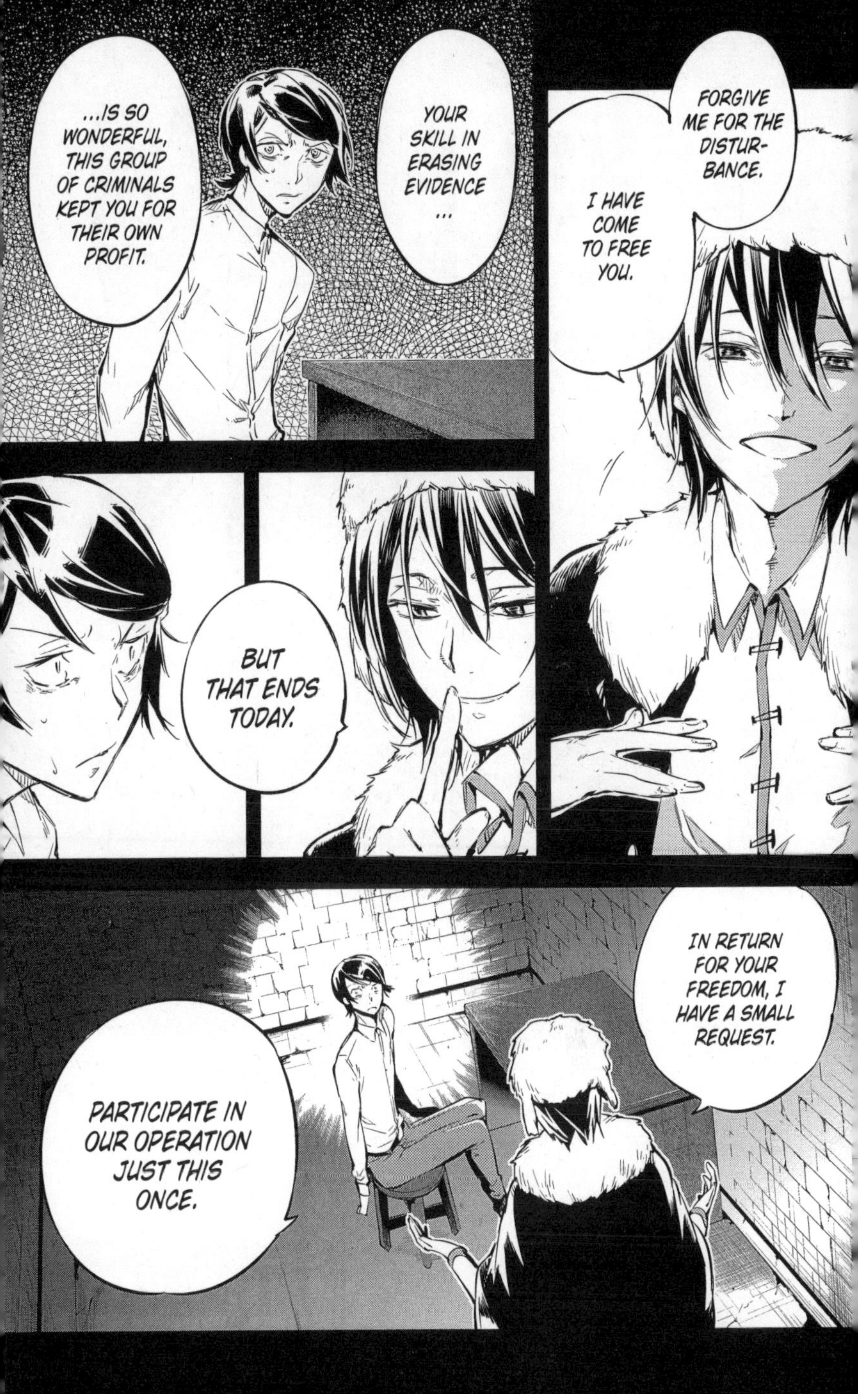
FORGIVE ME FOR THE DISTUR-BANCE.
I HAVE COME TO FREE YOU.
YOUR SKILL IN ERASING EVIDENCE ...
...IS SO WONDERFUL, THIS GROUP OF CRIMINALS KEPT YOU FOR THEIR OWN PROFIT.
BUT THAT ENDS TODAY.
IN RETURN FOR YOUR FREEDOM, I HAVE A SMALL REQUEST.
PARTICIPATE IN OUR OPERATION JUST THIS ONCE.

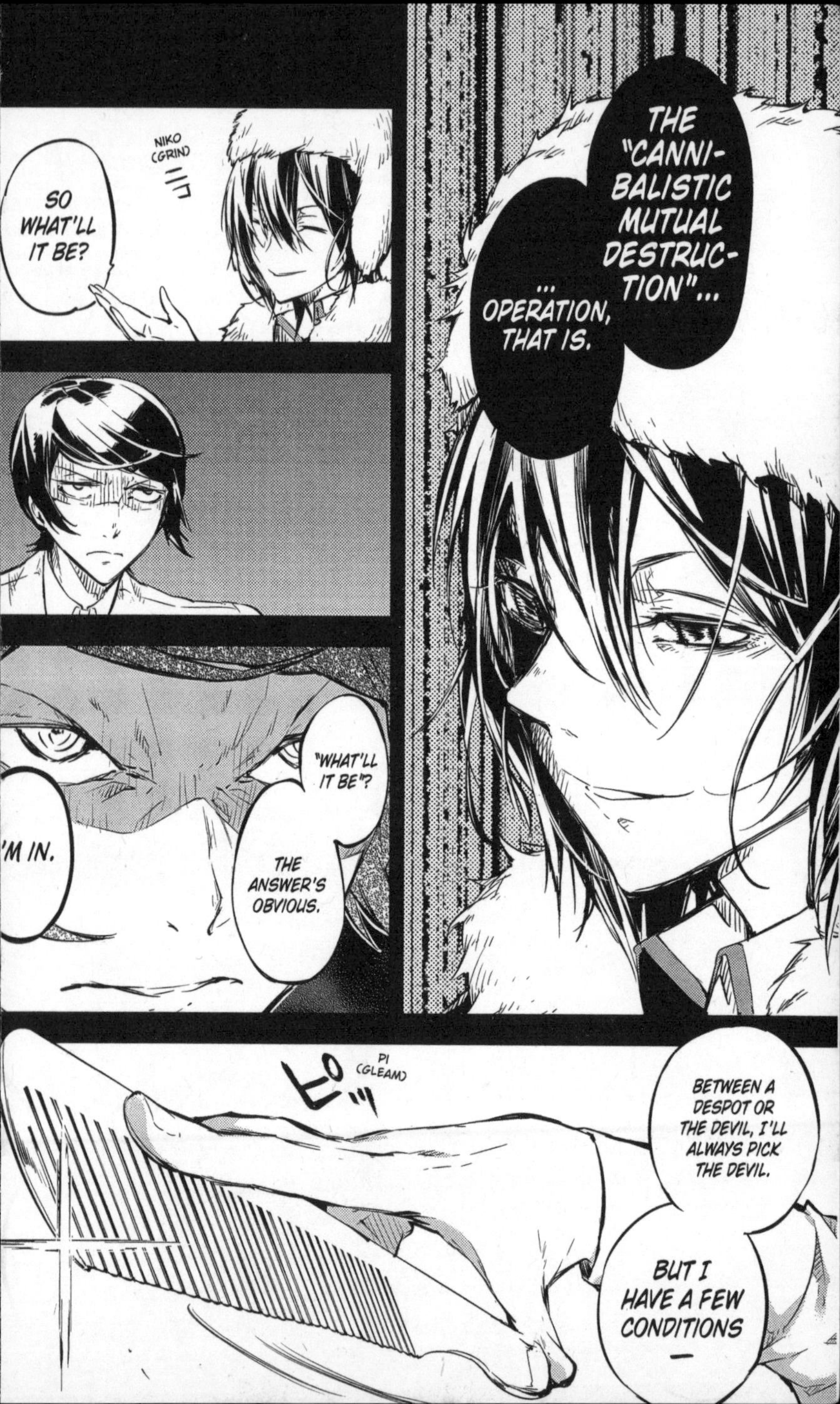
THE "CANNIBALISTIC MUTUAL DESTRUCTION"...
...OPERATION, THAT IS.
NIKO (GRIN)
SO WHAT'LL IT BE?
"WHAT'LL IT BE"?
THE ANSWER'S OBVIOUS.
'M IN.
PI (GLEAM)
BETWEEN A DESPOT OR THE DEVIL, I'LL ALWAYS PICK THE DEVIL.
BUT I HAVE A FEW CONDITIONS —

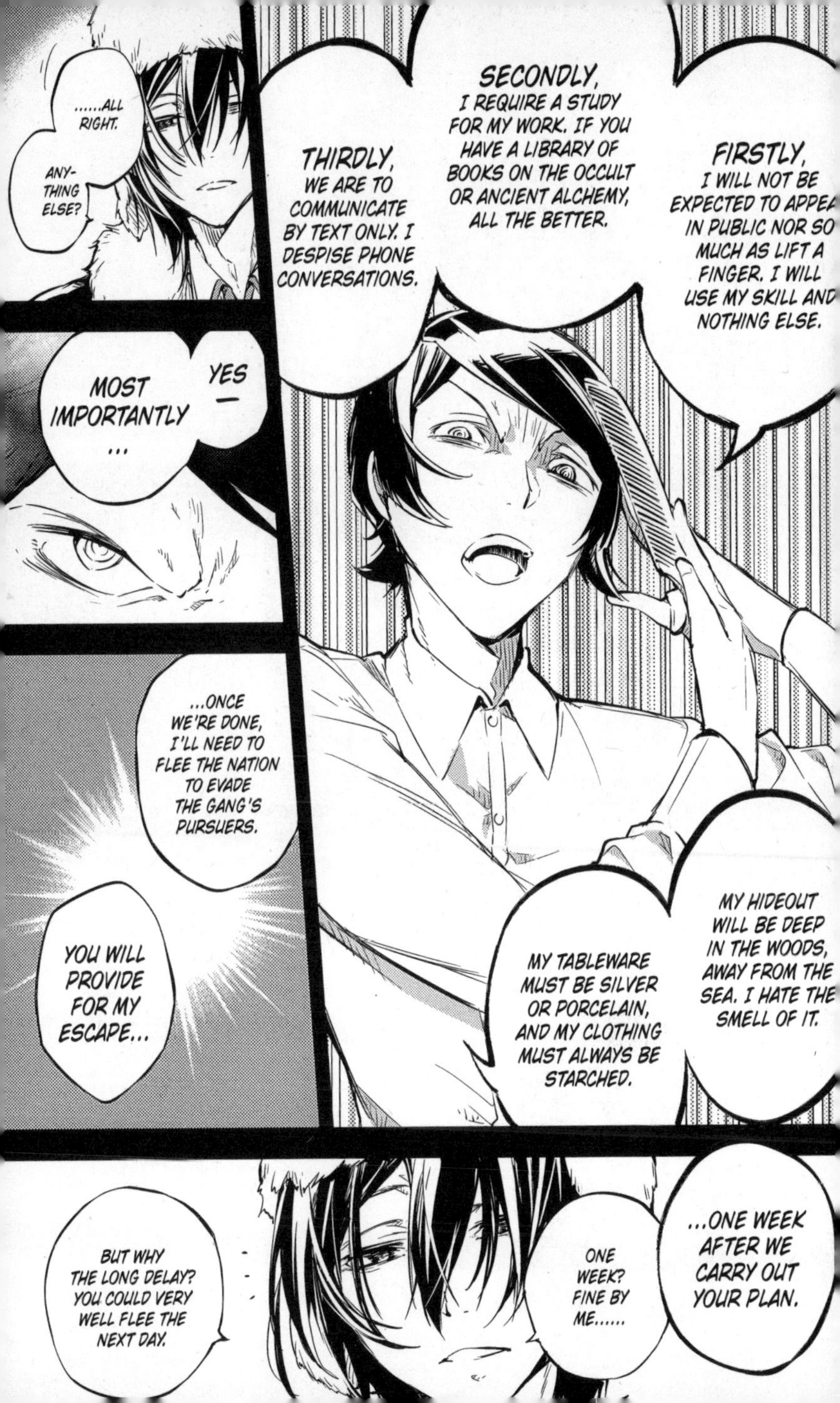
FIRSTLY, I WILL NOT BE EXPECTED TO APPEA IN PUBLIC NOR SO MUCH AS LIFT A FINGER. I WILL USE MY SKILL AND NOTHING ELSE.
SECONDLY, I REQUIRE A STUDY FOR MY WORK. IF YOU HAVE A LIBRARY OF BOOKS ON THE OCCULT OR ANCIENT ALCHEMY, ALL THE BETTER.
THIRDLY, WE ARE TO COMMUNICATE BY TEXT ONLY. I DESPISE PHONE CONVERSATIONS.
MY HIDEOUT WILL BE DEEP IN THE WOODS, AWAY FROM THE SEA. I HATE THE SMELL OF IT.
MY TABLEWARE MUST BE SILVER OR PORCELAIN, AND MY CLOTHING MUST ALWAYS BE STARCHED.
......ALL RIGHT.
ANY-THING ELSE?
YES —
MOST IMPORTANTLY ...
...ONCE WE'RE DONE, I'LL NEED TO FLEE THE NATION TO EVADE THE GANG'S PURSUERS.
YOU WILL PROVIDE FOR MY ESCAPE...
...ONE WEEK AFTER WE CARRY OUT YOUR PLAN.
ONE WEEK? FINE BY ME......
BUT WHY THE LONG DELAY? YOU COULD VERY WELL FLEE THE NEXT DAY.

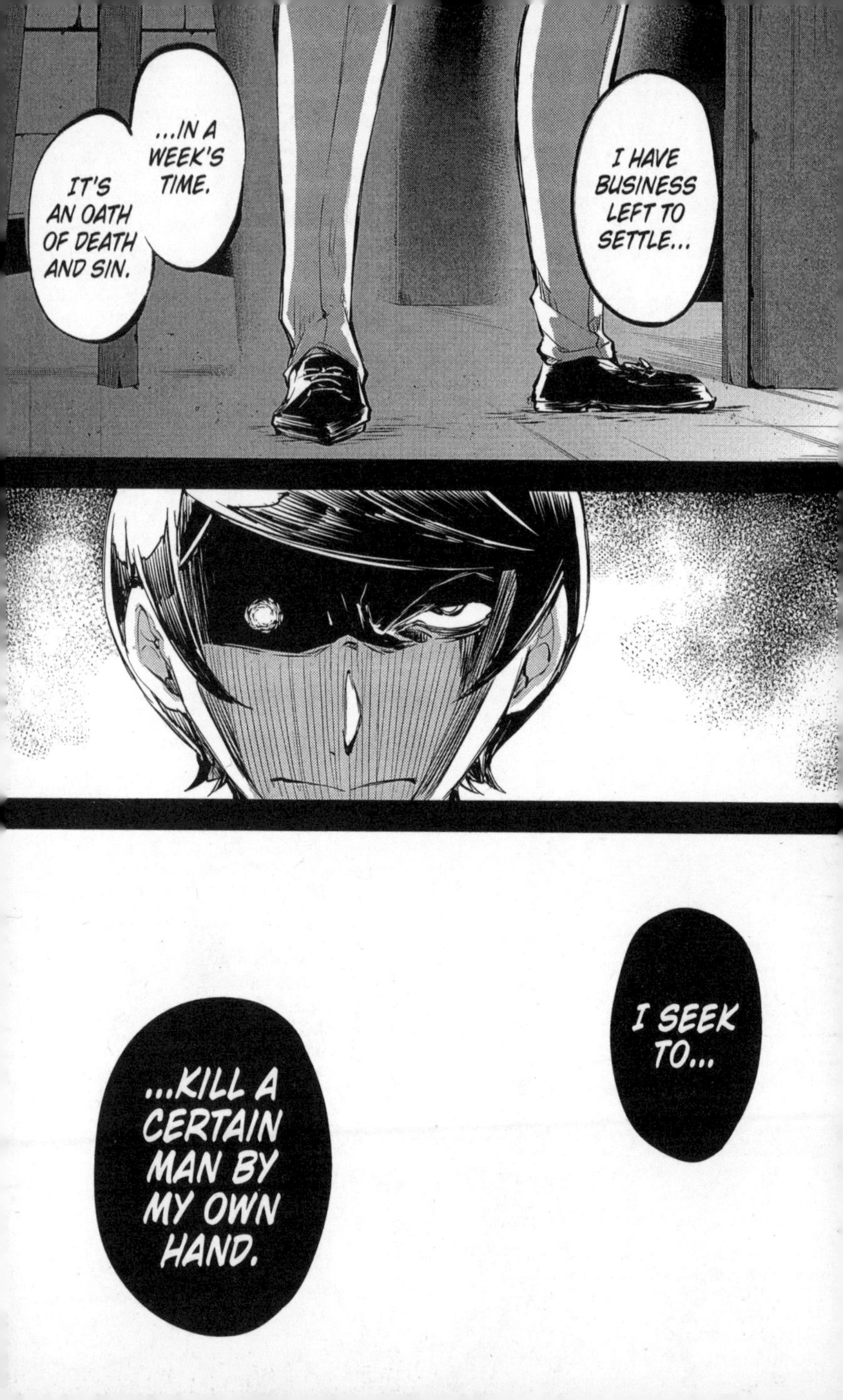
I HAVE BUSINESS LEFT TO SETTLE...
...IN A WEEK'S TIME.
IT'S AN OATH OF DEATH AND SIN.
I SEEK TO...
...KILL A CERTAIN MAN BY MY OWN HAND.

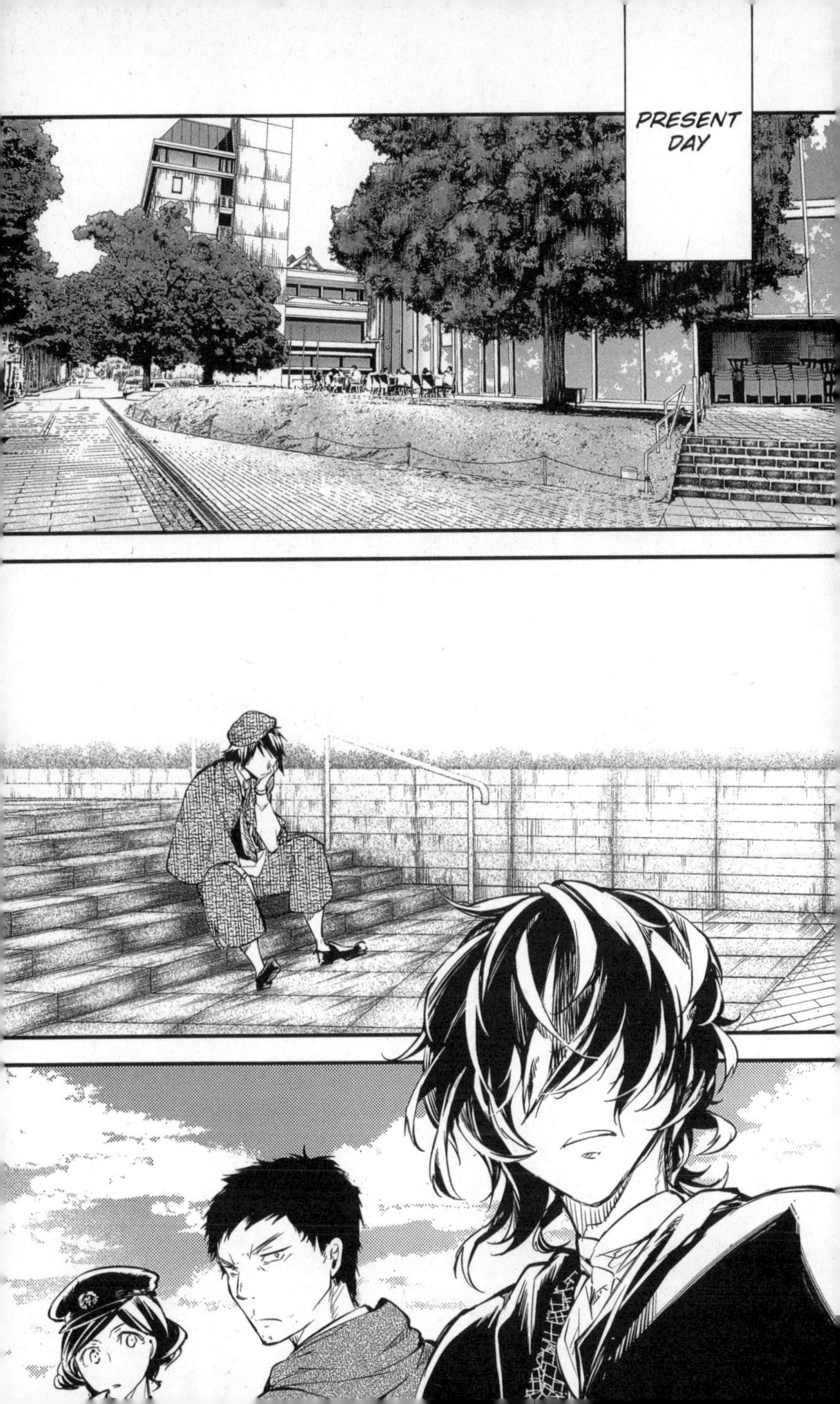
PRESENT DAY

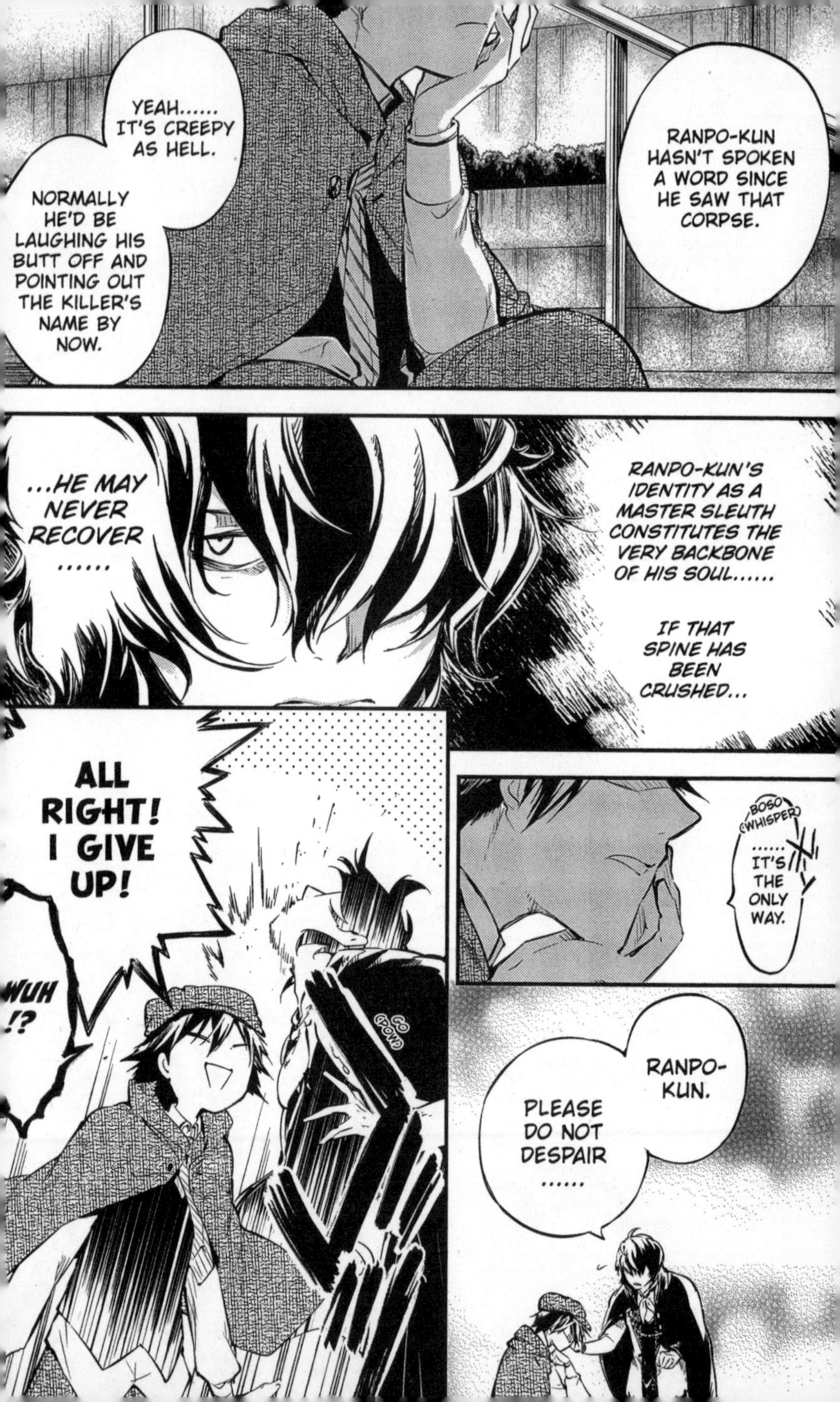
RANPO-KUN HASN'T SPOKEN A WORD SINCE HE SAW THAT CORPSE.
YEAH...... IT'S CREEPY AS HELL.
NORMALLY HE'D BE LAUGHING HIS BUTT OFF AND POINTING OUT THE KILLER'S NAME BY NOW.
RANPO-KUN'S IDENTITY AS A MASTER SLEUTH CONSTITUTES THE VERY BACKBONE OF HIS SOUL......
IF THAT SPINE HAS BEEN CRUSHED...
...HE MAY NEVER RECOVER ......
BOSO (WHISPER)
......IT'S THE ONLY WAY.
RANPO-KUN.
PLEASE DO NOT DESPAIR ......
ALL RIGHT! I GIVE UP!
GO (POW)
WUH !?

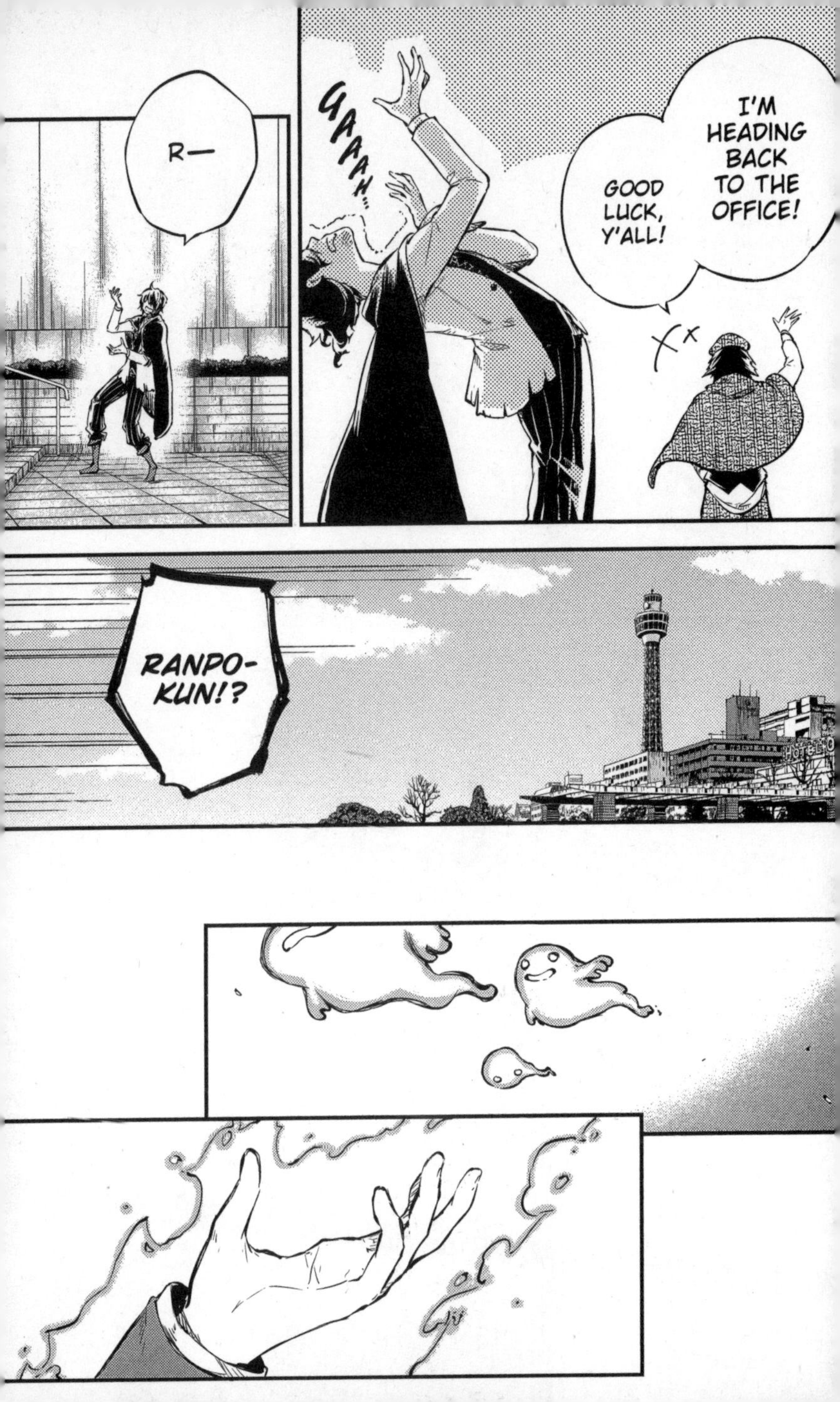
I'M HEADING BACK TO THE OFFICE!
GOOD LUCK, Y'ALL!
UAAAAH...
R—
RANPO-KUN!?

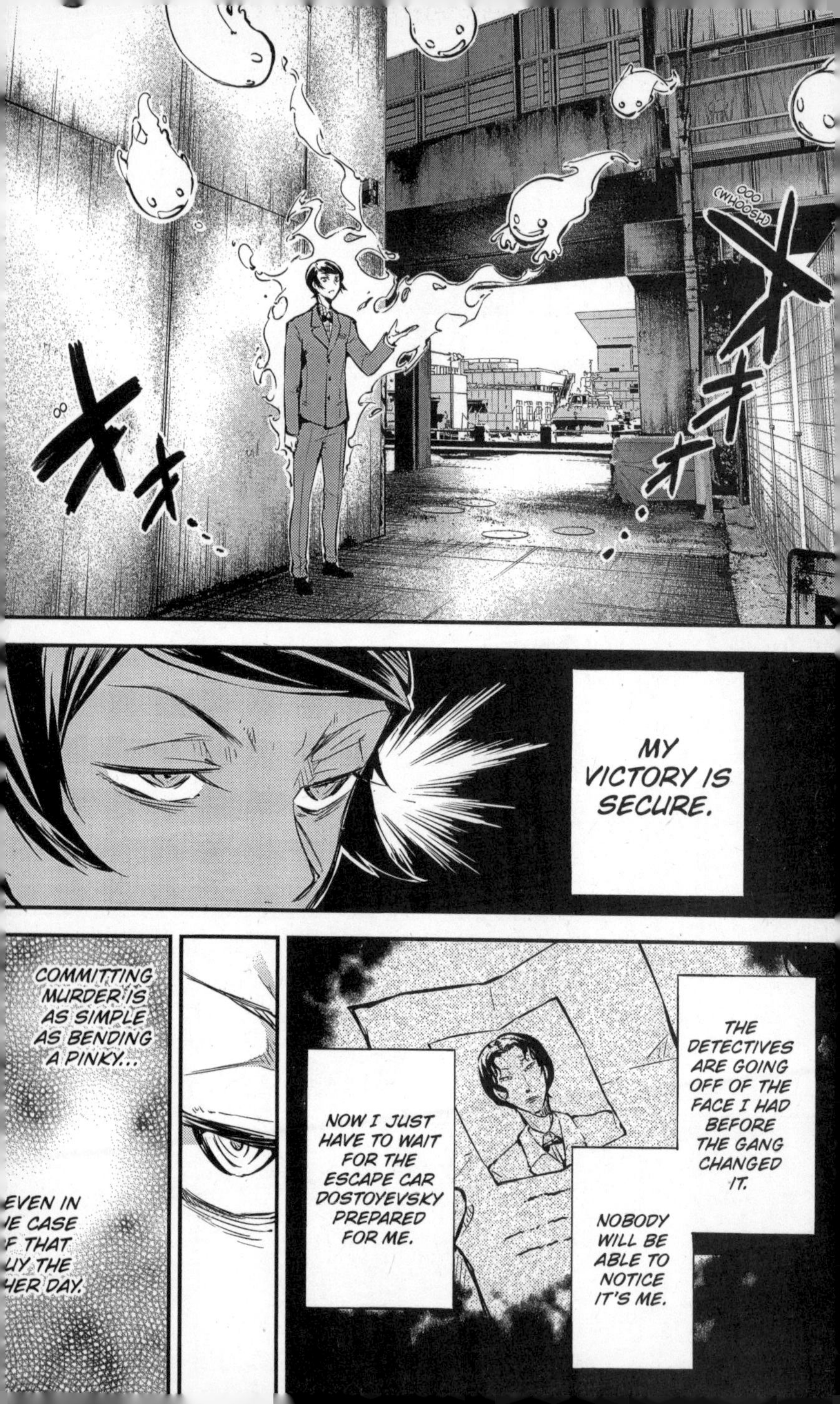
(WHOOSH) OOO
MY VICTORY IS SECURE.
THE DETECTIVES ARE GOING OFF OF THE FACE I HAD BEFORE THE GANG CHANGED IT.
NOBODY WILL BE ABLE TO NOTICE IT'S ME.
NOW I JUST HAVE TO WAIT FOR THE ESCAPE CAR DOSTOYEVSKY PREPARED FOR ME.
COMMITTING MURDER IS AS SIMPLE AS BENDING A PINKY...
EVEN IN
IE CASE
F THAT
UY THE
HER DAY.

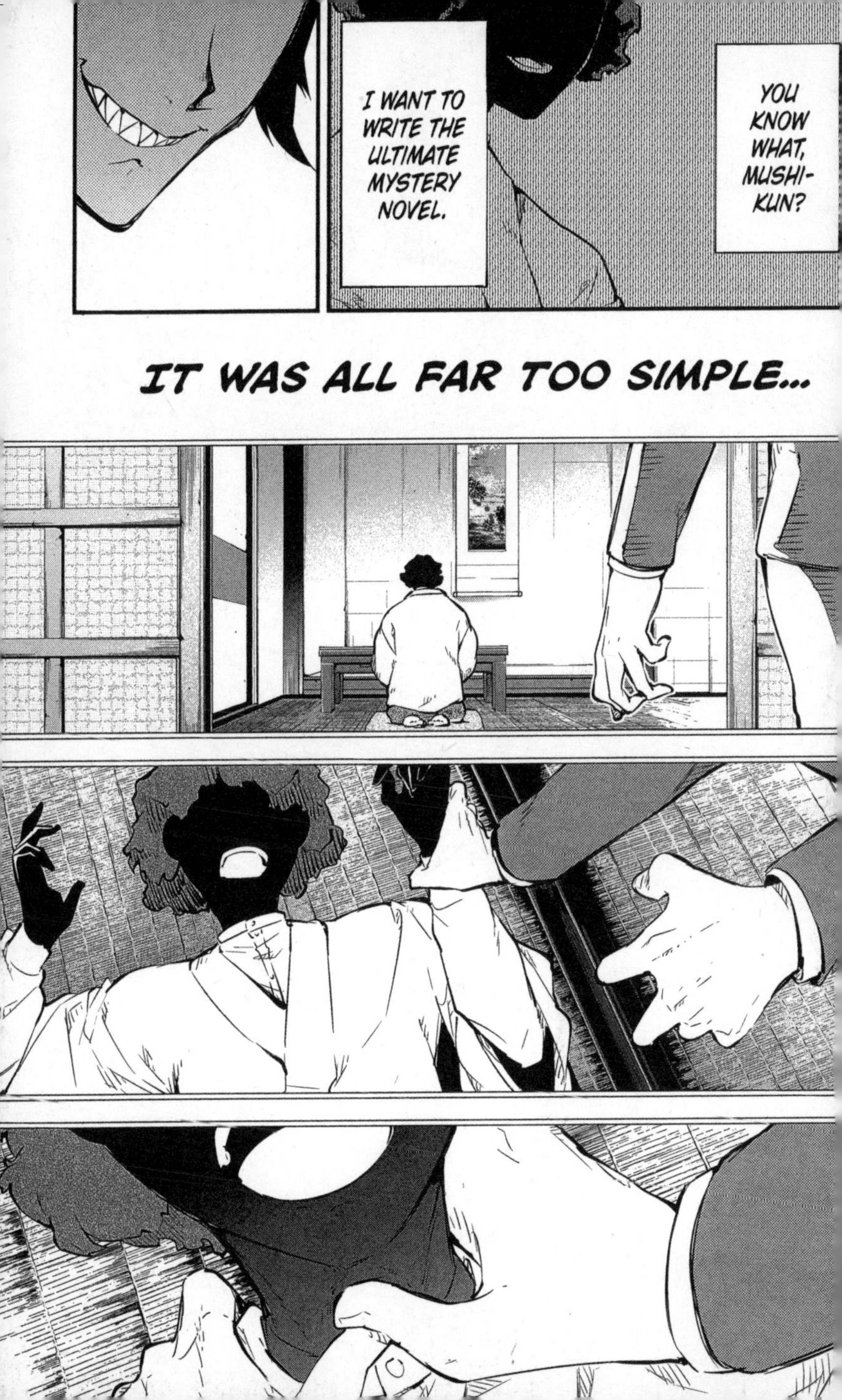
YOU KNOW WHAT, MUSHI-KUN?
I WANT TO WRITE THE ULTIMATE MYSTERY NOVEL.
IT WAS ALL FAR TOO SIMPLE...

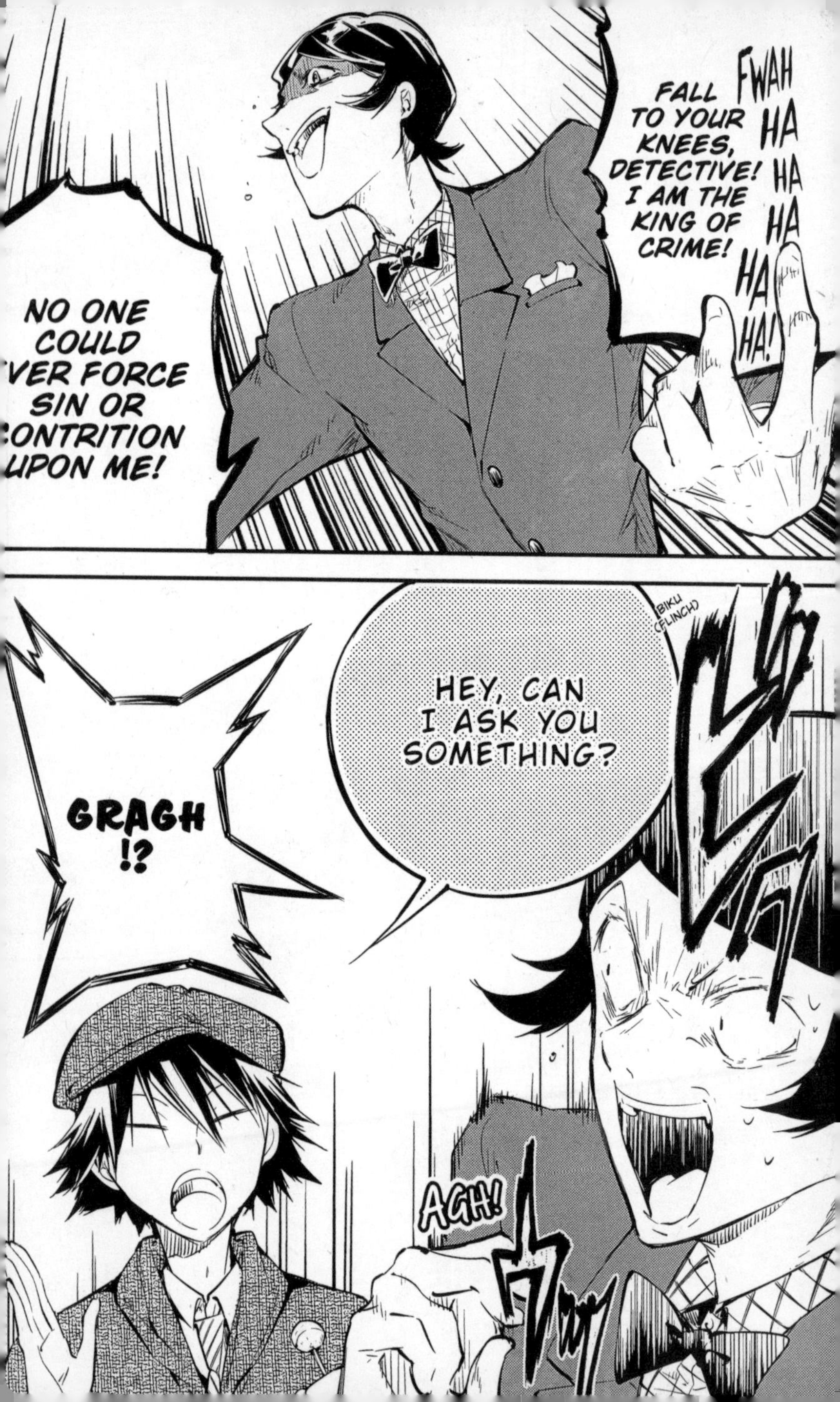
FWAH HA HA HA HA HA!
FALL TO YOUR KNEES, DETECTIVE! I AM THE KING OF CRIME!
NO ONE COULD VER FORCE SIN OR ONTRITION UPON ME!
BIKU (FLINCH)
HEY, CAN I ASK YOU SOMETHING?
GRAGH !?
AGH!

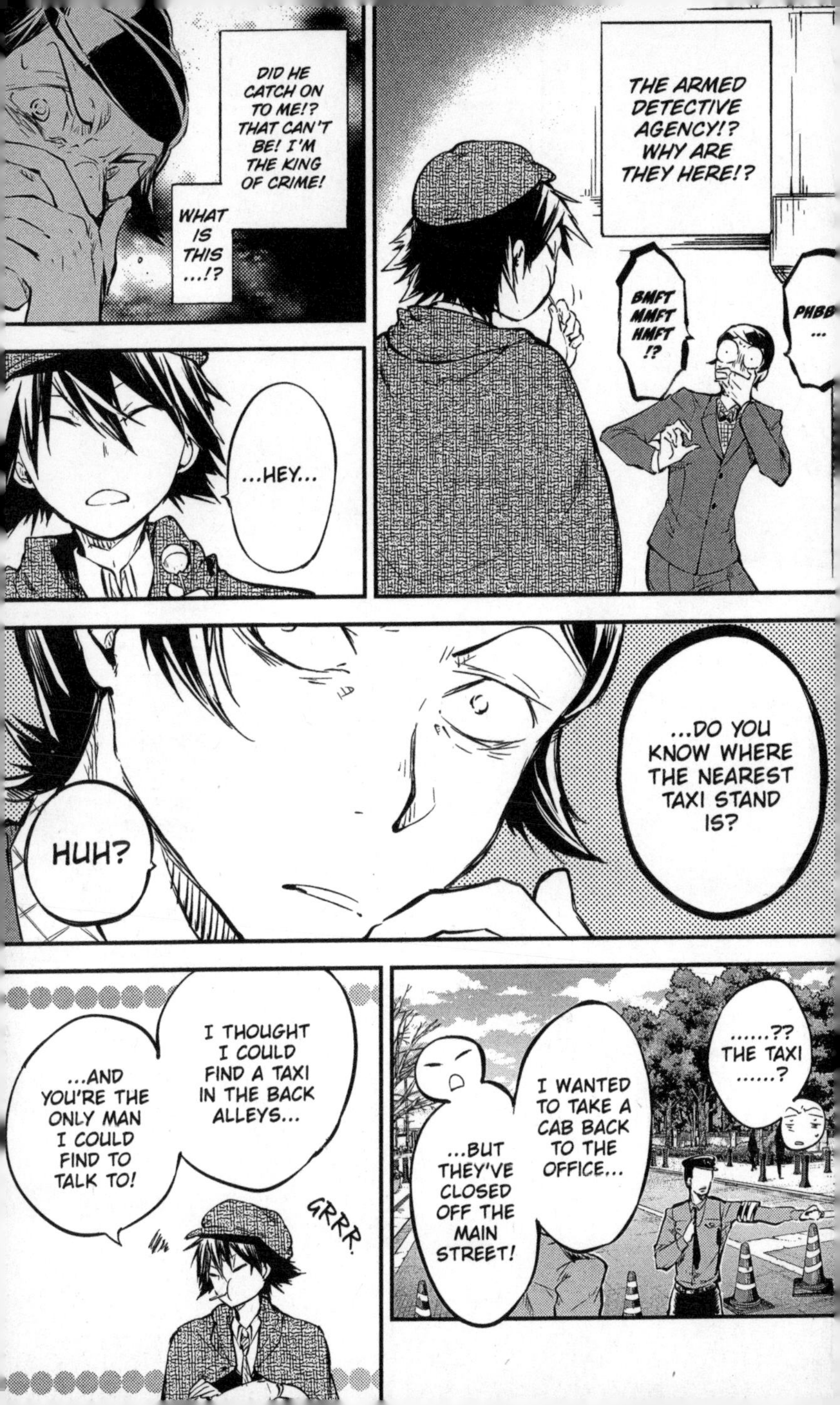
THE ARMED DETECTIVE AGENCY!? WHY ARE THEY HERE!?
PHBB ...
BMFT MMFT HMFT !?
DID HE CATCH ON TO ME!? THAT CAN'T BE! I'M THE KING OF CRIME!
WHAT IS THIS ...!?
...HEY...
...DO YOU KNOW WHERE THE NEAREST TAXI STAND IS?
HUH?
......?? THE TAXI ......?
I WANTED TO TAKE A CAB BACK TO THE OFFICE...
...BUT THEY'VE CLOSED OFF THE MAIN STREET!
I THOUGHT I COULD FIND A TAXI IN THE BACK ALLEYS...
...AND YOU'RE THE ONLY MAN I COULD FIND TO TALK TO!
GRRR

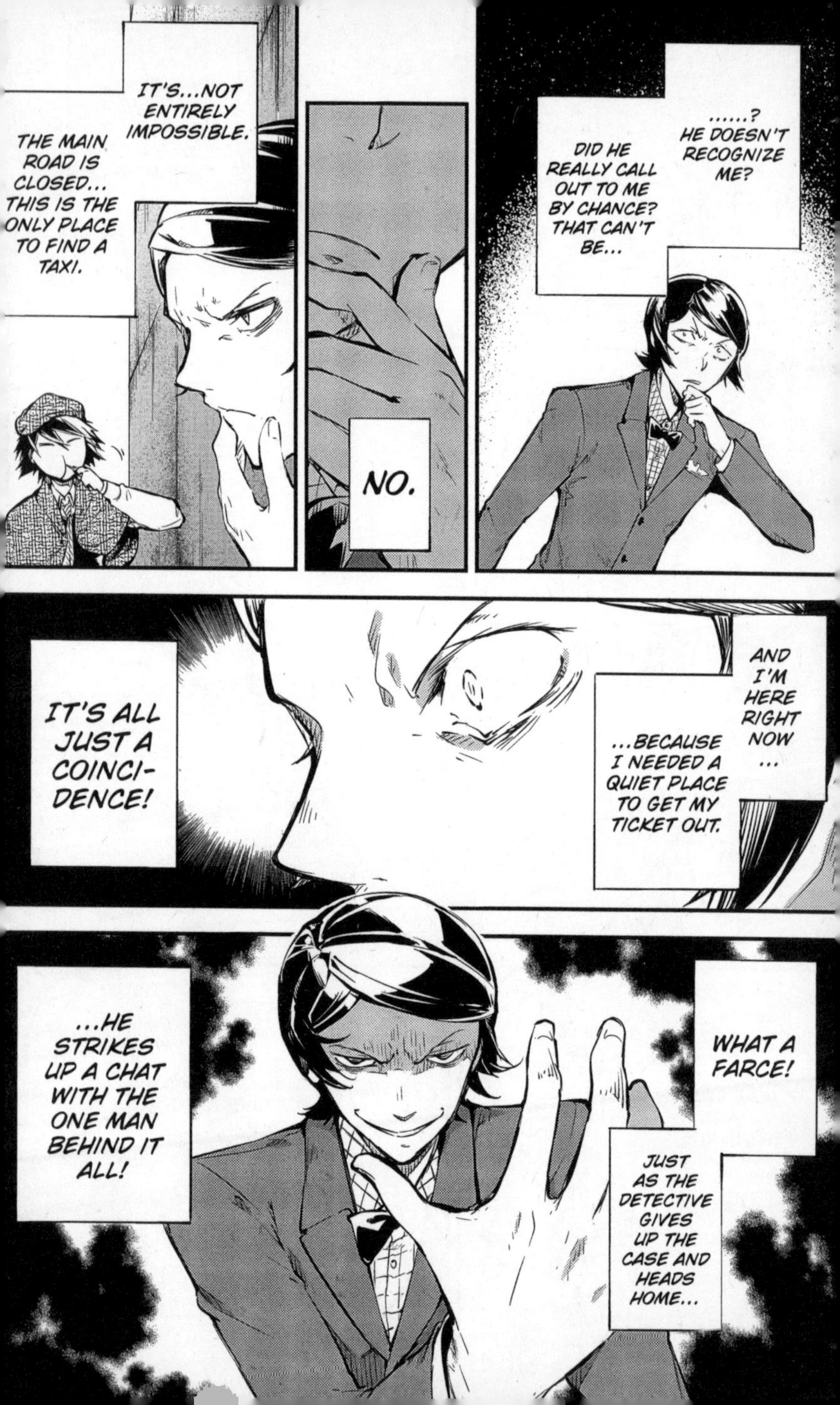

......? HE DOESN'T RECOGNIZE ME?
DID HE REALLY CALL OUT TO ME BY CHANCE? THAT CAN'T BE...
NO.
IT'S...NOT ENTIRELY IMPOSSIBLE.
THE MAIN ROAD IS CLOSED... THIS IS THE ONLY PLACE TO FIND A TAXI.
AND I'M HERE RIGHT NOW...
...BECAUSE I NEEDED A QUIET PLACE TO GET MY TICKET OUT.
IT'S ALL JUST A COINCI-DENCE!
WHAT A FARCE!
JUST AS THE DETECTIVE GIVES UP THE CASE AND HEADS HOME...
...HE STRIKES UP A CHAT WITH THE ONE MAN BEHIND IT ALL!

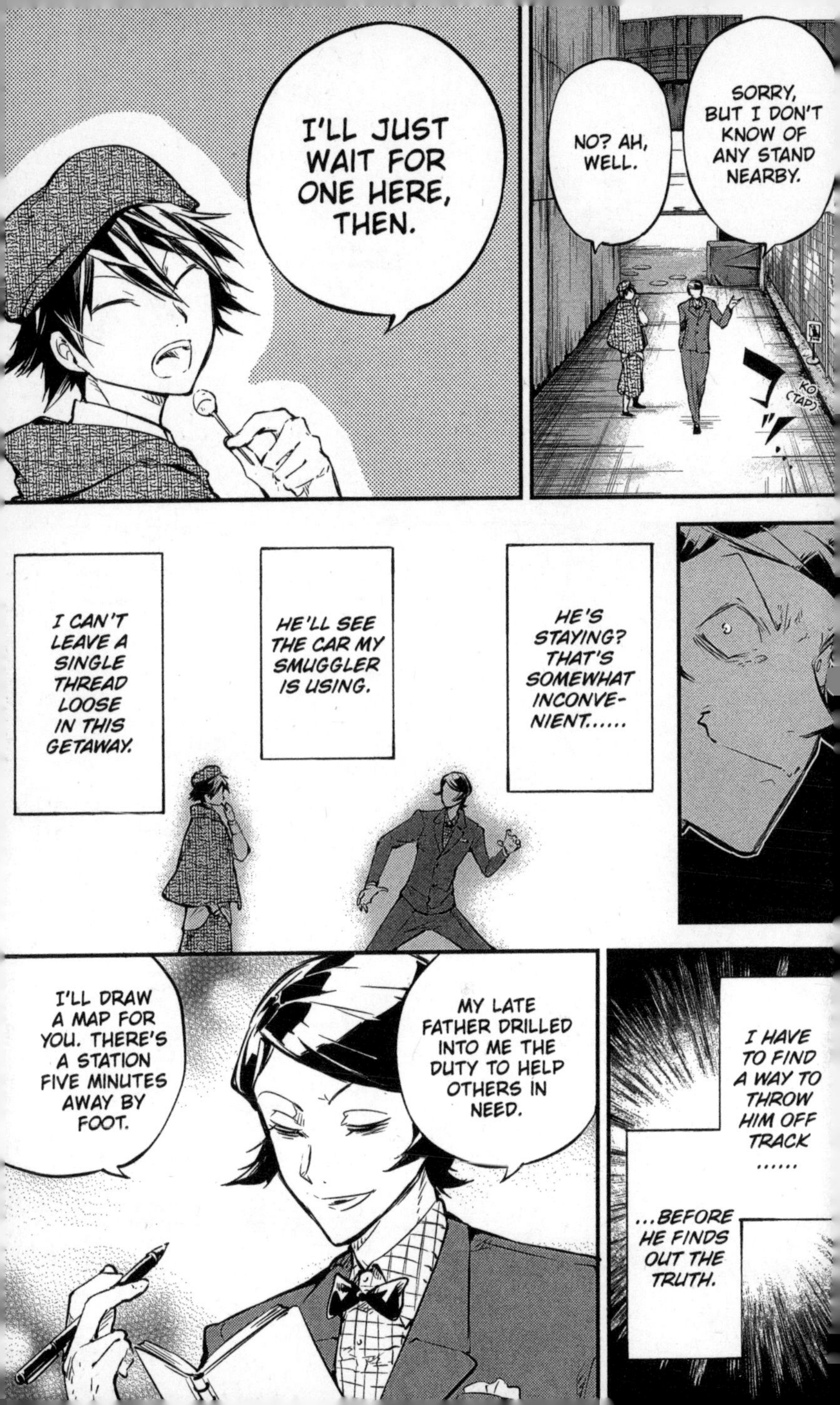
SORRY, BUT I DON'T KNOW OF ANY STAND NEARBY.
NO? AH, WELL.
KO (TAP)
I'LL JUST WAIT FOR ONE HERE, THEN.
HE'S STAYING? THAT'S SOMEWHAT INCONVENIENT......
HE'LL SEE THE CAR MY SMUGGLER IS USING.
I CAN'T LEAVE A SINGLE THREAD LOOSE IN THIS GETAWAY.
I HAVE TO FIND A WAY TO THROW HIM OFF TRACK......
...BEFORE HE FINDS OUT THE TRUTH.
MY LATE FATHER DRILLED INTO ME THE DUTY TO HELP OTHERS IN NEED.
I'LL DRAW A MAP FOR YOU. THERE'S A STATION FIVE MINUTES AWAY BY FOOT.

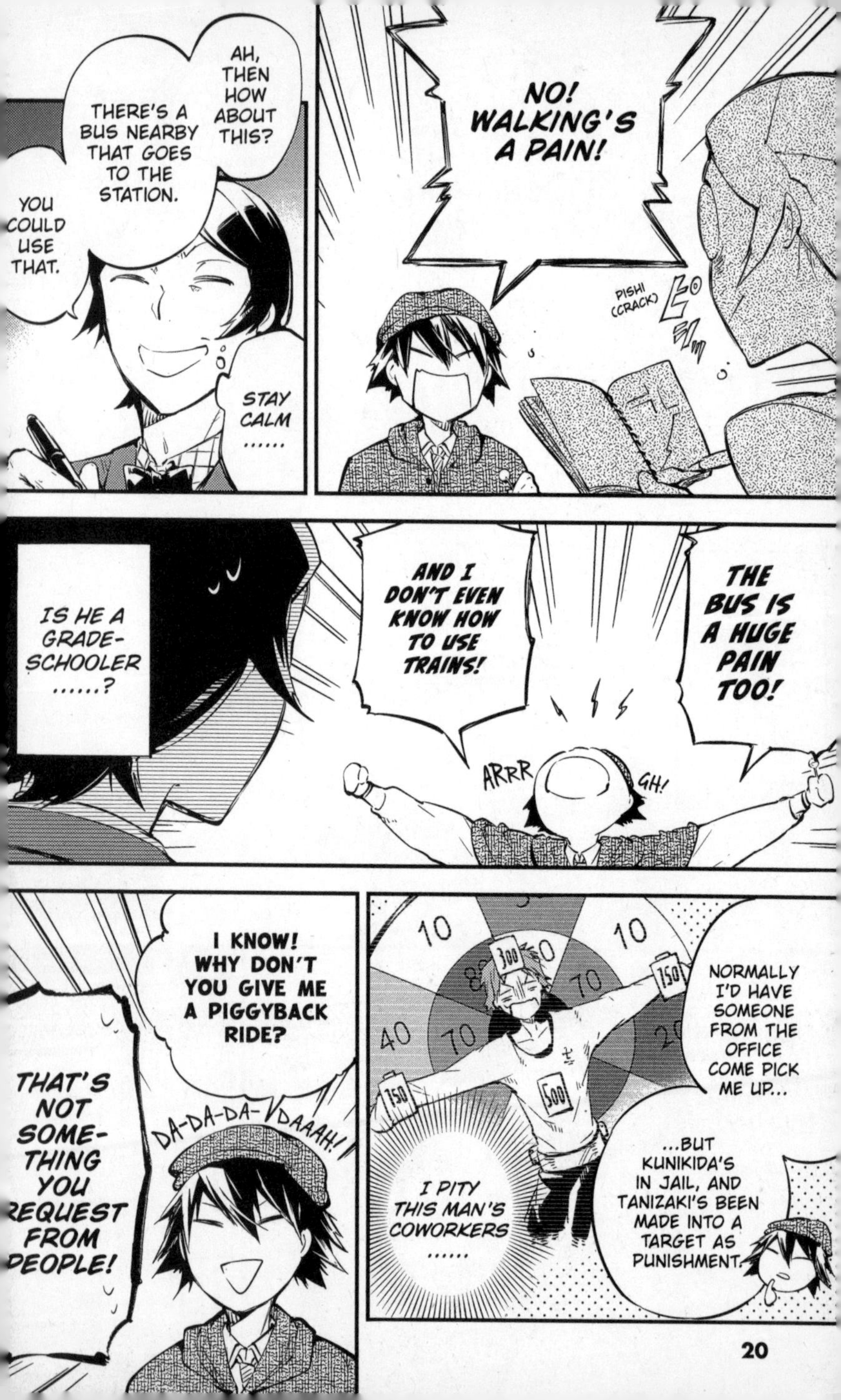

NO! WALKING'S A PAIN!
PISHI (CRACK)
AH, THEN HOW ABOUT THIS? THERE'S A BUS NEARBY THAT GOES TO THE STATION.
YOU COULD USE THAT.
STAY CALM ......
THE BUS IS A HUGE PAIN TOO!
AND I DON'T EVEN KNOW HOW TO USE TRAINS!
ARRRGH!
IS HE A GRADE-SCHOOLER ......?
NORMALLY I'D HAVE SOMEONE FROM THE OFFICE COME PICK ME UP...
...BUT KUNIKIDA'S IN JAIL, AND TANIZAKI'S BEEN MADE INTO A TARGET AS PUNISHMENT.
I PITY THIS MAN'S COWORKERS ......
I KNOW! WHY DON'T YOU GIVE ME A PIGGYBACK RIDE?
DA-DA-DA-DAAAH!
THAT'S NOT SOMETHING YOU REQUEST FROM PEOPLE!

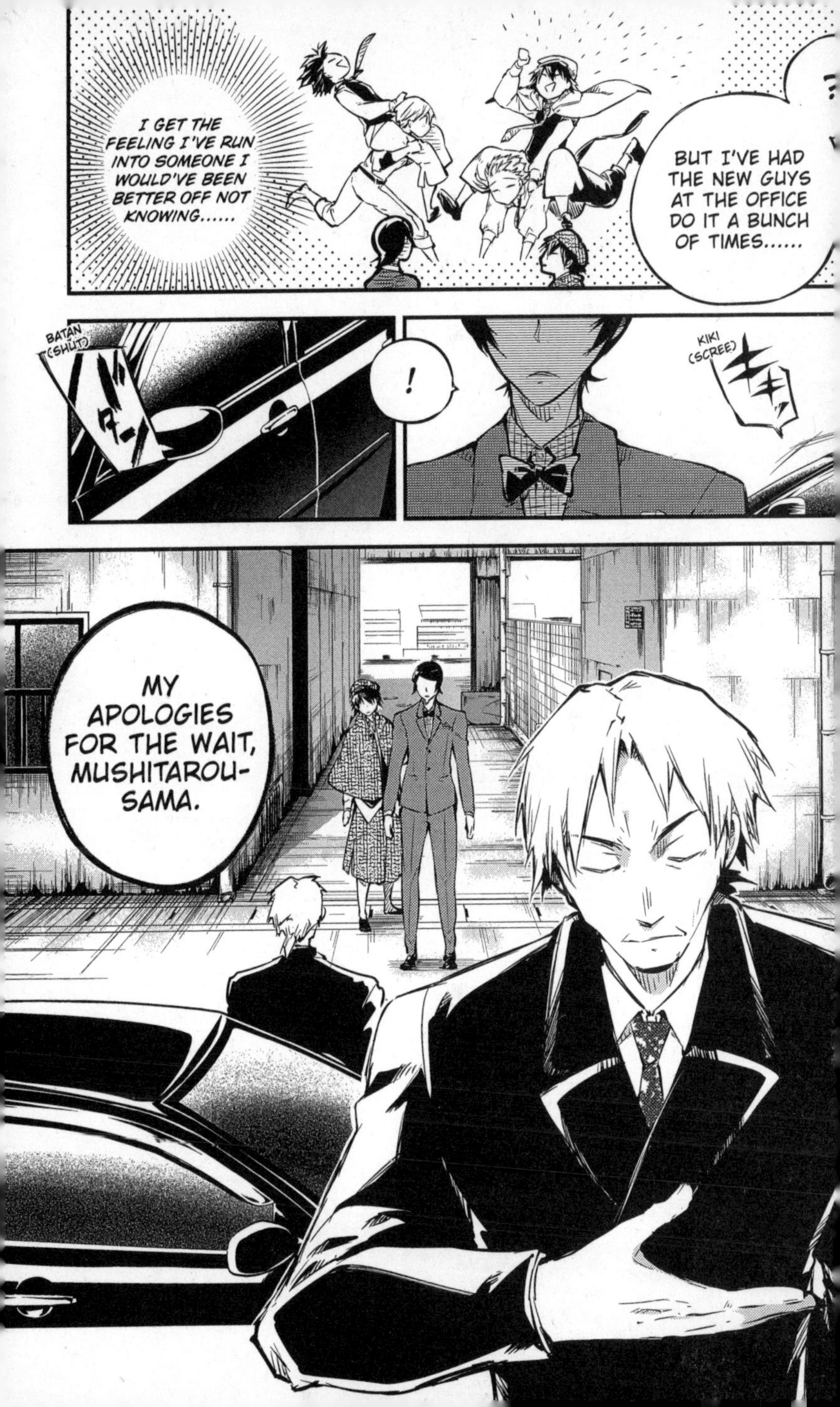
BUT I'VE HAD THE NEW GUYS AT THE OFFICE DO IT A BUNCH OF TIMES......
I GET THE FEELING I'VE RUN INTO SOMEONE I WOULD'VE BEEN BETTER OFF NOT KNOWING......
KIKI (SCREE)
BATAN (SHUT)
!
MY APOLOGIES FOR THE WAIT, MUSHITAROU-SAMA.

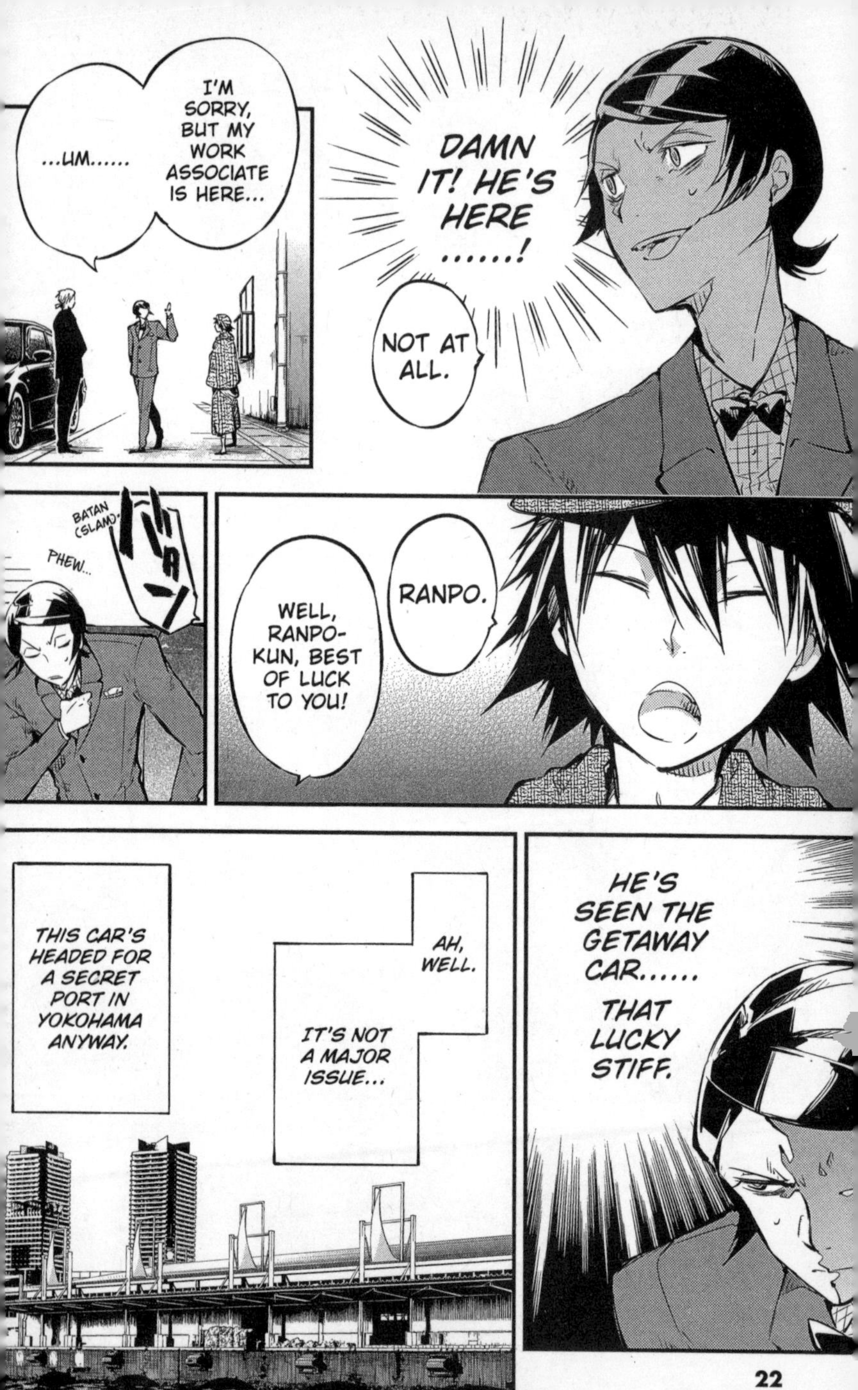

DAMN IT! HE'S HERE......!
NOT AT ALL.
...UM......
I'M SORRY, BUT MY WORK ASSOCIATE IS HERE...
RANPO.
WELL, RANPO-KUN, BEST OF LUCK TO YOU!
BATAN (SLAM)
PHEW...
HE'S SEEN THE GETAWAY CAR...... THAT LUCKY STIFF.
AH, WELL.
IT'S NOT A MAJOR ISSUE...
THIS CAR'S HEADED FOR A SECRET PORT IN YOKOHAMA ANYWAY.

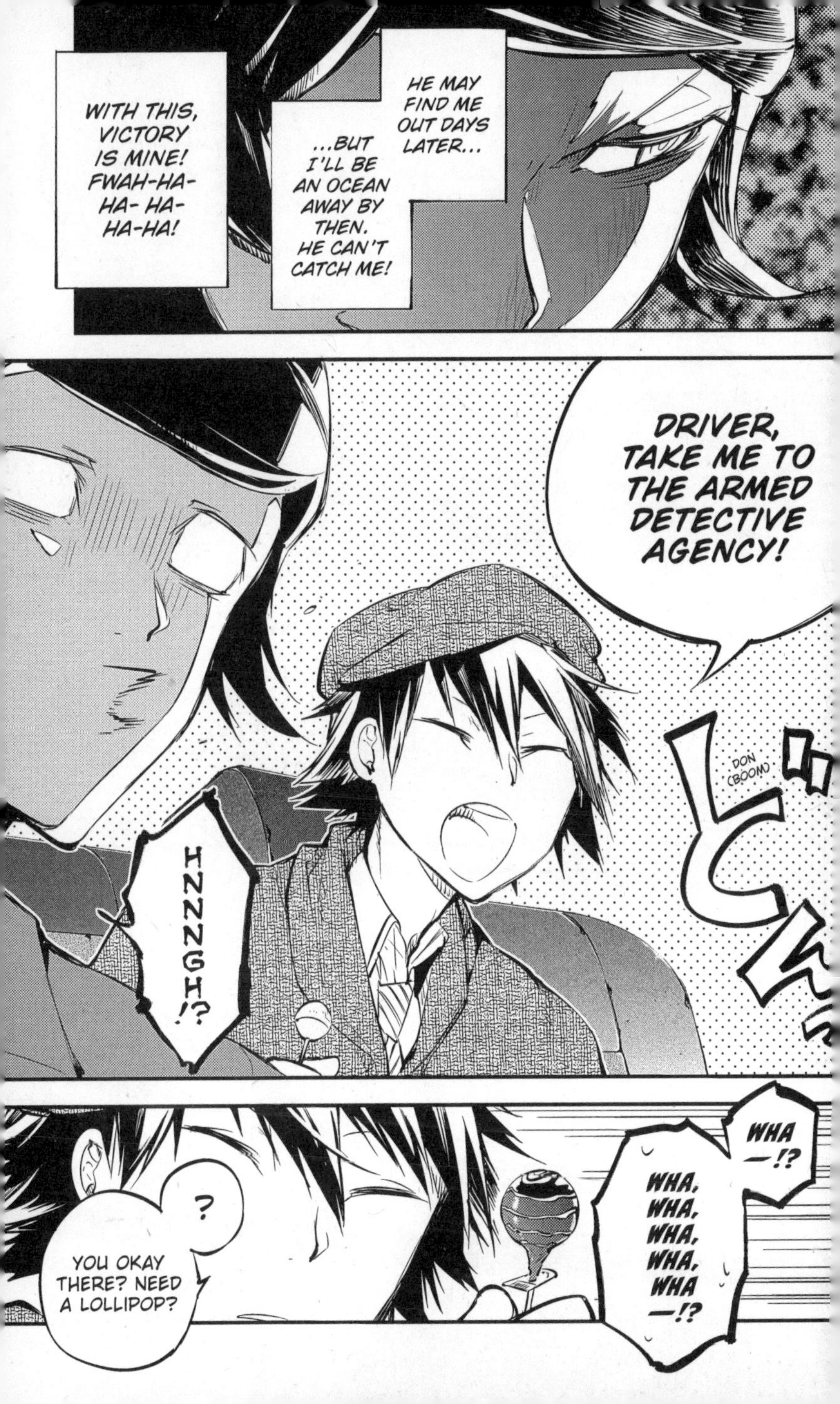
HE MAY FIND ME OUT DAYS LATER...
...BUT I'LL BE AN OCEAN AWAY BY THEN. HE CAN'T CATCH ME!
WITH THIS, VICTORY IS MINE! FWAH-HA-HA-HA-HA-HA!
DRIVER, TAKE ME TO THE ARMED DETECTIVE AGENCY!
DON (BOOM)
HNNNGH!?
WHA—!?
WHA, WHA, WHA, WHA, WHA—!?
?
YOU OKAY THERE? NEED A LOLLIPOP?

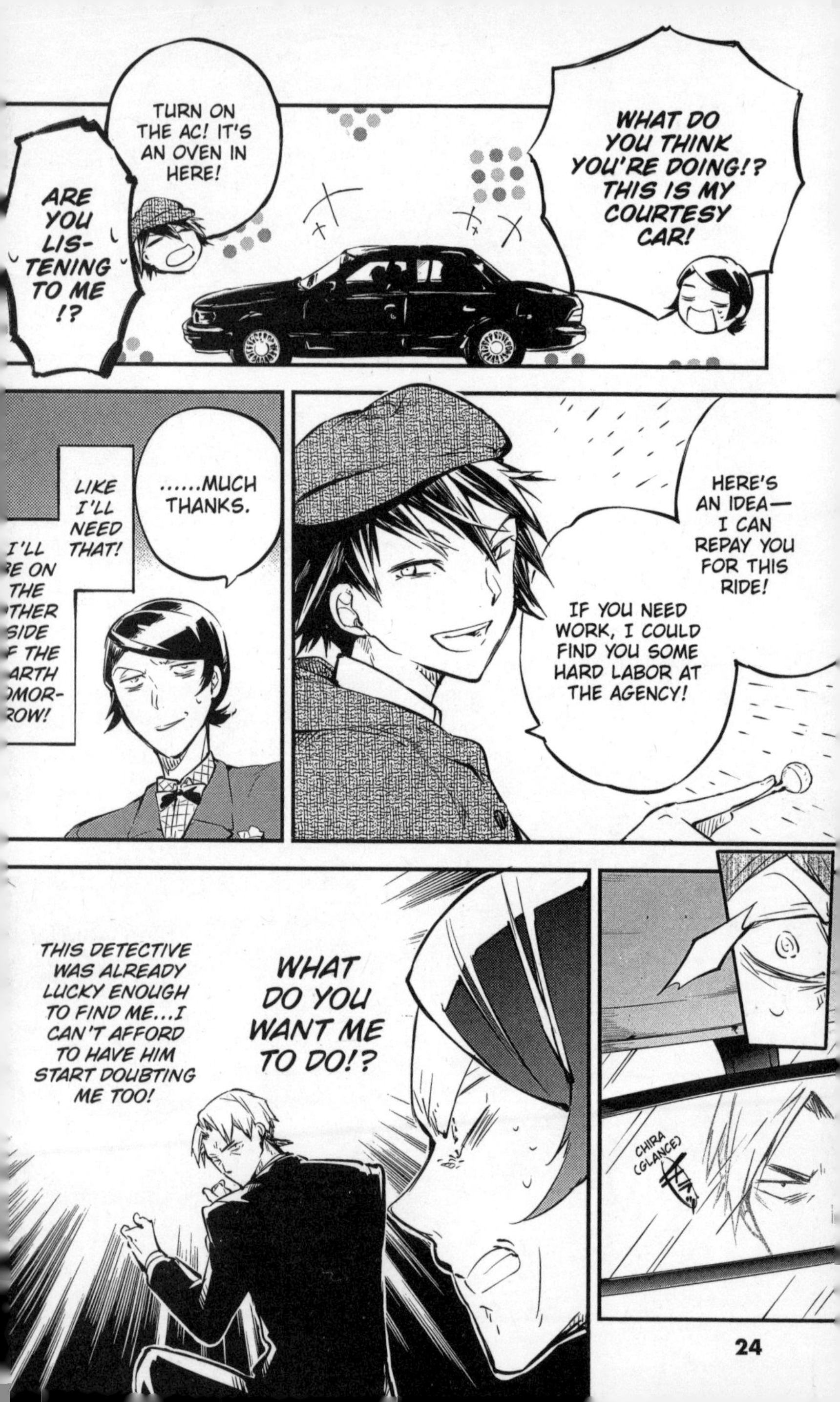
WHAT DO YOU THINK YOU'RE DOING!? THIS IS MY COURTESY CAR!
TURN ON THE AC! IT'S AN OVEN IN HERE!
ARE YOU LIS-TENING TO ME!?
HERE'S AN IDEA— I CAN REPAY YOU FOR THIS RIDE!
IF YOU NEED WORK, I COULD FIND YOU SOME HARD LABOR AT THE AGENCY!
......MUCH THANKS.
LIKE I'LL NEED THAT!
I'LL E ON THE THER SIDE F THE ARTH OMOR-ROW!
CHIRA (GLANCE)
WHAT DO YOU WANT ME TO DO!?
THIS DETECTIVE WAS ALREADY LUCKY ENOUGH TO FIND ME...I CAN'T AFFORD TO HAVE HIM START DOUBTING ME TOO!

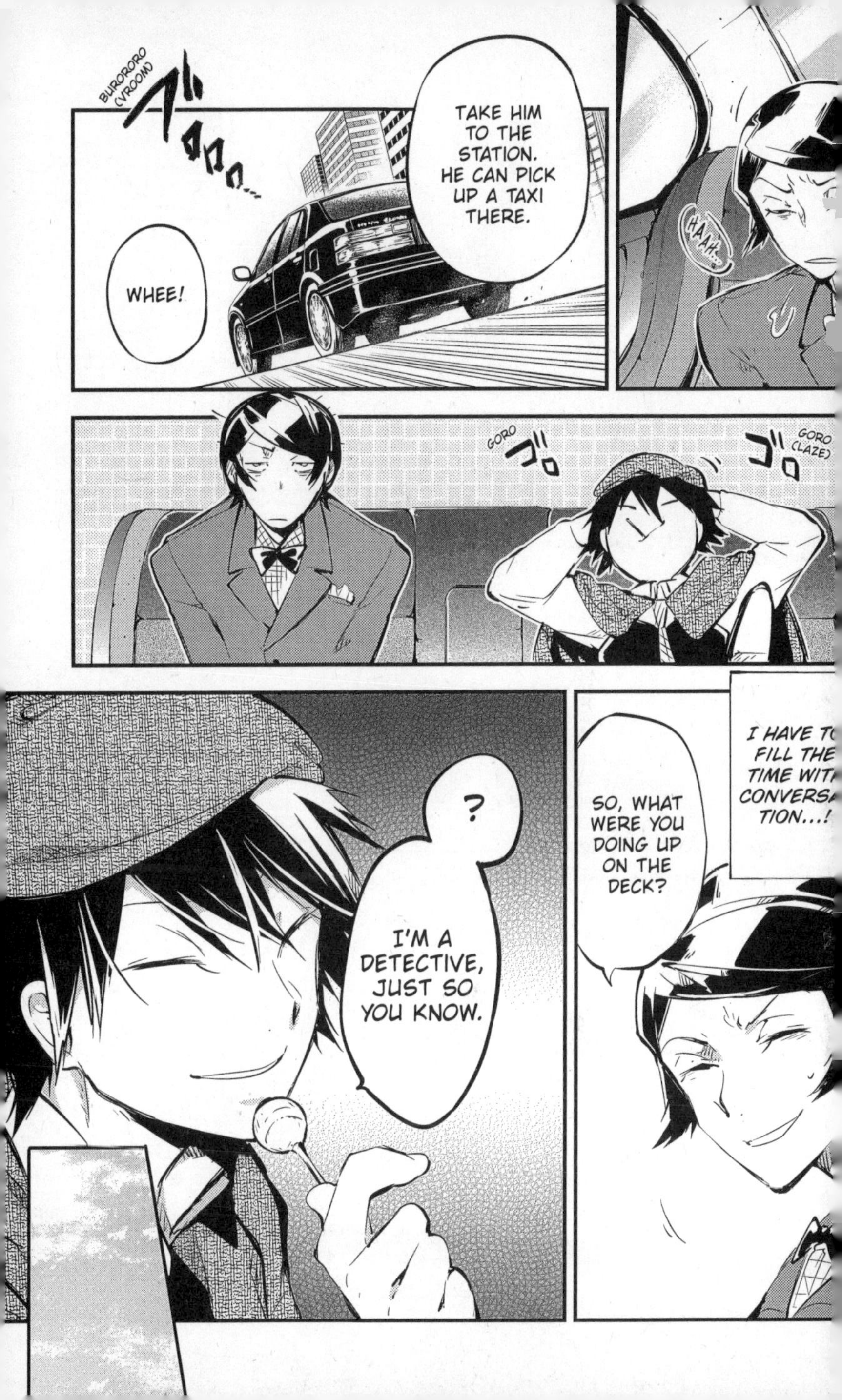
HAAAH...
TAKE HIM TO THE STATION. HE CAN PICK UP A TAXI THERE.
BURORORO (VROOM)
WHEE!
GORO (LAZE)
GORO
I HAVE TO FILL THE TIME WIT CONVERS TION...!
SO, WHAT WERE YOU DOING UP ON THE DECK?
?
I'M A DETECTIVE, JUST SO YOU KNOW.

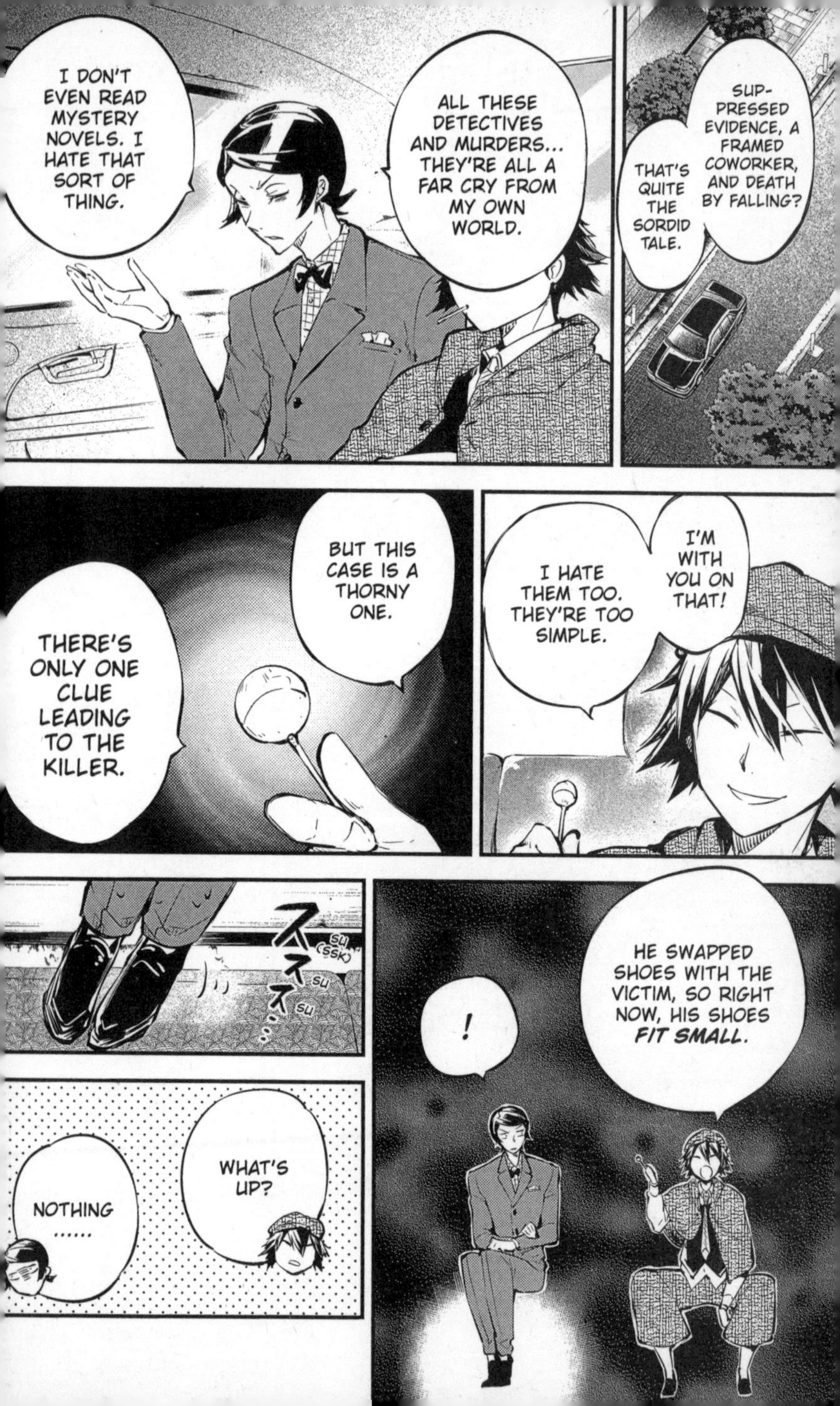

SUP-PRESSED EVIDENCE, A FRAMED COWORKER, AND DEATH BY FALLING?
THAT'S QUITE THE SORDID TALE.
ALL THESE DETECTIVES AND MURDERS... THEY'RE ALL A FAR CRY FROM MY OWN WORLD.
I DON'T EVEN READ MYSTERY NOVELS. I HATE THAT SORT OF THING.
I'M WITH YOU ON THAT!
I HATE THEM TOO. THEY'RE TOO SIMPLE.
BUT THIS CASE IS A THORNY ONE.
THERE'S ONLY ONE CLUE LEADING TO THE KILLER.
HE SWAPPED SHOES WITH THE VICTIM, SO RIGHT NOW, HIS SHOES *FIT SMALL*.
!
SU (SSK)
SU
SU
WHAT'S UP?
NOTHING ......

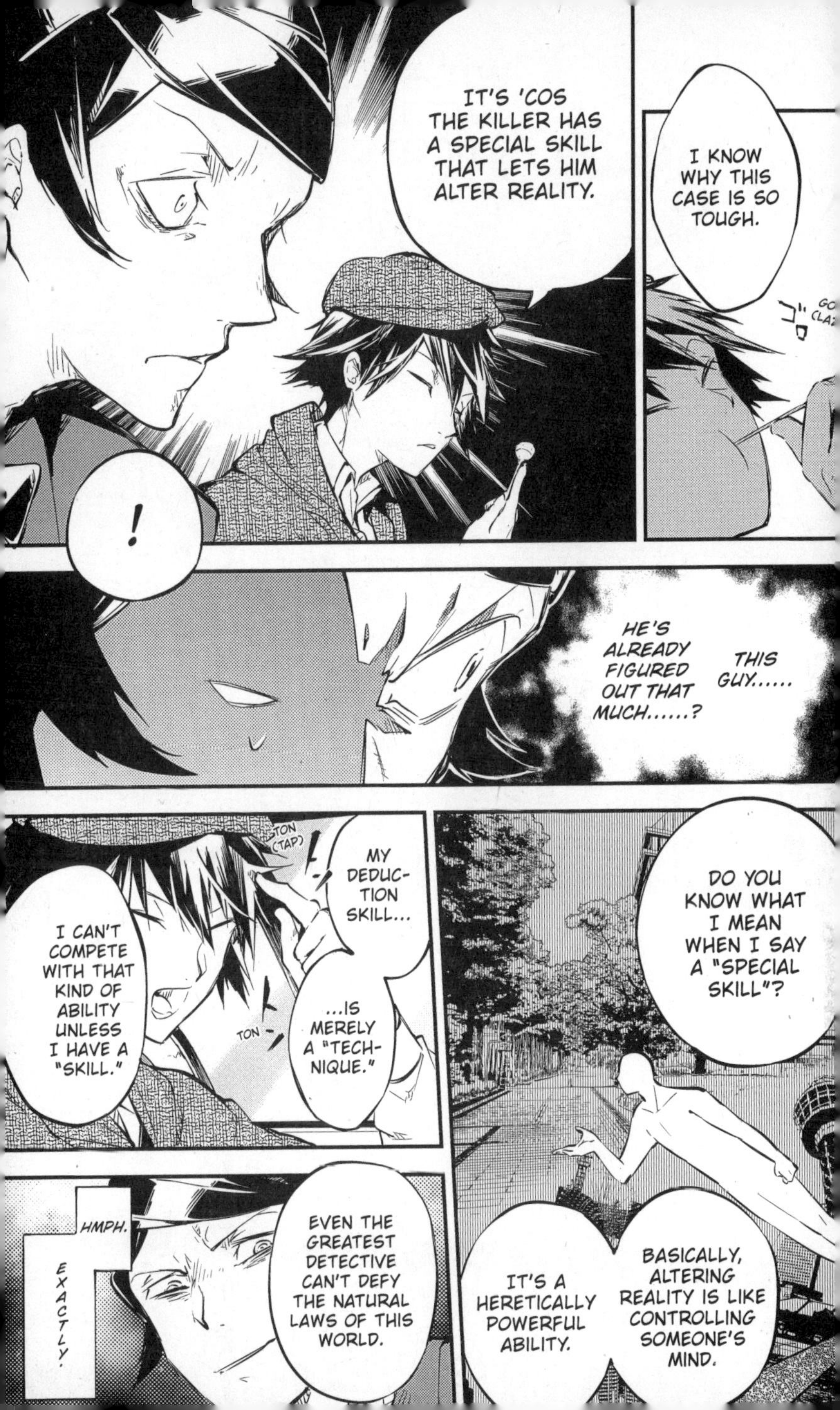
I KNOW WHY THIS CASE IS SO TOUGH.
IT'S 'COS THE KILLER HAS A SPECIAL SKILL THAT LETS HIM ALTER REALITY.
!
THIS GUY......
HE'S ALREADY FIGURED OUT THAT MUCH......?
DO YOU KNOW WHAT I MEAN WHEN I SAY A "SPECIAL SKILL"?
BASICALLY, ALTERING REALITY IS LIKE CONTROLLING SOMEONE'S MIND.
IT'S A HERETICALLY POWERFUL ABILITY.
TON (TAP)
MY DEDUC-TION SKILL...
...IS MERELY A "TECH-NIQUE."
TON
I CAN'T COMPETE WITH THAT KIND OF ABILITY UNLESS I HAVE A "SKILL."
EVEN THE GREATEST DETECTIVE CAN'T DEFY THE NATURAL LAWS OF THIS WORLD.
HMPH.
EXACTLY.

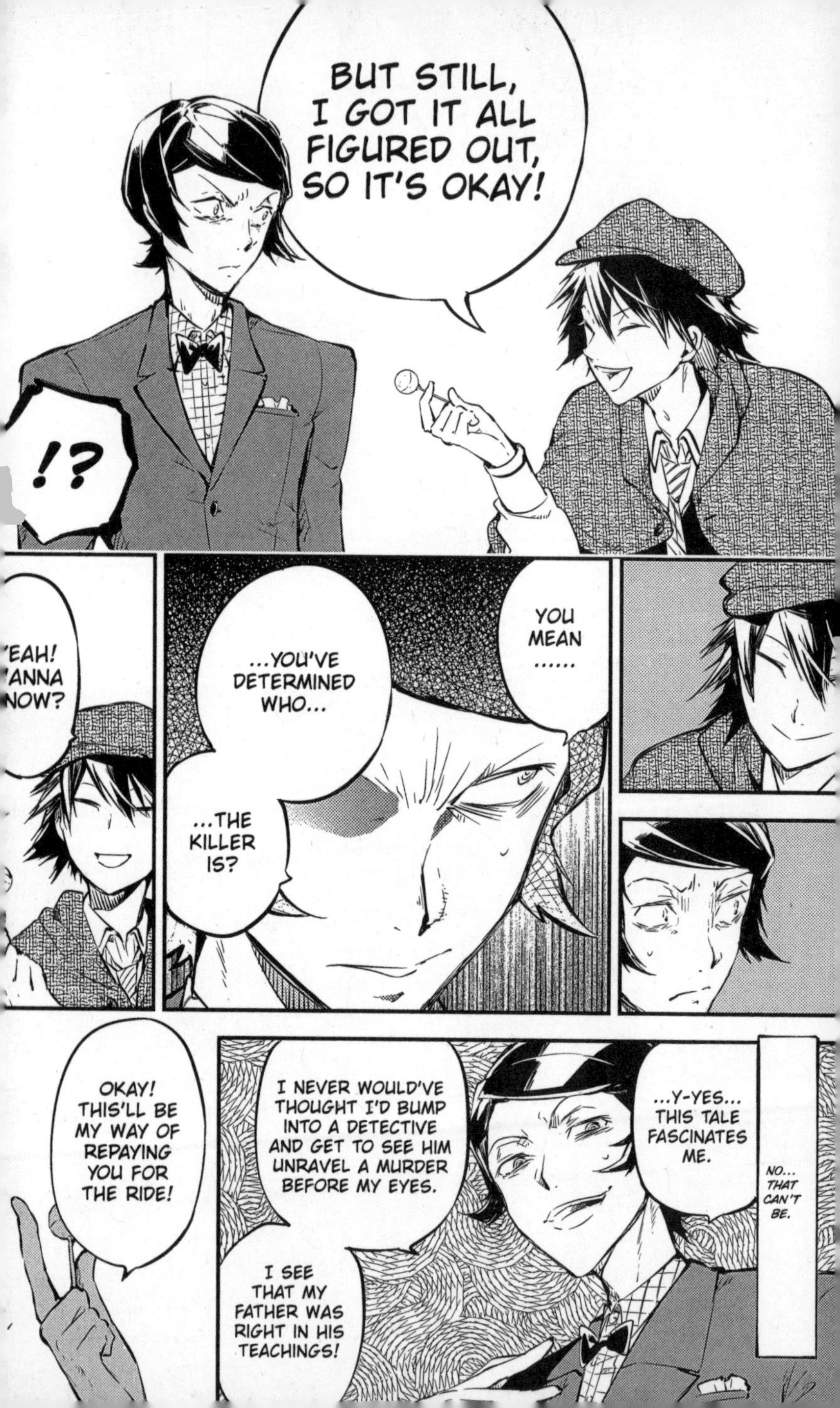
BUT STILL, I GOT IT ALL FIGURED OUT, SO IT'S OKAY!
!?
YOU MEAN ......
...YOU'VE DETERMINED WHO...
...THE KILLER IS?
EAH! ANNA NOW?
NO... THAT CAN'T BE.
...Y-YES... THIS TALE FASCINATES ME.
I NEVER WOULD'VE THOUGHT I'D BUMP INTO A DETECTIVE AND GET TO SEE HIM UNRAVEL A MURDER BEFORE MY EYES.
I SEE THAT MY FATHER WAS RIGHT IN HIS TEACHINGS!
OKAY! THIS'LL BE MY WAY OF REPAYING YOU FOR THE RIDE!

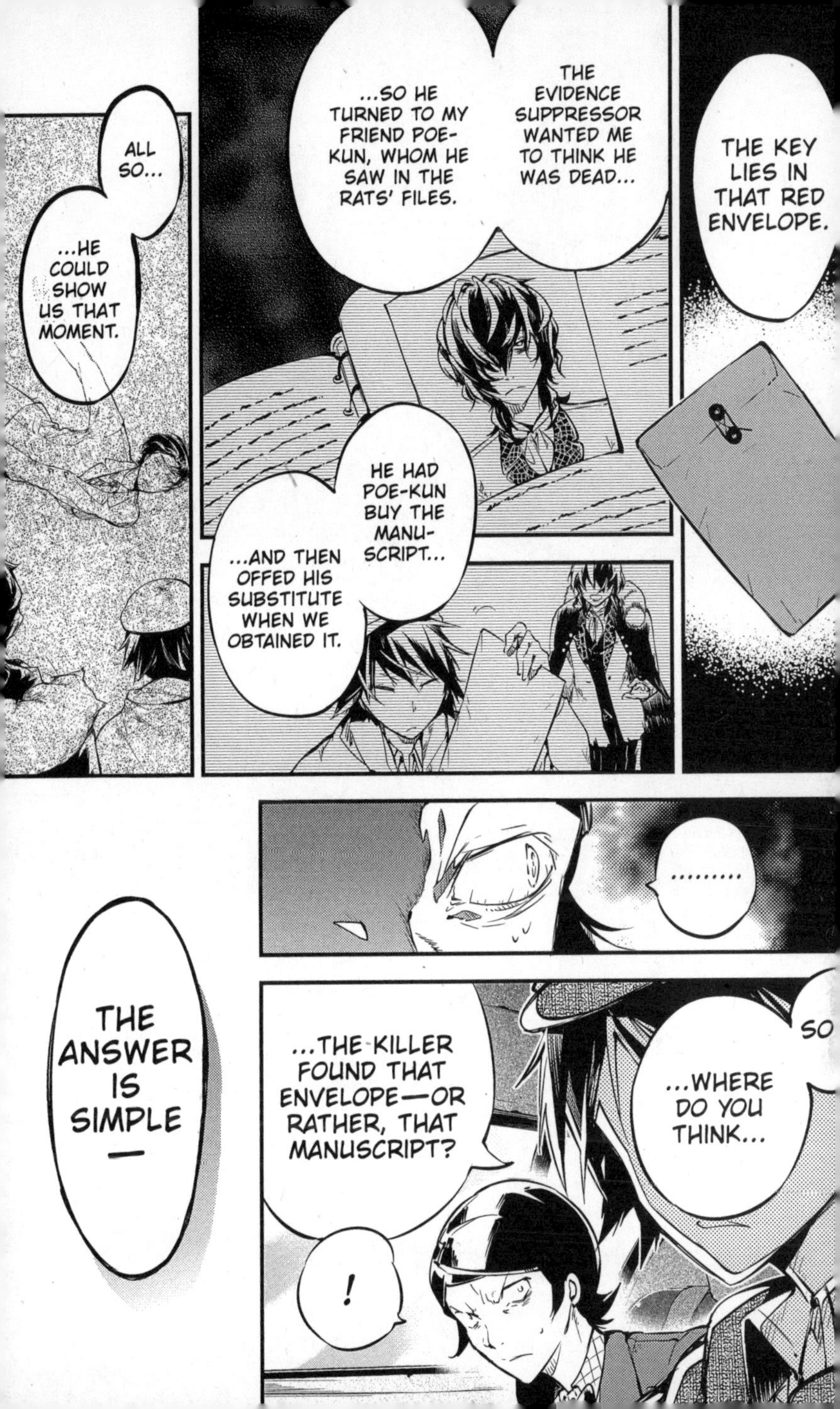
THE KEY LIES IN THAT RED ENVELOPE.
THE EVIDENCE SUPPRESSOR WANTED ME TO THINK HE WAS DEAD...
...SO HE TURNED TO MY FRIEND POE-KUN, WHOM HE SAW IN THE RATS' FILES.
HE HAD POE-KUN BUY THE MANU-SCRIPT...
...AND THEN OFFED HIS SUBSTITUTE WHEN WE OBTAINED IT.
ALL SO...
...HE COULD SHOW US THAT MOMENT.
....
SO
...WHERE DO YOU THINK...
...THE KILLER FOUND THAT ENVELOPE—OR RATHER, THAT MANUSCRIPT?
!
THE ANSWER IS SIMPLE —

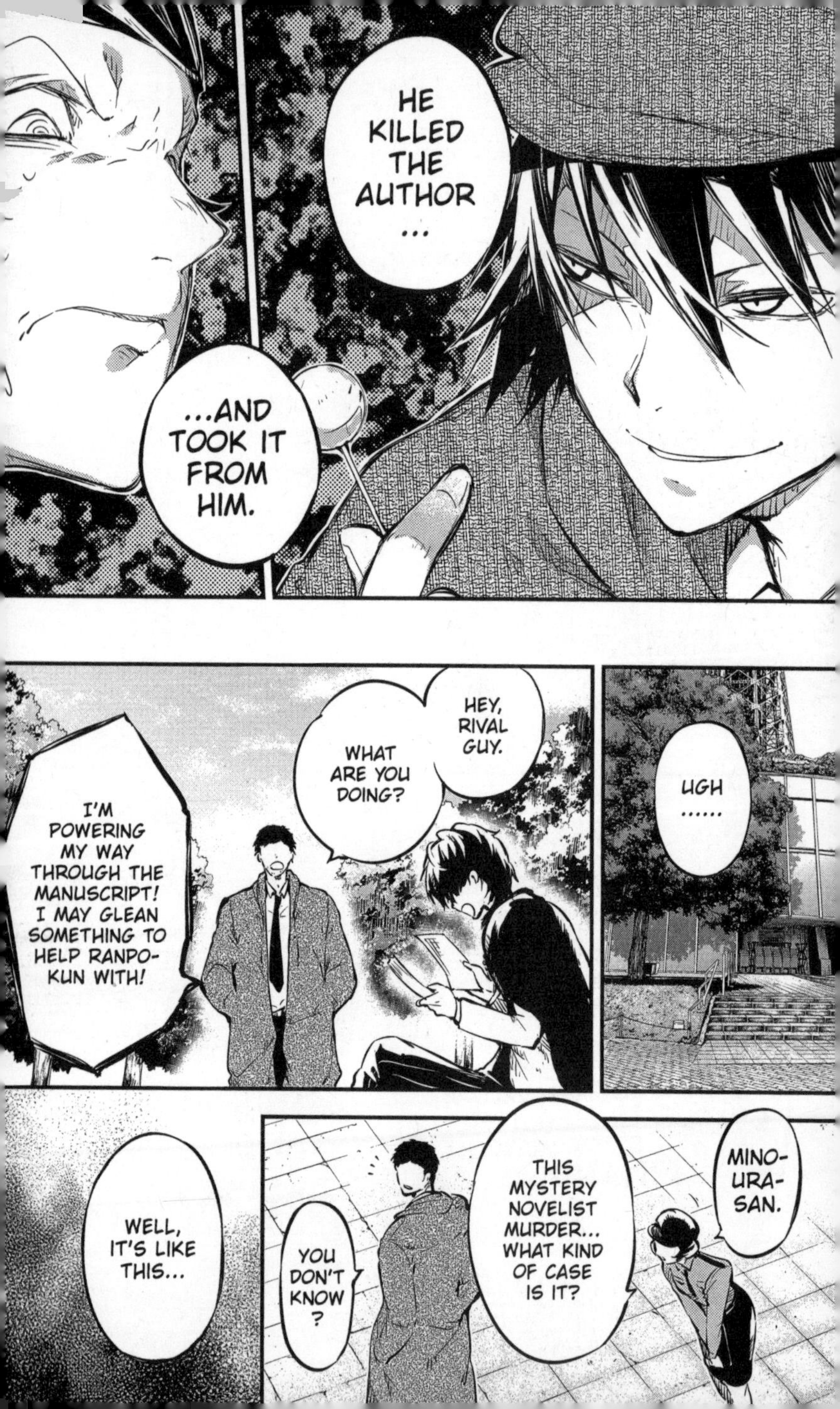
HE KILLED THE AUTHOR ...
...AND TOOK IT FROM HIM.
UGH ......
HEY, RIVAL GUY.
WHAT ARE YOU DOING?
I'M POWERING MY WAY THROUGH THE MANUSCRIPT! I MAY GLEAN SOMETHING TO HELP RANPO-KUN WITH!
MINOURA-SAN.
THIS MYSTERY NOVELIST MURDER... WHAT KIND OF CASE IS IT?
YOU DON'T KNOW ?
WELL, IT'S LIKE THIS...

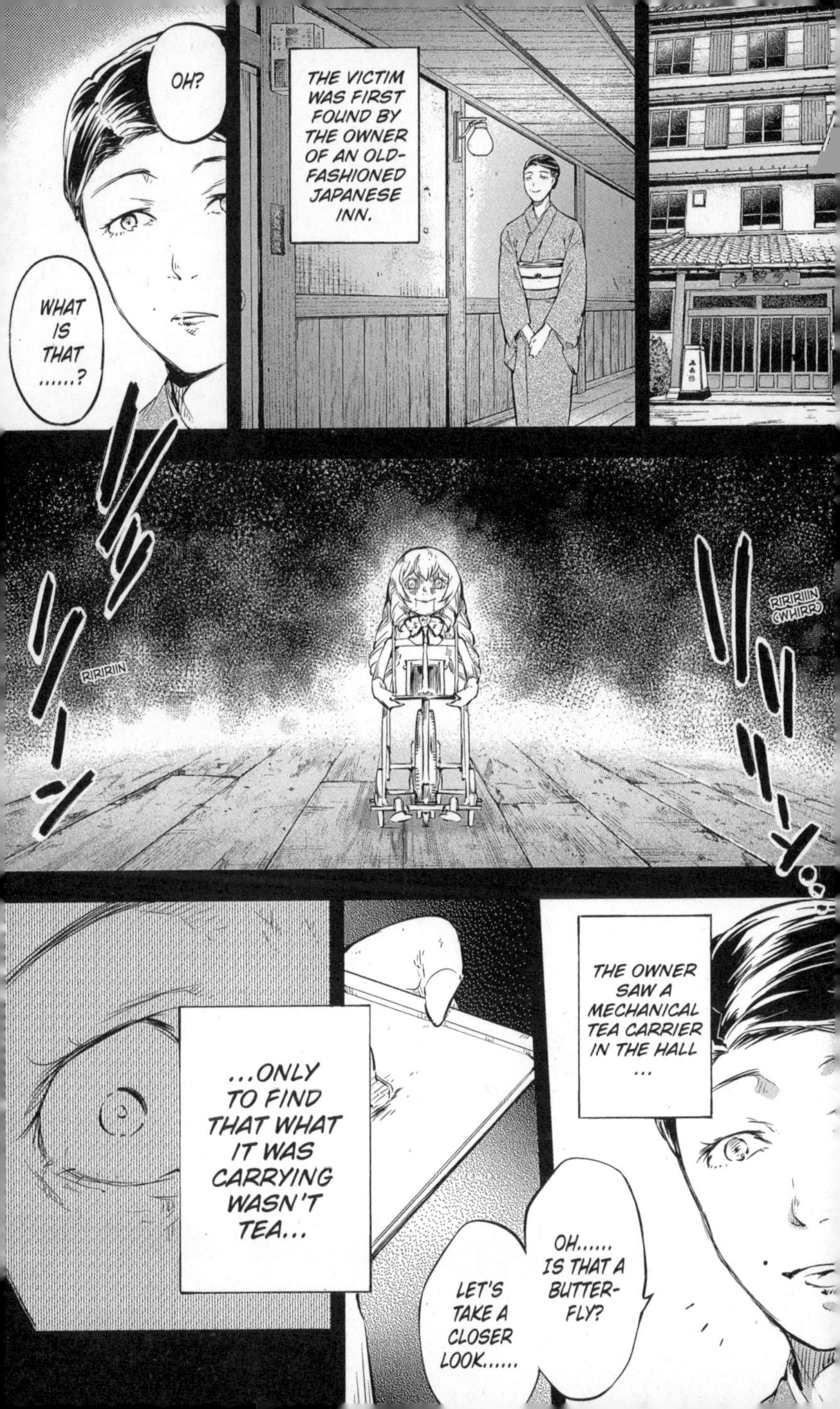
THE VICTIM WAS FIRST FOUND BY THE OWNER OF AN OLD-FASHIONED JAPANESE INN.
OH?
WHAT IS THAT......?
RIRIRIIN (WHIRR)
RIRIRIIN
THE OWNER SAW A MECHANICAL TEA CARRIER IN THE HALL...
OH...... IS THAT A BUTTERFLY?
LET'S TAKE A CLOSER LOOK......
...ONLY TO FIND THAT WHAT IT WAS CARRYING WASN'T TEA...

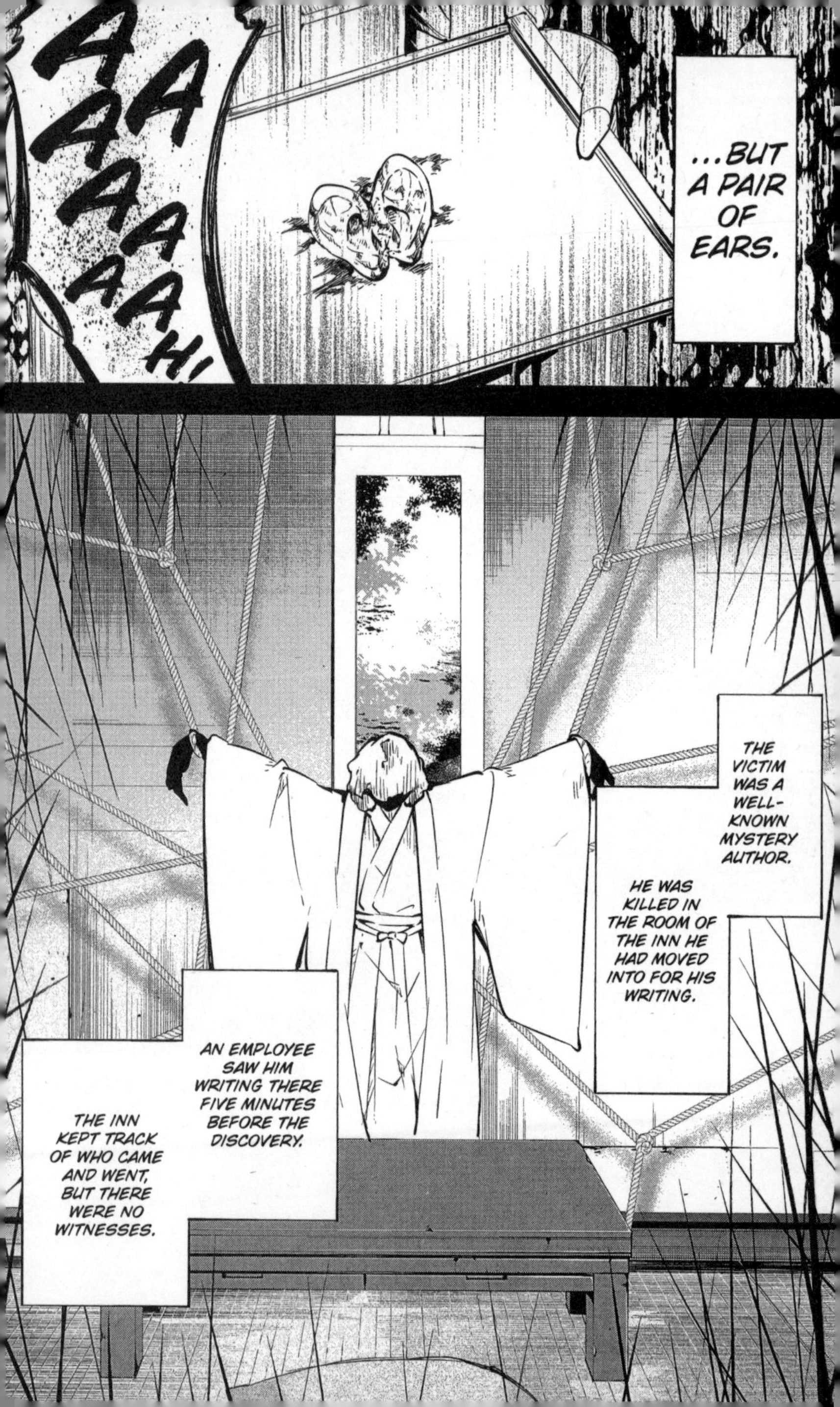
...BUT A PAIR OF EARS.
AAAAAAAAAAH!
THE VICTIM WAS A WELL-KNOWN MYSTERY AUTHOR.
HE WAS KILLED IN THE ROOM OF THE INN HE HAD MOVED INTO FOR HIS WRITING.
AN EMPLOYEE SAW HIM WRITING THERE FIVE MINUTES BEFORE THE DISCOVERY.
THE INN KEPT TRACK OF WHO CAME AND WENT, BUT THERE WERE NO WITNESSES.

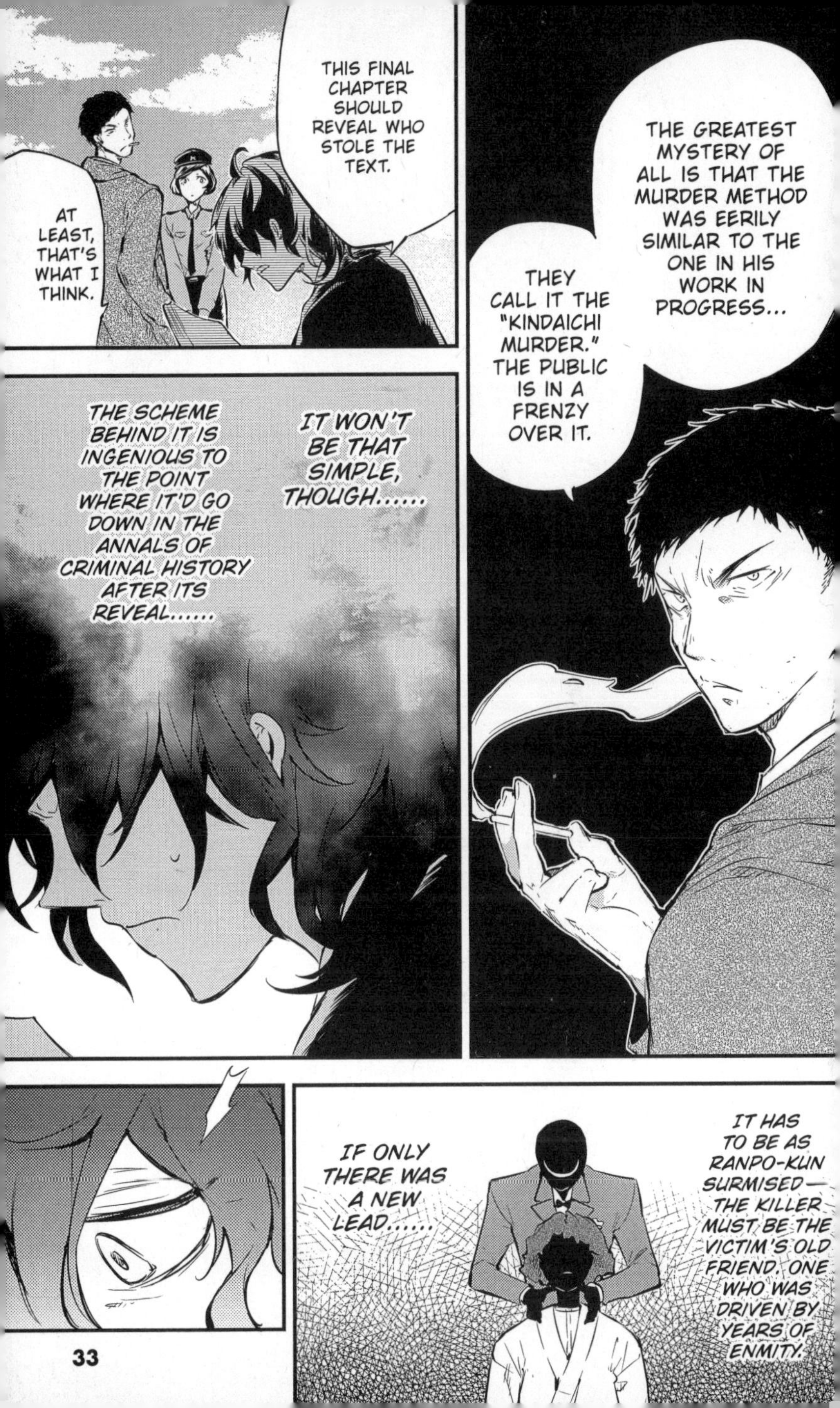
THE GREATEST MYSTERY OF ALL IS THAT THE MURDER METHOD WAS EERILY SIMILAR TO THE ONE IN HIS WORK IN PROGRESS...
THEY CALL IT THE "KINDAICHI MURDER." THE PUBLIC IS IN A FRENZY OVER IT.
THIS FINAL CHAPTER SHOULD REVEAL WHO STOLE THE TEXT.
AT LEAST, THAT'S WHAT I THINK.
IT WON'T BE THAT SIMPLE, THOUGH......
THE SCHEME BEHIND IT IS INGENIOUS TO THE POINT WHERE IT'D GO DOWN IN THE ANNALS OF CRIMINAL HISTORY AFTER ITS REVEAL......
IT HAS TO BE AS RANPO-KUN SURMISED—THE KILLER MUST BE THE VICTIM'S OLD FRIEND, ONE WHO WAS DRIVEN BY YEARS OF ENMITY.
IF ONLY THERE WAS A NEW LEAD......

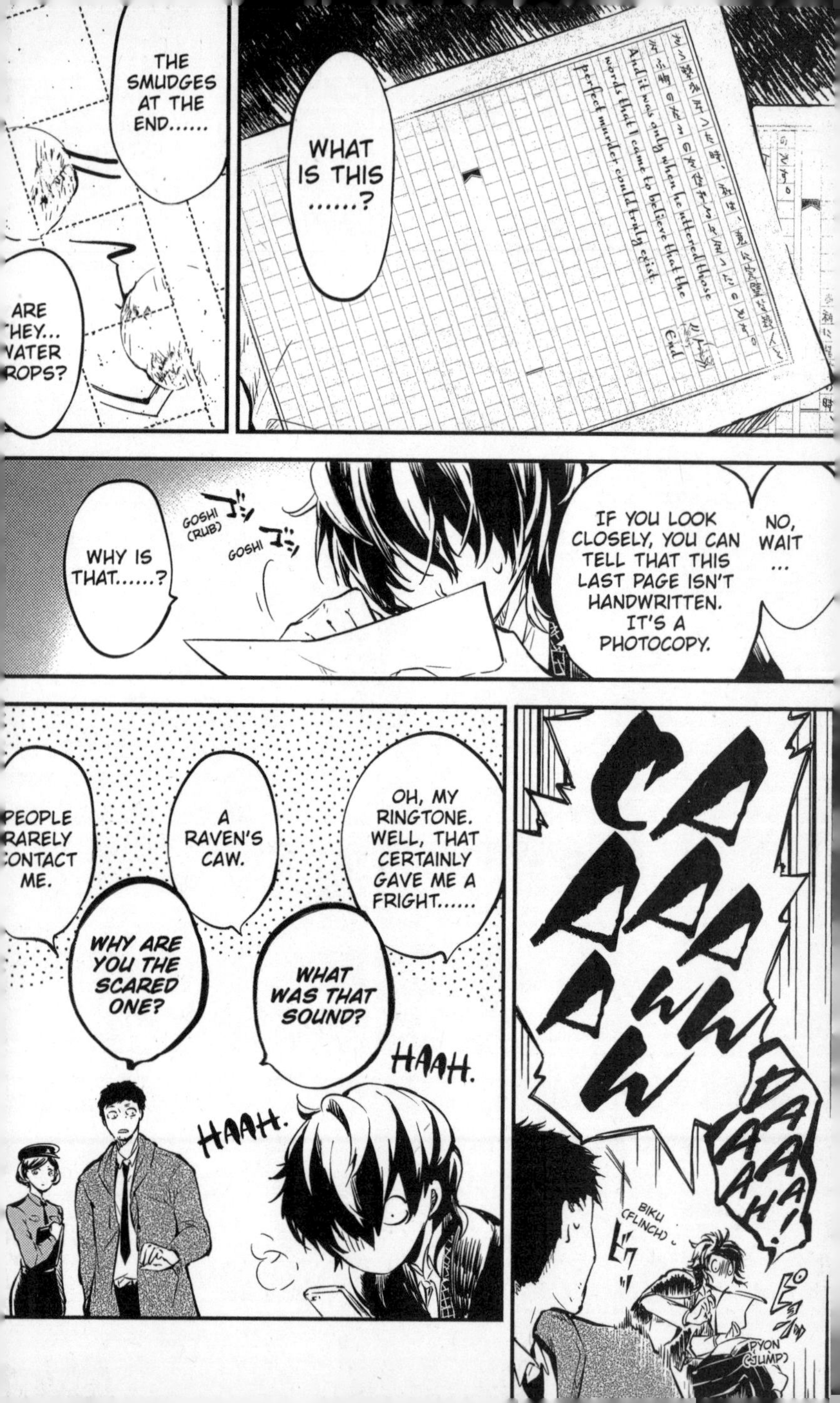
WHAT IS THIS ......?
And it was only when he uttered those words that I came to believe that the perfect murder could truly exist.
The End
THE SMUDGES AT THE END......
ARE HEY... VATER ROPS?
NO, WAIT ...
IF YOU LOOK CLOSELY, YOU CAN TELL THAT THIS LAST PAGE ISN'T HANDWRITTEN. IT'S A PHOTOCOPY.
GOSHI (RUB)
GOSHI
WHY IS THAT......?
CAAAAAAAWWW
DAAAAAAH!
BIKU (FLINCH)
PYON (JUMP)
OH, MY RINGTONE. WELL, THAT CERTAINLY GAVE ME A FRIGHT......
A RAVEN'S CAW.
PEOPLE RARELY CONTACT ME.
WHAT WAS THAT SOUND?
WHY ARE YOU THE SCARED ONE?
HAAH.
HAAH.

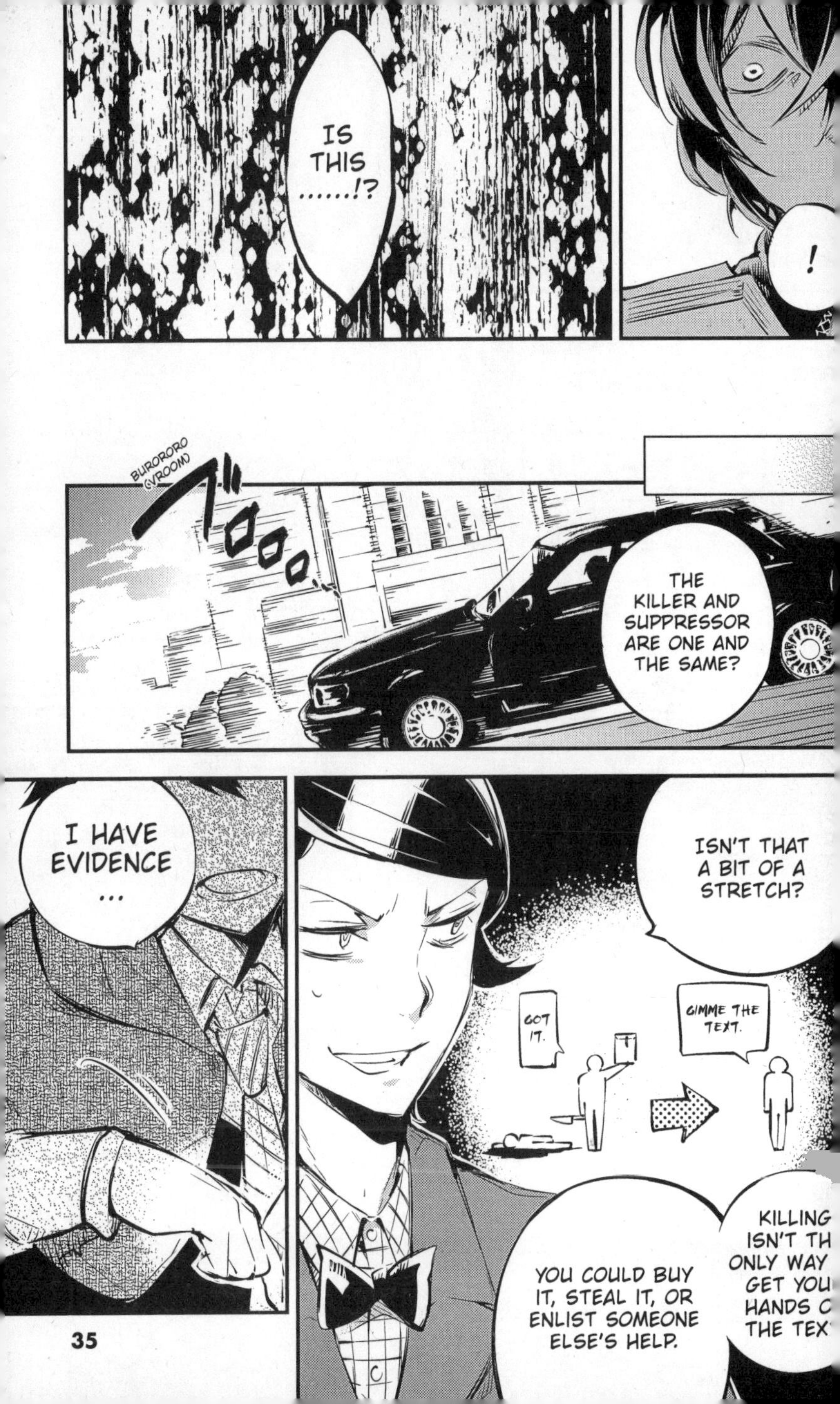
!
IS THIS ......!?
BURORORO (VROOM)
THE KILLER AND SUPPRESSOR ARE ONE AND THE SAME?
ISN'T THAT A BIT OF A STRETCH?
GIMME THE TEXT.
GOT IT.
KILLING ISN'T TH ONLY WAY GET YOU HANDS C THE TEX
YOU COULD BUY IT, STEAL IT, OR ENLIST SOMEONE ELSE'S HELP.
I HAVE EVIDENCE ...

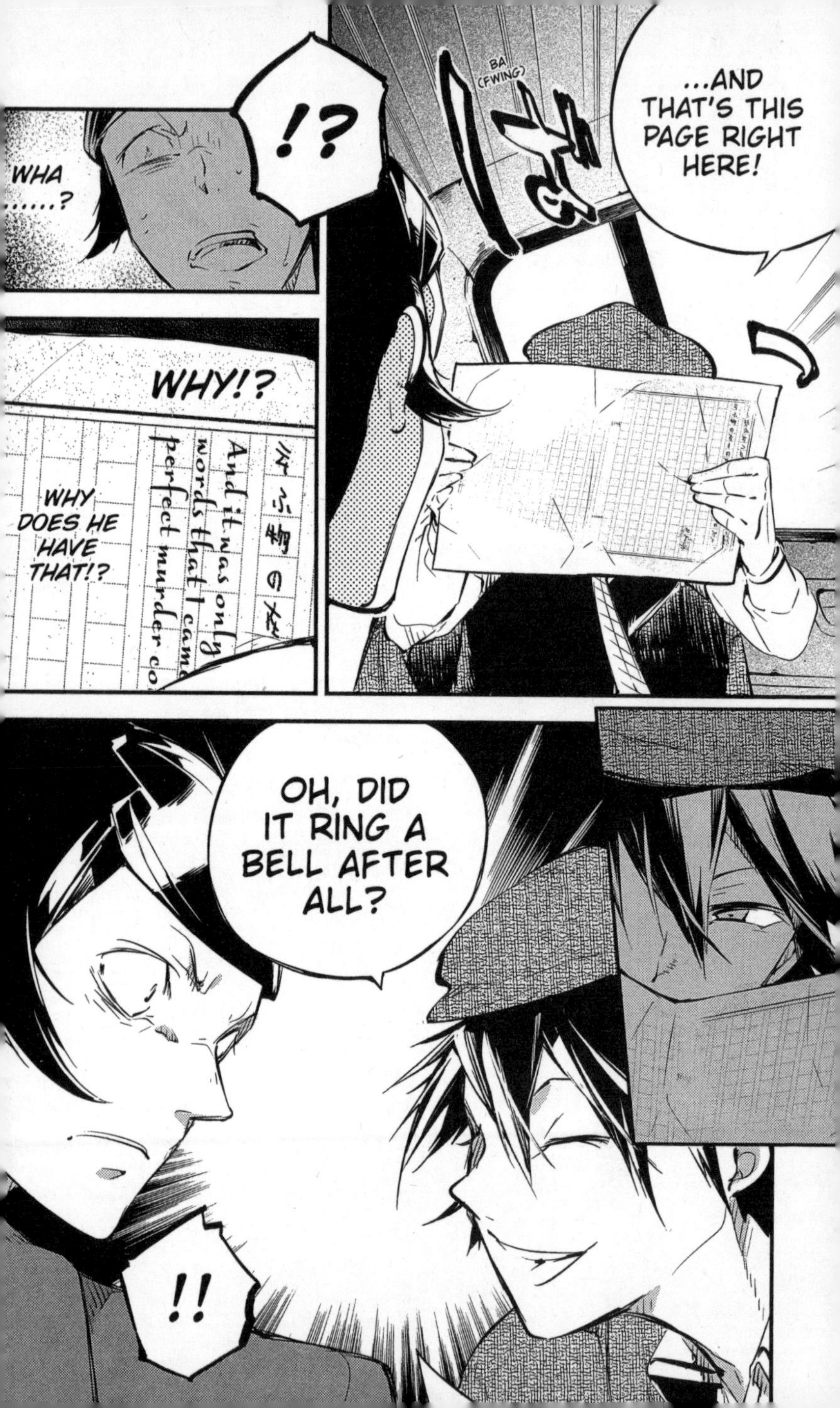
BA (FWING)
...AND THAT'S THIS PAGE RIGHT HERE!
!?
WHA ......?
WHY!?
And it was only
words that I came
perfect murder co
WHY DOES HE HAVE THAT!?
OH, DID IT RING A BELL AFTER ALL?
!!

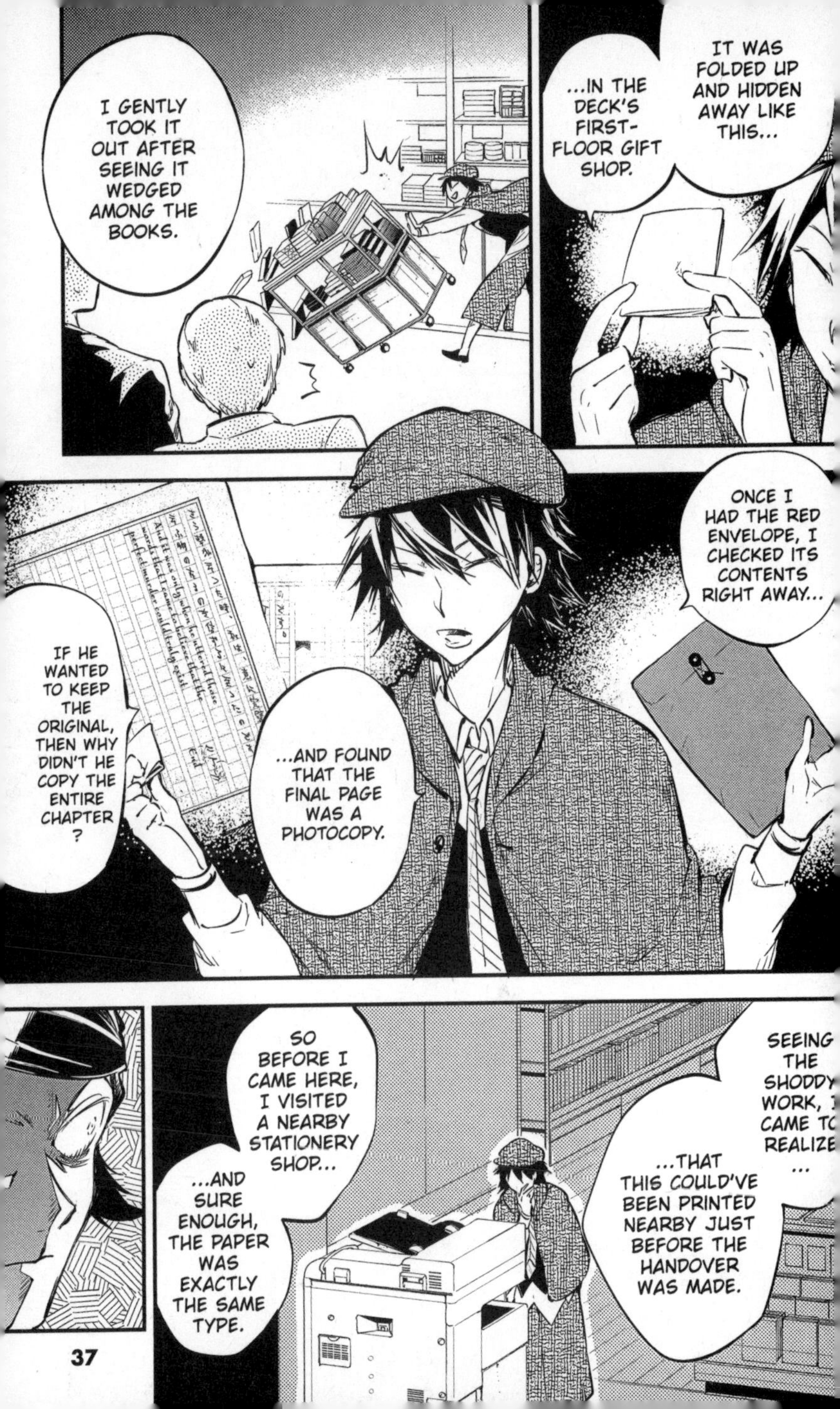
IT WAS FOLDED UP AND HIDDEN AWAY LIKE THIS...
...IN THE DECK'S FIRST-FLOOR GIFT SHOP.
I GENTLY TOOK IT OUT AFTER SEEING IT WEDGED AMONG THE BOOKS.
ONCE I HAD THE RED ENVELOPE, I CHECKED ITS CONTENTS RIGHT AWAY...
...AND FOUND THAT THE FINAL PAGE WAS A PHOTOCOPY.
IF HE WANTED TO KEEP THE ORIGINAL, THEN WHY DIDN'T HE COPY THE ENTIRE CHAPTER?
SEEING THE SHODDY WORK, I CAME TO REALIZE...
...THAT THIS COULD'VE BEEN PRINTED NEARBY JUST BEFORE THE HANDOVER WAS MADE.
SO BEFORE I CAME HERE, I VISITED A NEARBY STATIONERY SHOP...
...AND SURE ENOUGH, THE PAPER WAS EXACTLY THE SAME TYPE.

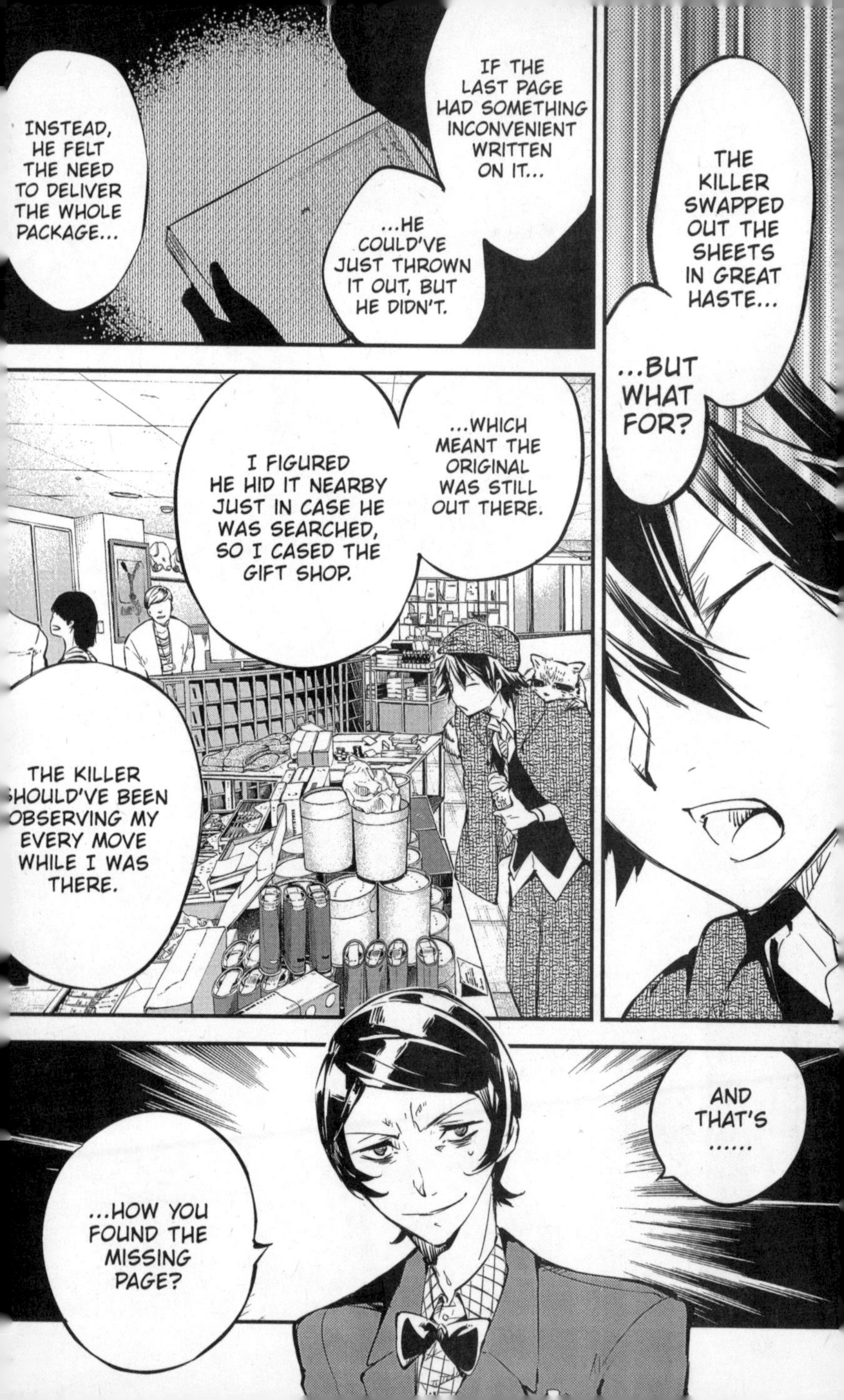
THE KILLER SWAPPED OUT THE SHEETS IN GREAT HASTE...
...BUT WHAT FOR?
IF THE LAST PAGE HAD SOMETHING INCONVENIENT WRITTEN ON IT...
...HE COULD'VE JUST THROWN IT OUT, BUT HE DIDN'T.
INSTEAD, HE FELT THE NEED TO DELIVER THE WHOLE PACKAGE...
...WHICH MEANT THE ORIGINAL WAS STILL OUT THERE.
I FIGURED HE HID IT NEARBY JUST IN CASE HE WAS SEARCHED, SO I CASED THE GIFT SHOP.
THE KILLER SHOULD'VE BEEN OBSERVING MY EVERY MOVE WHILE I WAS THERE.
AND THAT'S......
...HOW YOU FOUND THE MISSING PAGE?

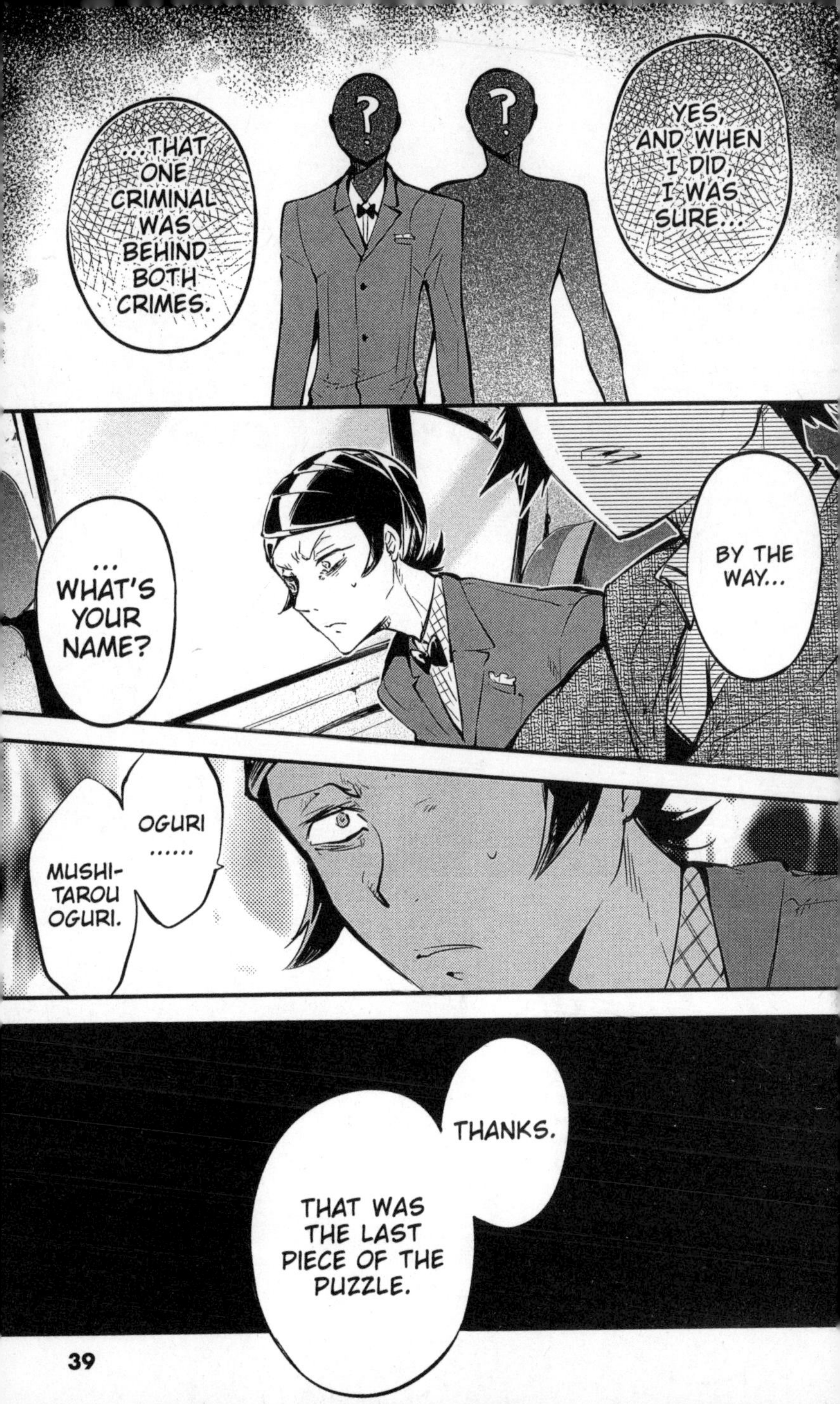
YES, AND WHEN I DID, I WAS SURE...
...THAT ONE CRIMINAL WAS BEHIND BOTH CRIMES.
BY THE WAY...
... WHAT'S YOUR NAME?
OGURI ...... MUSHI-TAROU OGURI.
THANKS.
THAT WAS THE LAST PIECE OF THE PUZZLE.

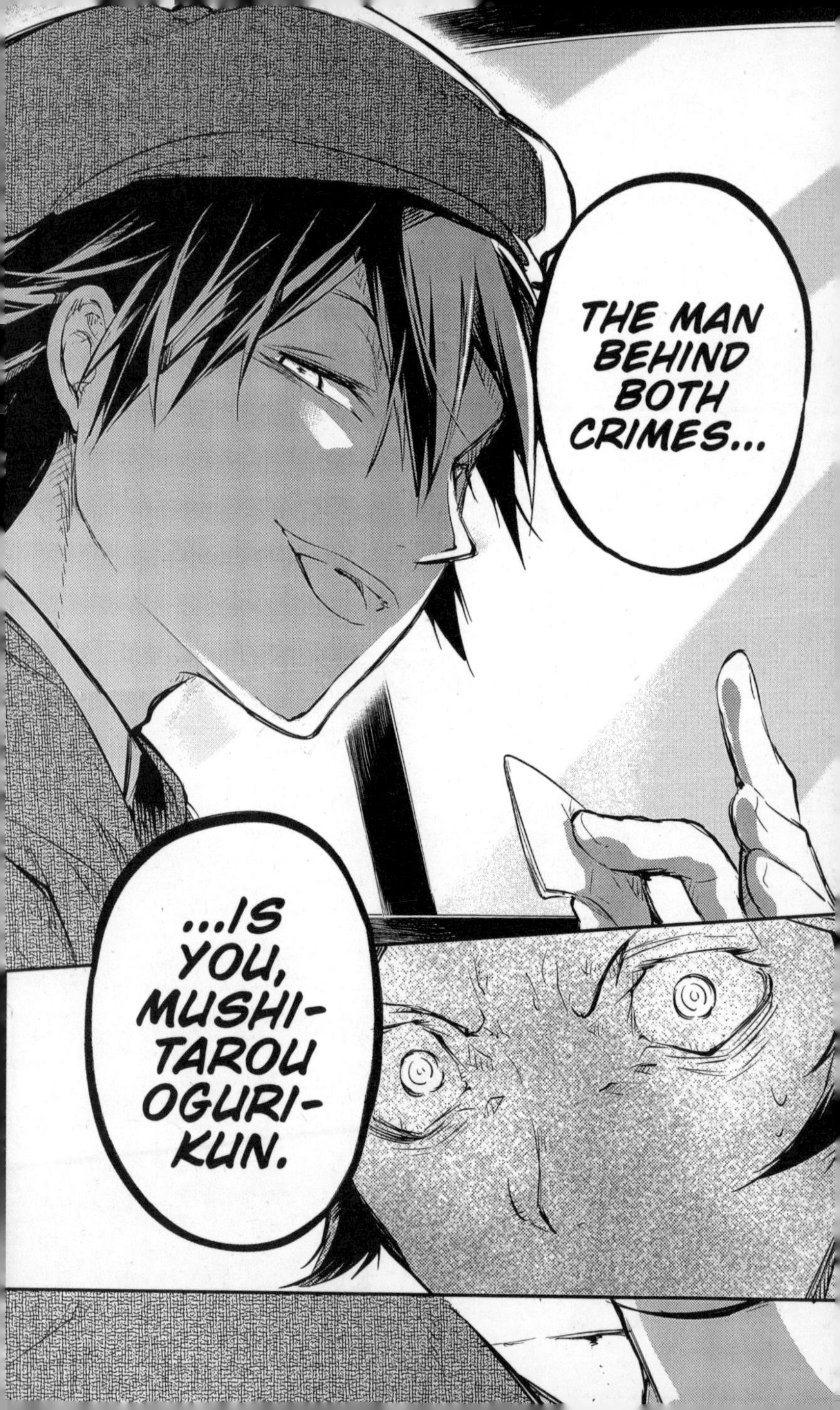
THE MAN BEHIND BOTH CRIMES...
...IS YOU, MUSHI-TAROU OGURI-KUN.

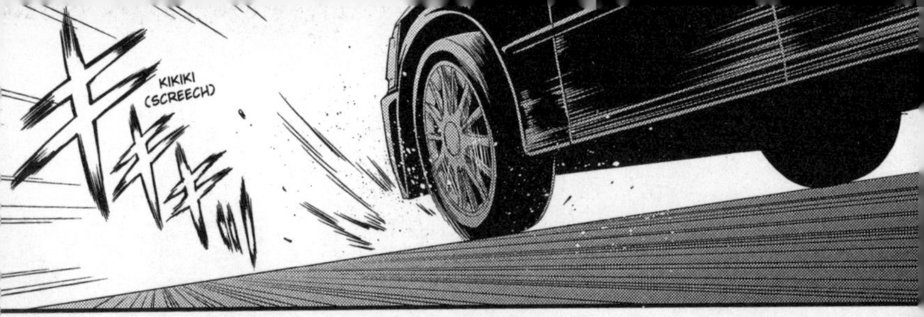
KIKIKI (SCREECH)

CHAPTER 5
The Perfect Murde
the Perfect Killer, Part

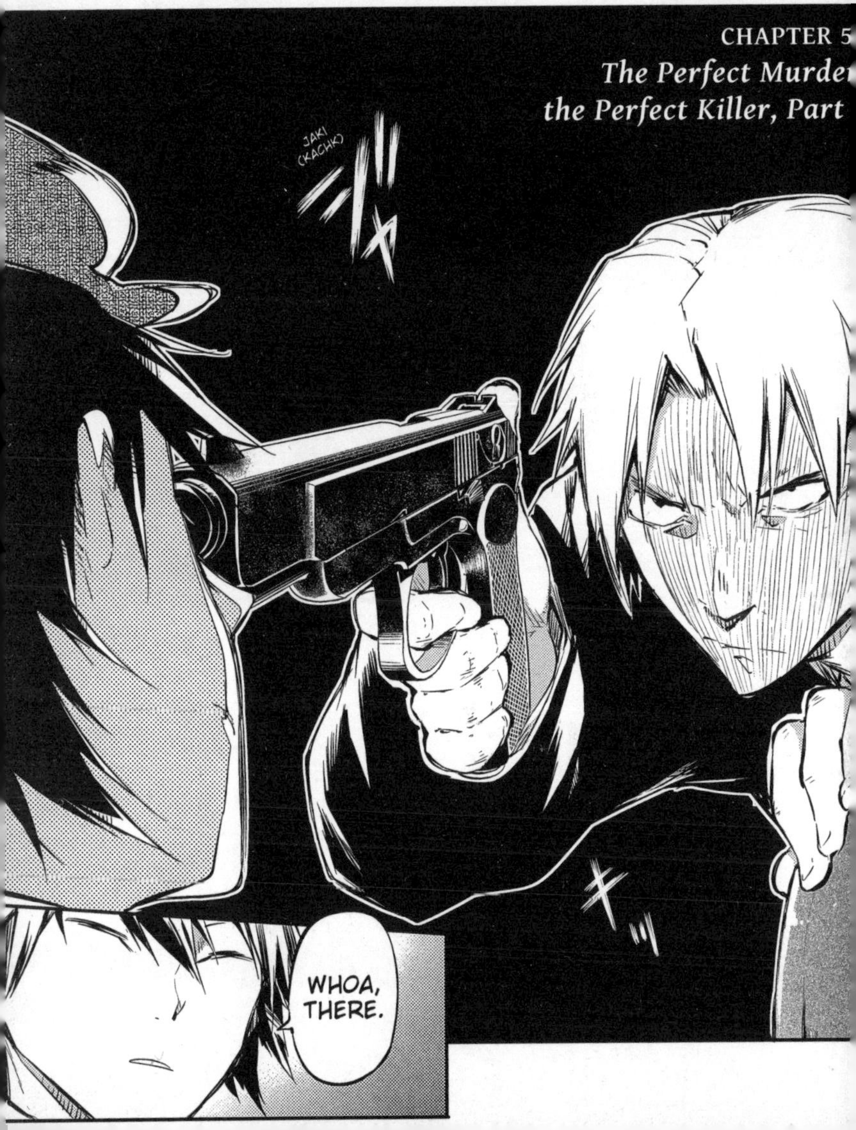
JAKI (KACHK)
WHOA, THERE.

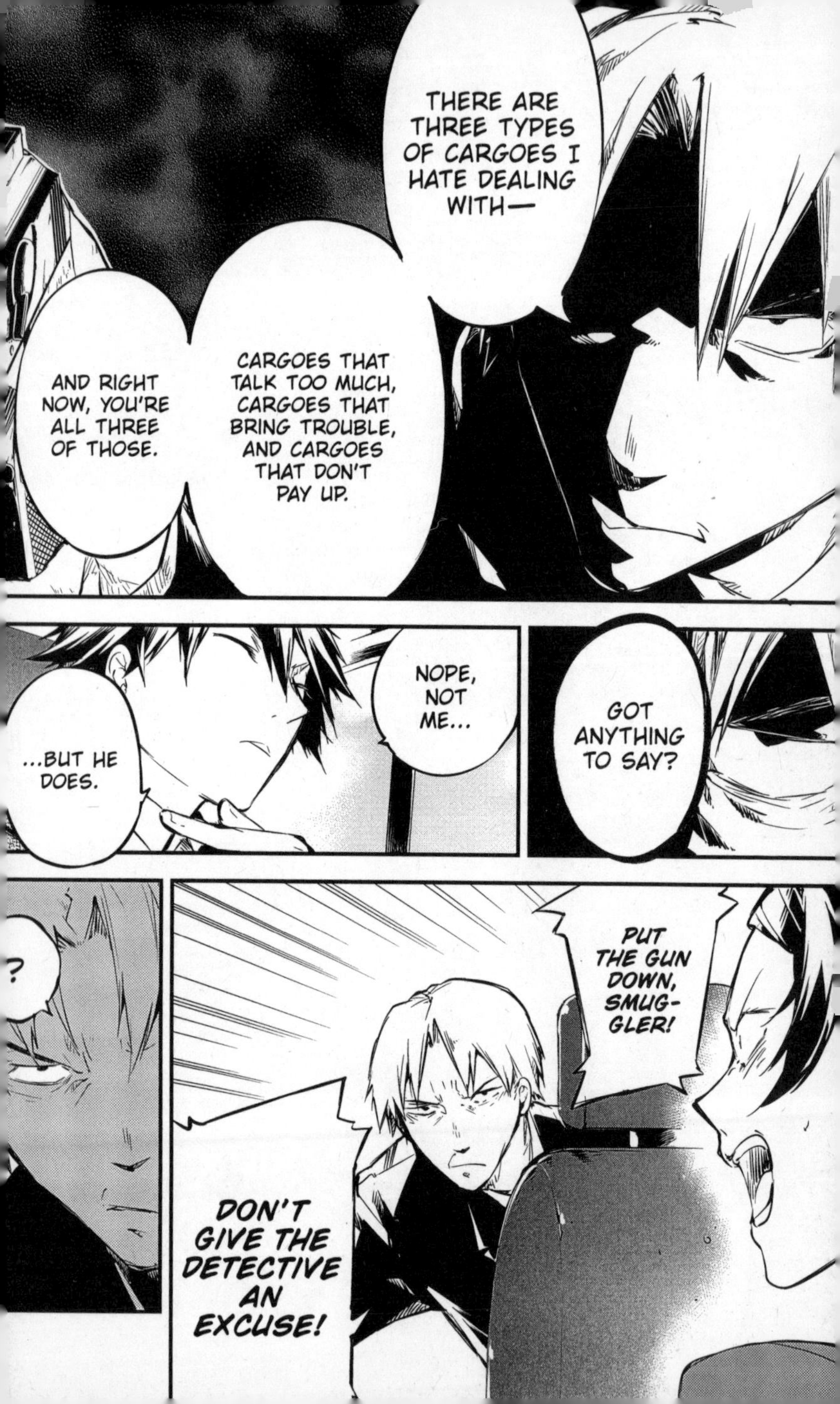
THERE ARE THREE TYPES OF CARGOES I HATE DEALING WITH—
CARGOES THAT TALK TOO MUCH, CARGOES THAT BRING TROUBLE, AND CARGOES THAT DON'T PAY UP.
AND RIGHT NOW, YOU'RE ALL THREE OF THOSE.
GOT ANYTHING TO SAY?
NOPE, NOT ME...
...BUT HE DOES.
PUT THE GUN DOWN, SMUG-GLER!
DON'T GIVE THE DETECTIVE AN EXCUSE!
?

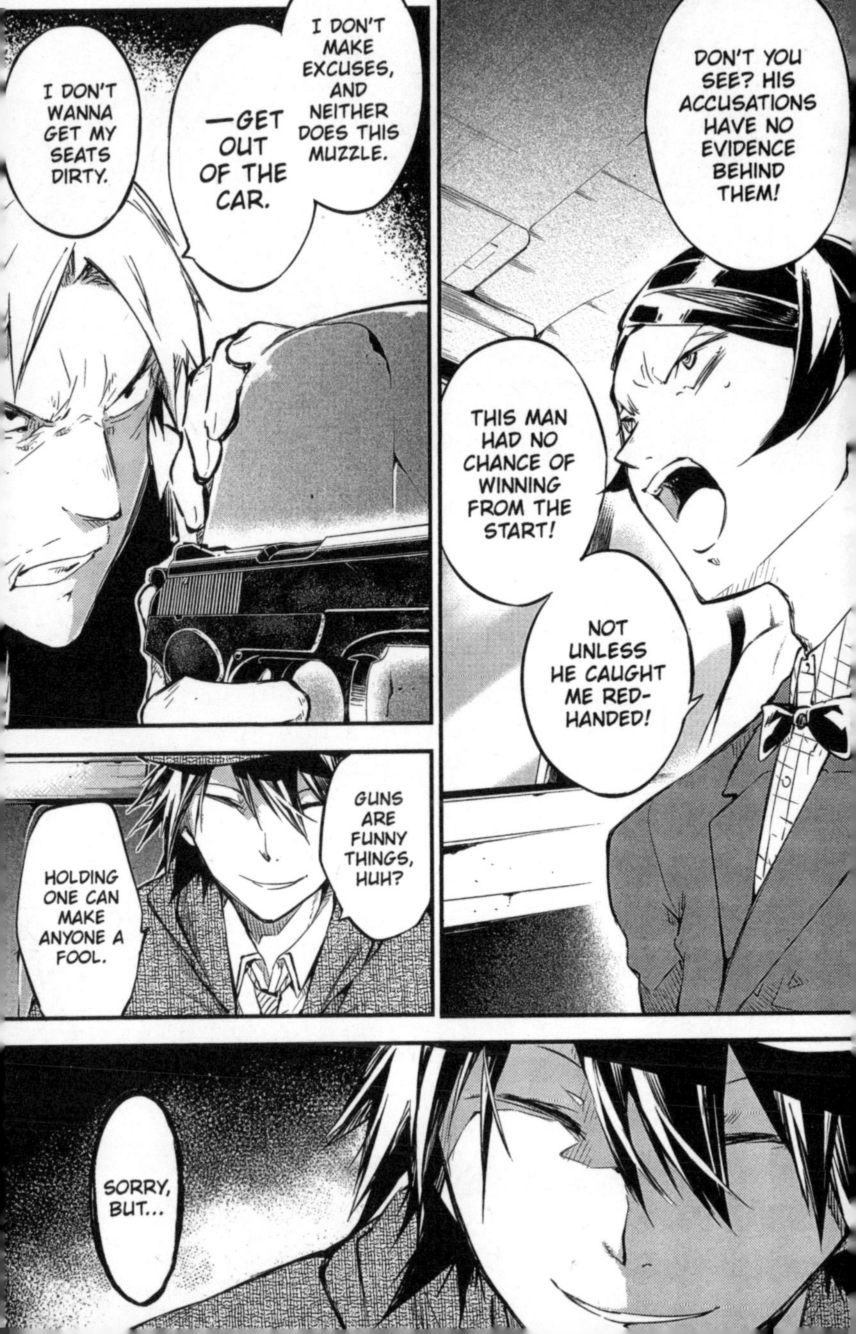
DON'T YOU SEE? HIS ACCUSATIONS HAVE NO EVIDENCE BEHIND THEM!
THIS MAN HAD NO CHANCE OF WINNING FROM THE START!
NOT UNLESS HE CAUGHT ME RED-HANDED!
I DON'T MAKE EXCUSES, AND NEITHER DOES THIS MUZZLE.
—GET OUT OF THE CAR.
I DON'T WANNA GET MY SEATS DIRTY.
GUNS ARE FUNNY THINGS, HUH?
HOLDING ONE CAN MAKE ANYONE A FOOL.
SORRY, BUT...

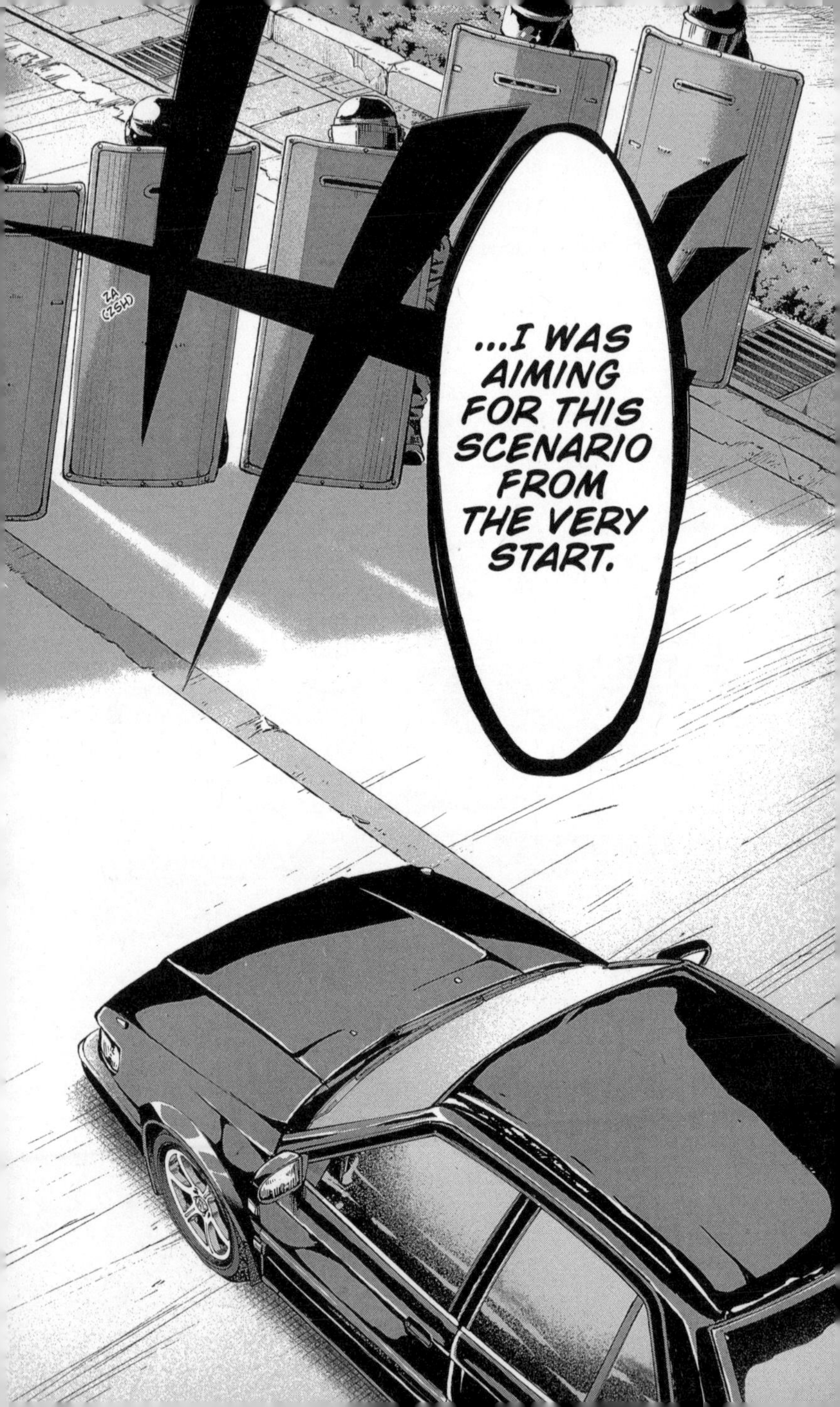
...I WAS AIMING FOR THIS SCENARIO FROM THE VERY START.
ZA (ZSH)

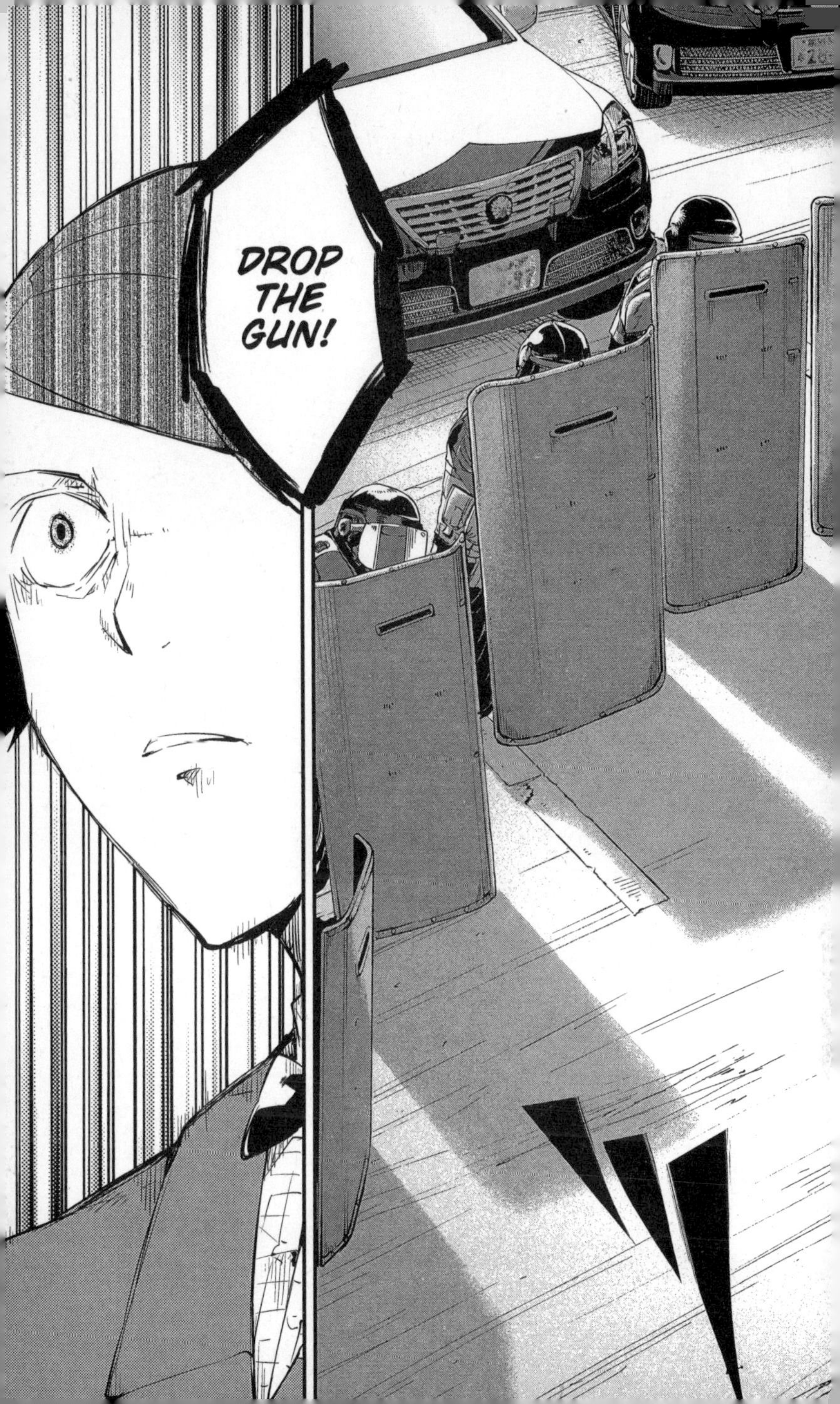
DROP THE GUN!

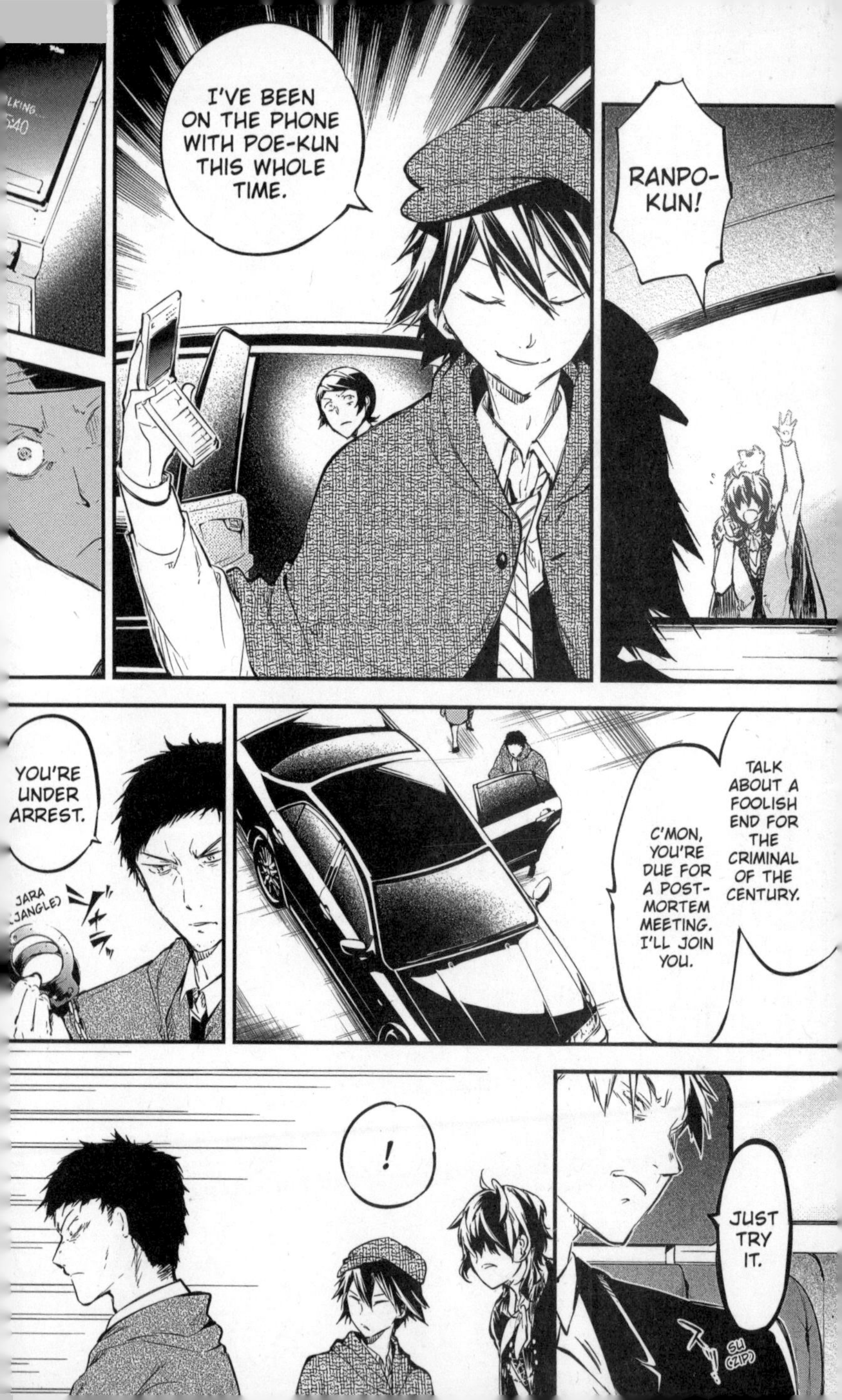
RANPO-KUN!
I'VE BEEN ON THE PHONE WITH POE-KUN THIS WHOLE TIME.
TALK ABOUT A FOOLISH END FOR THE CRIMINAL OF THE CENTURY.
C'MON, YOU'RE DUE FOR A POST-MORTEM MEETING. I'LL JOIN YOU.
YOU'RE UNDER ARREST.
JARA (JANGLE)
JUST TRY IT.
SU (ZIP)
!

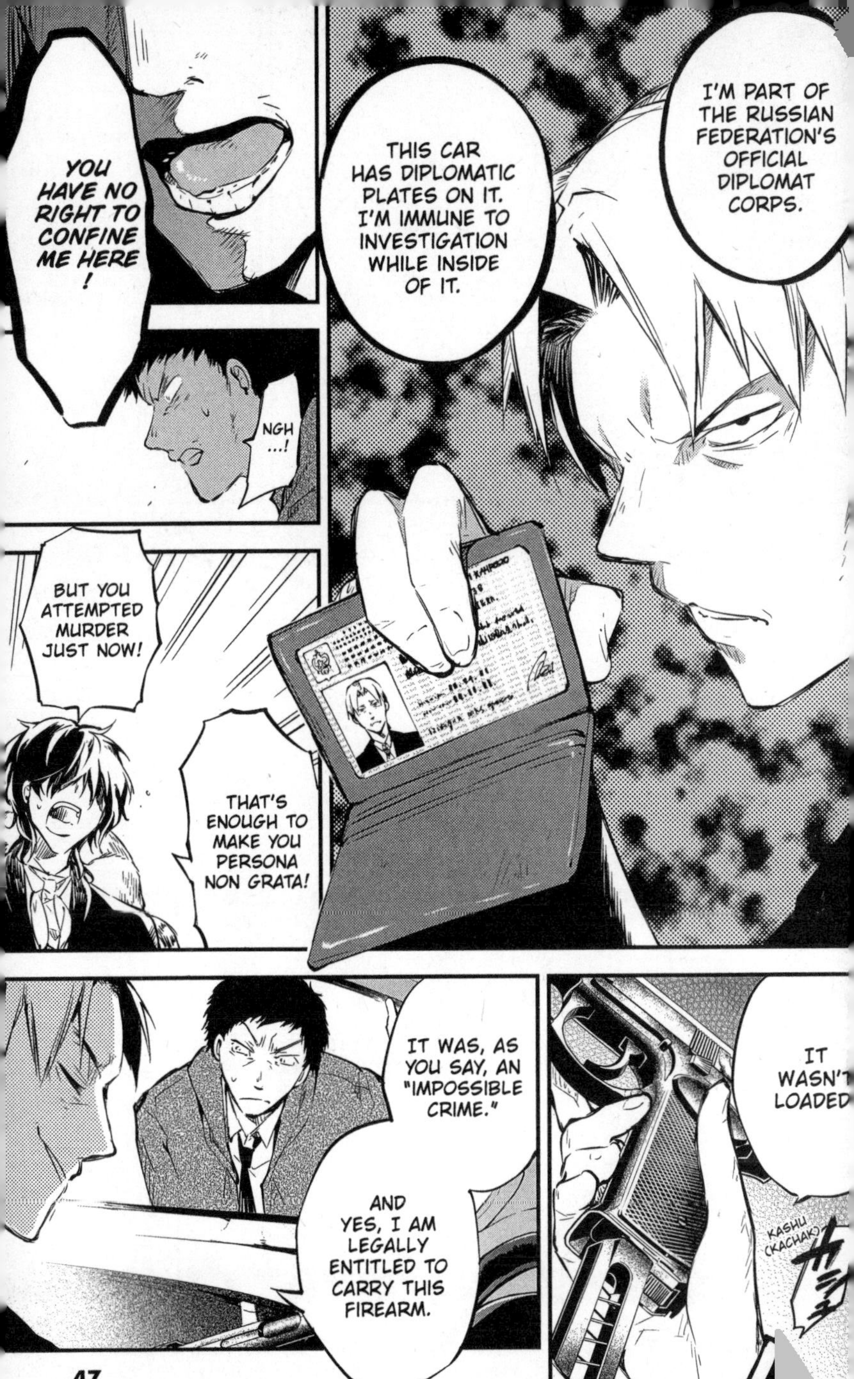
I'M PART OF THE RUSSIAN FEDERATION'S OFFICIAL DIPLOMAT CORPS.
THIS CAR HAS DIPLOMATIC PLATES ON IT. I'M IMMUNE TO INVESTIGATION WHILE INSIDE OF IT.
YOU HAVE NO RIGHT TO CONFINE ME HERE!
NGH ...!
BUT YOU ATTEMPTED MURDER JUST NOW!
THAT'S ENOUGH TO MAKE YOU PERSONA NON GRATA!
IT WASN'T LOADED
KASHU (KACHAK)
IT WAS, AS YOU SAY, AN "IMPOSSIBLE CRIME."
AND YES, I AM LEGALLY ENTITLED TO CARRY THIS FIREARM.

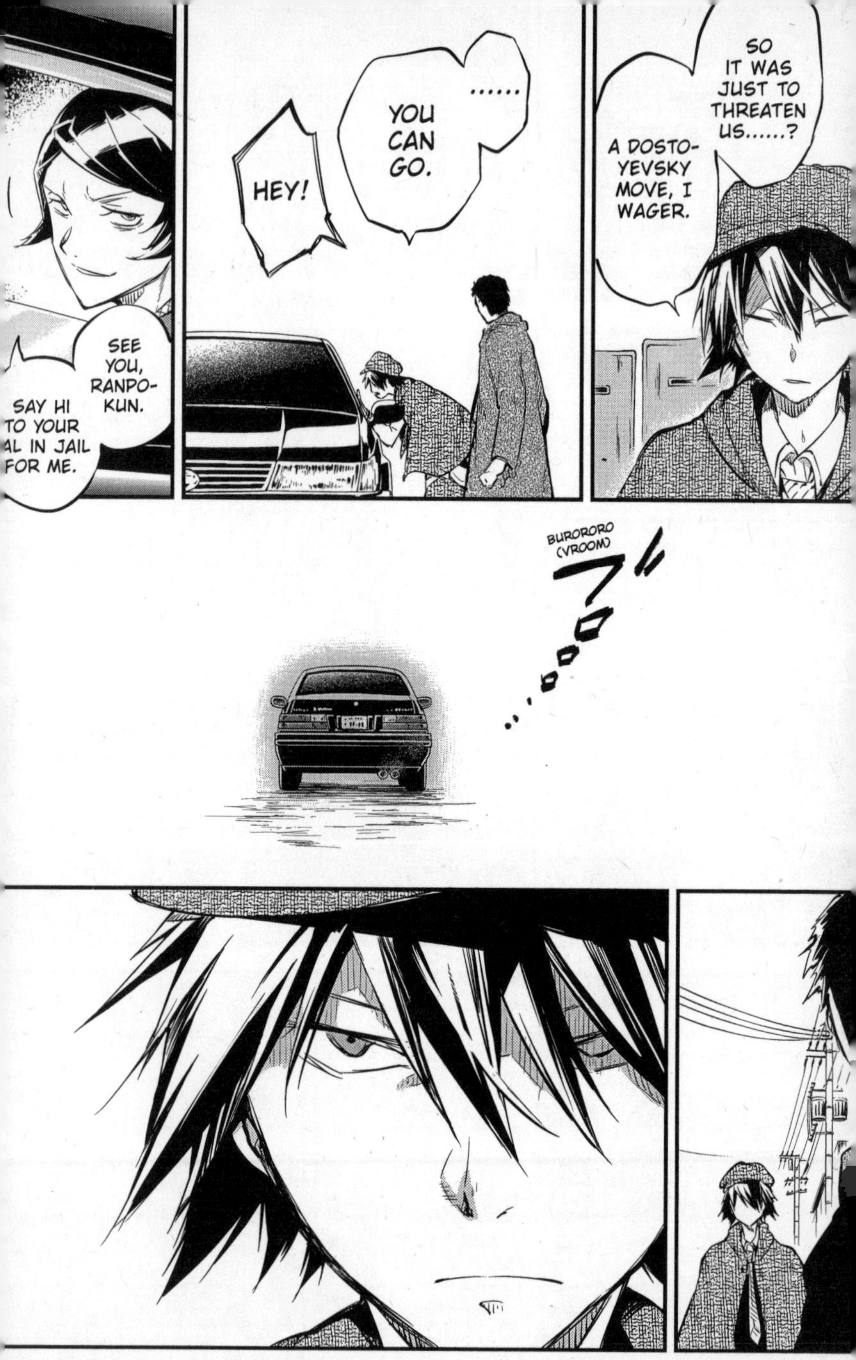
SO IT WAS JUST TO THREATEN US......?
A DOSTO-YEVSKY MOVE, I WAGER.
......
YOU CAN GO.
HEY!
SEE YOU, RANPO-KUN.
SAY HI TO YOUR AL IN JAIL FOR ME.
BURORORO (VROOM)

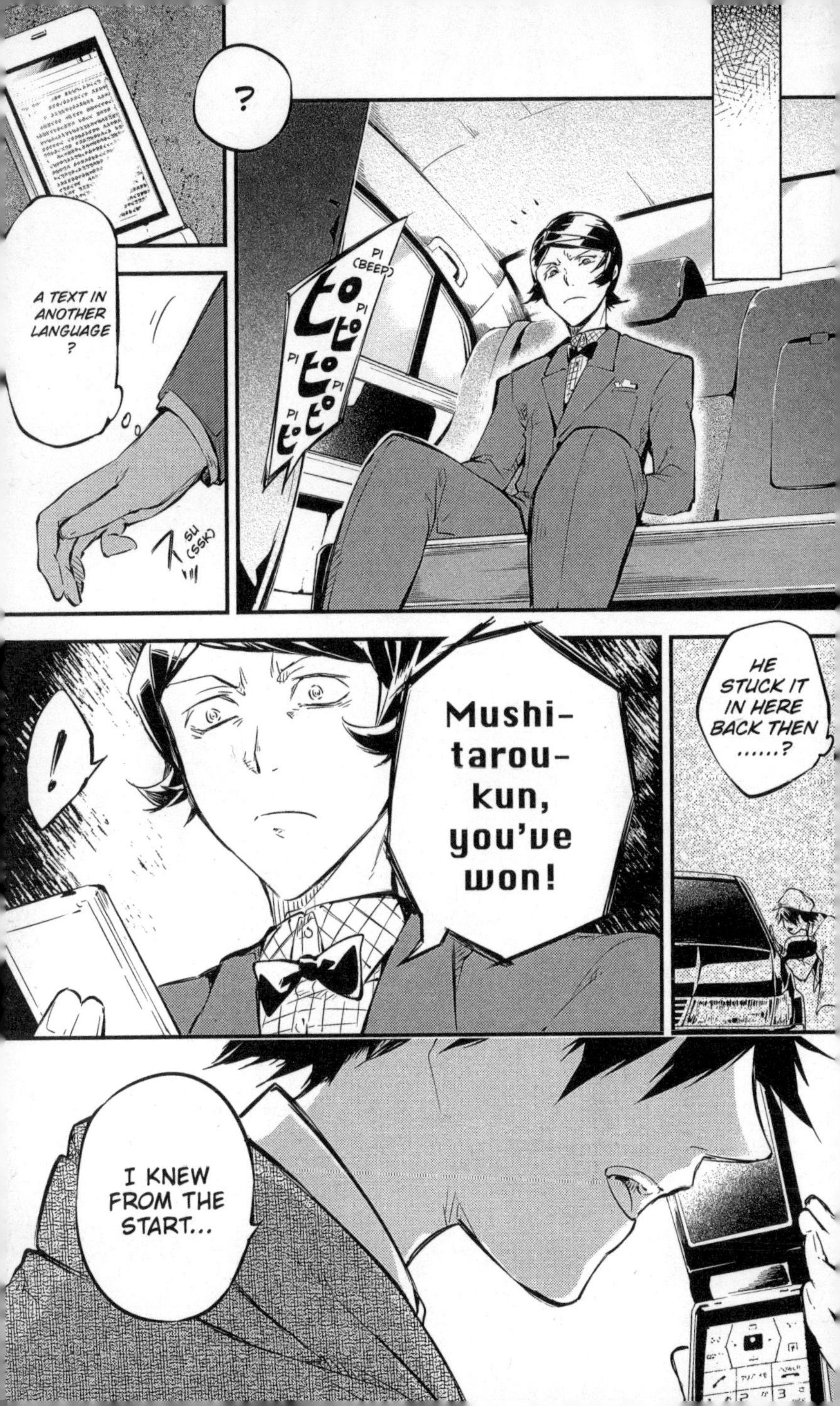
PI (BEEP)
PI
PI
PI
PI
?
A TEXT IN ANOTHER LANGUAGE?
SU (SSK)
HE STUCK IT IN HERE BACK THEN......?
!
Mushi-tarou-kun, you've won!
I KNEW FROM THE START...

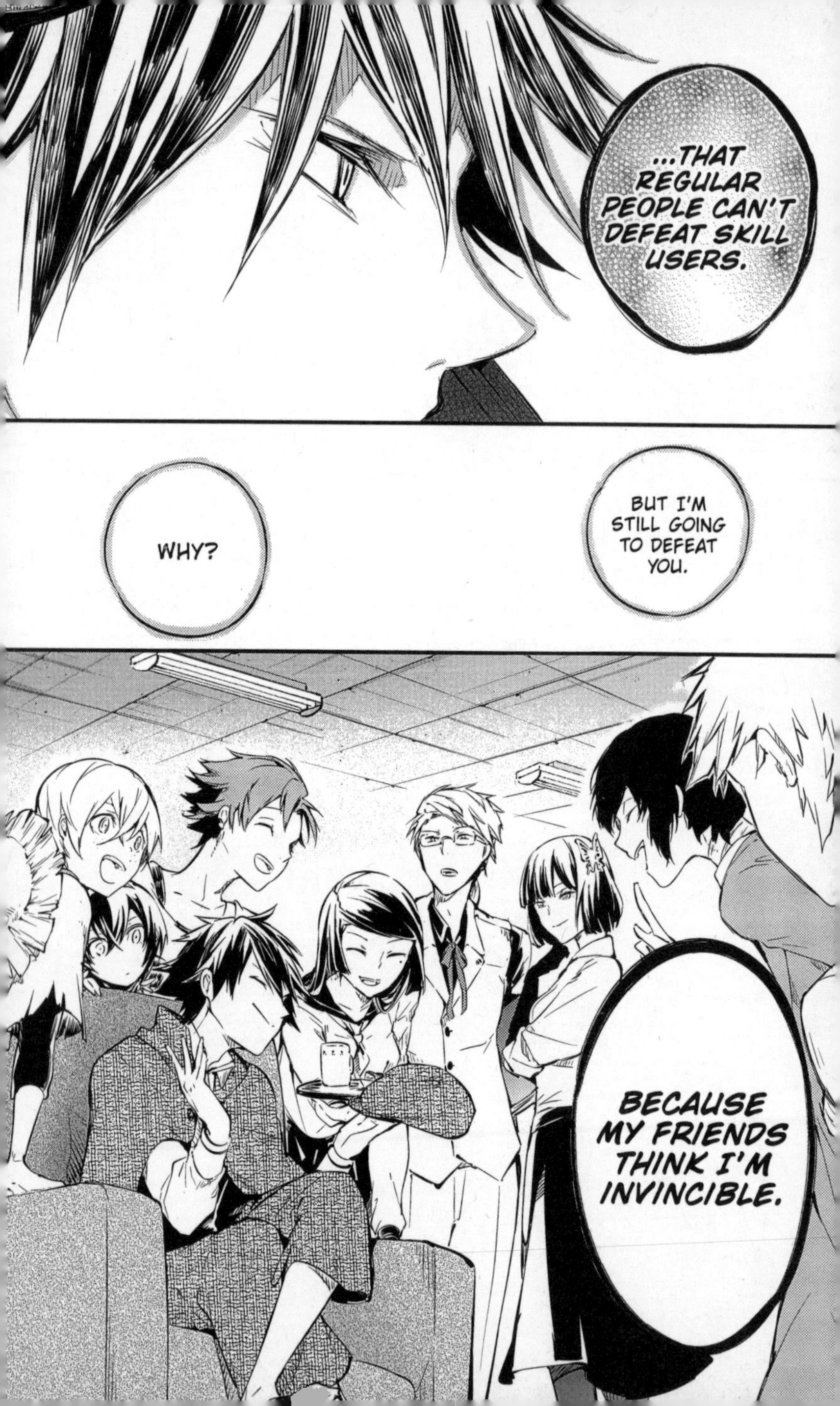
...THAT REGULAR PEOPLE CAN'T DEFEAT SKILL USERS.
BUT I'M STILL GOING TO DEFEAT YOU.
WHY?
BECAUSE MY FRIENDS THINK I'M INVINCIBLE.

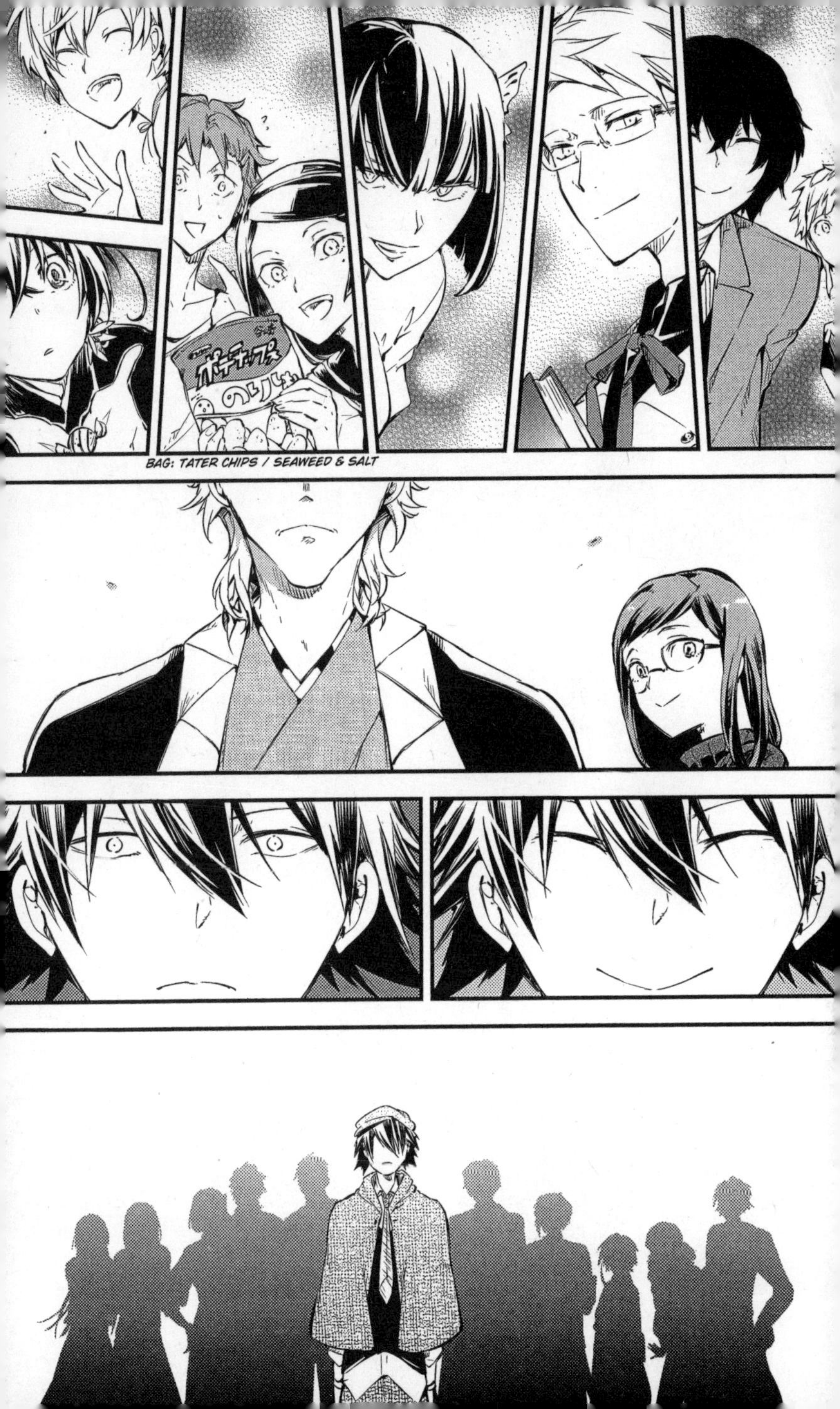
ポテチップス
のりしお
BAG: TATER CHIPS / SEAWEED & SALT

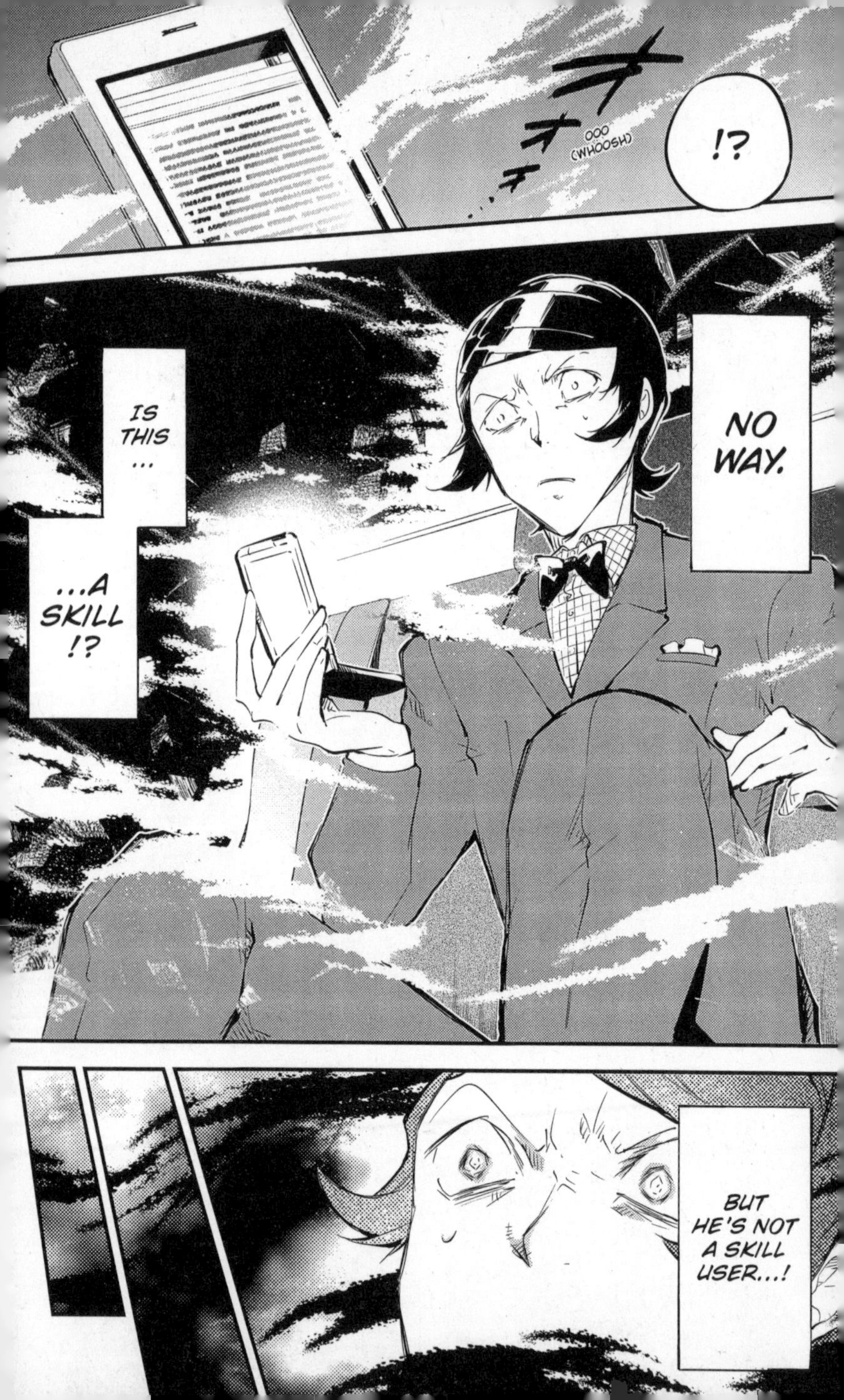
!?
OOO (WHOOSH)
NO WAY.
IS THIS ...
...A SKILL !?
BUT HE'S NOT A SKILL USER...!

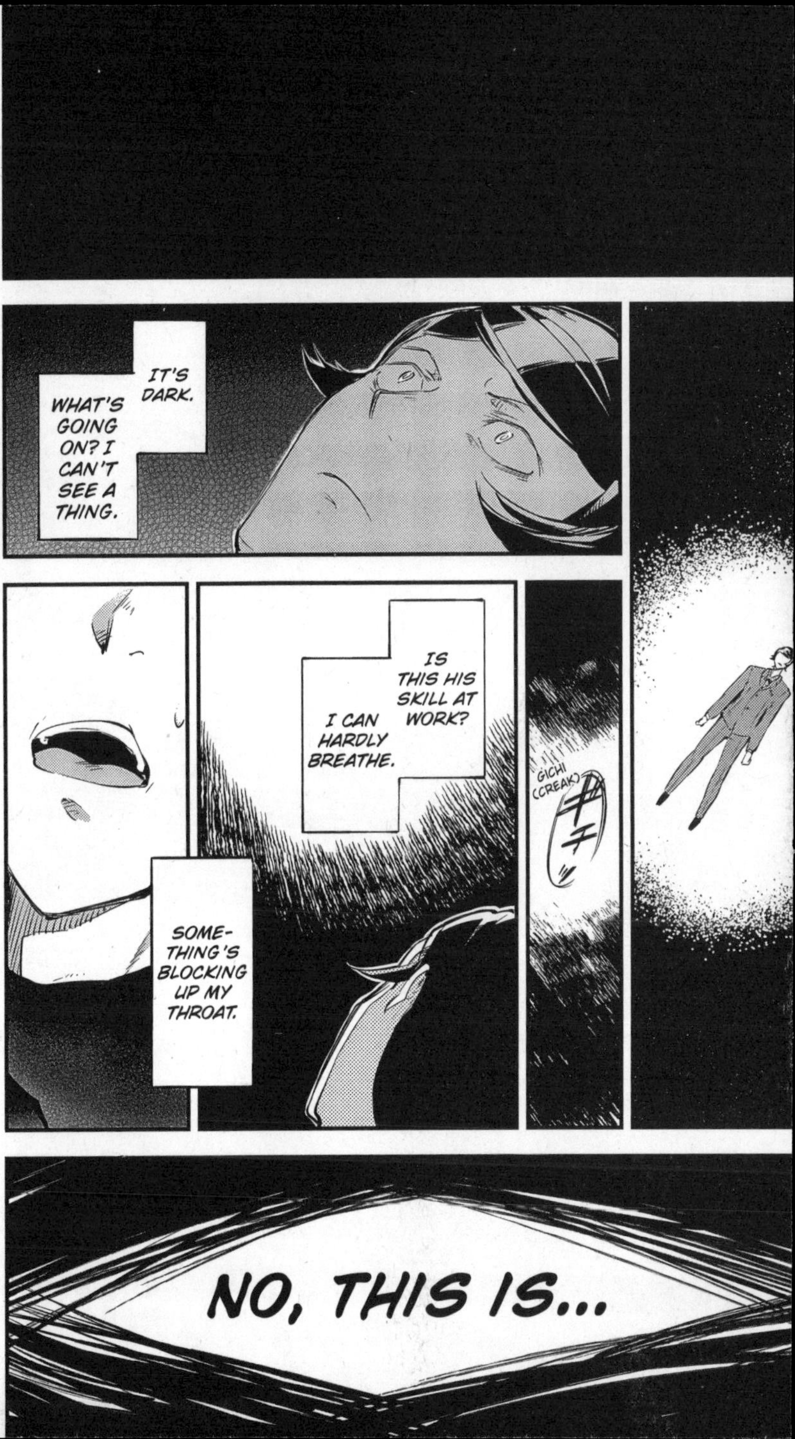
IT'S DARK.
WHAT'S GOING ON? I CAN'T SEE A THING.
GICHI (CREAK)
IS THIS HIS SKILL AT WORK?
I CAN HARDLY BREATHE.
SOME-THING'S BLOCKING UP MY THROAT.
NO, THIS IS...

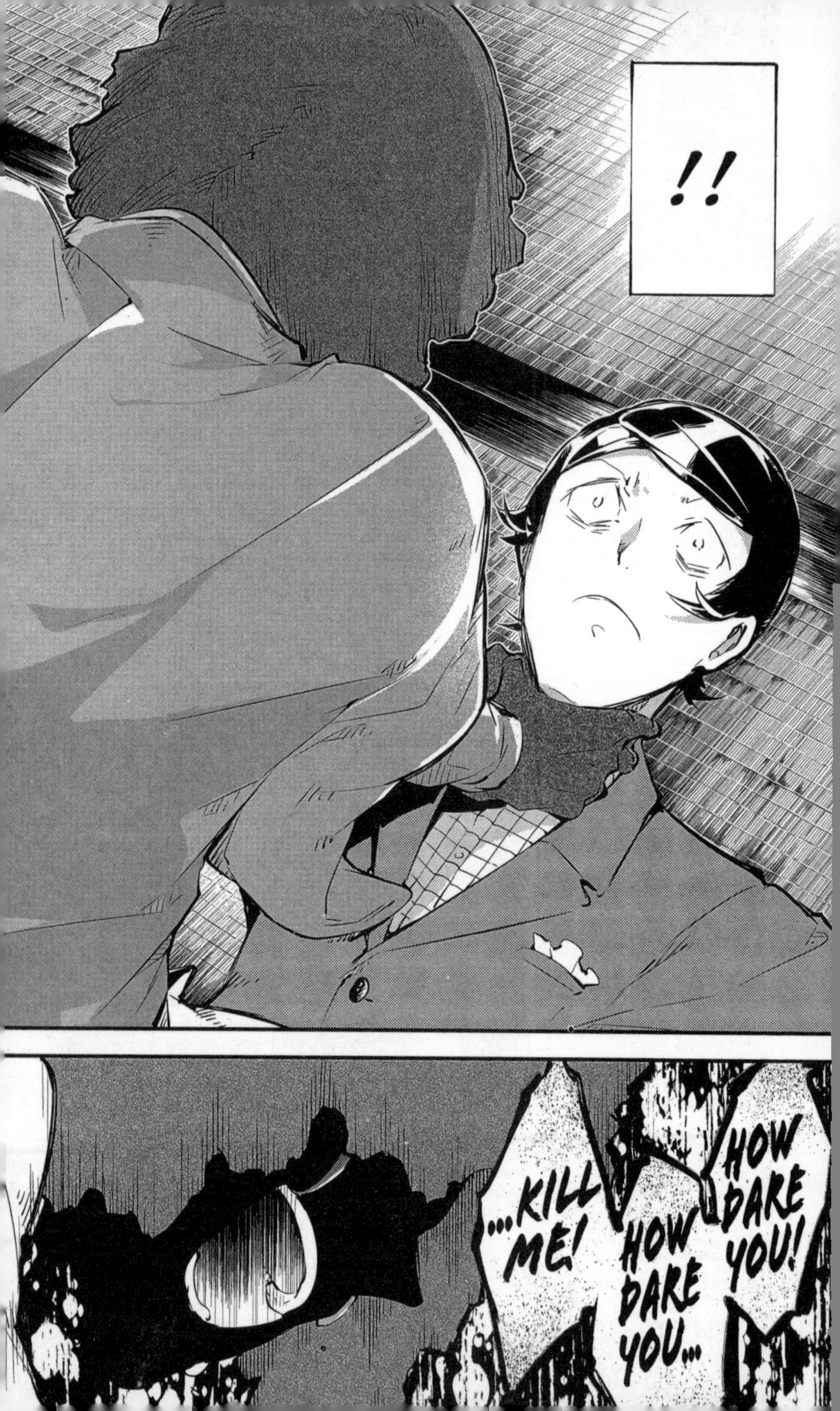
!!
HOW DARE YOU!
HOW DARE YOU...
...KILL ME!

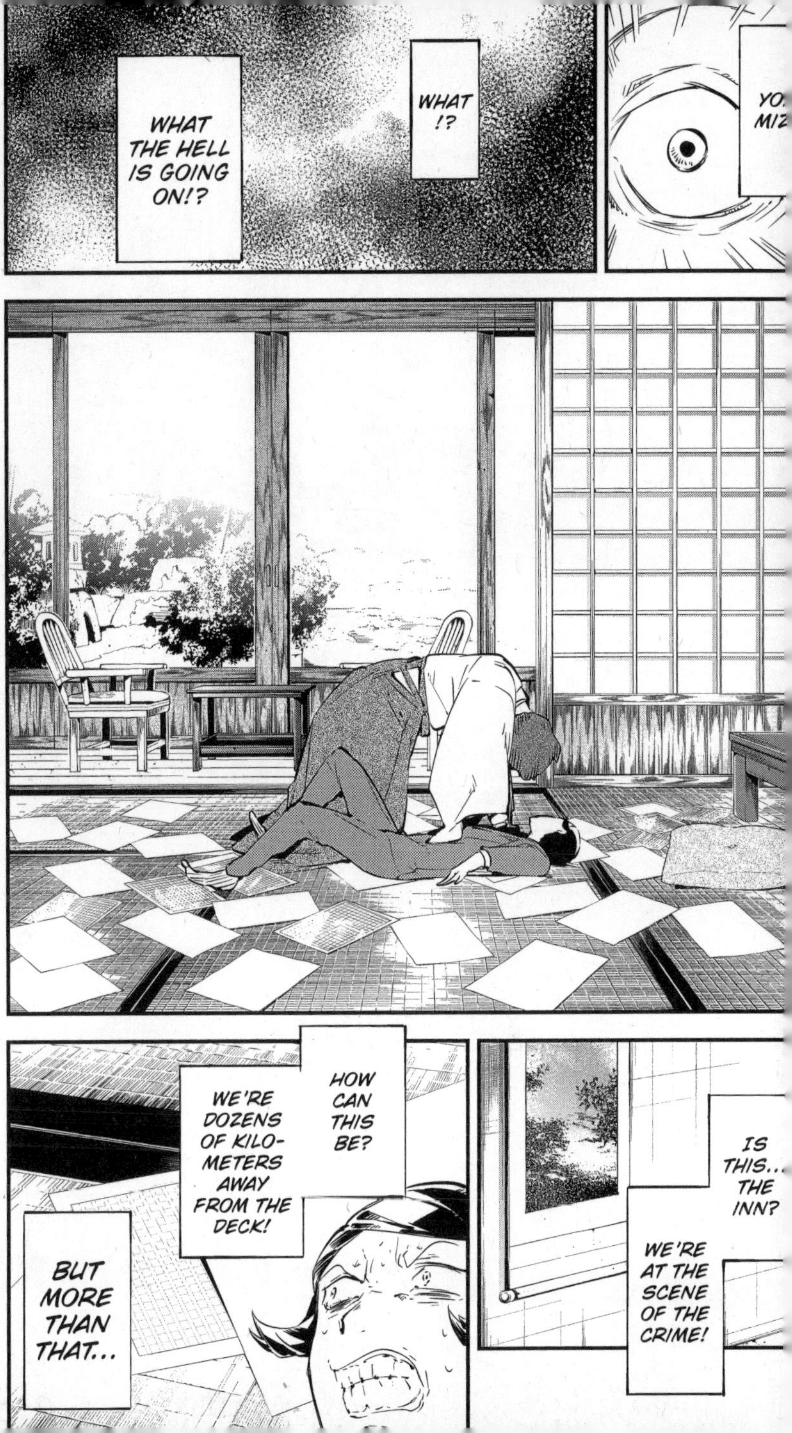
WHAT !?
WHAT THE HELL IS GOING ON!?
IS THIS... THE INN?
WE'RE AT THE SCENE OF THE CRIME!
HOW CAN THIS BE?
WE'RE DOZENS OF KILO-METERS AWAY FROM THE DECK!
BUT MORE THAN THAT...

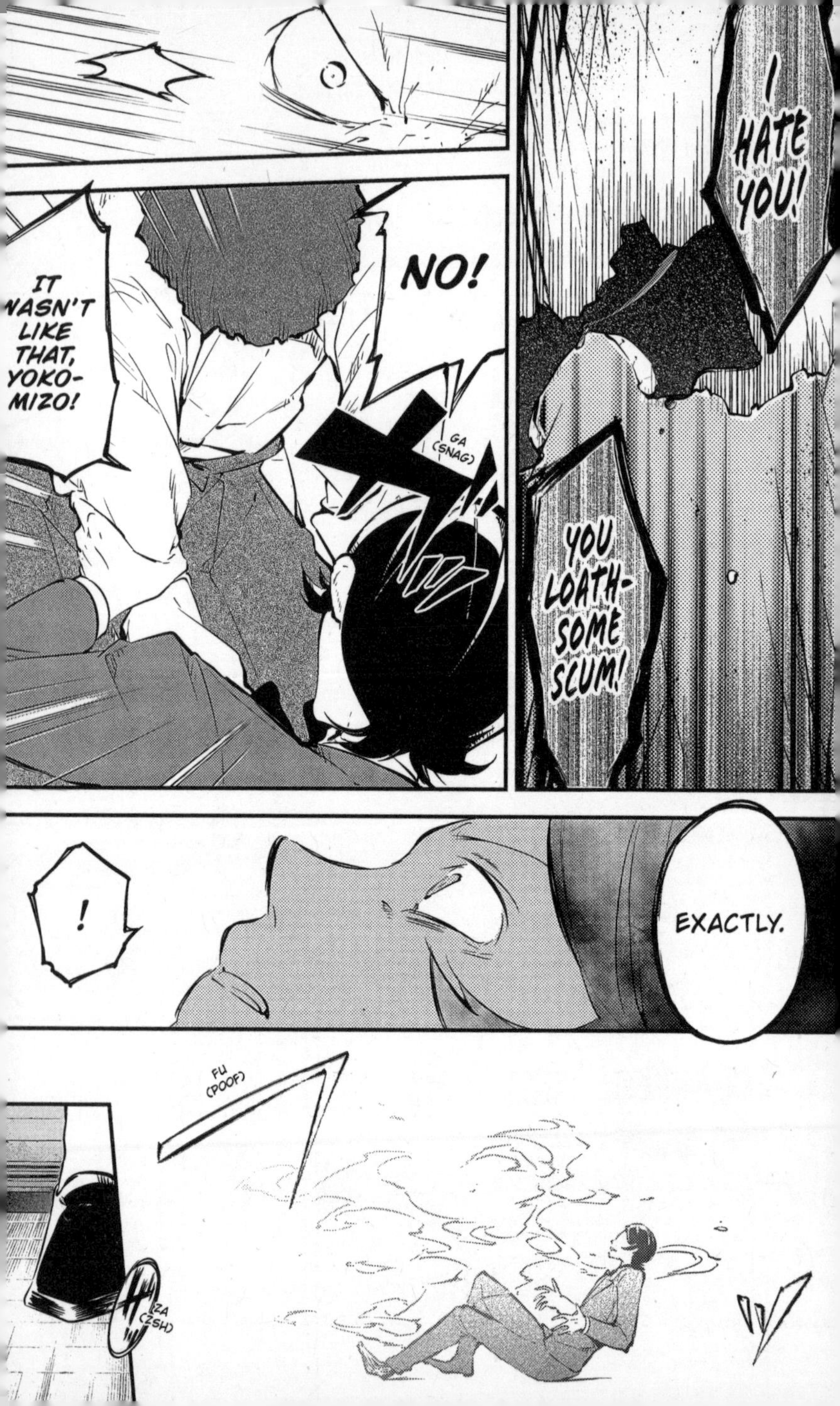
I HATE YOU!
YOU LOATH-SOME SCUM!
NO!
GA (SNAG)
IT WASN'T LIKE THAT, YOKO-MIZO!
EXACTLY.
!
FU (POOF)
ZA (ZSH)

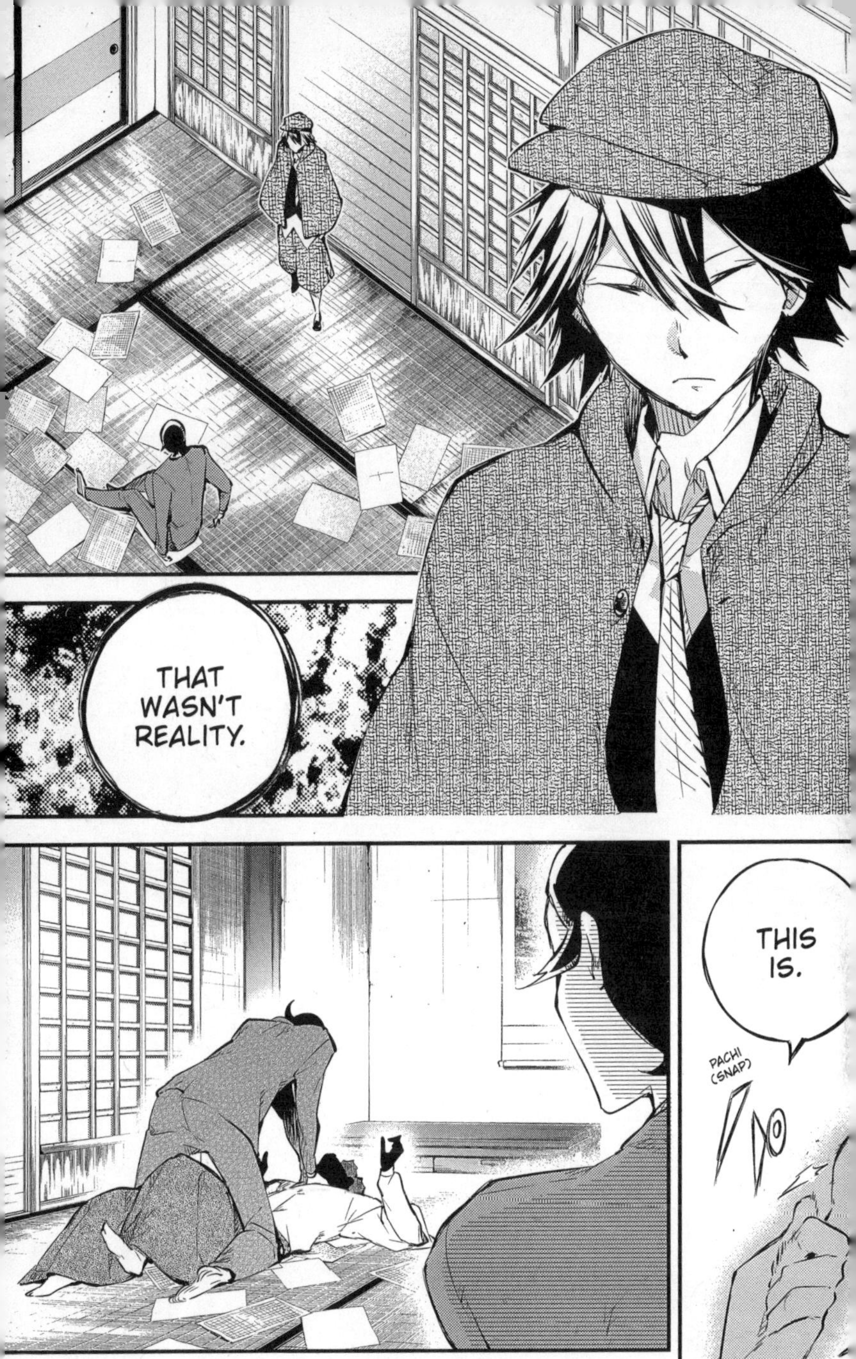
THAT WASN'T REALITY.
THIS IS.
PACHI (SNAP)

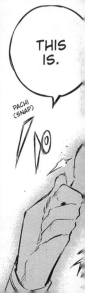

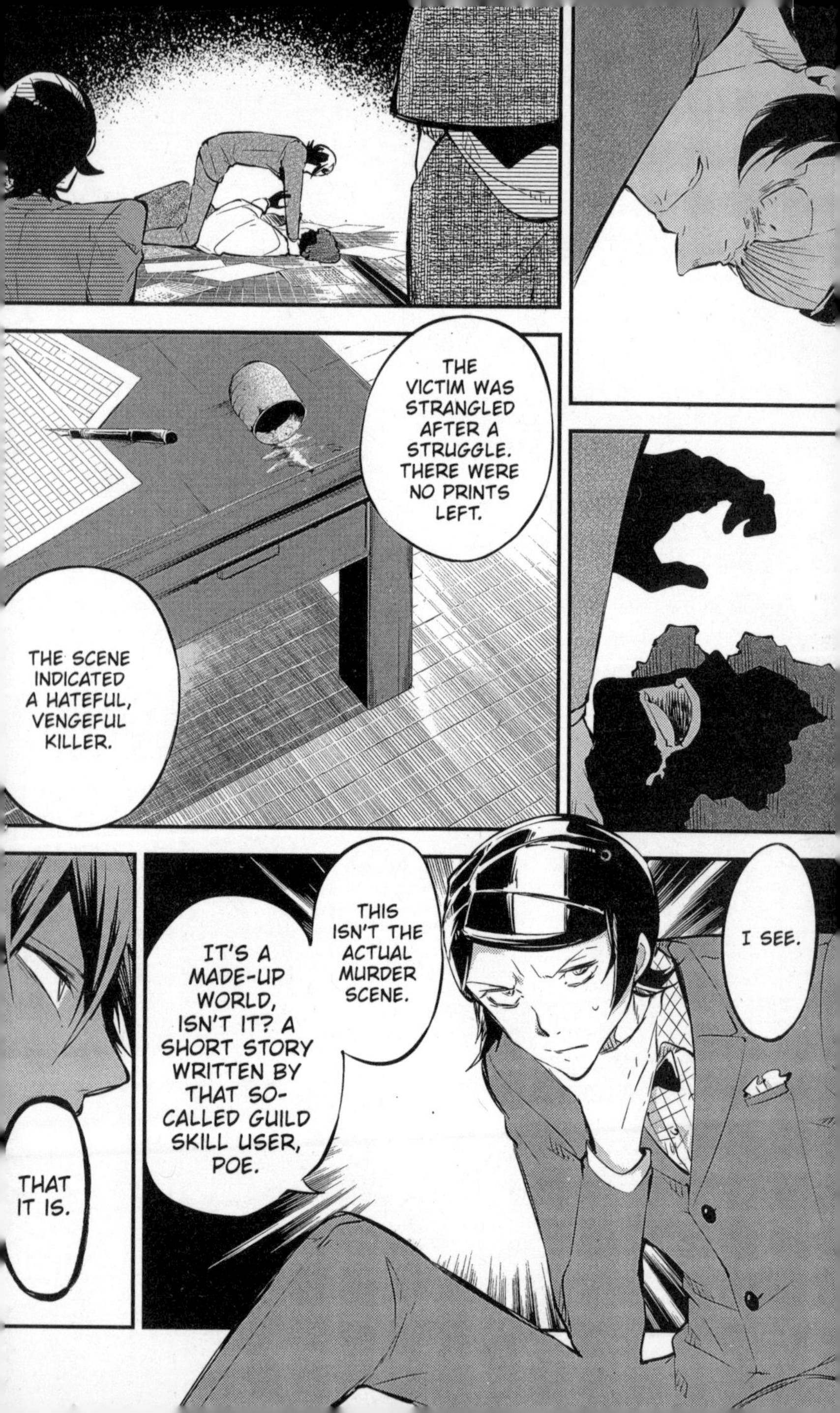
THE VICTIM WAS STRANGLED AFTER A STRUGGLE. THERE WERE NO PRINTS LEFT.
THE SCENE INDICATED A HATEFUL, VENGEFUL KILLER.
I SEE.
THIS ISN'T THE ACTUAL MURDER SCENE.
IT'S A MADE-UP WORLD, ISN'T IT? A SHORT STORY WRITTEN BY THAT SO-CALLED GUILD SKILL USER, POE.
THAT IT IS.

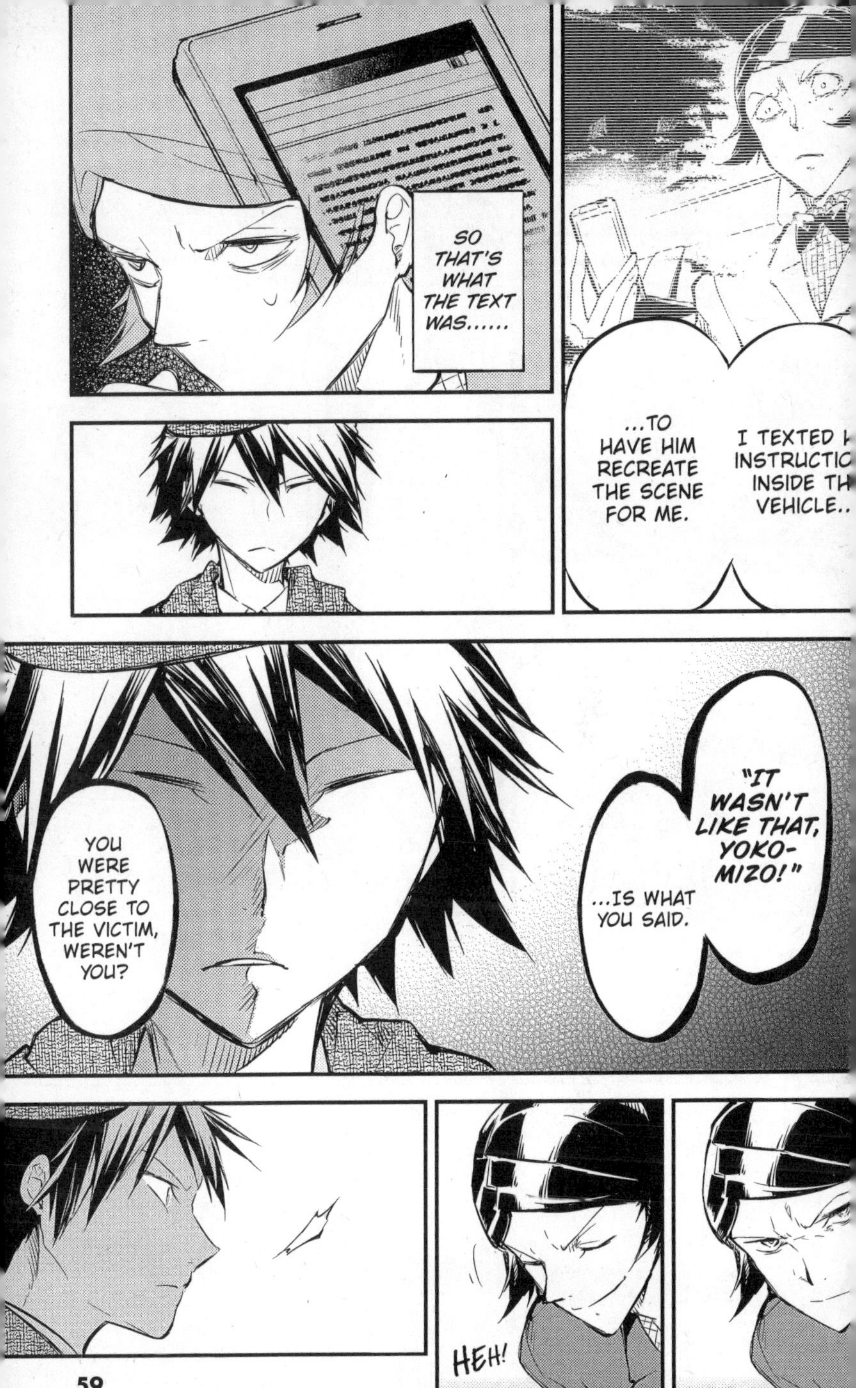
I TEXTED H
INSTRUCTIC
INSIDE TH
VEHICLE..
...TO HAVE HIM RECREATE THE SCENE FOR ME.
SO THAT'S WHAT THE TEXT WAS......
"IT WASN'T LIKE THAT, YOKO-MIZO!"
...IS WHAT YOU SAID.
YOU WERE PRETTY CLOSE TO THE VICTIM, WEREN'T YOU?
HEH!

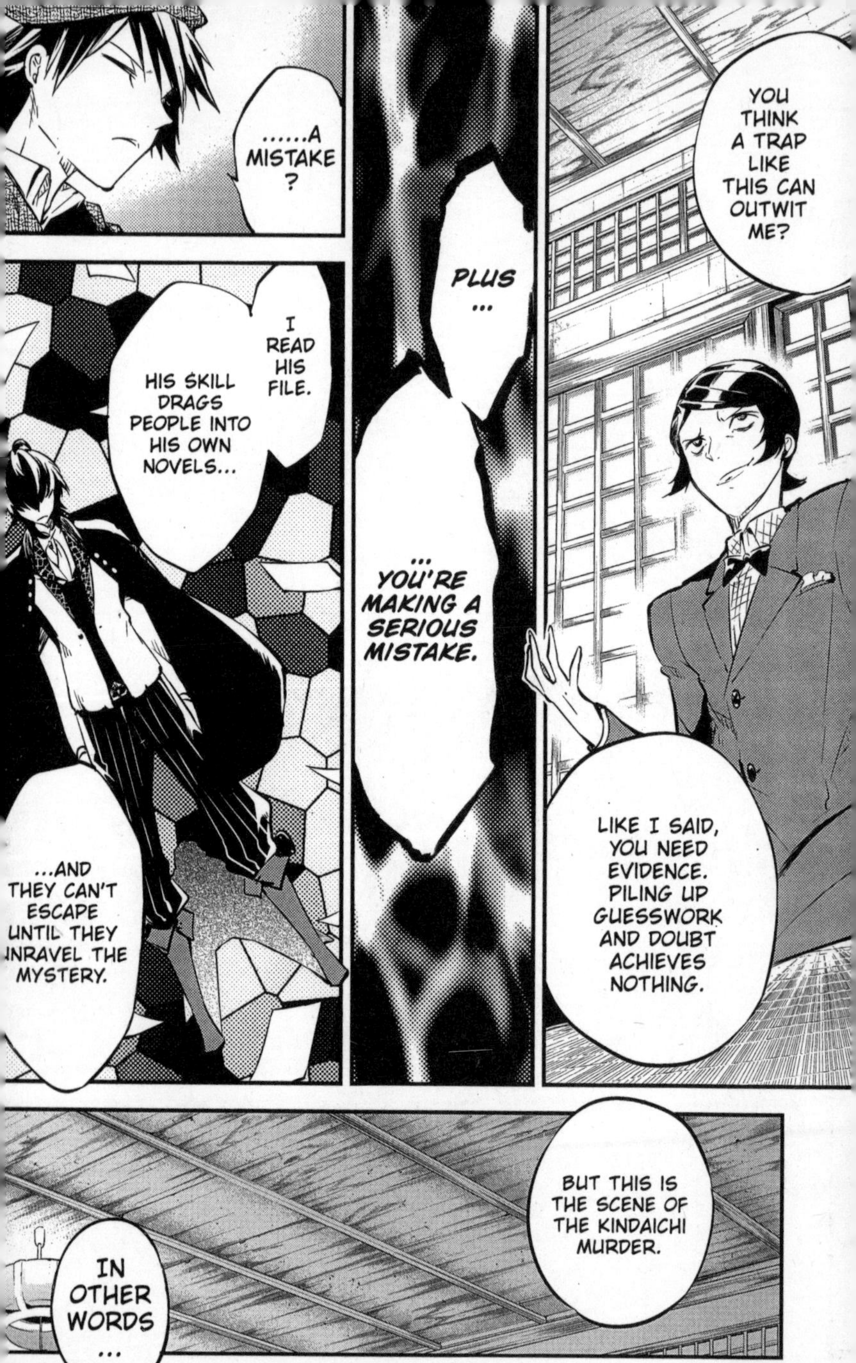
YOU THINK A TRAP LIKE THIS CAN OUTWIT ME?
LIKE I SAID, YOU NEED EVIDENCE. PILING UP GUESSWORK AND DOUBT ACHIEVES NOTHING.
PLUS ...
... YOU'RE MAKING A SERIOUS MISTAKE.
......A MISTAKE?
I READ HIS FILE.
HIS SKILL DRAGS PEOPLE INTO HIS OWN NOVELS...
...AND THEY CAN'T ESCAPE UNTIL THEY UNRAVEL THE MYSTERY.
BUT THIS IS THE SCENE OF THE KINDAICHI MURDER.
IN OTHER WORDS ...

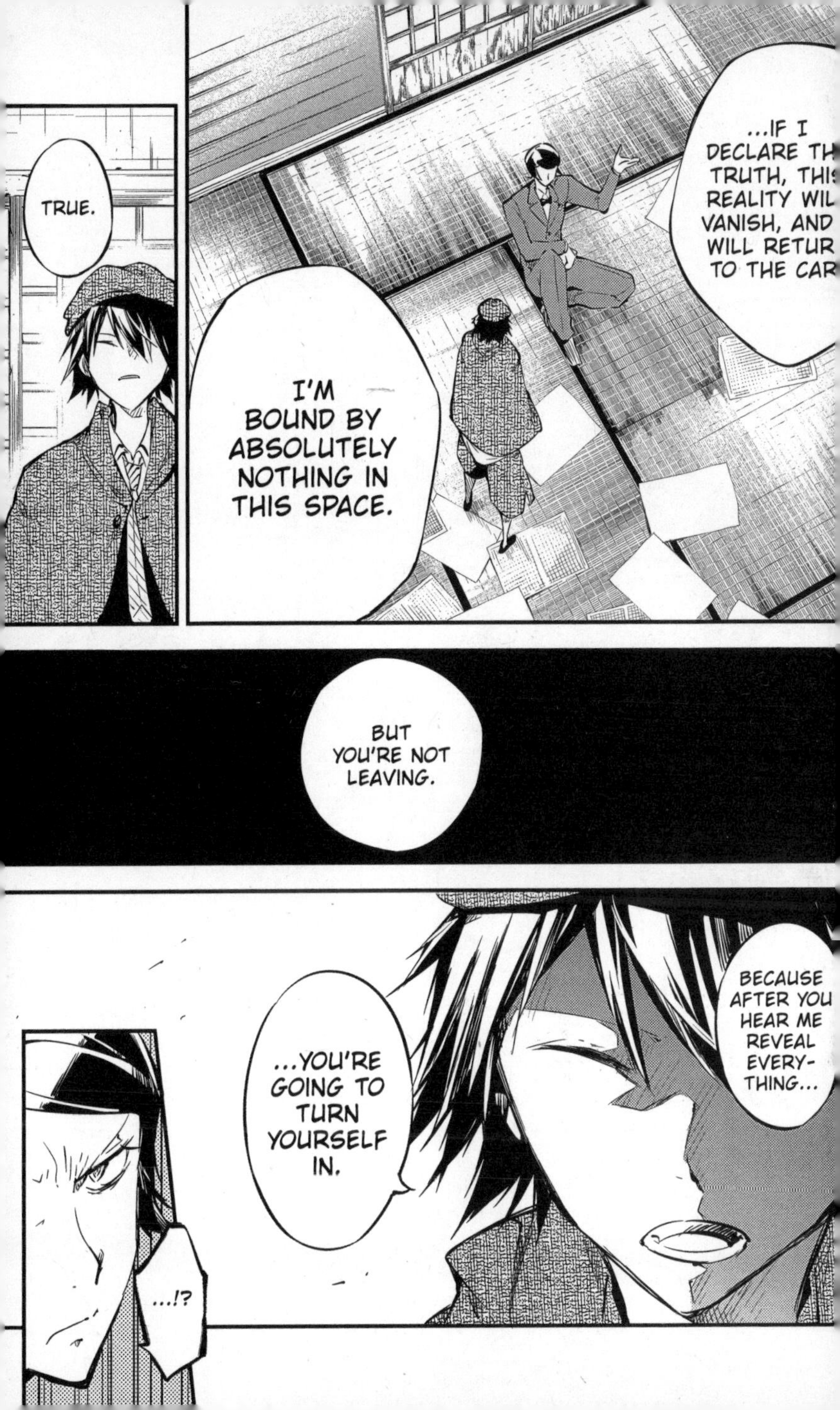
...IF I DECLARE TH TRUTH, THI REALITY WIL VANISH, AND WILL RETUR TO THE CAR
I'M BOUND BY ABSOLUTELY NOTHING IN THIS SPACE.
TRUE.
BUT YOU'RE NOT LEAVING.
BECAUSE AFTER YOU HEAR ME REVEAL EVERY-THING...
...YOU'RE GOING TO TURN YOURSELF IN.
...!?

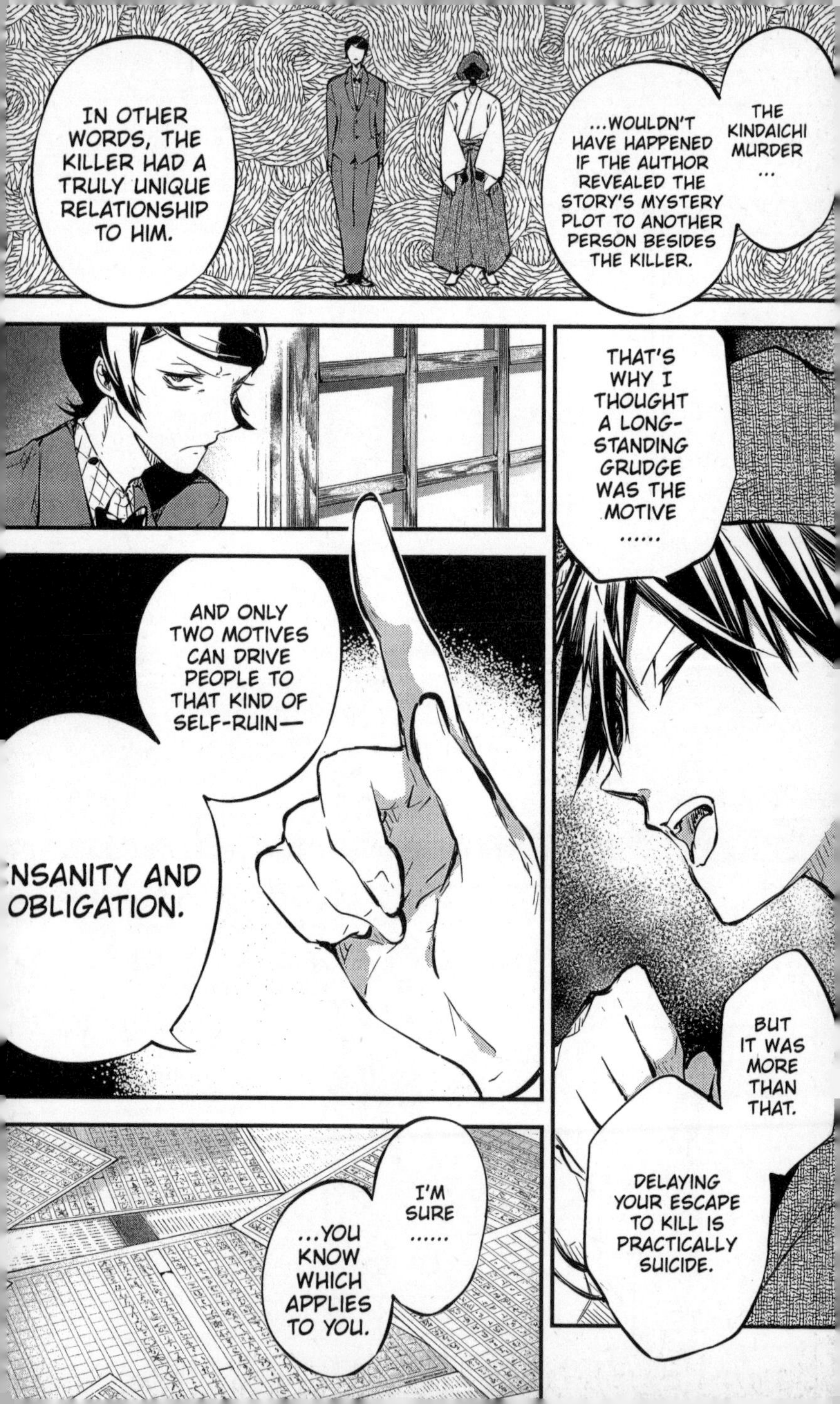
THE KINDAICHI MURDER ...
...WOULDN'T HAVE HAPPENED IF THE AUTHOR REVEALED THE STORY'S MYSTERY PLOT TO ANOTHER PERSON BESIDES THE KILLER.
IN OTHER WORDS, THE KILLER HAD A TRULY UNIQUE RELATIONSHIP TO HIM.
THAT'S WHY I THOUGHT A LONG-STANDING GRUDGE WAS THE MOTIVE ......
BUT IT WAS MORE THAN THAT.
DELAYING YOUR ESCAPE TO KILL IS PRACTICALLY SUICIDE.
AND ONLY TWO MOTIVES CAN DRIVE PEOPLE TO THAT KIND OF SELF-RUIN—
INSANITY AND OBLIGATION.
I'M SURE ......
...YOU KNOW WHICH APPLIES TO YOU.

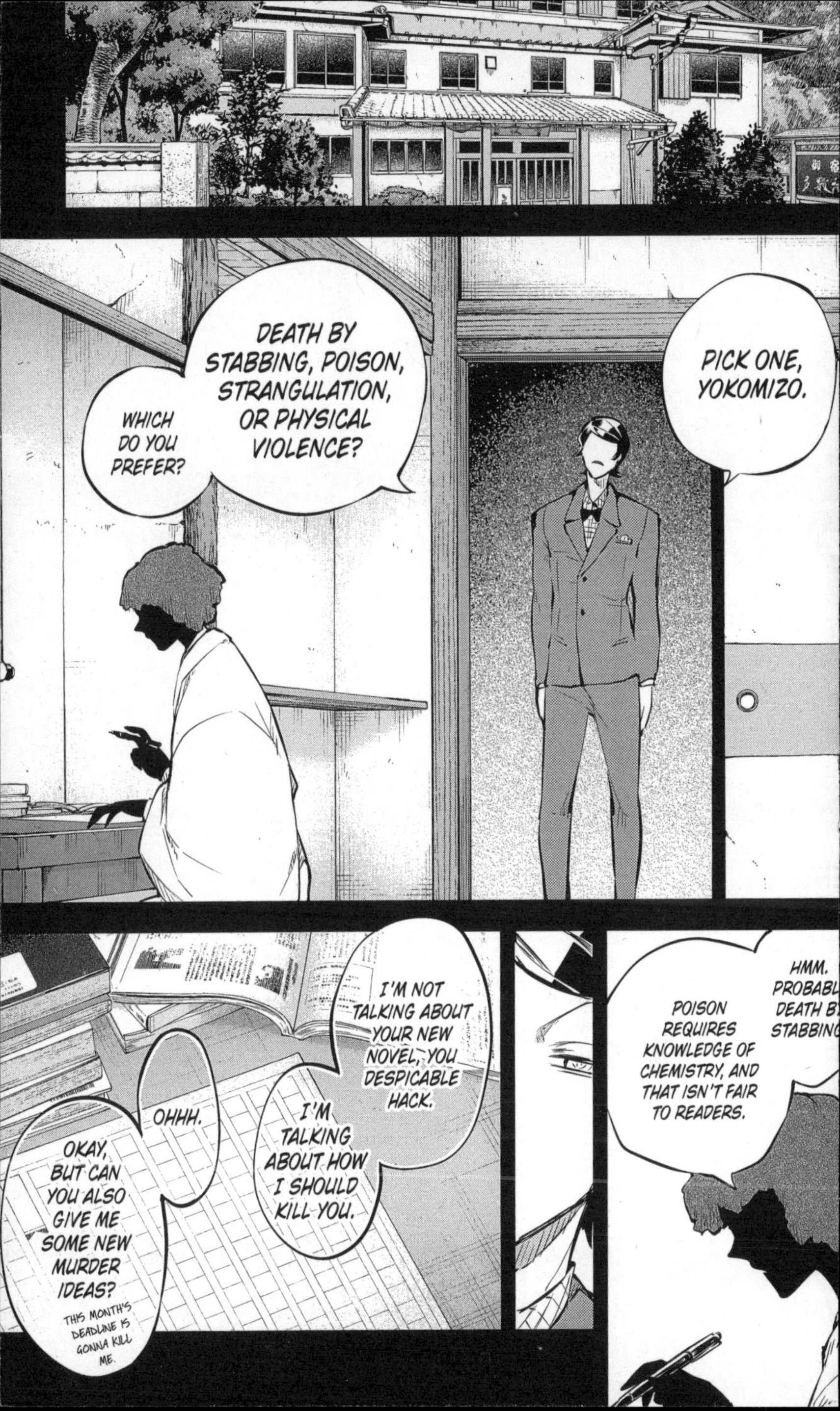
PICK ONE, YOKOMIZO.
DEATH BY STABBING, POISON, STRANGULATION, OR PHYSICAL VIOLENCE?
WHICH DO YOU PREFER?
HMM. PROBABL DEATH B STABBIN
POISON REQUIRES KNOWLEDGE OF CHEMISTRY, AND THAT ISN'T FAIR TO READERS.
I'M NOT TALKING ABOUT YOUR NEW NOVEL, YOU DESPICABLE HACK.
I'M TALKING ABOUT HOW I SHOULD KILL YOU.
OHHH.
OKAY, BUT CAN YOU ALSO GIVE ME SOME NEW MURDER IDEAS?
THIS MONTH'S DEADLINE IS GONNA KILL ME.

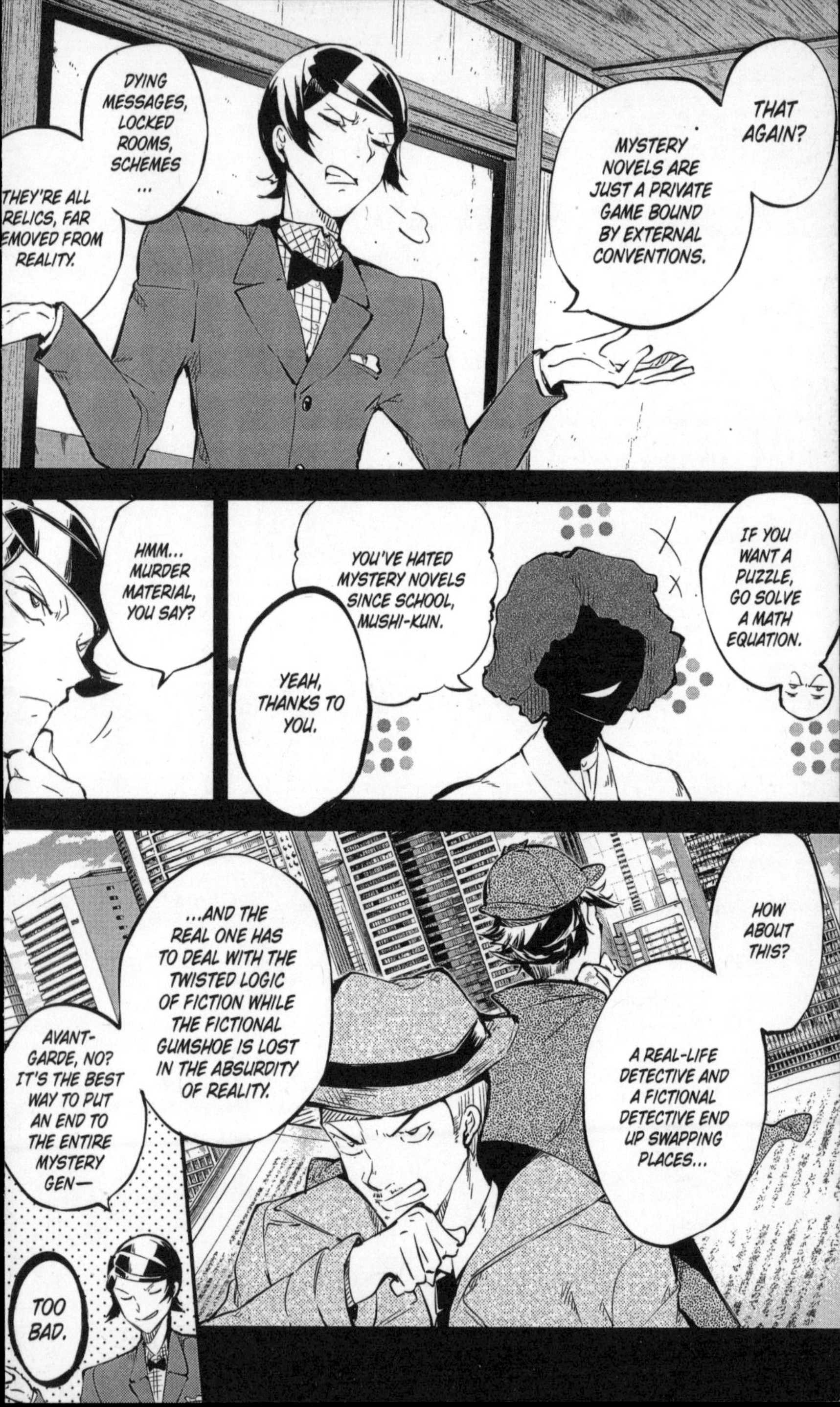
THAT AGAIN?
MYSTERY NOVELS ARE JUST A PRIVATE GAME BOUND BY EXTERNAL CONVENTIONS.
DYING MESSAGES, LOCKED ROOMS, SCHEMES ...
THEY'RE ALL RELICS, FAR EMOVED FROM REALITY.
IF YOU WANT A PUZZLE, GO SOLVE A MATH EQUATION.
YOU'VE HATED MYSTERY NOVELS SINCE SCHOOL, MUSHI-KUN.
YEAH, THANKS TO YOU.
HMM... MURDER MATERIAL, YOU SAY?
HOW ABOUT THIS?
A REAL-LIFE DETECTIVE AND A FICTIONAL DETECTIVE END UP SWAPPING PLACES...
...AND THE REAL ONE HAS TO DEAL WITH THE TWISTED LOGIC OF FICTION WHILE THE FICTIONAL GUMSHOE IS LOST IN THE ABSURDITY OF REALITY.
AVANT-GARDE, NO? IT'S THE BEST WAY TO PUT AN END TO THE ENTIRE MYSTERY GEN—
TOO BAD.

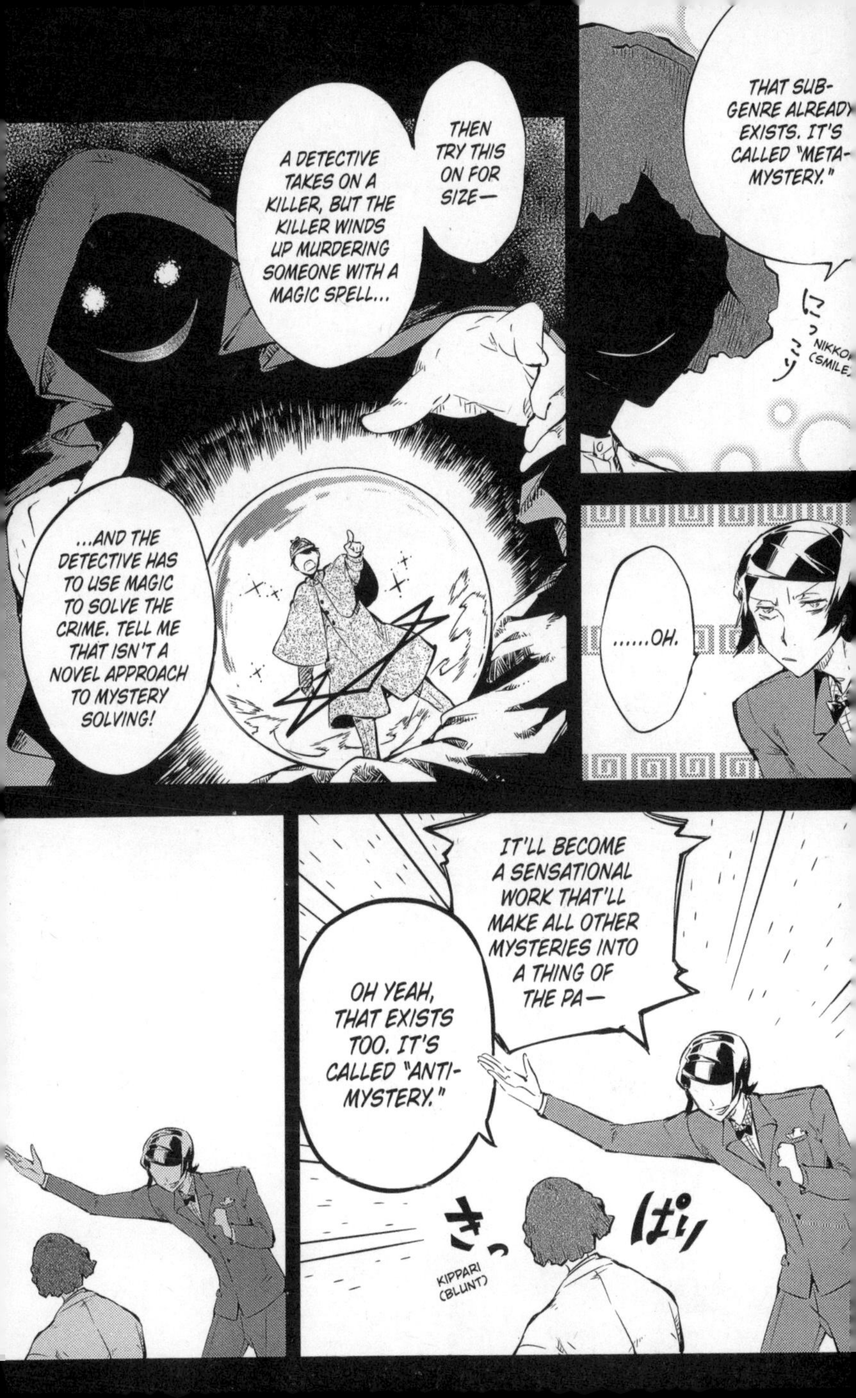
THEN TRY THIS ON FOR SIZE—
A DETECTIVE TAKES ON A KILLER, BUT THE KILLER WINDS UP MURDERING SOMEONE WITH A MAGIC SPELL...
...AND THE DETECTIVE HAS TO USE MAGIC TO SOLVE THE CRIME. TELL ME THAT ISN'T A NOVEL APPROACH TO MYSTERY SOLVING!
THAT SUB-GENRE ALREADY EXISTS. IT'S CALLED "META-MYSTERY."
にっこり
NIKKO (SMILE
......OH.
IT'LL BECOME A SENSATIONAL WORK THAT'LL MAKE ALL OTHER MYSTERIES INTO A THING OF THE PA—
OH YEAH, THAT EXISTS TOO. IT'S CALLED "ANTI-MYSTERY."
きっぱり
KIPPARI (BLUNT)

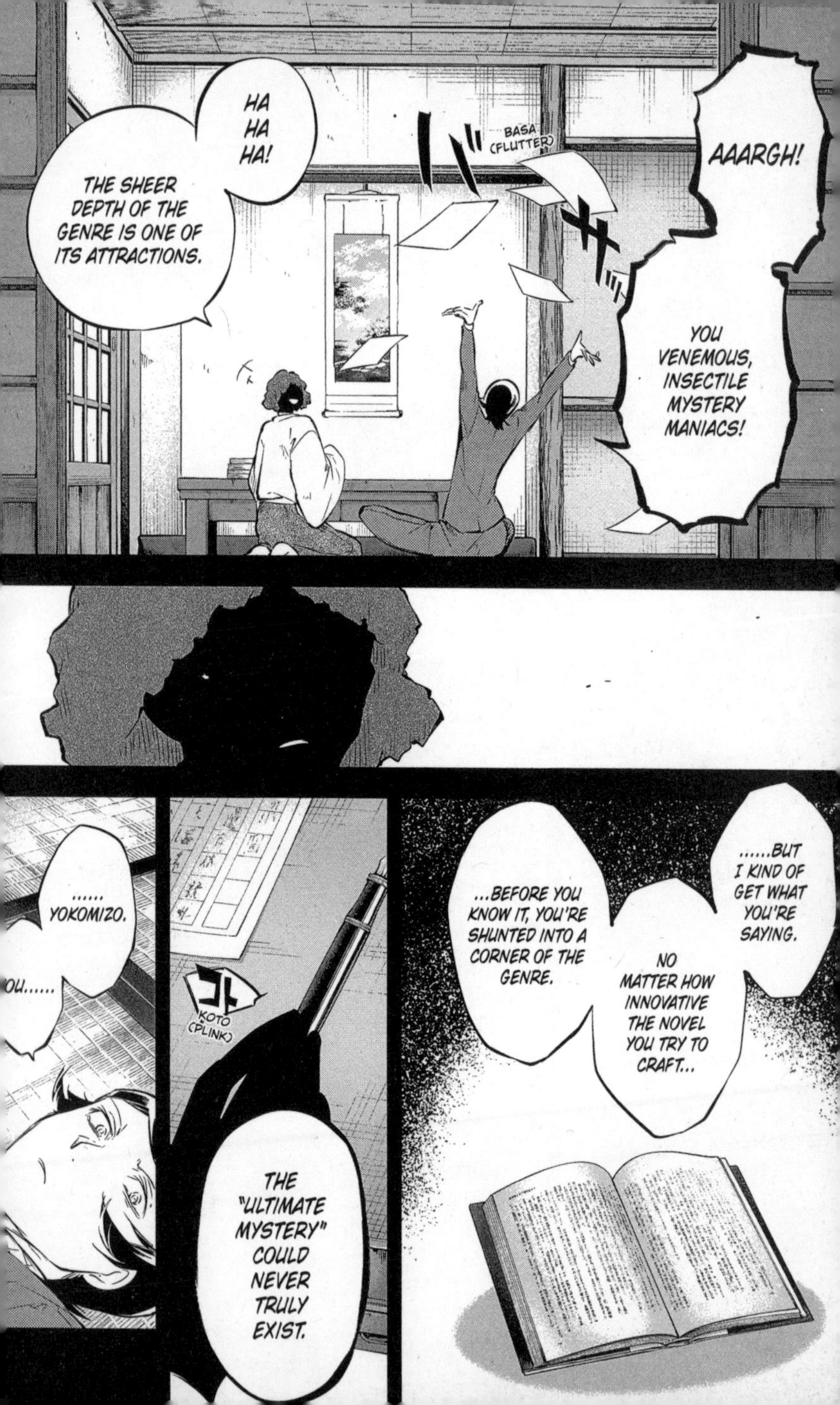
AAARGH!
YOU VENEMOUS, INSECTILE MYSTERY MANIACS!
BASA (FLUTTER)
HA HA HA!
THE SHEER DEPTH OF THE GENRE IS ONE OF ITS ATTRACTIONS.
......BUT I KIND OF GET WHAT YOU'RE SAYING.
NO MATTER HOW INNOVATIVE THE NOVEL YOU TRY TO CRAFT...
...BEFORE YOU KNOW IT, YOU'RE SHUNTED INTO A CORNER OF THE GENRE.
KOTO (PLINK)
THE "ULTIMATE MYSTERY" COULD NEVER TRULY EXIST.
...... YOKOMIZO.
OU......

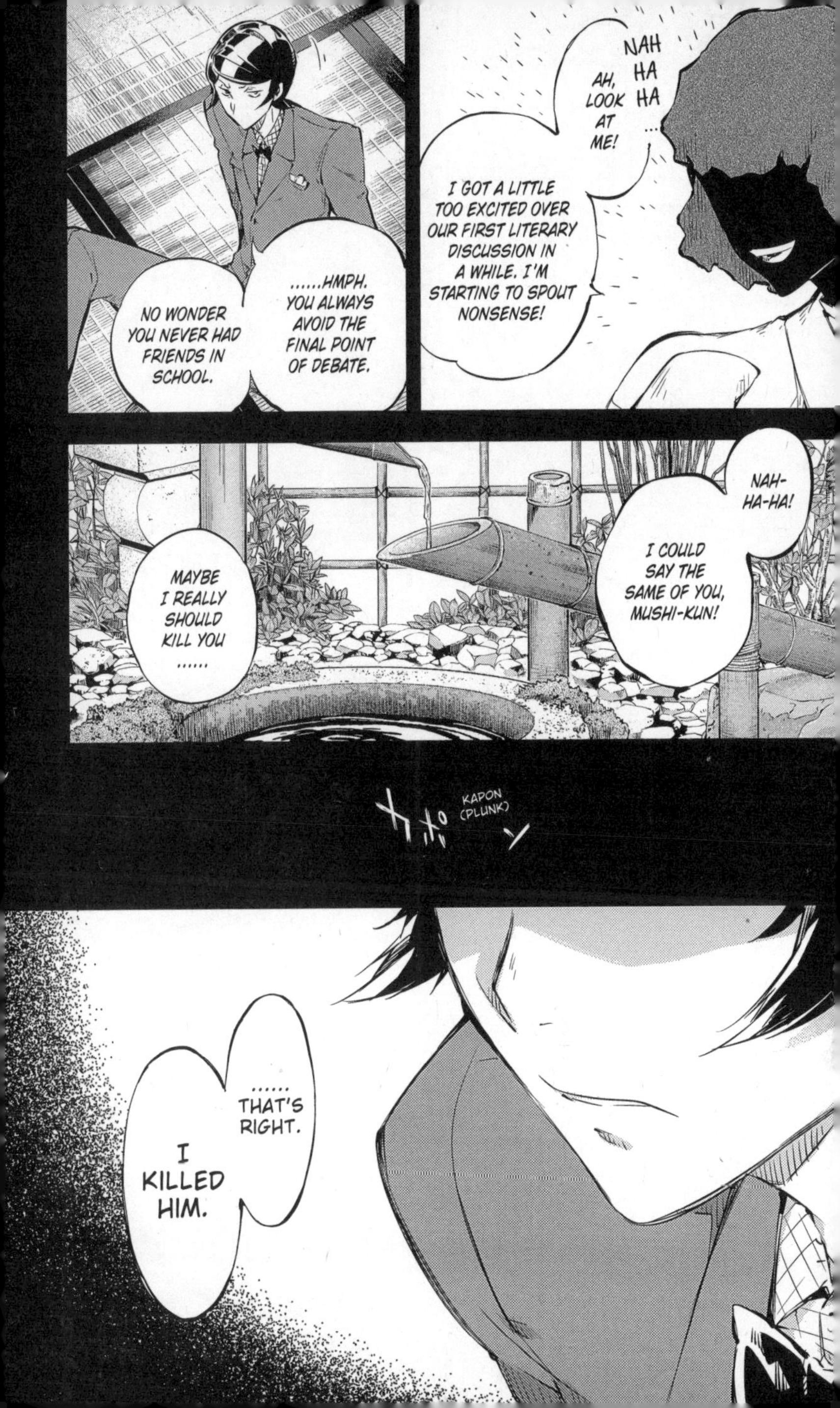
NAH HA HA ...
AH, LOOK AT ME!
I GOT A LITTLE TOO EXCITED OVER OUR FIRST LITERARY DISCUSSION IN A WHILE. I'M STARTING TO SPOUT NONSENSE!
......HMPH. YOU ALWAYS AVOID THE FINAL POINT OF DEBATE.
NO WONDER YOU NEVER HAD FRIENDS IN SCHOOL.
NAH-HA-HA!
I COULD SAY THE SAME OF YOU, MUSHI-KUN!
MAYBE I REALLY SHOULD KILL YOU ......
KAPON (PLUNK)
...... THAT'S RIGHT.
I KILLED HIM.

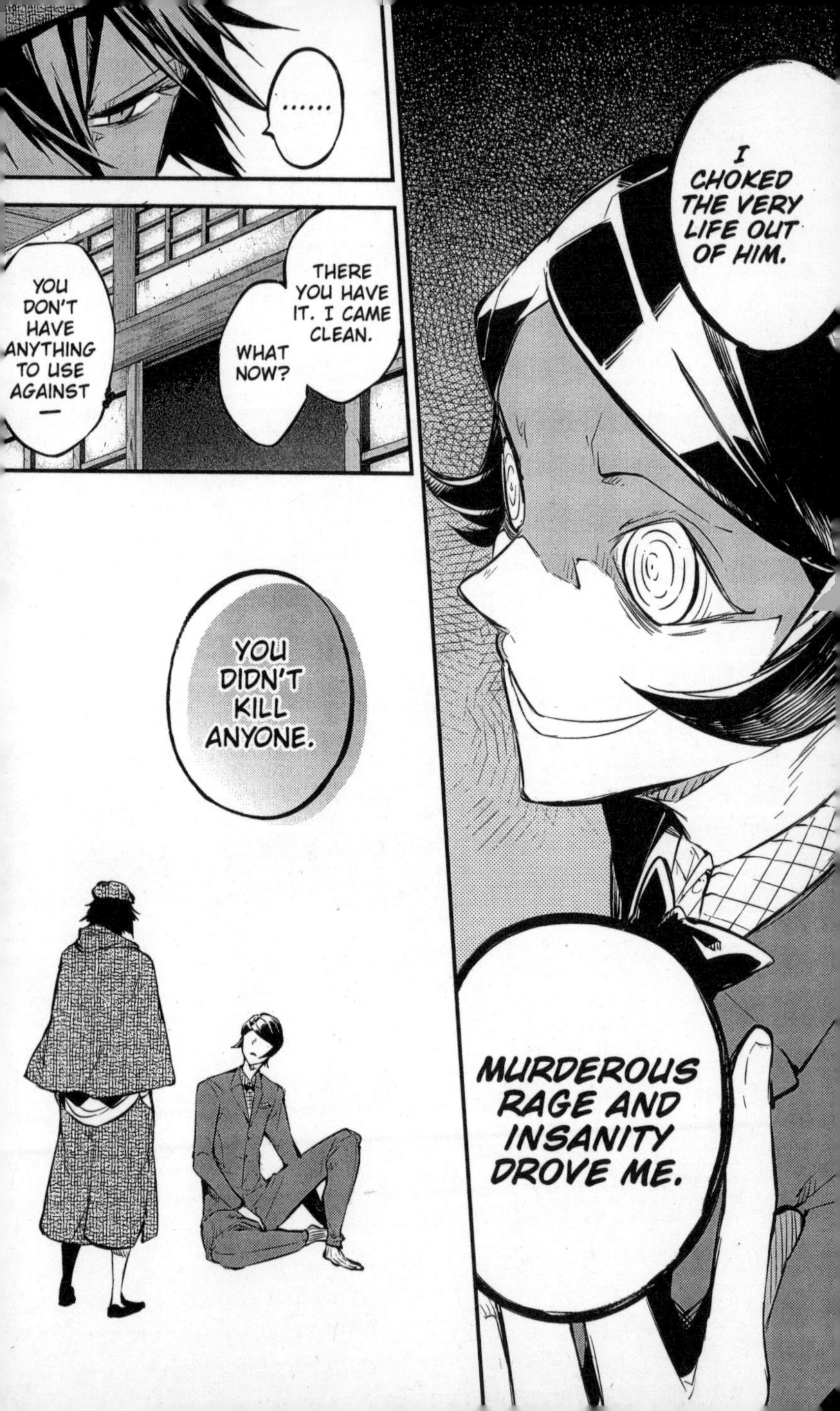
I CHOKED THE VERY LIFE OUT OF HIM.
MURDEROUS RAGE AND INSANITY DROVE ME.
......
THERE YOU HAVE IT. I CAME CLEAN.
WHAT NOW?
YOU DON'T HAVE ANYTHING TO USE AGAINST —
YOU DIDN'T KILL ANYONE.

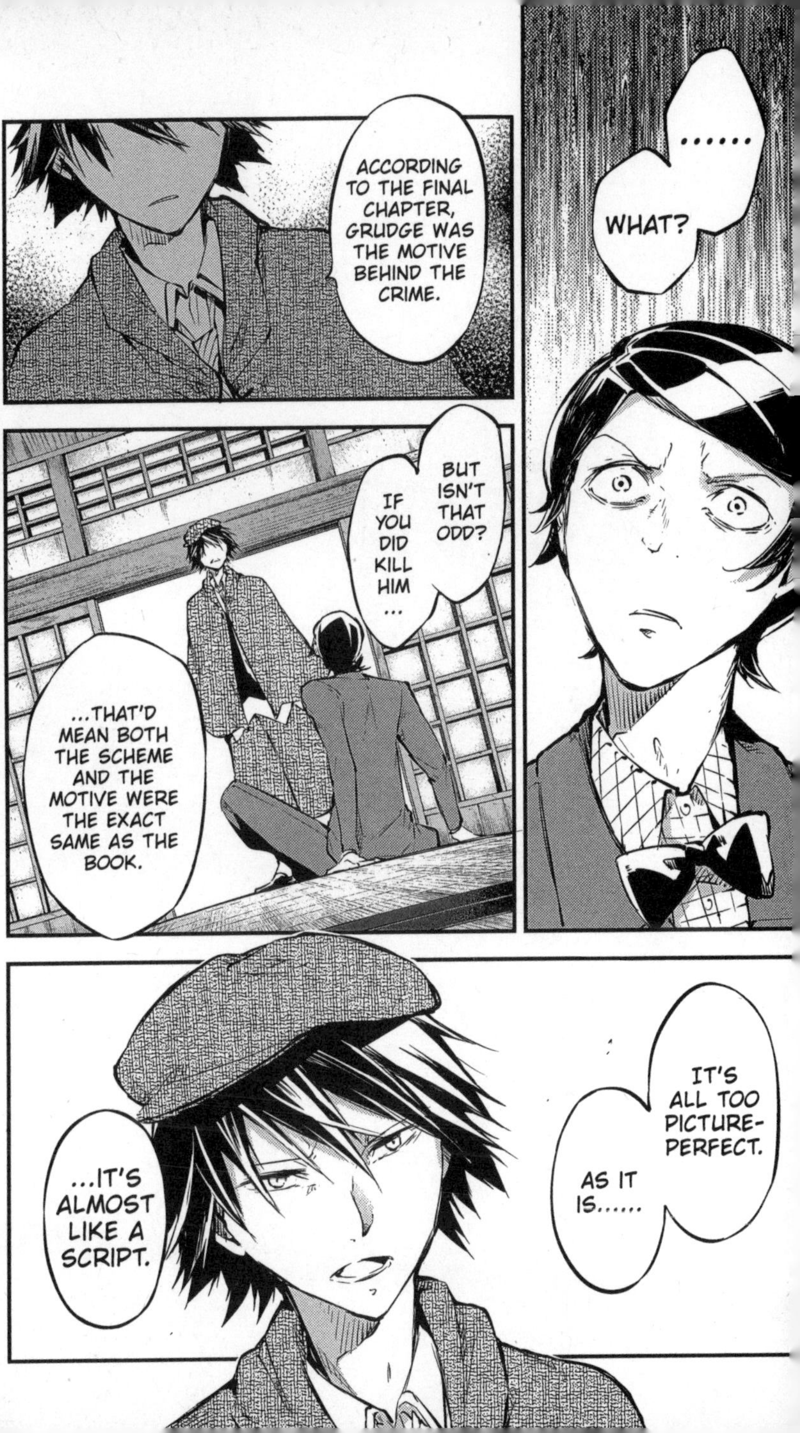
......
WHAT?
ACCORDING TO THE FINAL CHAPTER, GRUDGE WAS THE MOTIVE BEHIND THE CRIME.
BUT ISN'T THAT ODD?
IF YOU DID KILL HIM...
...THAT'D MEAN BOTH THE SCHEME AND THE MOTIVE WERE THE EXACT SAME AS THE BOOK.
IT'S ALL TOO PICTURE-PERFECT.
AS IT IS......
...IT'S ALMOST LIKE A SCRIPT.

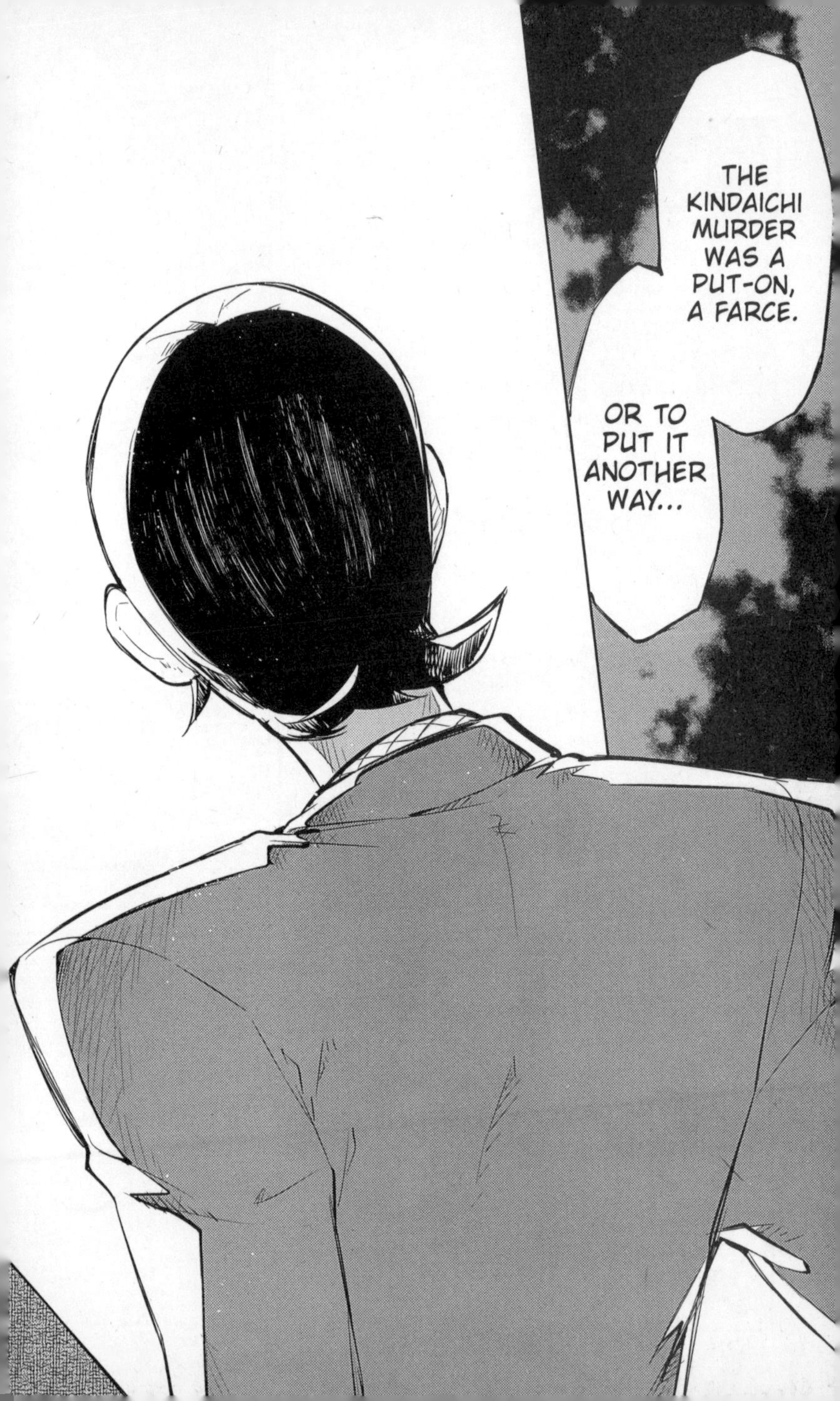
THE KINDAICHI MURDER WAS A PUT-ON, A FARCE.
OR TO PUT IT ANOTHER WAY...

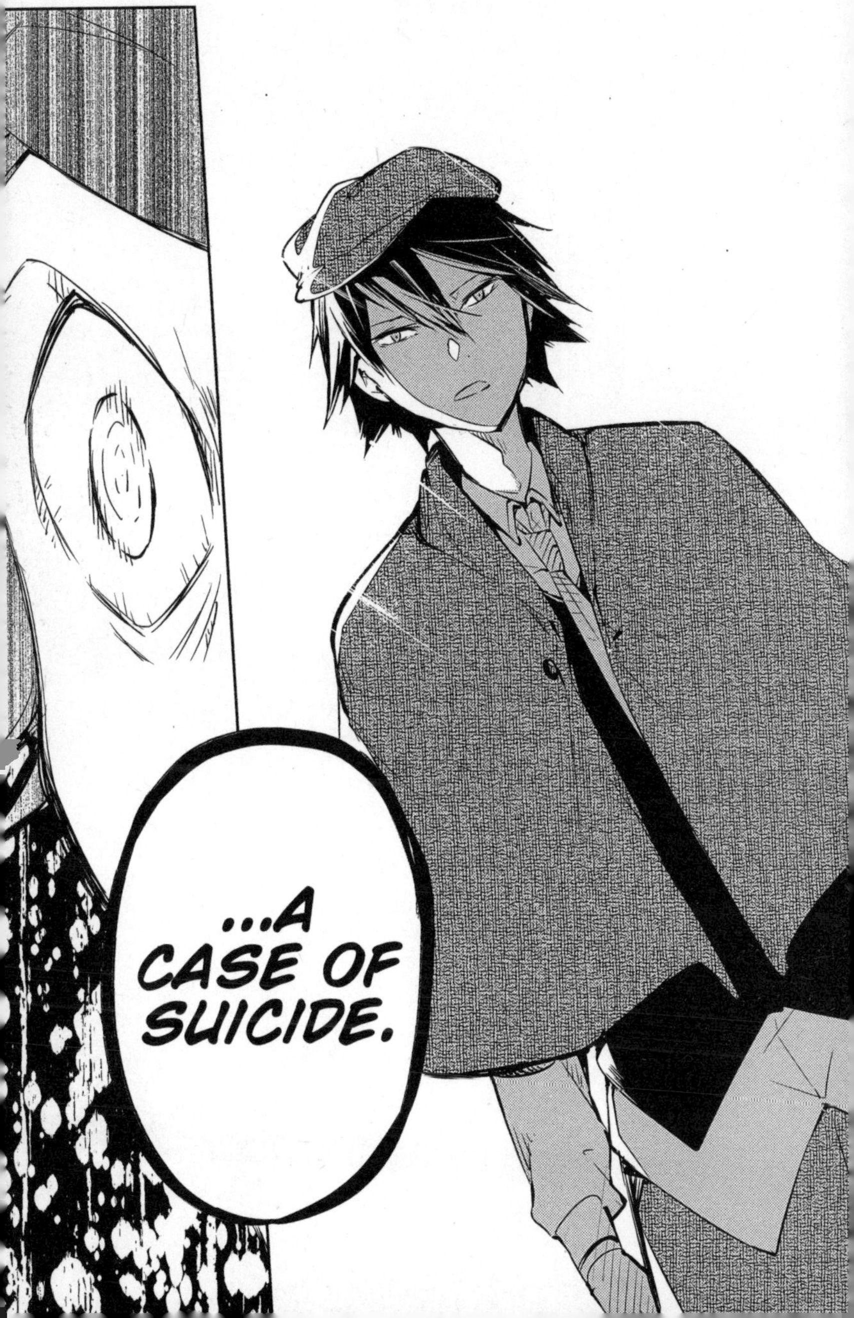
...A CASE OF SUICIDE.

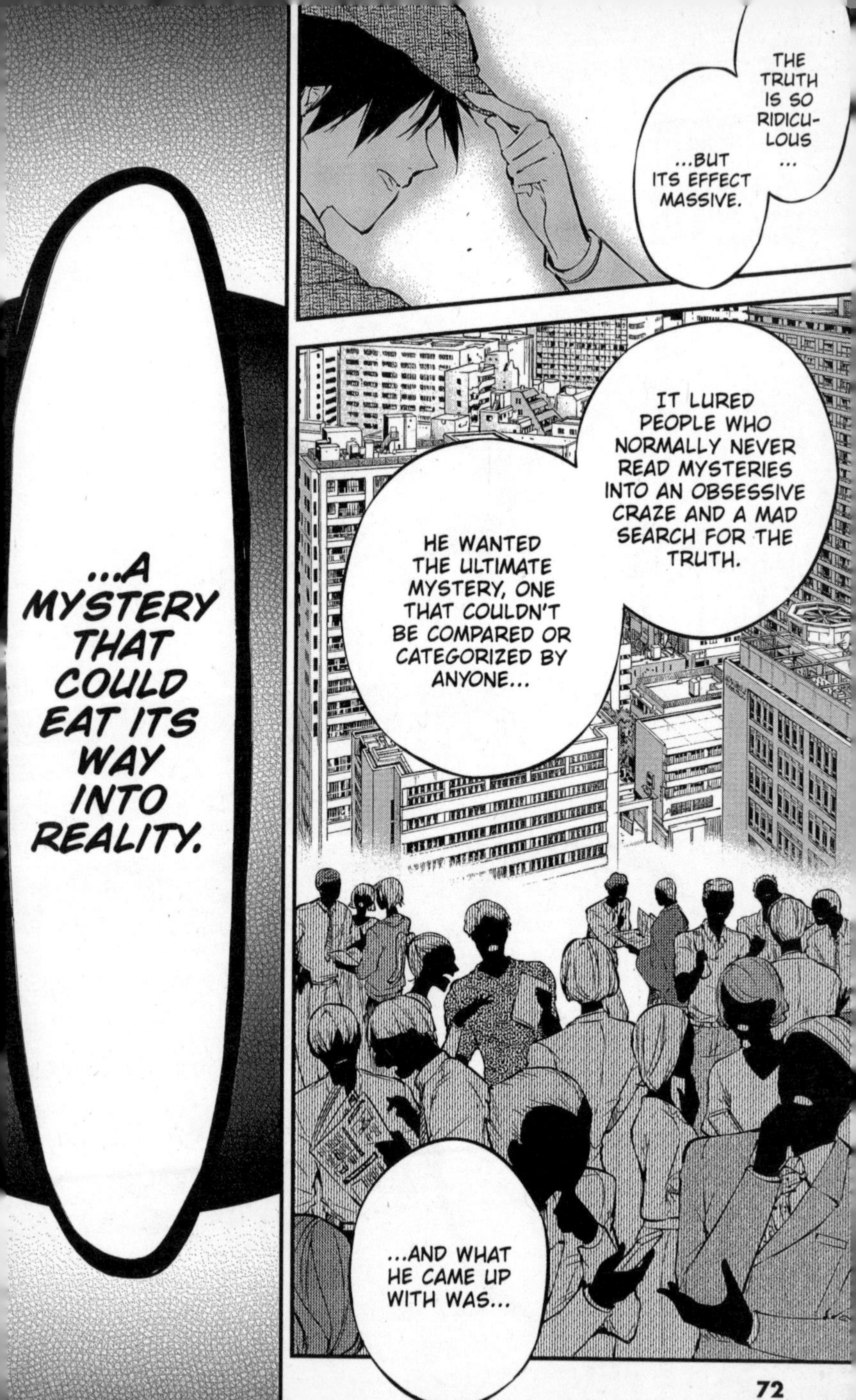
THE TRUTH IS SO RIDICULOUS...
...BUT ITS EFFECT MASSIVE.
IT LURED PEOPLE WHO NORMALLY NEVER READ MYSTERIES INTO AN OBSESSIVE CRAZE AND A MAD SEARCH FOR THE TRUTH.
HE WANTED THE ULTIMATE MYSTERY, ONE THAT COULDN'T BE COMPARED OR CATEGORIZED BY ANYONE...
...AND WHAT HE CAME UP WITH WAS...
...A MYSTERY THAT COULD EAT ITS WAY INTO REALITY.

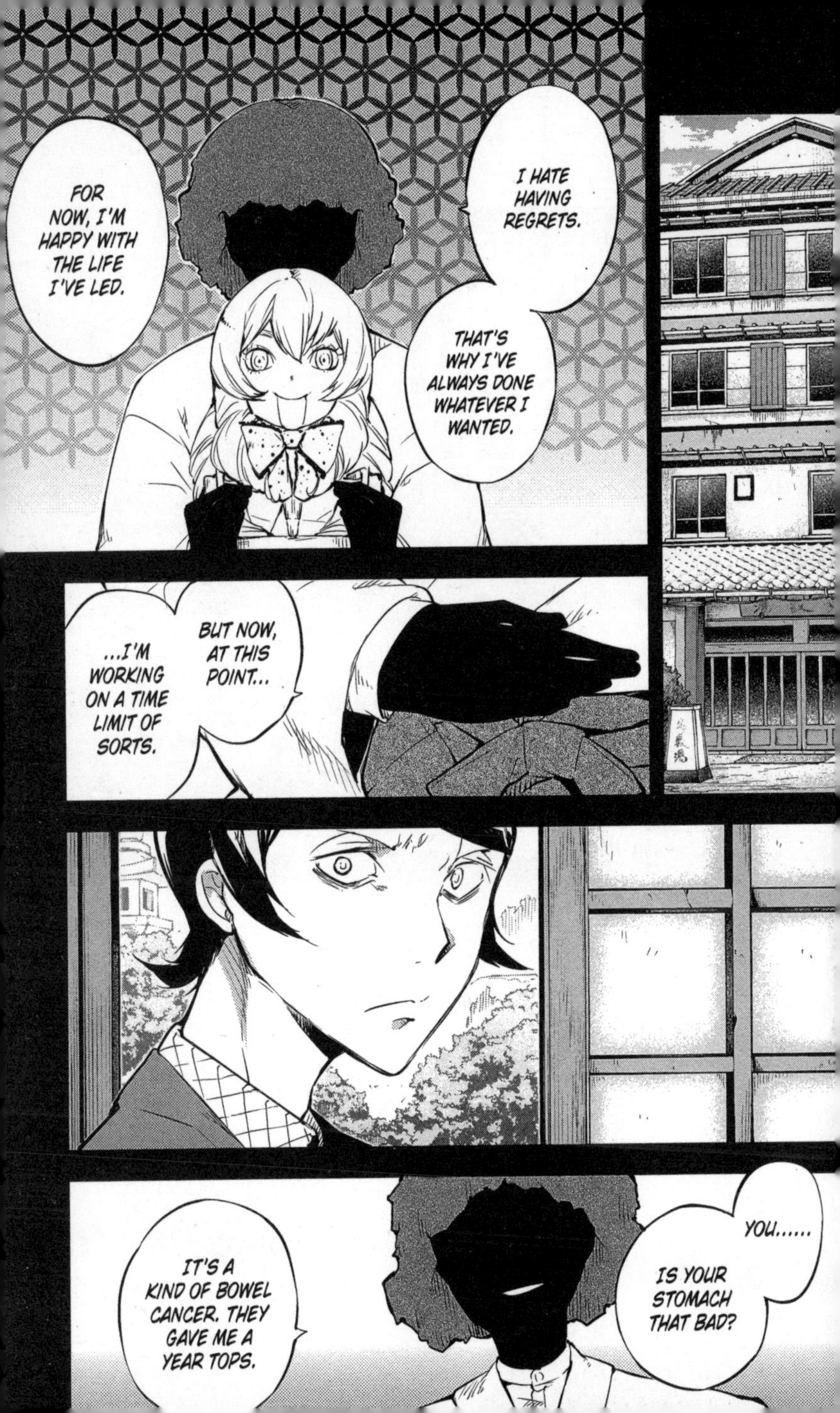
I HATE HAVING REGRETS.
THAT'S WHY I'VE ALWAYS DONE WHATEVER I WANTED.
FOR NOW, I'M HAPPY WITH THE LIFE I'VE LED.
BUT NOW, AT THIS POINT...
...I'M WORKING ON A TIME LIMIT OF SORTS.
YOU......
IS YOUR STOMACH THAT BAD?
IT'S A KIND OF BOWEL CANCER. THEY GAVE ME A YEAR TOPS.

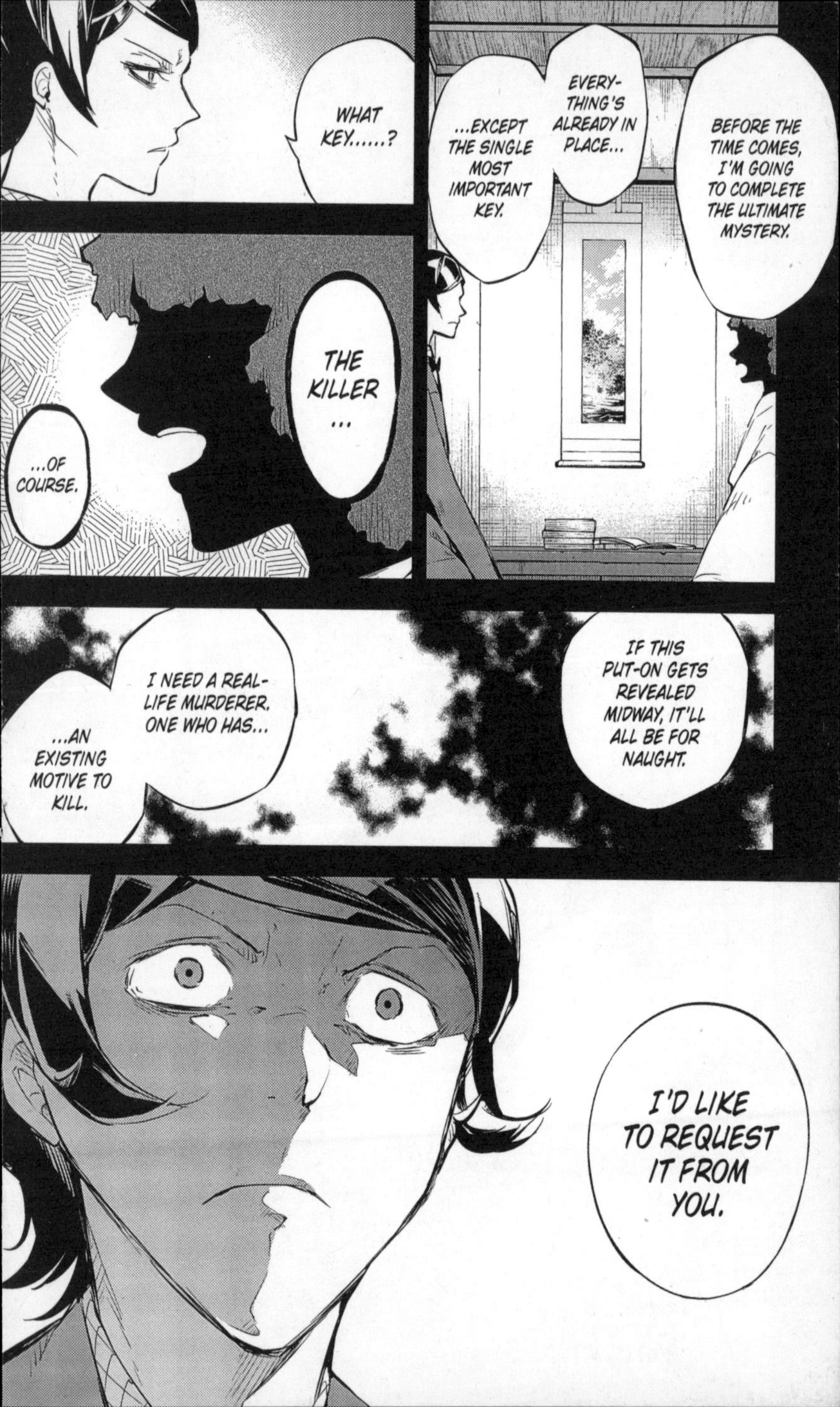
BEFORE THE TIME COMES, I'M GOING TO COMPLETE THE ULTIMATE MYSTERY.
EVERYTHING'S ALREADY IN PLACE...
...EXCEPT THE SINGLE MOST IMPORTANT KEY.
WHAT KEY......?
THE KILLER...
...OF COURSE.
IF THIS PUT-ON GETS REVEALED MIDWAY, IT'LL ALL BE FOR NAUGHT.
I NEED A REAL-LIFE MURDERER. ONE WHO HAS...
...AN EXISTING MOTIVE TO KILL.
I'D LIKE TO REQUEST IT FROM YOU.

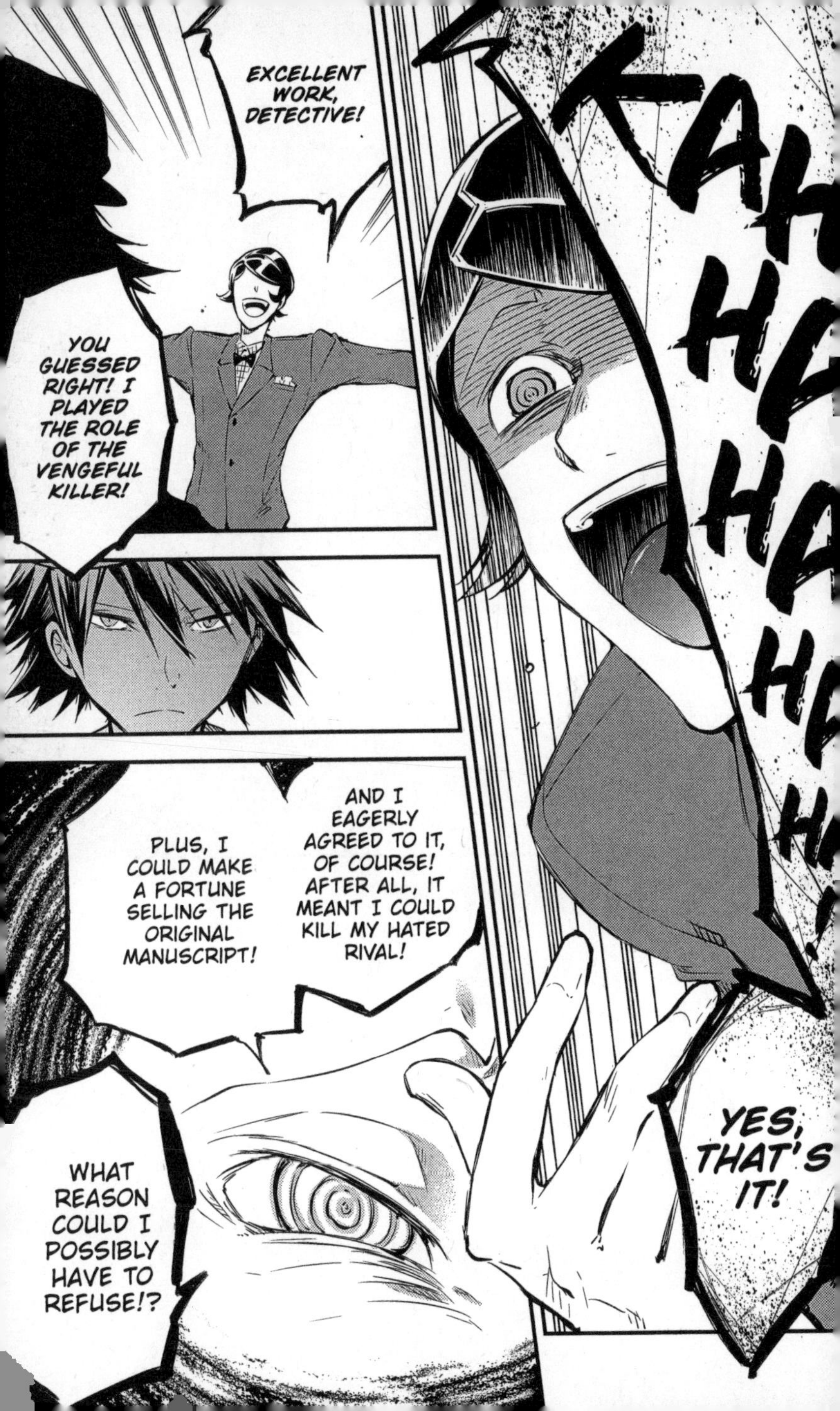
KAH HA HA HA HA HA!
EXCELLENT WORK, DETECTIVE!
YOU GUESSED RIGHT! I PLAYED THE ROLE OF THE VENGEFUL KILLER!
AND I EAGERLY AGREED TO IT, OF COURSE! AFTER ALL, IT MEANT I COULD KILL MY HATED RIVAL!
PLUS, I COULD MAKE A FORTUNE SELLING THE ORIGINAL MANUSCRIPT!
YES, THAT'S IT!
WHAT REASON COULD I POSSIBLY HAVE TO REFUSE!?

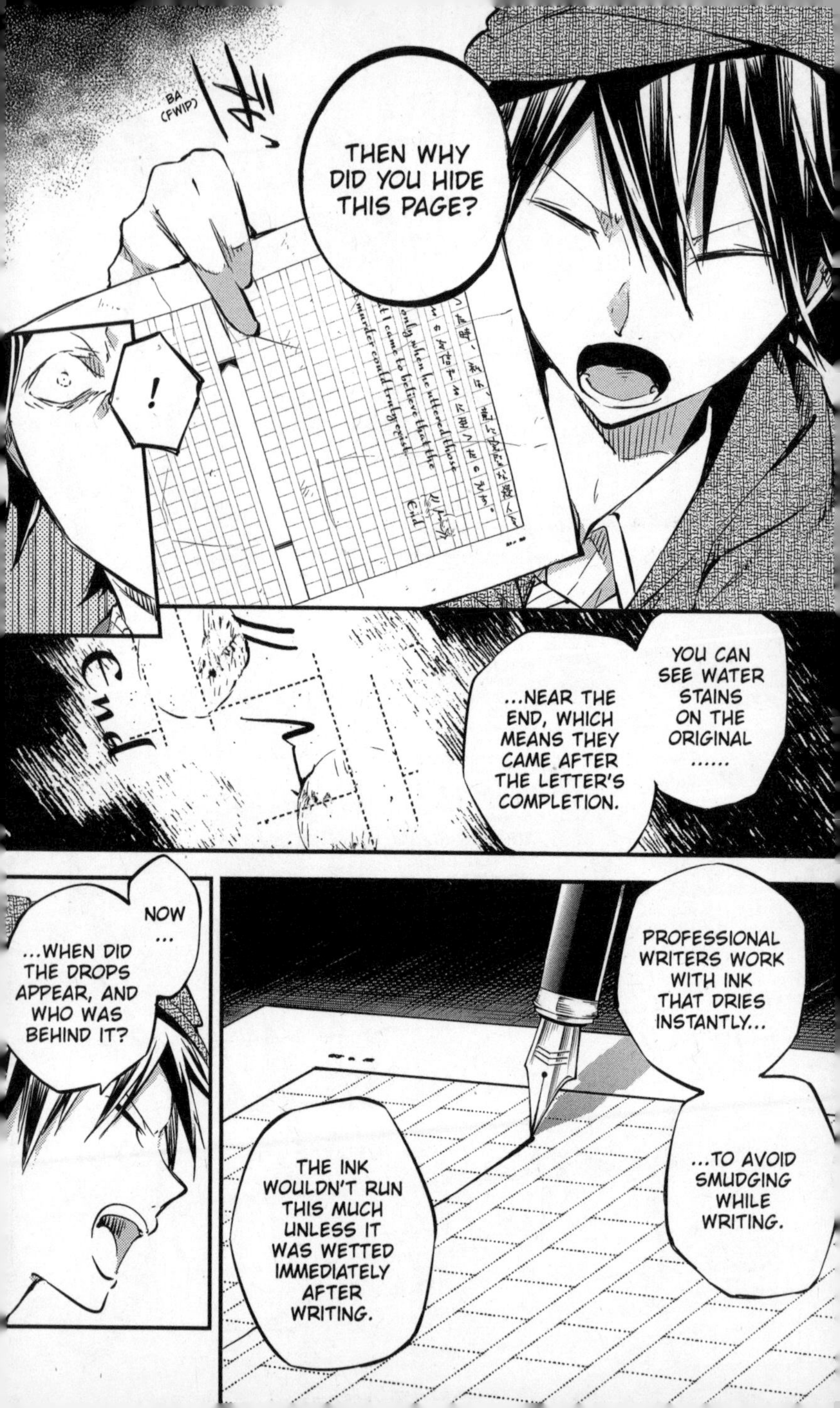
THEN WHY DID YOU HIDE THIS PAGE?
BA (FWIP)
only when he uttered those
that I came to believe that the
murder could truly exist
End
!
YOU CAN SEE WATER STAINS ON THE ORIGINAL ......
...NEAR THE END, WHICH MEANS THEY CAME AFTER THE LETTER'S COMPLETION.
End
PROFESSIONAL WRITERS WORK WITH INK THAT DRIES INSTANTLY...
...TO AVOID SMUDGING WHILE WRITING.
THE INK WOULDN'T RUN THIS MUCH UNLESS IT WAS WETTED IMMEDIATELY AFTER WRITING.
NOW ...
...WHEN DID THE DROPS APPEAR, AND WHO WAS BEHIND IT?

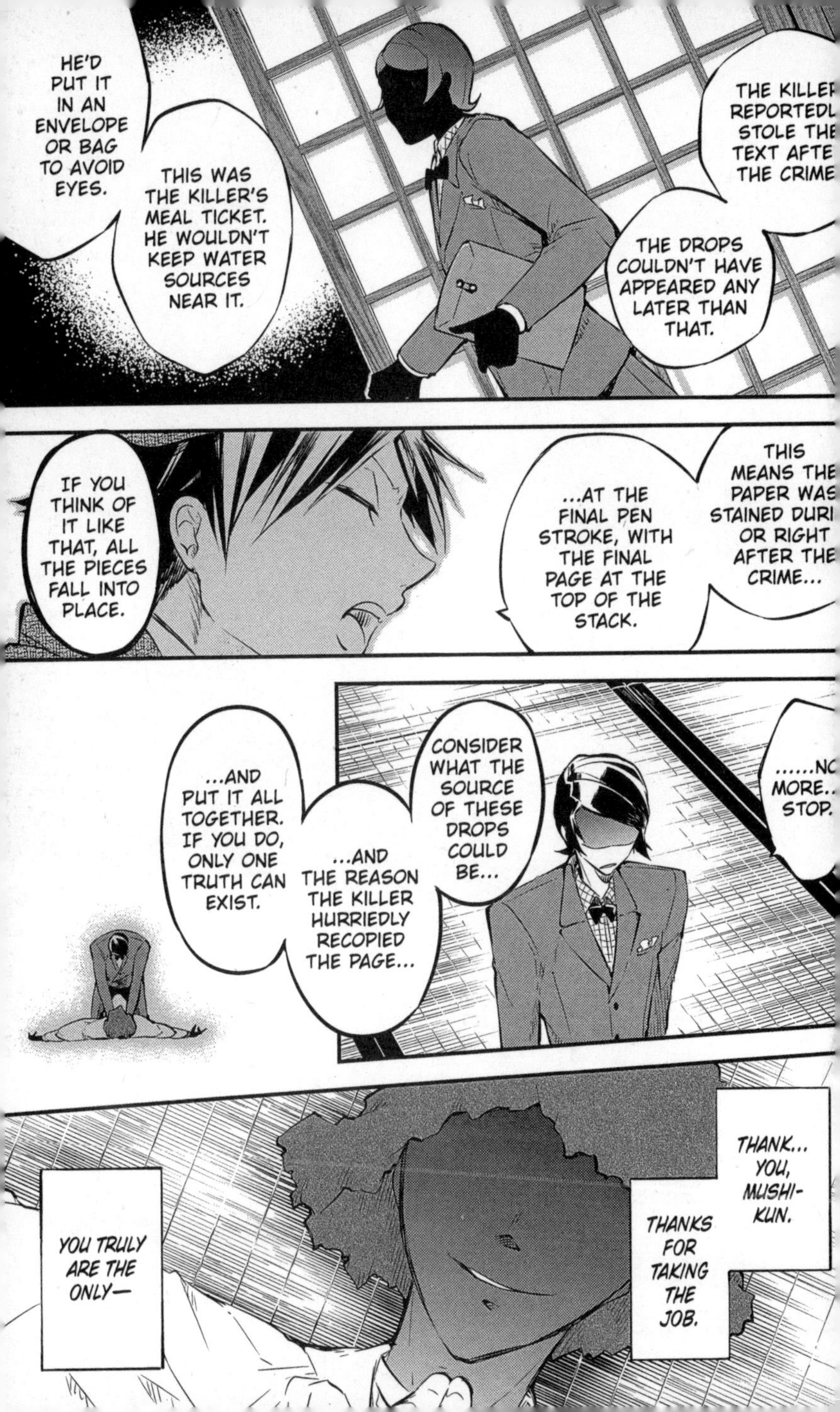

THE KILLEF REPORTEDL STOLE THE TEXT AFTE THE CRIME
THE DROPS COULDN'T HAVE APPEARED ANY LATER THAN THAT.
THIS WAS THE KILLER'S MEAL TICKET. HE WOULDN'T KEEP WATER SOURCES NEAR IT.
HE'D PUT IT IN AN ENVELOPE OR BAG TO AVOID EYES.
THIS MEANS THE PAPER WAS STAINED DURI OR RIGHT AFTER THE CRIME...
...AT THE FINAL PEN STROKE, WITH THE FINAL PAGE AT THE TOP OF THE STACK.
IF YOU THINK OF IT LIKE THAT, ALL THE PIECES FALL INTO PLACE.
......NC MORE.. STOP.
CONSIDER WHAT THE SOURCE OF THESE DROPS COULD BE...
...AND THE REASON THE KILLER HURRIEDLY RECOPIED THE PAGE...
...AND PUT IT ALL TOGETHER. IF YOU DO, ONLY ONE TRUTH CAN EXIST.
THANK... YOU, MUSHI-KUN.
THANKS FOR TAKING THE JOB.
YOU TRULY ARE THE ONLY—

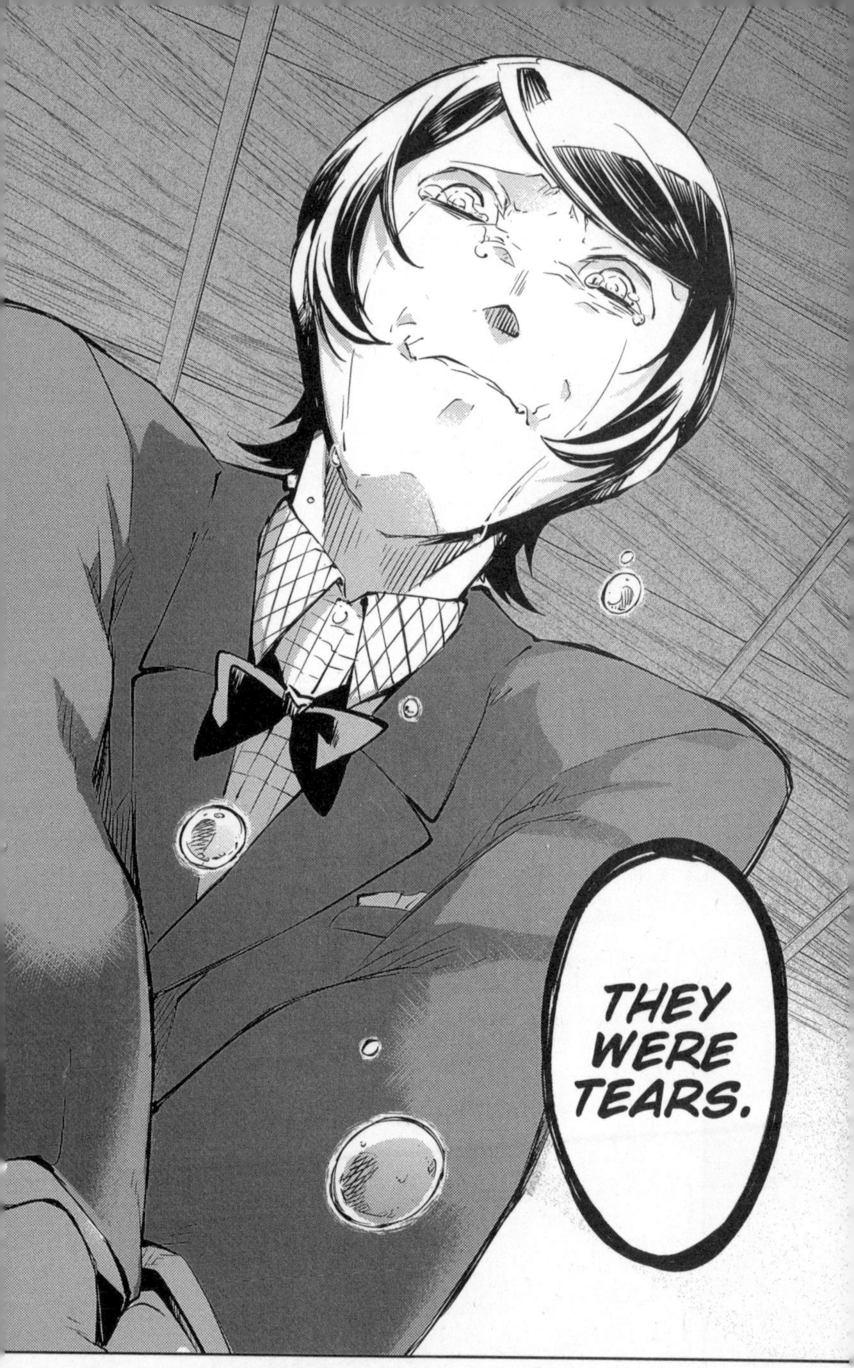
THEY WERE TEARS.

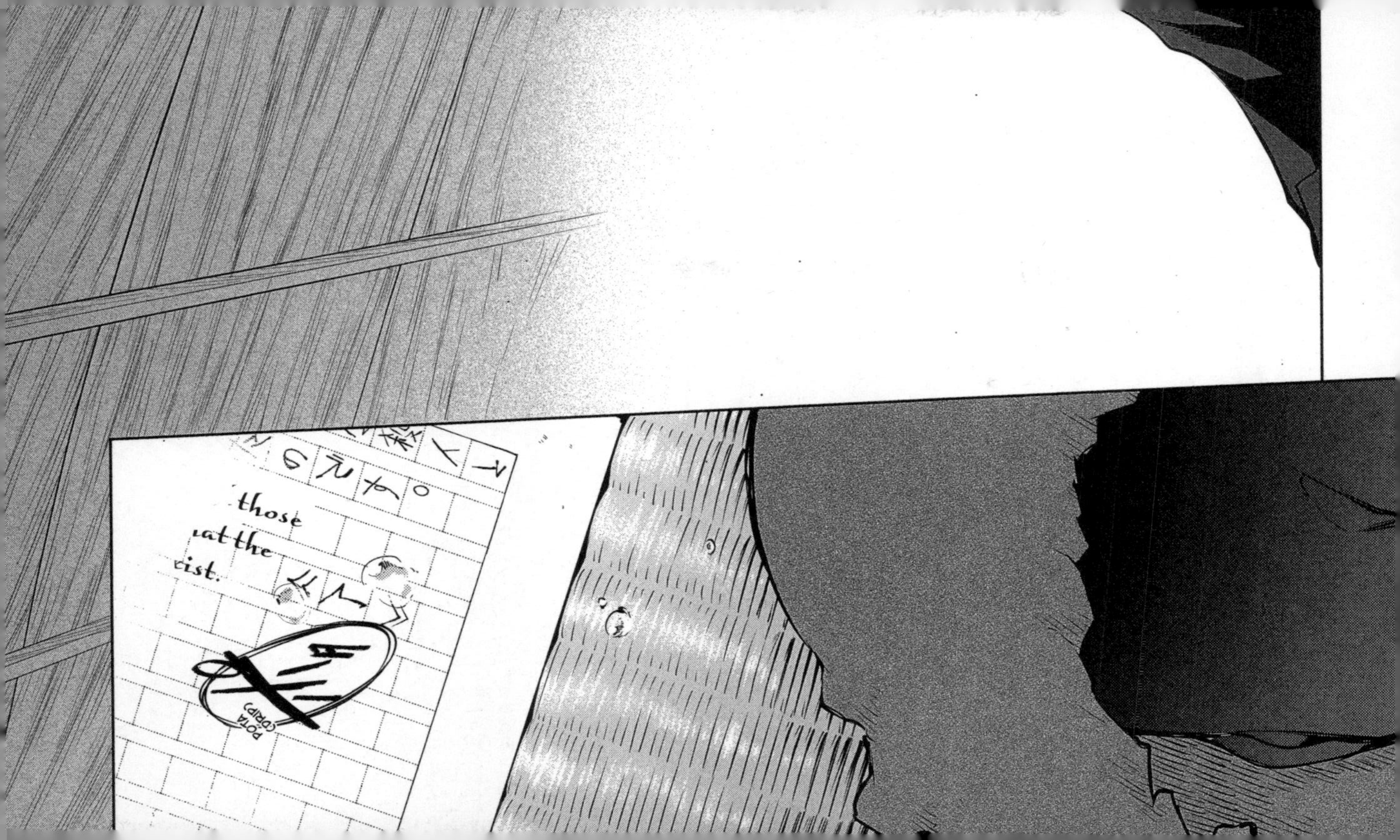
those
at the
ist.
POTA (DRIP)

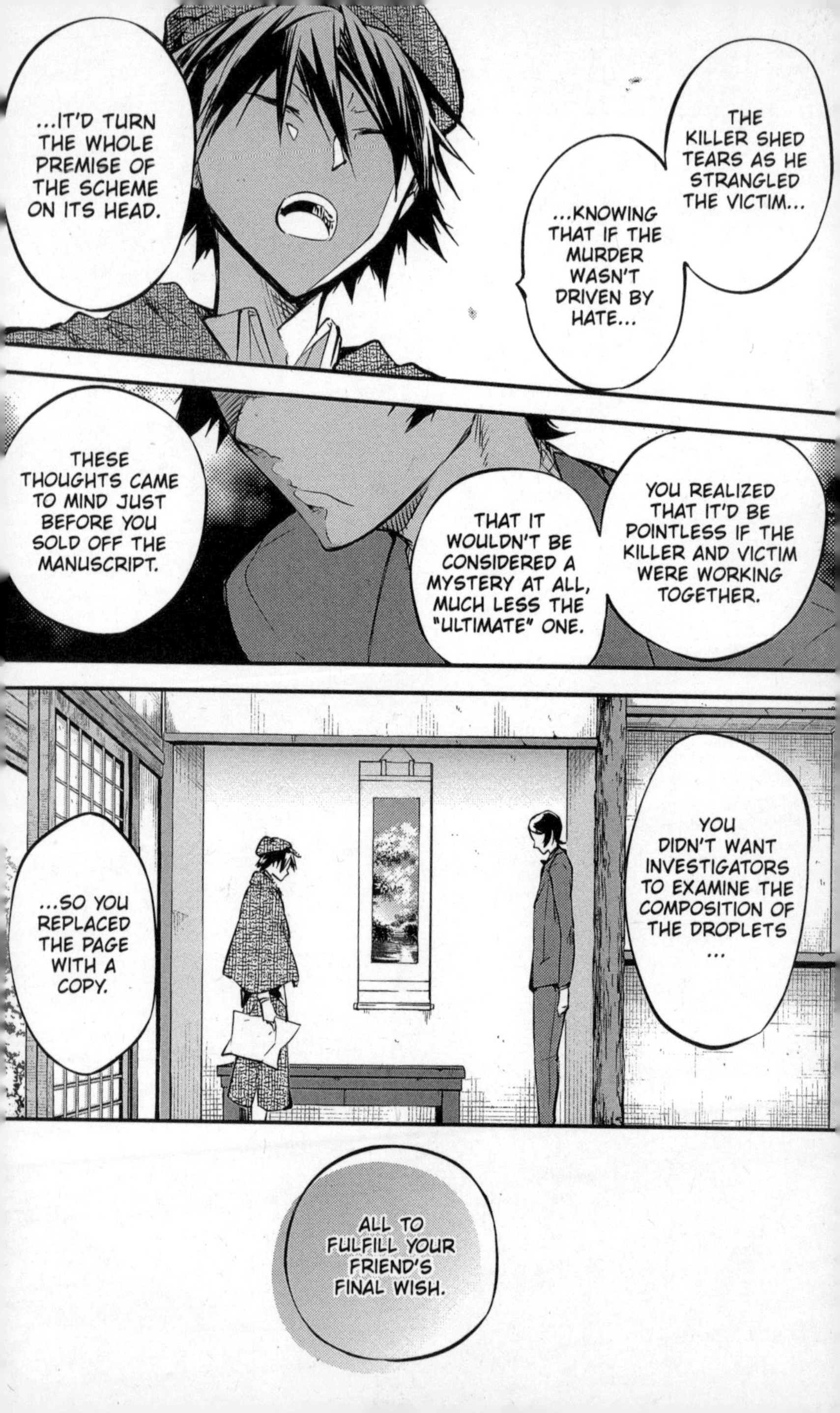
THE KILLER SHED TEARS AS HE STRANGLED THE VICTIM...
...KNOWING THAT IF THE MURDER WASN'T DRIVEN BY HATE...
...IT'D TURN THE WHOLE PREMISE OF THE SCHEME ON ITS HEAD.
YOU REALIZED THAT IT'D BE POINTLESS IF THE KILLER AND VICTIM WERE WORKING TOGETHER.
THAT IT WOULDN'T BE CONSIDERED A MYSTERY AT ALL, MUCH LESS THE "ULTIMATE" ONE.
THESE THOUGHTS CAME TO MIND JUST BEFORE YOU SOLD OFF THE MANUSCRIPT.
YOU DIDN'T WANT INVESTIGATORS TO EXAMINE THE COMPOSITION OF THE DROPLETS ...
...SO YOU REPLACED THE PAGE WITH A COPY.
ALL TO FULFILL YOUR FRIEND'S FINAL WISH.

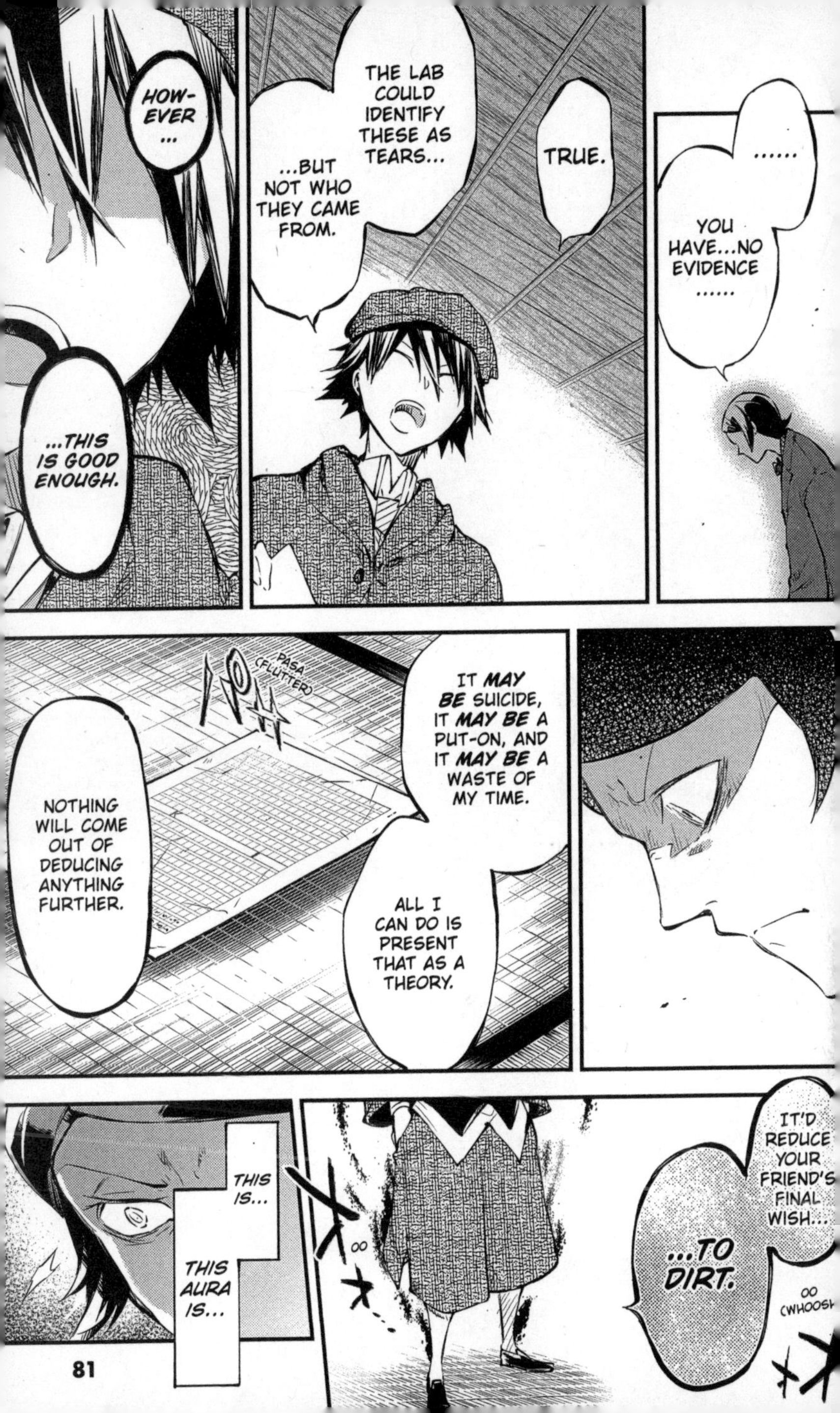
......
YOU HAVE...NO EVIDENCE ......
TRUE.
THE LAB COULD IDENTIFY THESE AS TEARS...
...BUT NOT WHO THEY CAME FROM.
HOW-EVER...
...THIS IS GOOD ENOUGH.
IT MAY BE SUICIDE, IT MAY BE A PUT-ON, AND IT MAY BE A WASTE OF MY TIME.
PASA (FLUTTER)
ALL I CAN DO IS PRESENT THAT AS A THEORY.
NOTHING WILL COME OUT OF DEDUCING ANYTHING FURTHER.
IT'D REDUCE YOUR FRIEND'S FINAL WISH...
...TO DIRT.
OO (WHOOSH
OO
THIS IS...
THIS AURA IS...

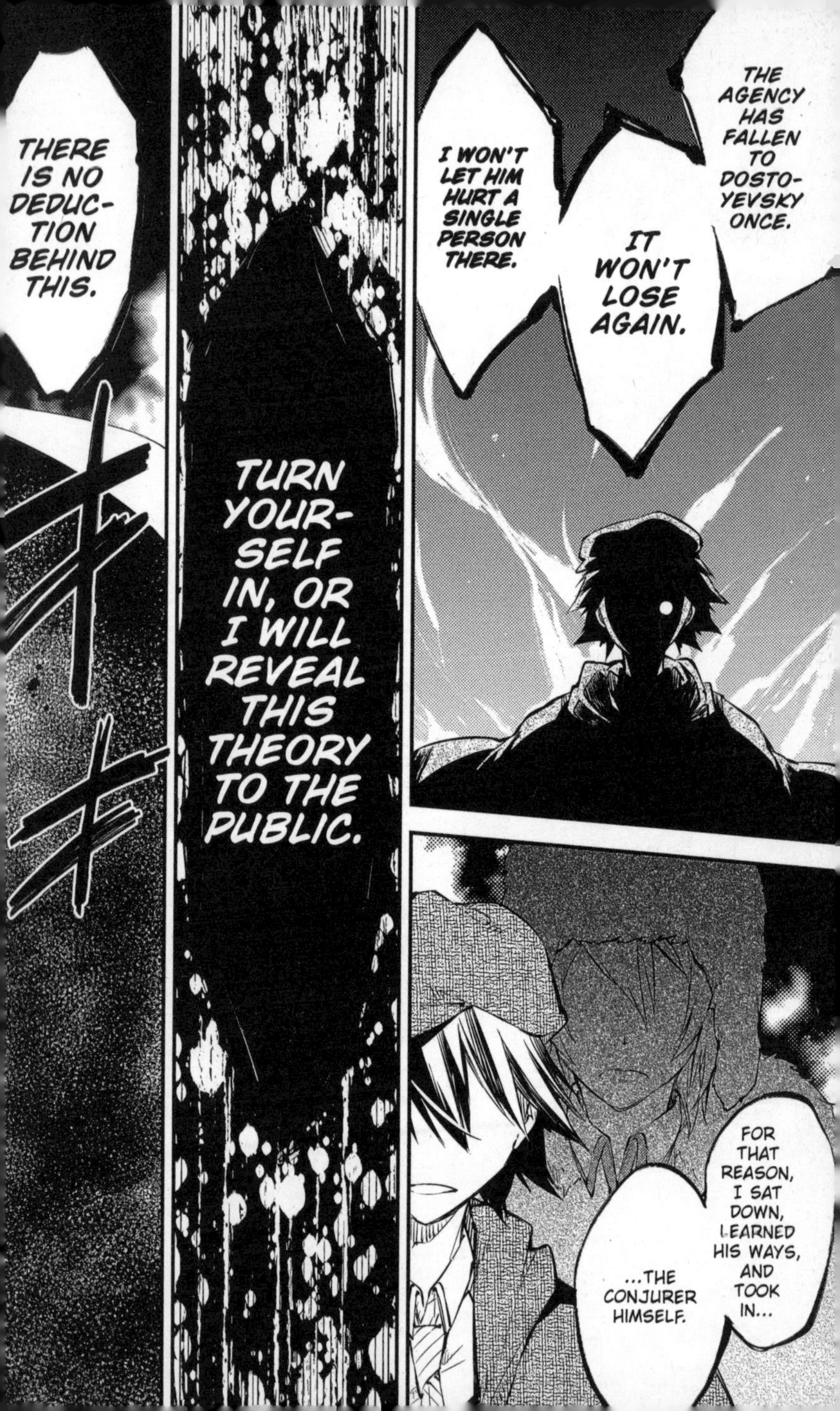
THE AGENCY HAS FALLEN TO DOSTO-YEVSKY ONCE.
IT WON'T LOSE AGAIN.
I WON'T LET HIM HURT A SINGLE PERSON THERE.
FOR THAT REASON, I SAT DOWN, LEARNED HIS WAYS, AND TOOK IN...
...THE CONJURER HIMSELF.
TURN YOUR-SELF IN, OR I WILL REVEAL THIS THEORY TO THE PUBLIC.
THERE IS NO DEDUC-TION BEHIND THIS.

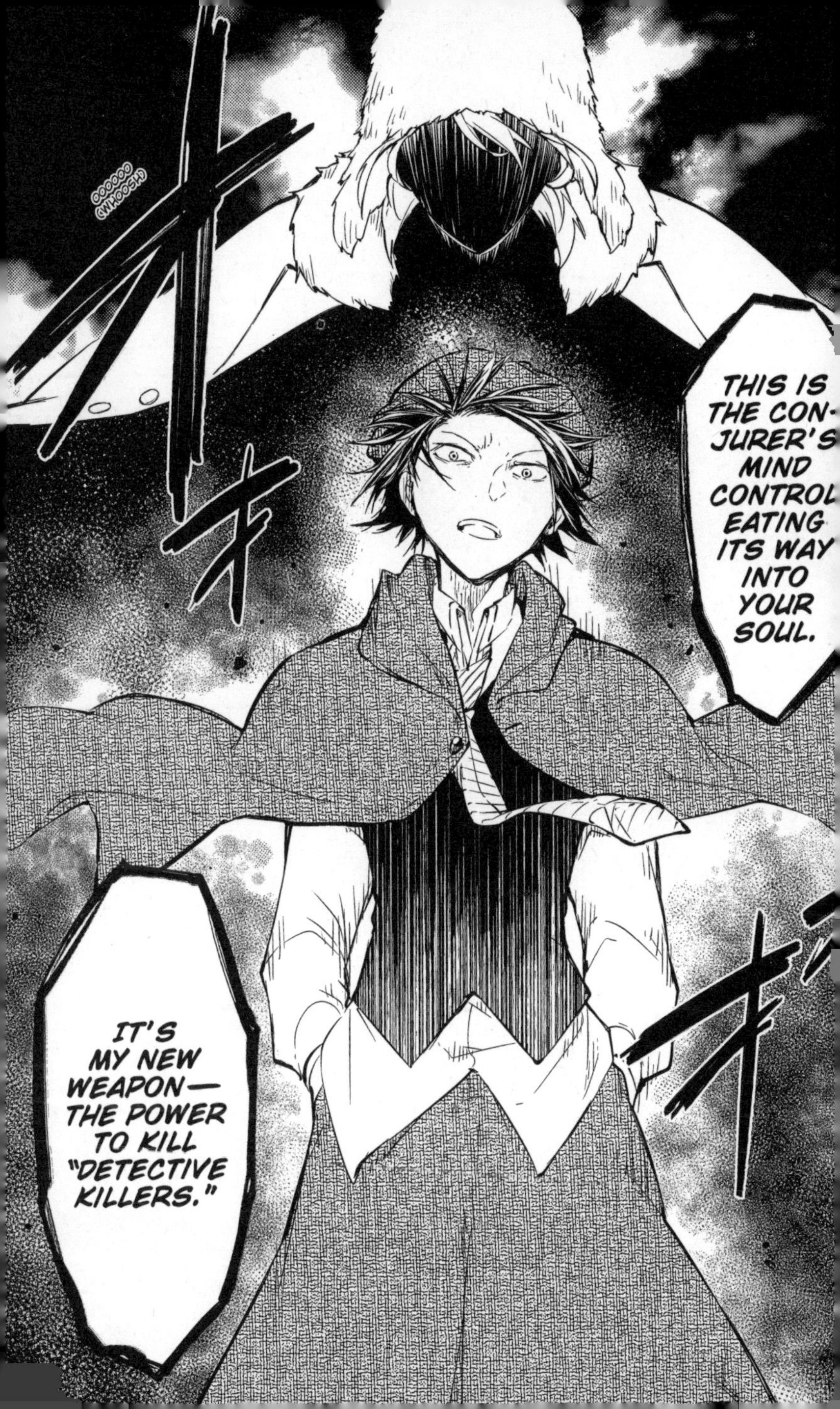

THIS IS THE CON-JURER'S MIND CONTROL EATING ITS WAY INTO YOUR SOUL.
OOOOOO (WHOOSH)
IT'S MY NEW WEAPON—THE POWER TO KILL "DETECTIVE KILLERS."

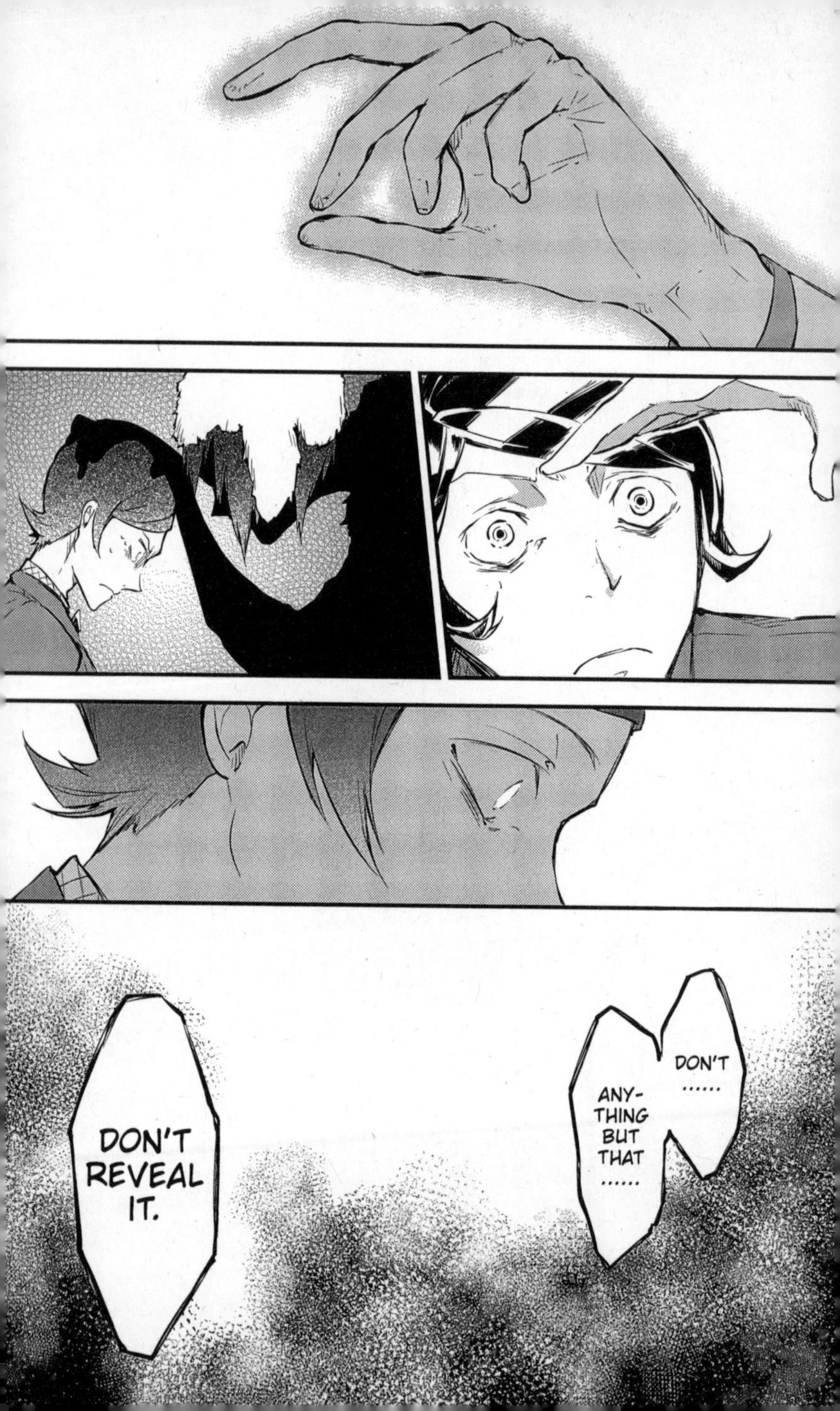
DON'T …… ANY-THING BUT THAT ……
DON'T REVEAL IT.

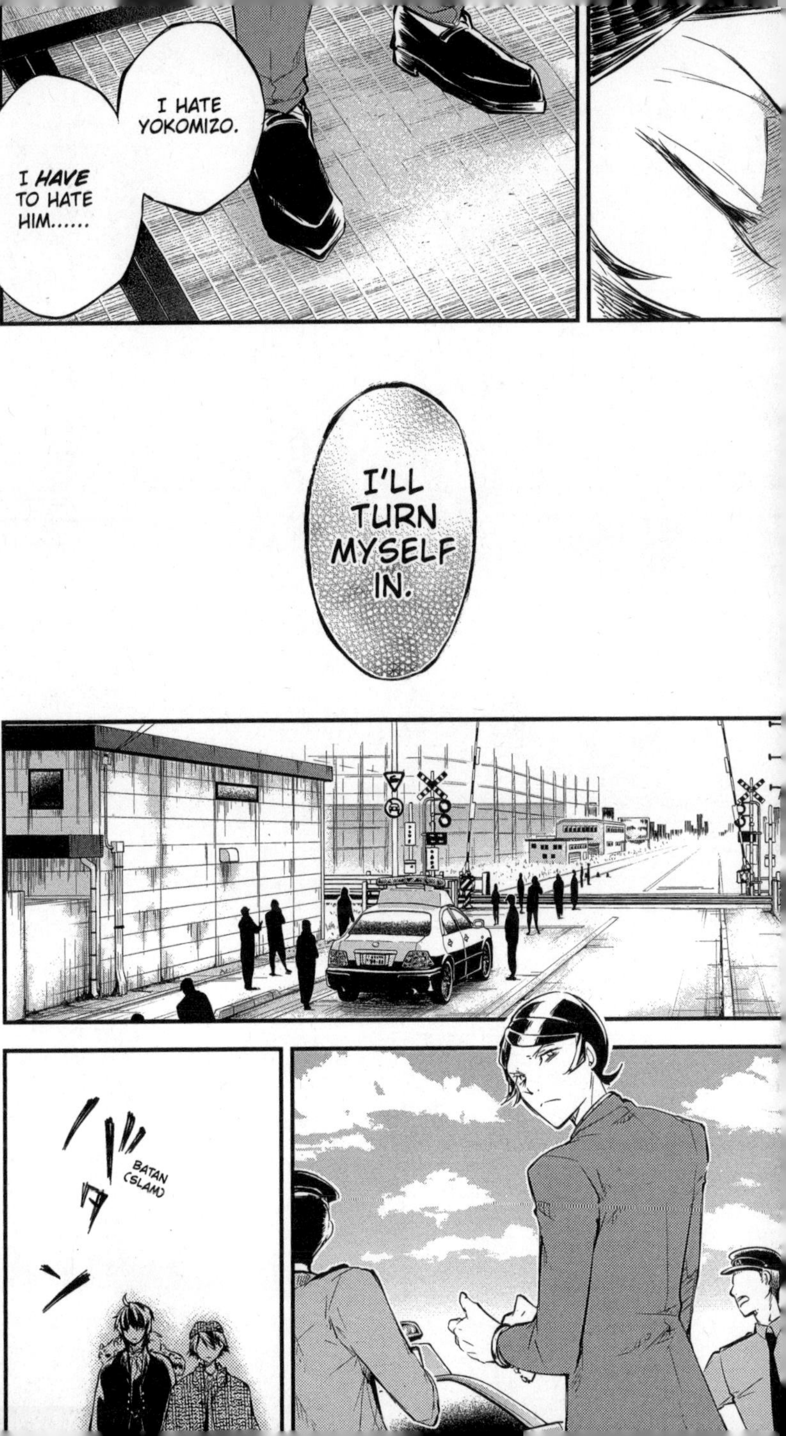
I HATE YOKOMIZO.
I *HAVE* TO HATE HIM......
I'LL TURN MYSELF IN.
BATAN (SLAM)

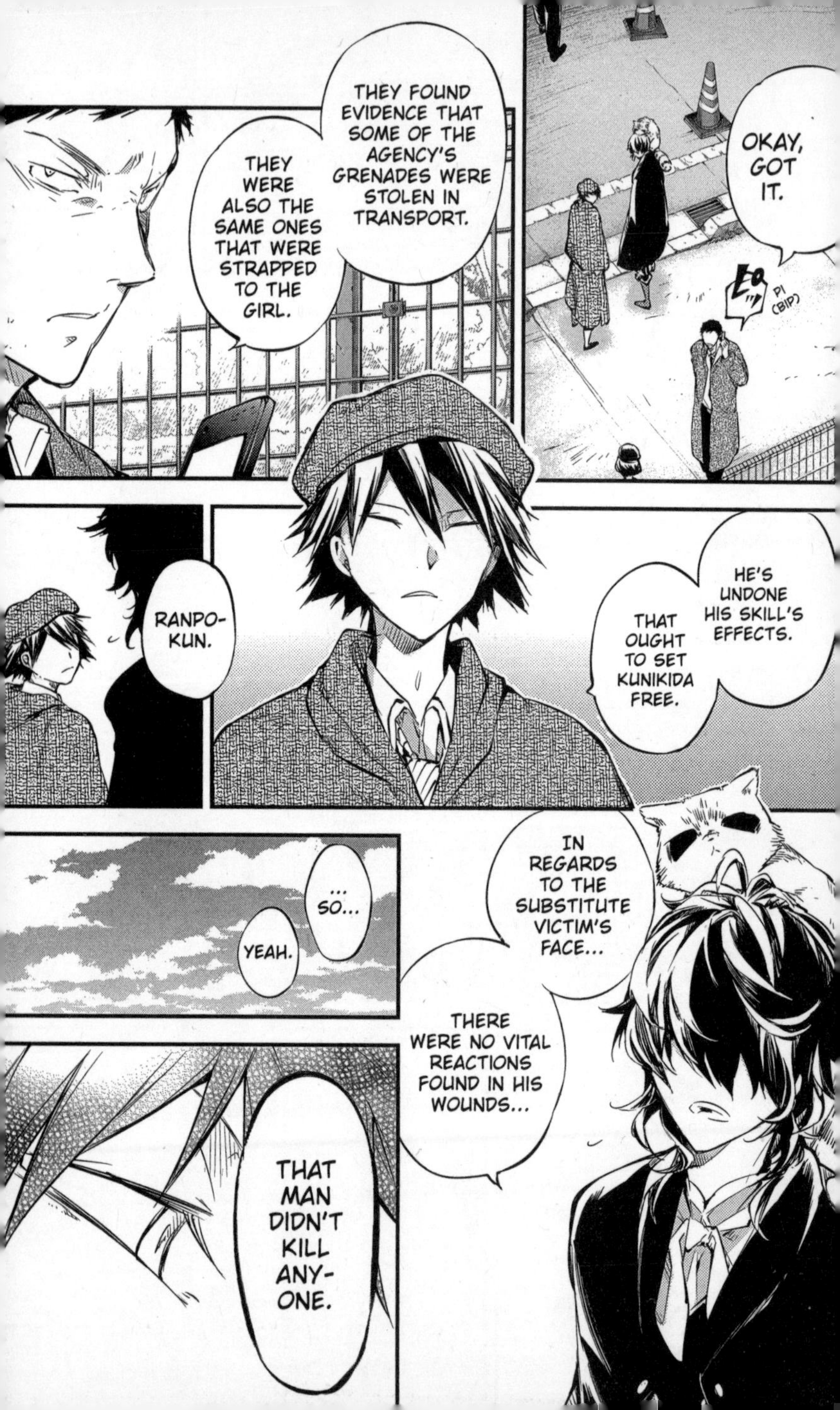
OKAY, GOT IT.
PI (BIP)
THEY FOUND EVIDENCE THAT SOME OF THE AGENCY'S GRENADES WERE STOLEN IN TRANSPORT.
THEY WERE ALSO THE SAME ONES THAT WERE STRAPPED TO THE GIRL.
HE'S UNDONE HIS SKILL'S EFFECTS.
THAT OUGHT TO SET KUNIKIDA FREE.
RANPO-KUN.
IN REGARDS TO THE SUBSTITUTE VICTIM'S FACE...
THERE WERE NO VITAL REACTIONS FOUND IN HIS WOUNDS...
...SO...
YEAH.
THAT MAN DIDN'T KILL ANY-ONE.

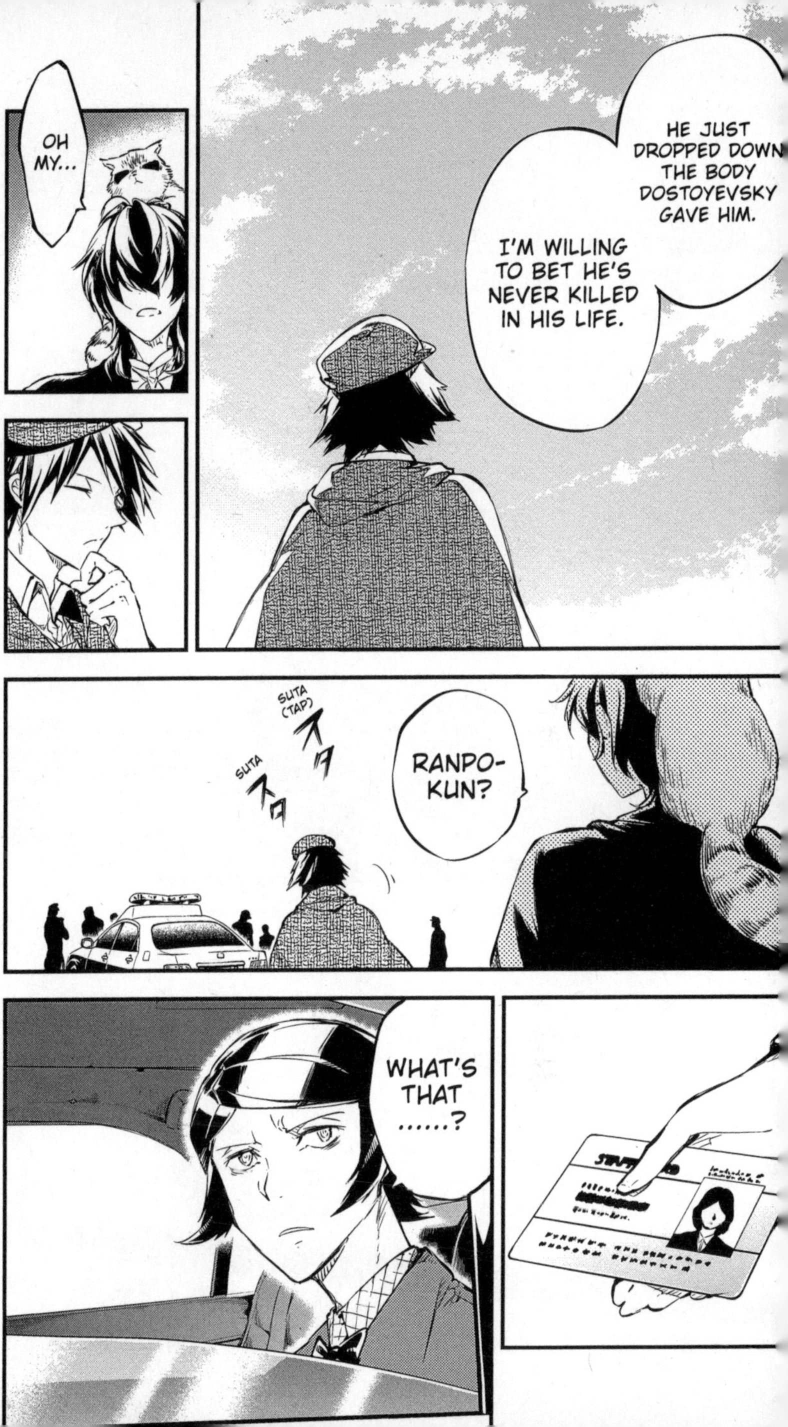
HE JUST DROPPED DOWN THE BODY DOSTOYEVSKY GAVE HIM.
I'M WILLING TO BET HE'S NEVER KILLED IN HIS LIFE.
OH MY...
RANPO-KUN?
SUTA (TAP)
スタ
SUTA
スタ
WHAT'S THAT ......?

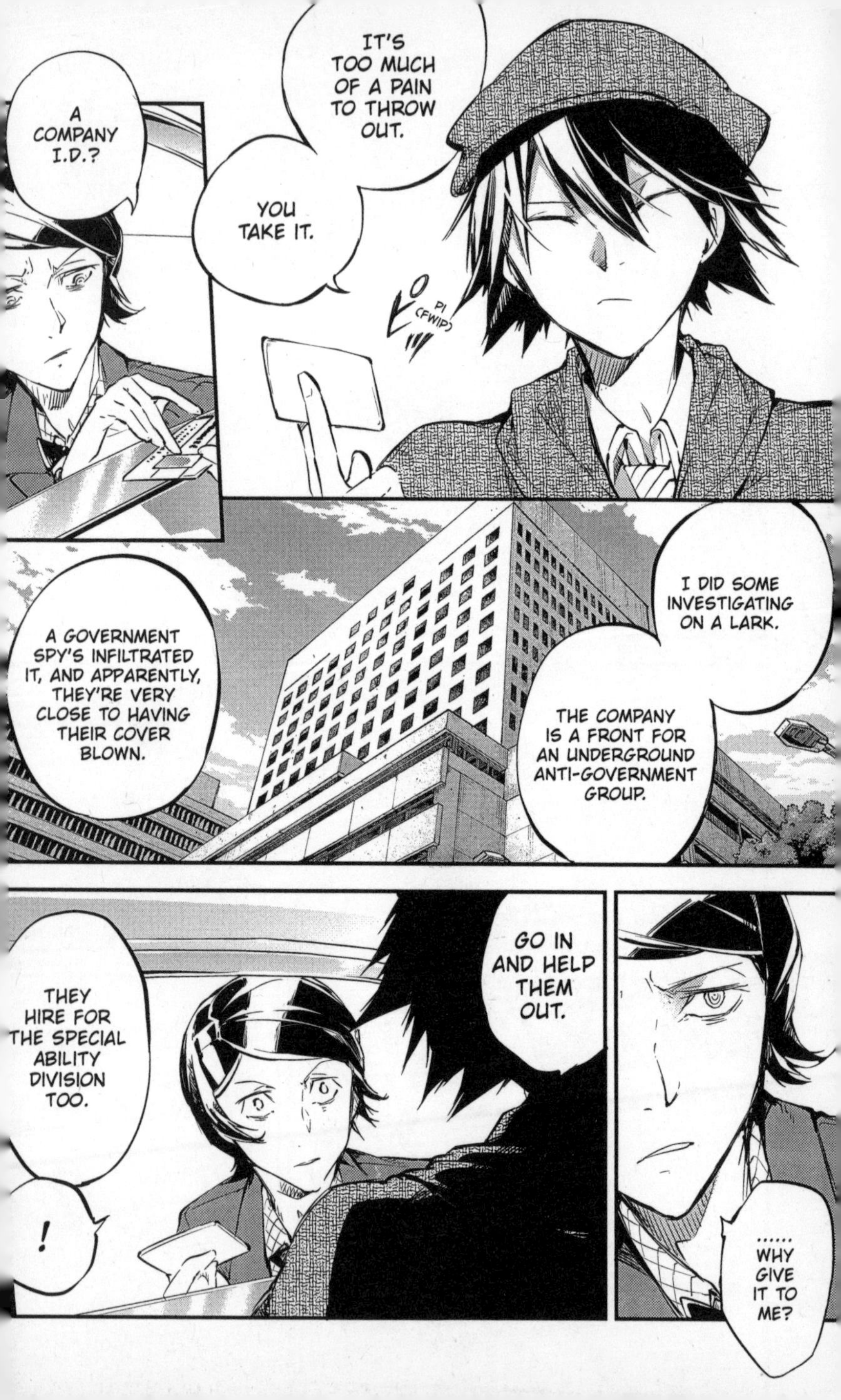
IT'S TOO MUCH OF A PAIN TO THROW OUT.
YOU TAKE IT.
PI (FWIP)
A COMPANY I.D.?
I DID SOME INVESTIGATING ON A LARK.
THE COMPANY IS A FRONT FOR AN UNDERGROUND ANTI-GOVERNMENT GROUP.
A GOVERNMENT SPY'S INFILTRATED IT, AND APPARENTLY, THEY'RE VERY CLOSE TO HAVING THEIR COVER BLOWN.
......WHY GIVE IT TO ME?
GO IN AND HELP THEM OUT.
THEY HIRE FOR THE SPECIAL ABILITY DIVISION TOO.
!

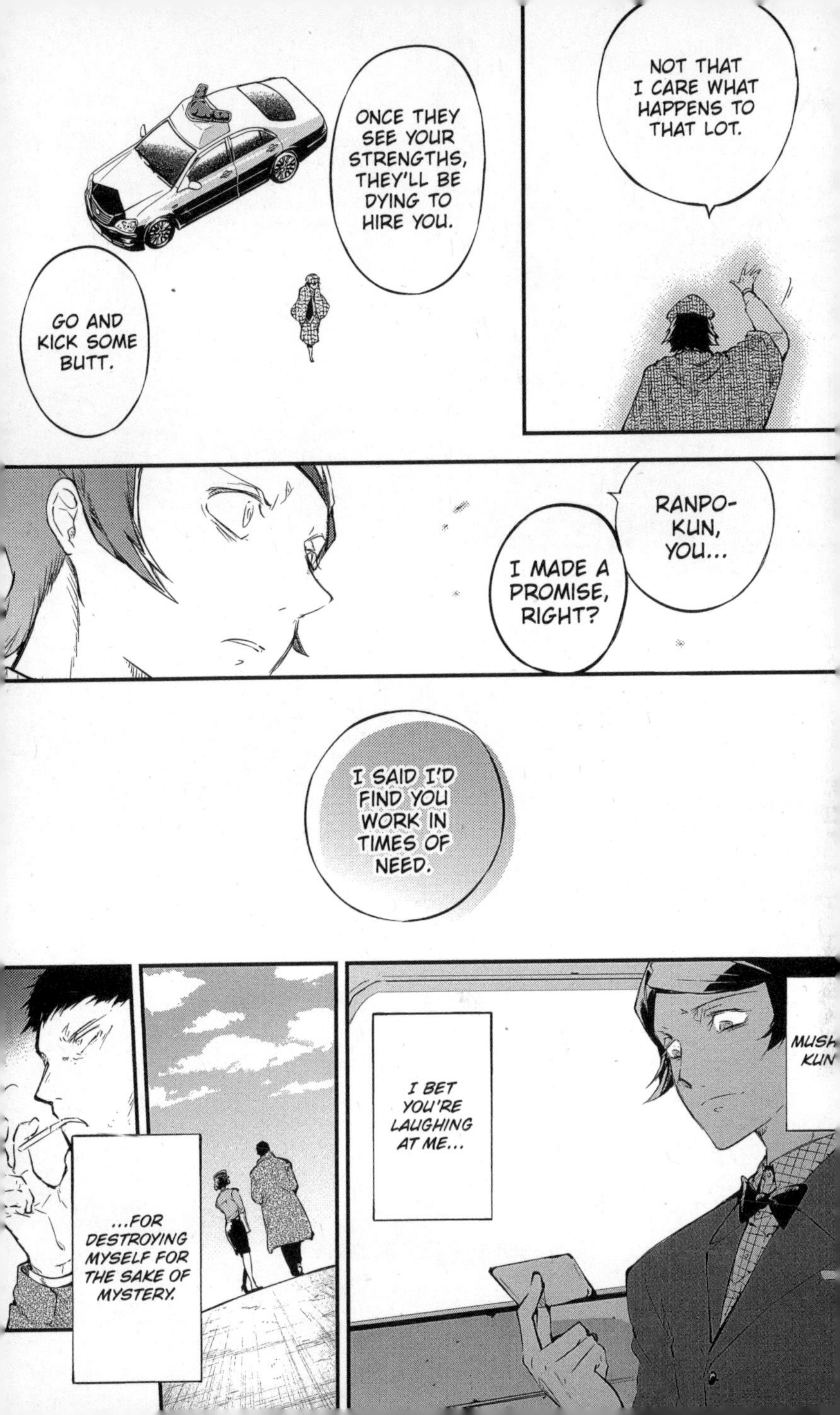
NOT THAT I CARE WHAT HAPPENS TO THAT LOT.
ONCE THEY SEE YOUR STRENGTHS, THEY'LL BE DYING TO HIRE YOU.
GO AND KICK SOME BUTT.
RANPO-KUN, YOU...
I MADE A PROMISE, RIGHT?
I SAID I'D FIND YOU WORK IN TIMES OF NEED.
MUSH KUN
I BET YOU'RE LAUGHING AT ME...
...FOR DESTROYING MYSELF FOR THE SAKE OF MYSTERY.

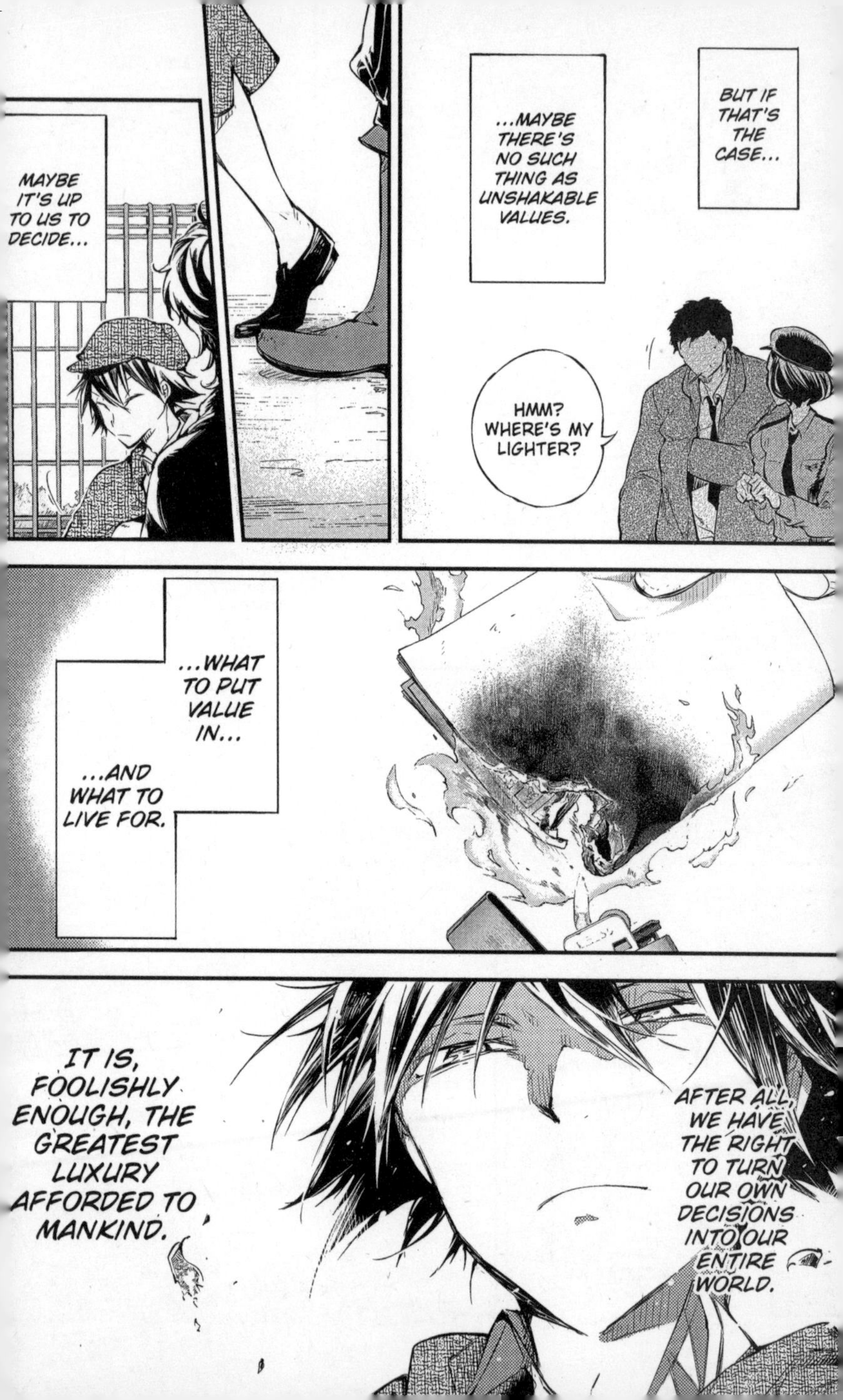
BUT IF THAT'S THE CASE...
...MAYBE THERE'S NO SUCH THING AS UNSHAKABLE VALUES.
HMM? WHERE'S MY LIGHTER?
MAYBE IT'S UP TO US TO DECIDE...
...WHAT TO PUT VALUE IN...
...AND WHAT TO LIVE FOR.
AFTER ALL, WE HAVE THE RIGHT TO TURN OUR OWN DECISIONS INTO OUR ENTIRE WORLD.
IT IS, FOOLISHLY ENOUGH, THE GREATEST LUXURY AFFORDED TO MANKIND.

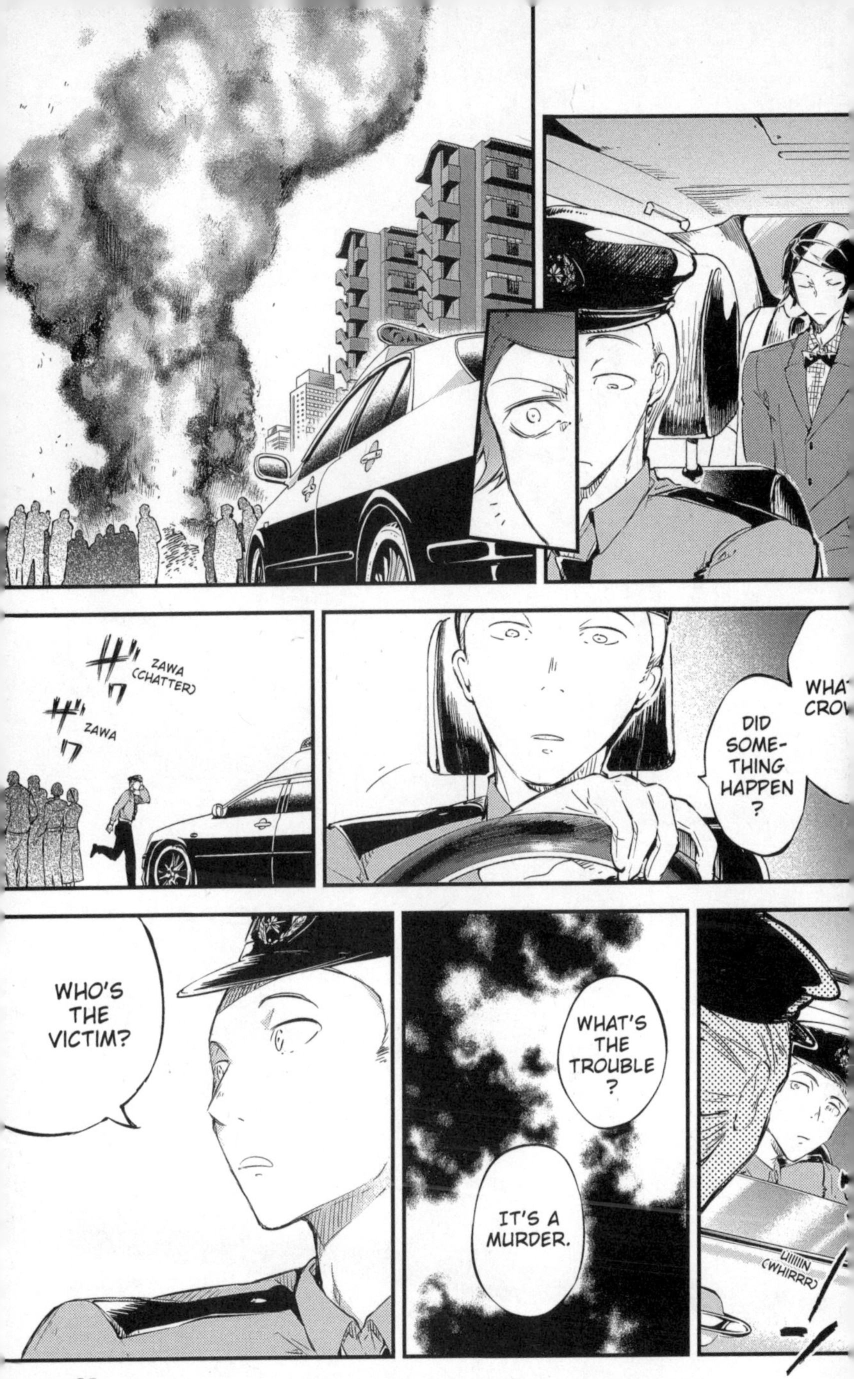
WHAT CROW
DID SOMETHING HAPPEN?
ZAWA (CHATTER)
ZAWA
UIIIIIN (WHIRRR)
WHAT'S THE TROUBLE?
IT'S A MURDER.
WHO'S THE VICTIM?

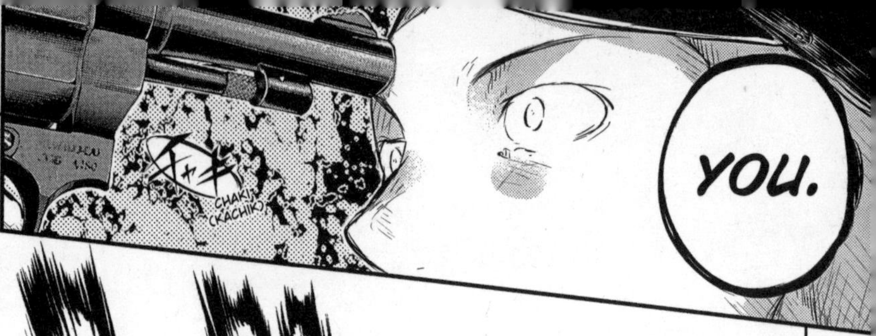
YOU.
CHAKI
(KACHIK)
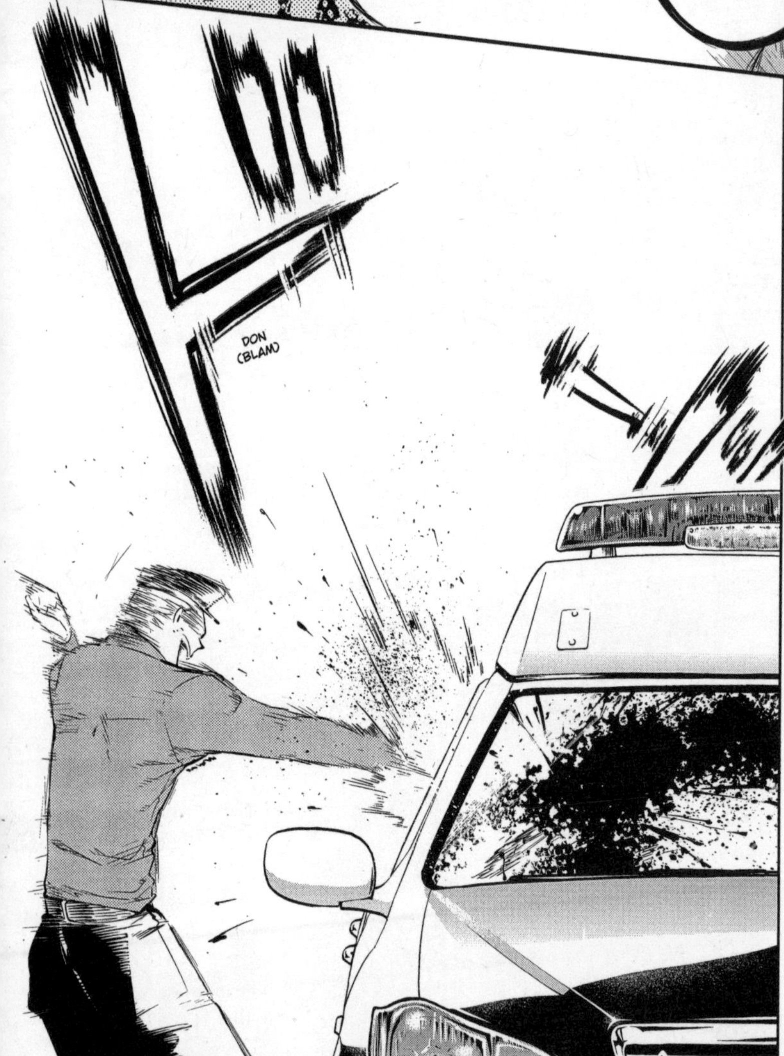
DON
(BLAM)

CHAPTER 57

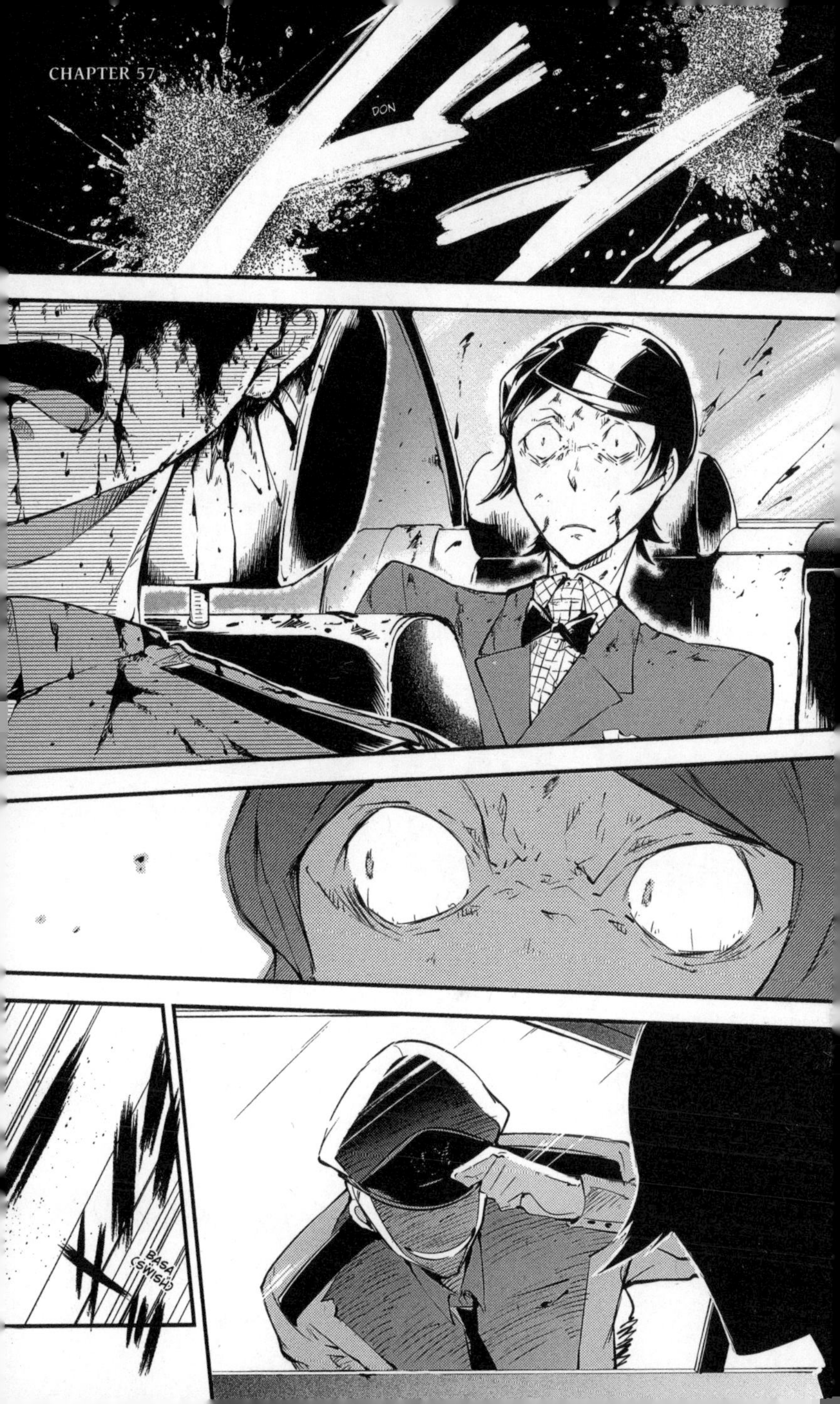
DON
BASA (SWISH)

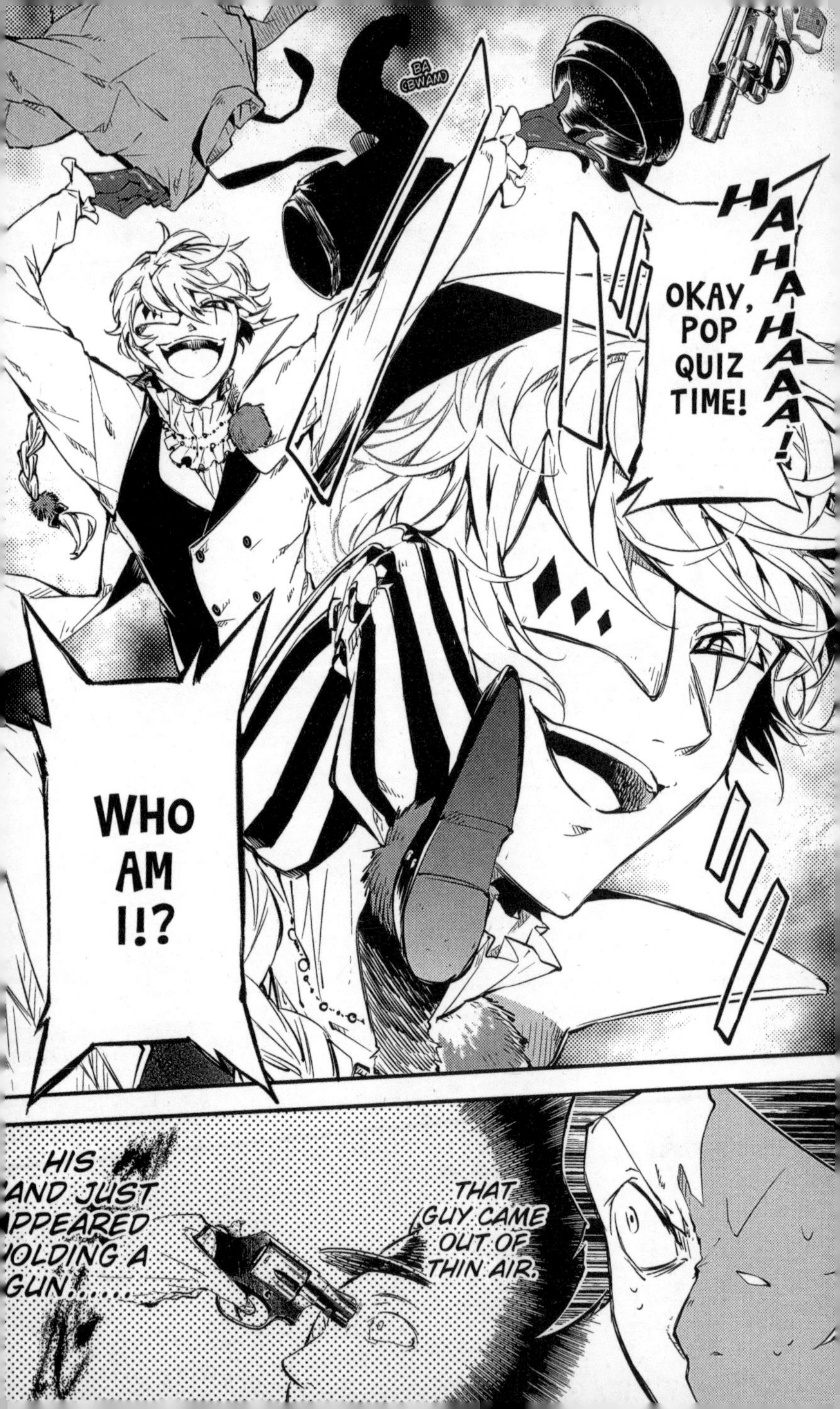
HAHAHAHAAA!!
OKAY, POP QUIZ TIME!
BA (BWAM)
WHO AM I!?
THAT GUY CAME OUT OF THIN AIR.
HIS
AND JUST
PPEARED
OLDING A
GUN......

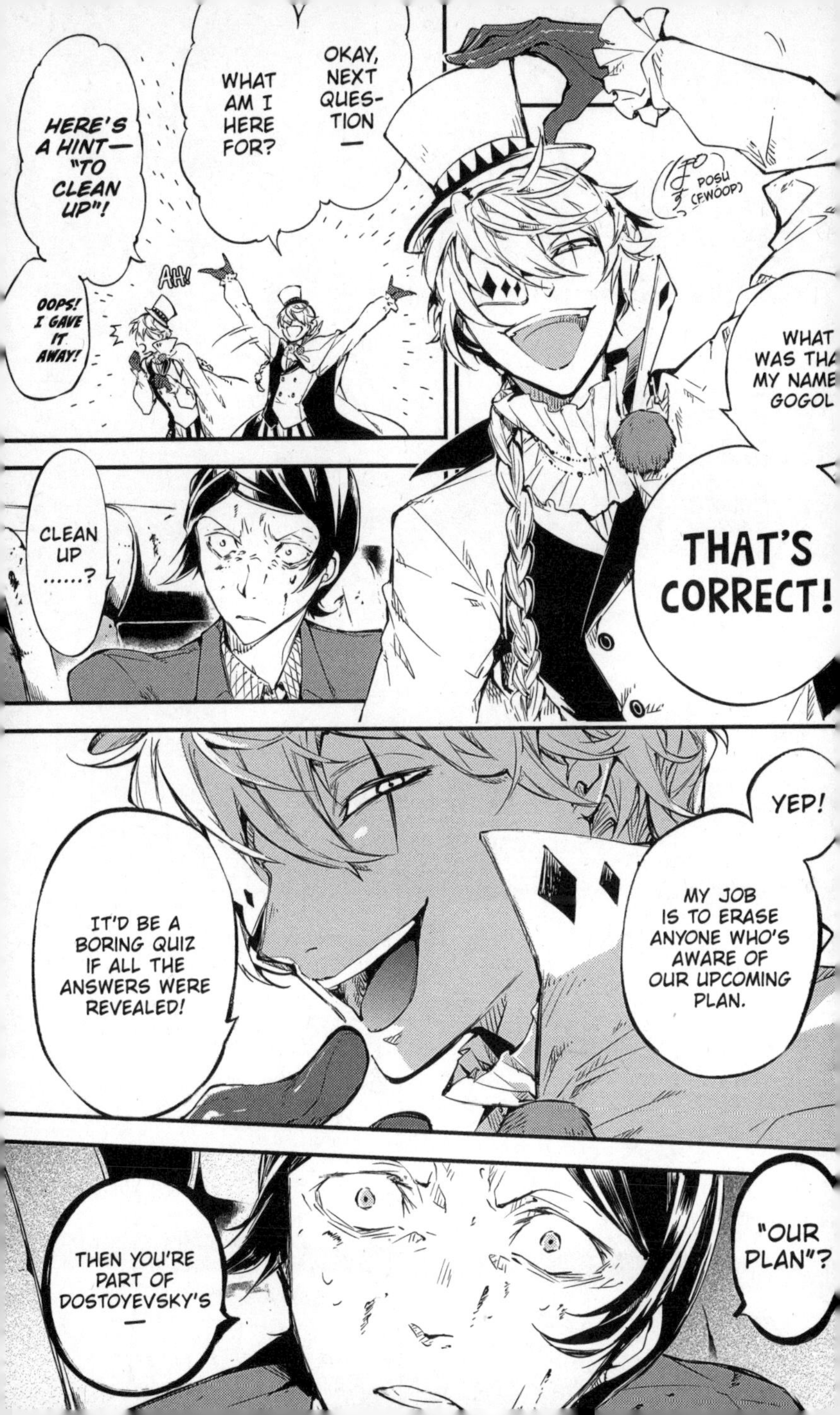
POSU (FWOOP)
WHAT WAS THA MY NAME GOGOL
THAT'S CORRECT!
OKAY, NEXT QUES-TION—
WHAT AM I HERE FOR?
HERE'S A HINT—"TO CLEAN UP"!
AH!
OOPS! I GAVE IT AWAY!
CLEAN UP ......?
YEP!
MY JOB IS TO ERASE ANYONE WHO'S AWARE OF OUR UPCOMING PLAN.
IT'D BE A BORING QUIZ IF ALL THE ANSWERS WERE REVEALED!
"OUR PLAN"?
THEN YOU'RE PART OF DOSTOYEVSKY'S—

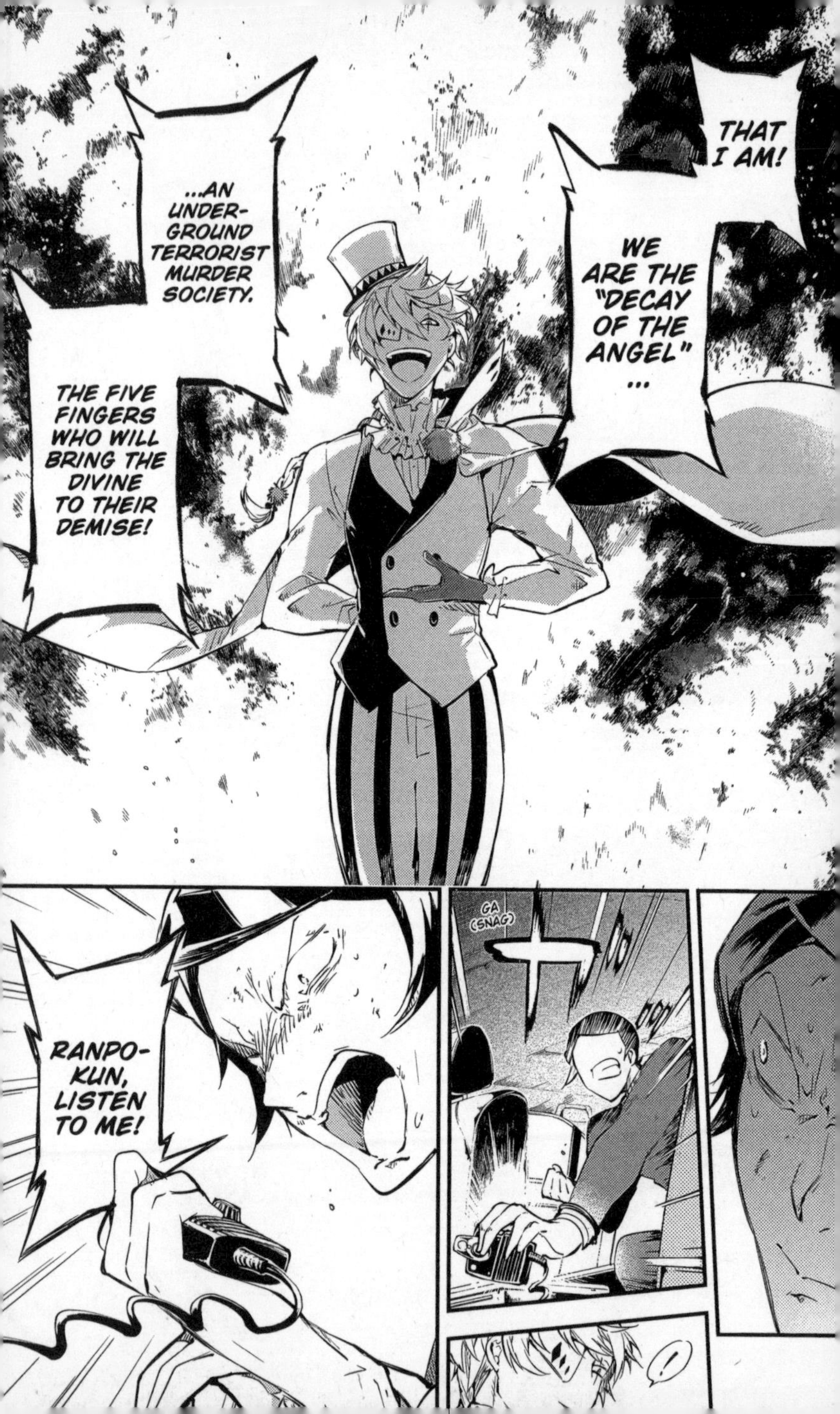
THAT I AM!
WE ARE THE "DECAY OF THE ANGEL"...
...AN UNDERGROUND TERRORIST MURDER SOCIETY.
THE FIVE FINGERS WHO WILL BRING THE DIVINE TO THEIR DEMISE!
GA (SNAG)
!
RANPO-KUN, LISTEN TO ME!

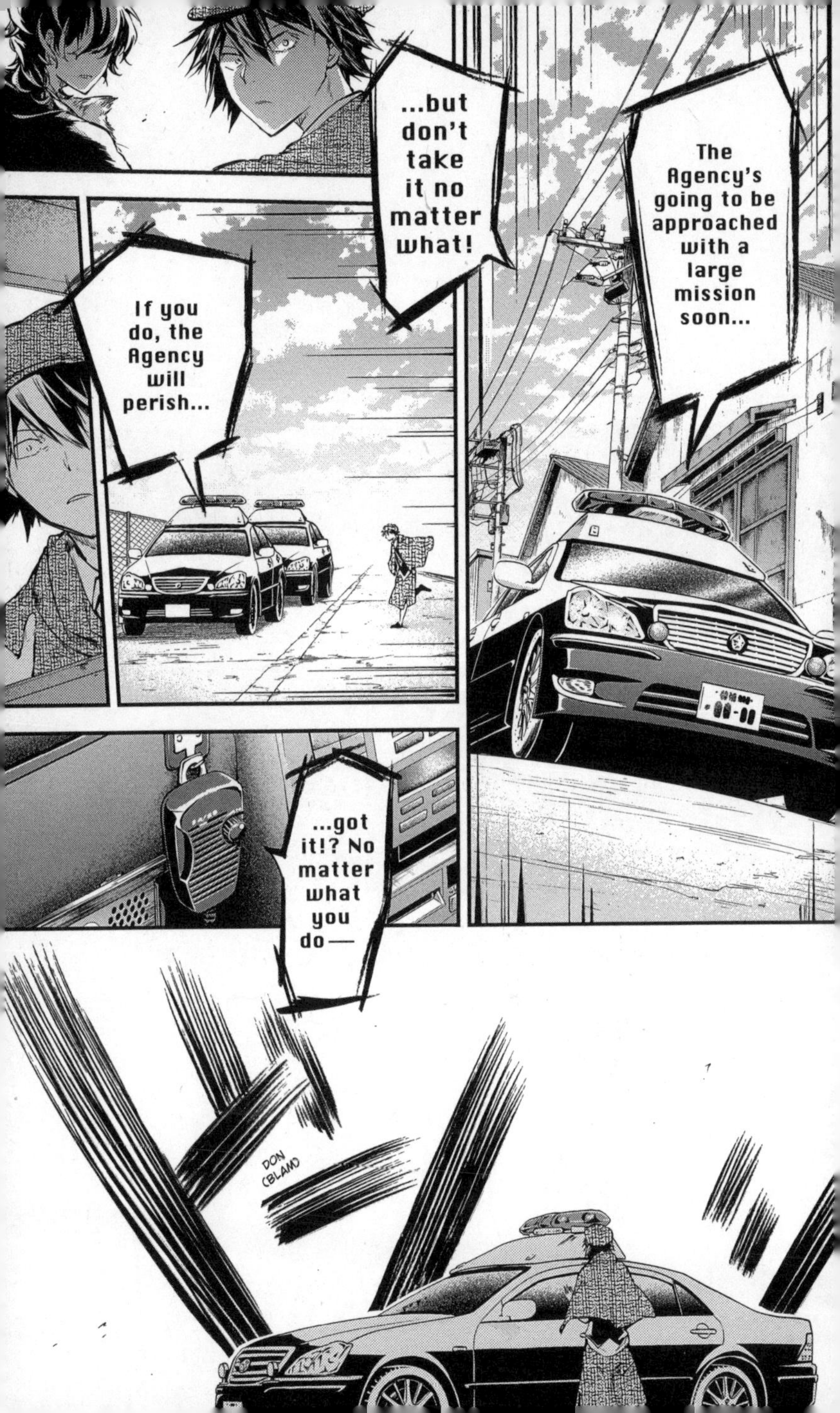
The Agency's going to be approached with a large mission soon...
...but don't take it no matter what!
If you do, the Agency will perish...
...got it!? No matter what you do—
DON
(BLAM)

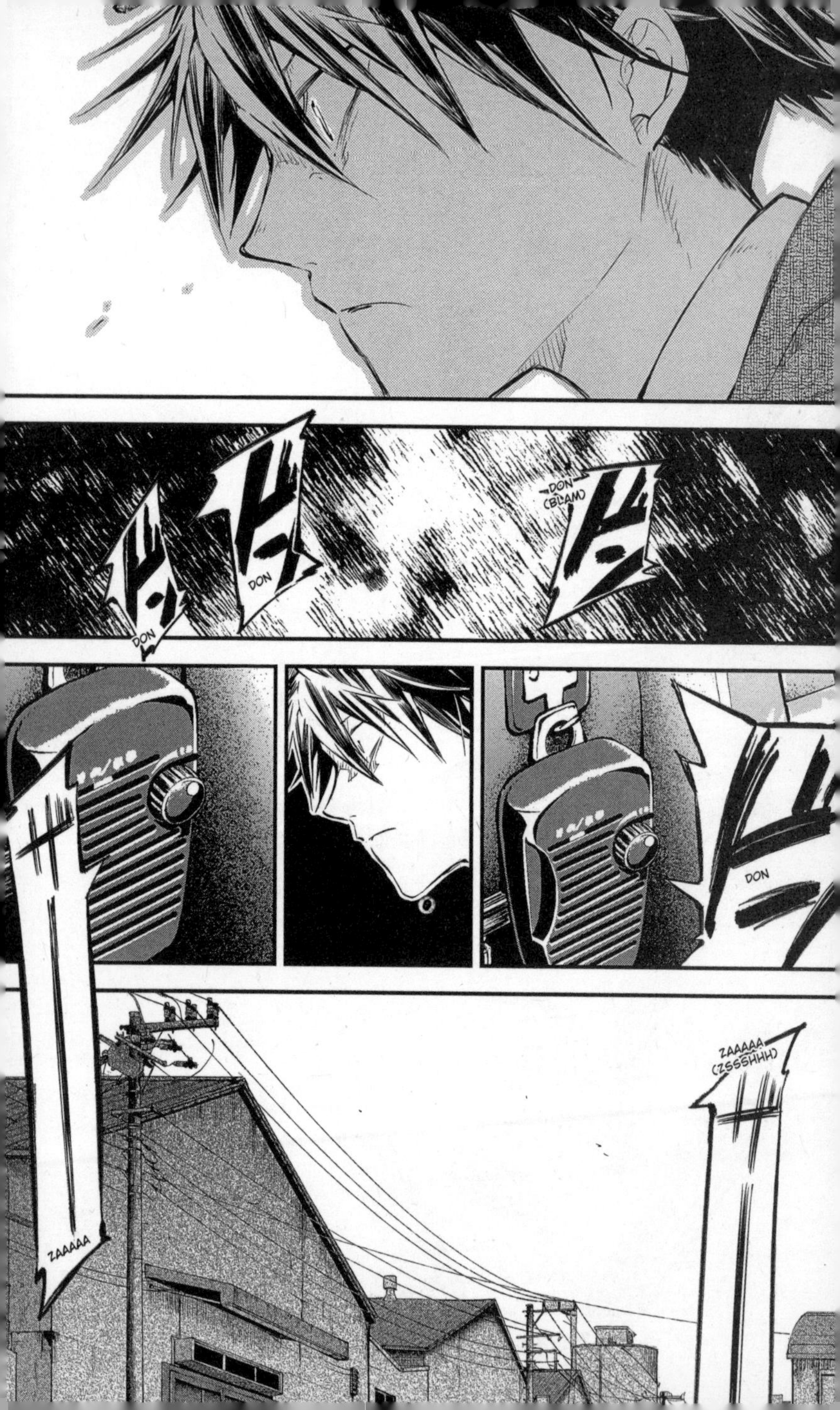
DON
(BLAM)
DON
DON
DON
ZAAAAA
(ZSSSHHH)
ZAAAAA

CHAPTER 57

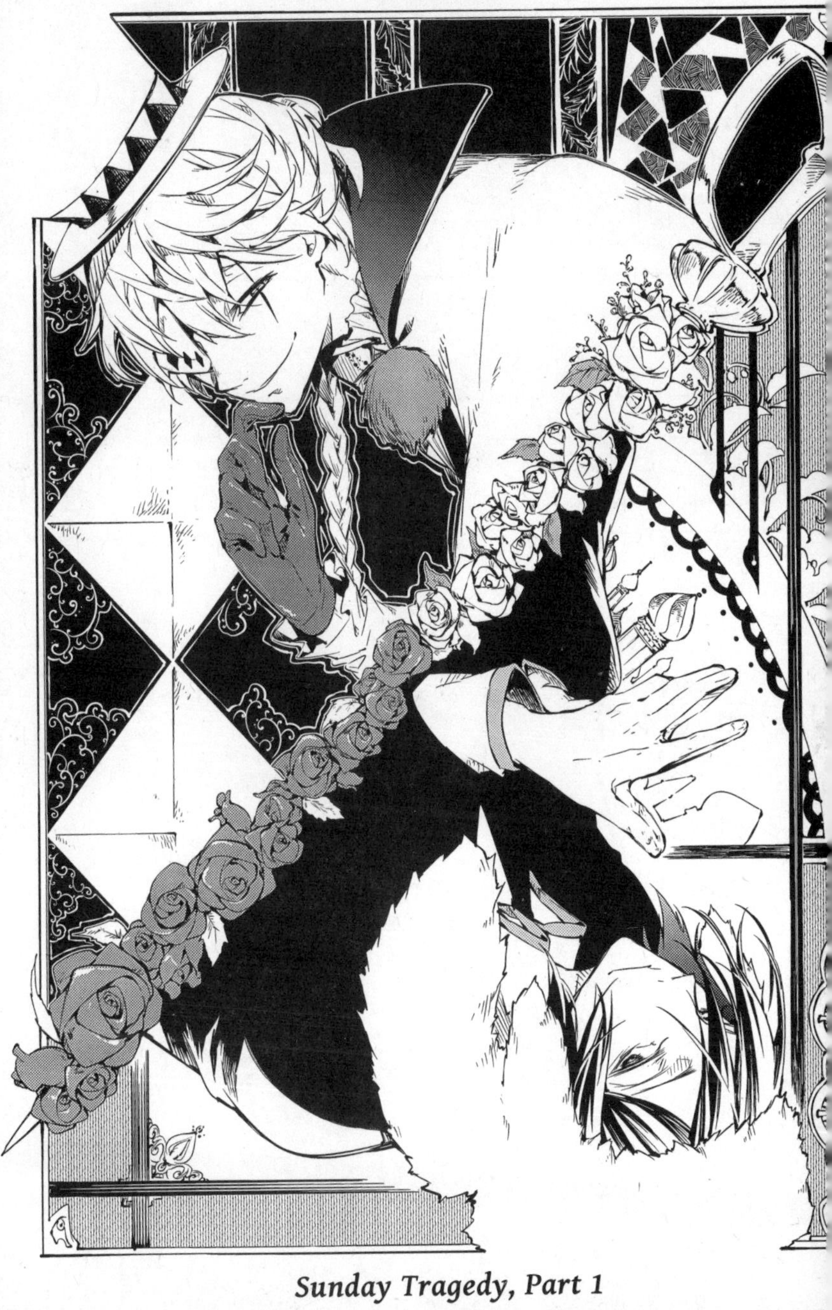

Sunday Tragedy, Part 1

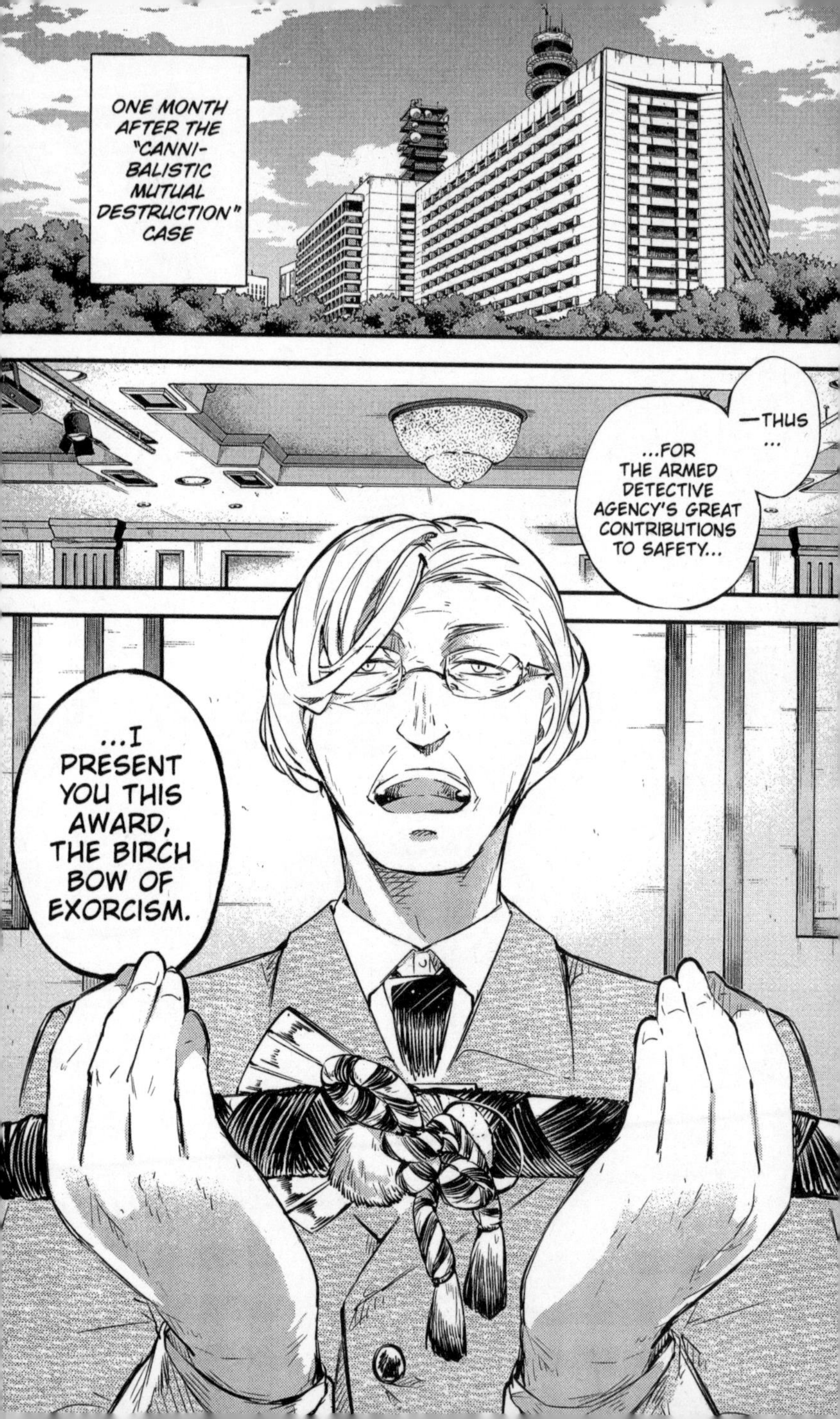
ONE MONTH AFTER THE "CANNIBALISTIC MUTUAL DESTRUCTION" CASE
—THUS ...
...FOR THE ARMED DETECTIVE AGENCY'S GREAT CONTRIBUTIONS TO SAFETY...
...I PRESENT YOU THIS AWARD, THE BIRCH BOW OF EXORCISM.

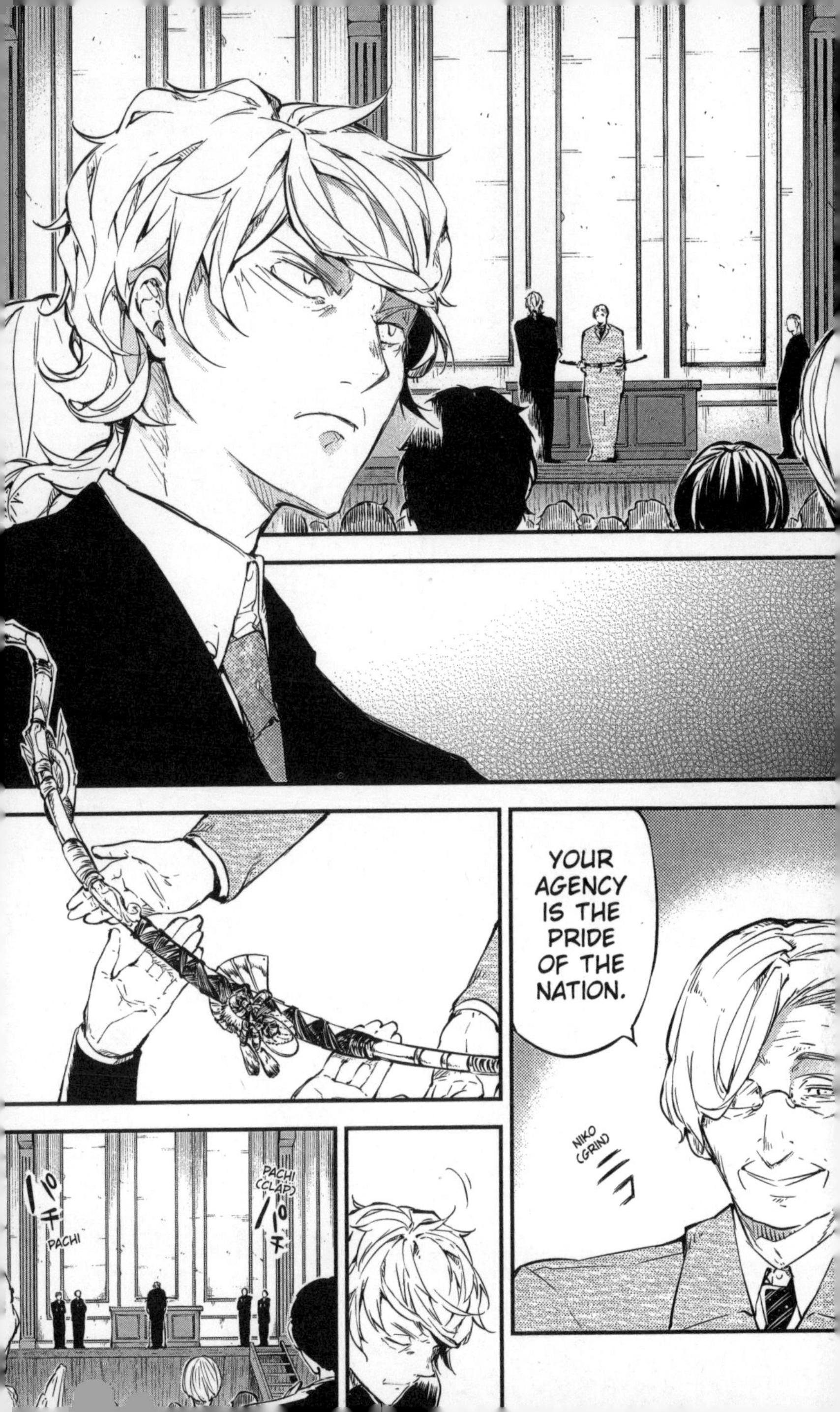
YOUR AGENCY IS THE PRIDE OF THE NATION.
NIKO (GRIN)
PACHI (CLAP)
PACHI

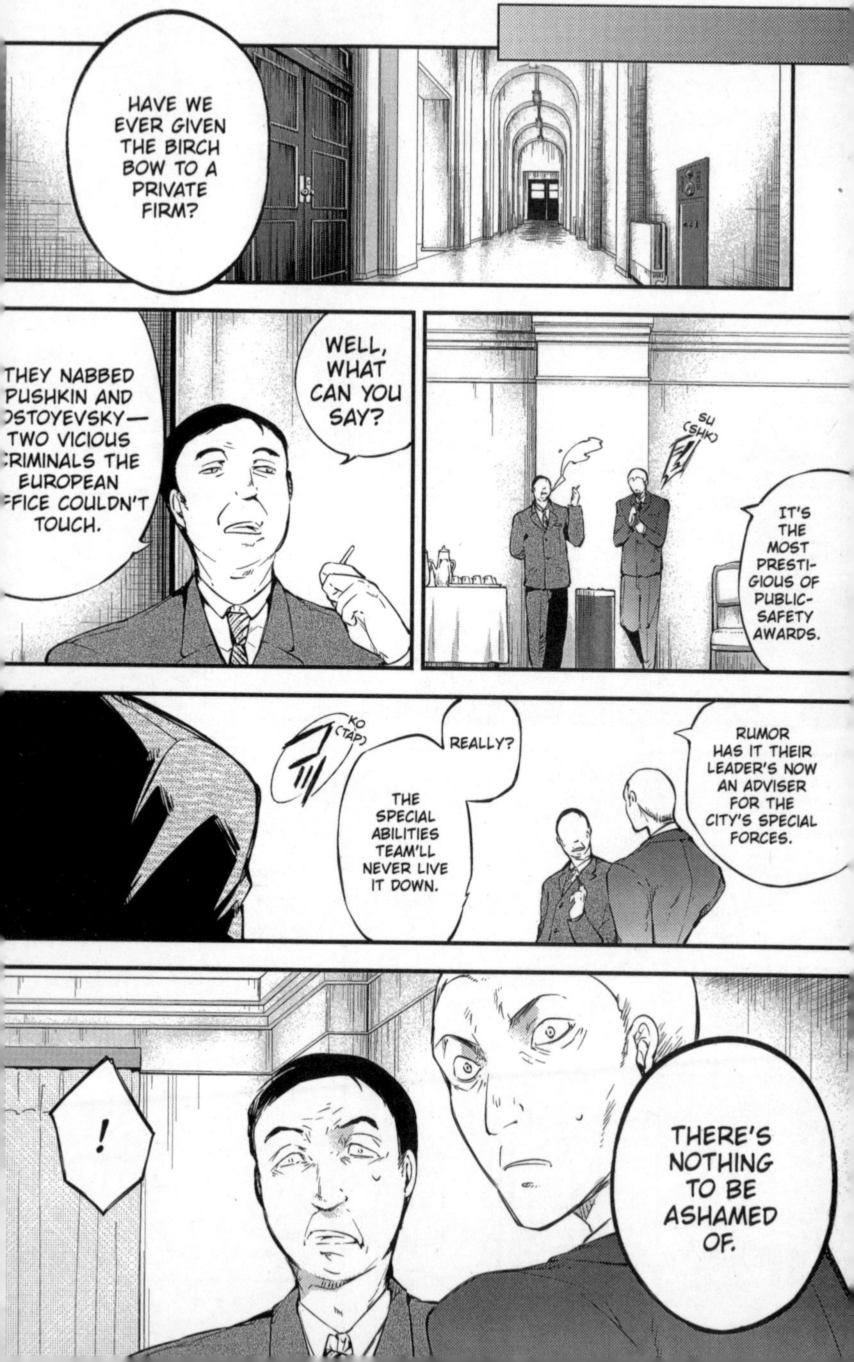
HAVE WE EVER GIVEN THE BIRCH BOW TO A PRIVATE FIRM?
SU (SHK)
IT'S THE MOST PRESTI-GIOUS OF PUBLIC-SAFETY AWARDS.
WELL, WHAT CAN YOU SAY?
THEY NABBED PUSHKIN AND DOSTOYEVSKY—TWO VICIOUS CRIMINALS THE EUROPEAN OFFICE COULDN'T TOUCH.
RUMOR HAS IT THEIR LEADER'S NOW AN ADVISER FOR THE CITY'S SPECIAL FORCES.
REALLY?
THE SPECIAL ABILITIES TEAM'LL NEVER LIVE IT DOWN.
KO (TAP)
THERE'S NOTHING TO BE ASHAMED OF.
!

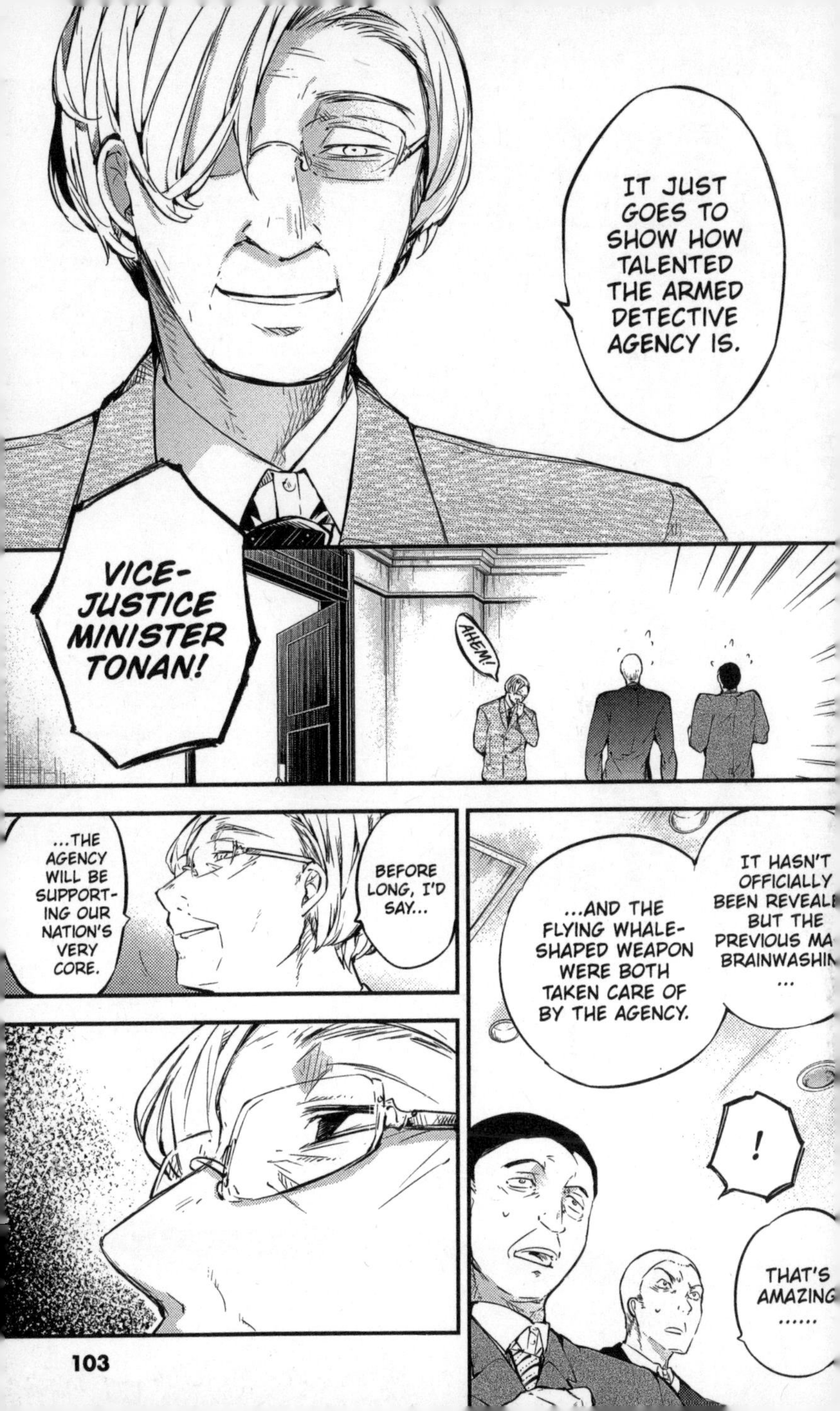
IT JUST GOES TO SHOW HOW TALENTED THE ARMED DETECTIVE AGENCY IS.
VICE-JUSTICE MINISTER TONAN!
AHEM!
IT HASN'T OFFICIALLY BEEN REVEALE BUT THE PREVIOUS MA BRAINWASHIN ...
...AND THE FLYING WHALE-SHAPED WEAPON WERE BOTH TAKEN CARE OF BY THE AGENCY.
!
THAT'S AMAZING ......
BEFORE LONG, I'D SAY...
...THE AGENCY WILL BE SUPPORTING OUR NATION'S VERY CORE.

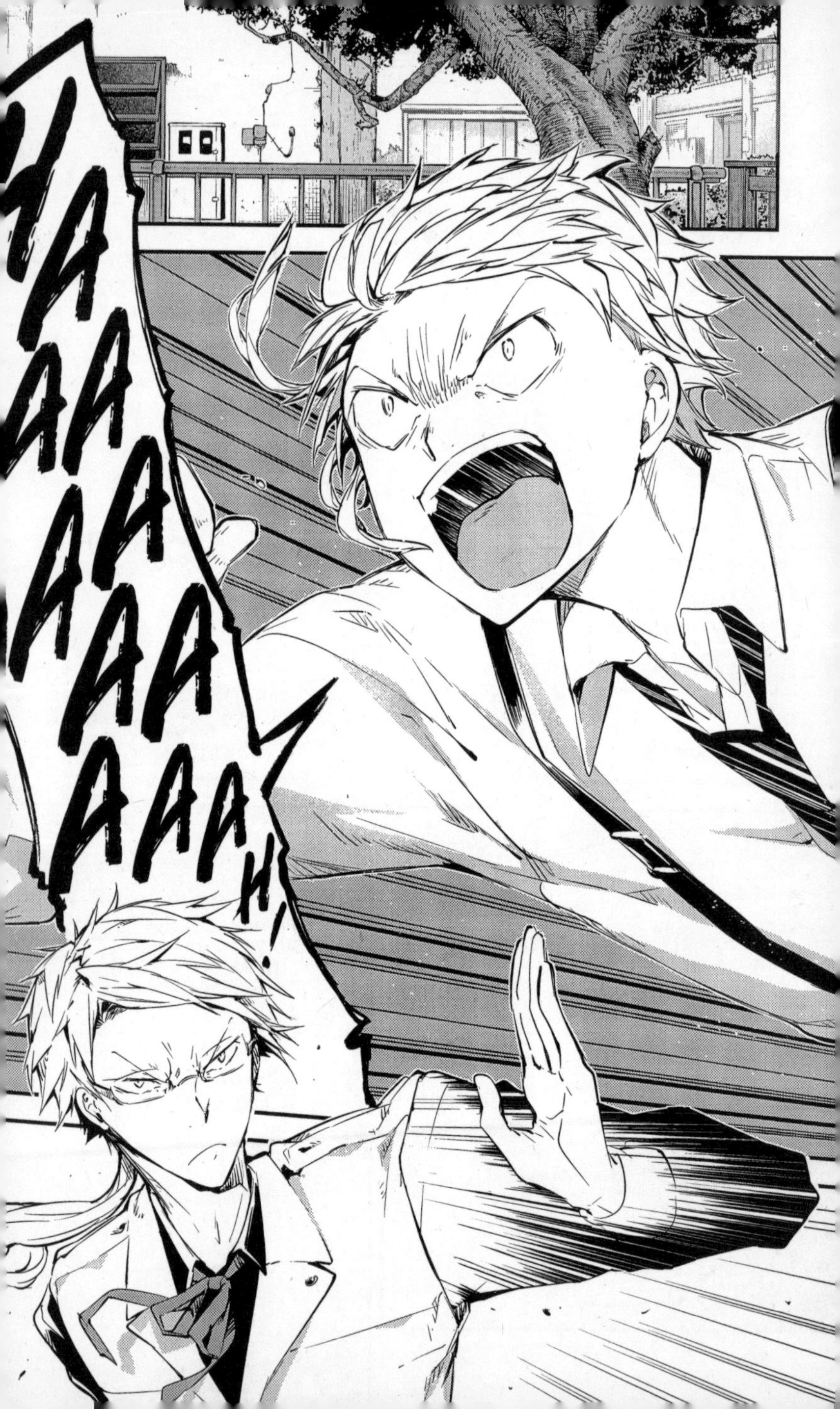
WAAAAAAAAAAAAAAAAH!

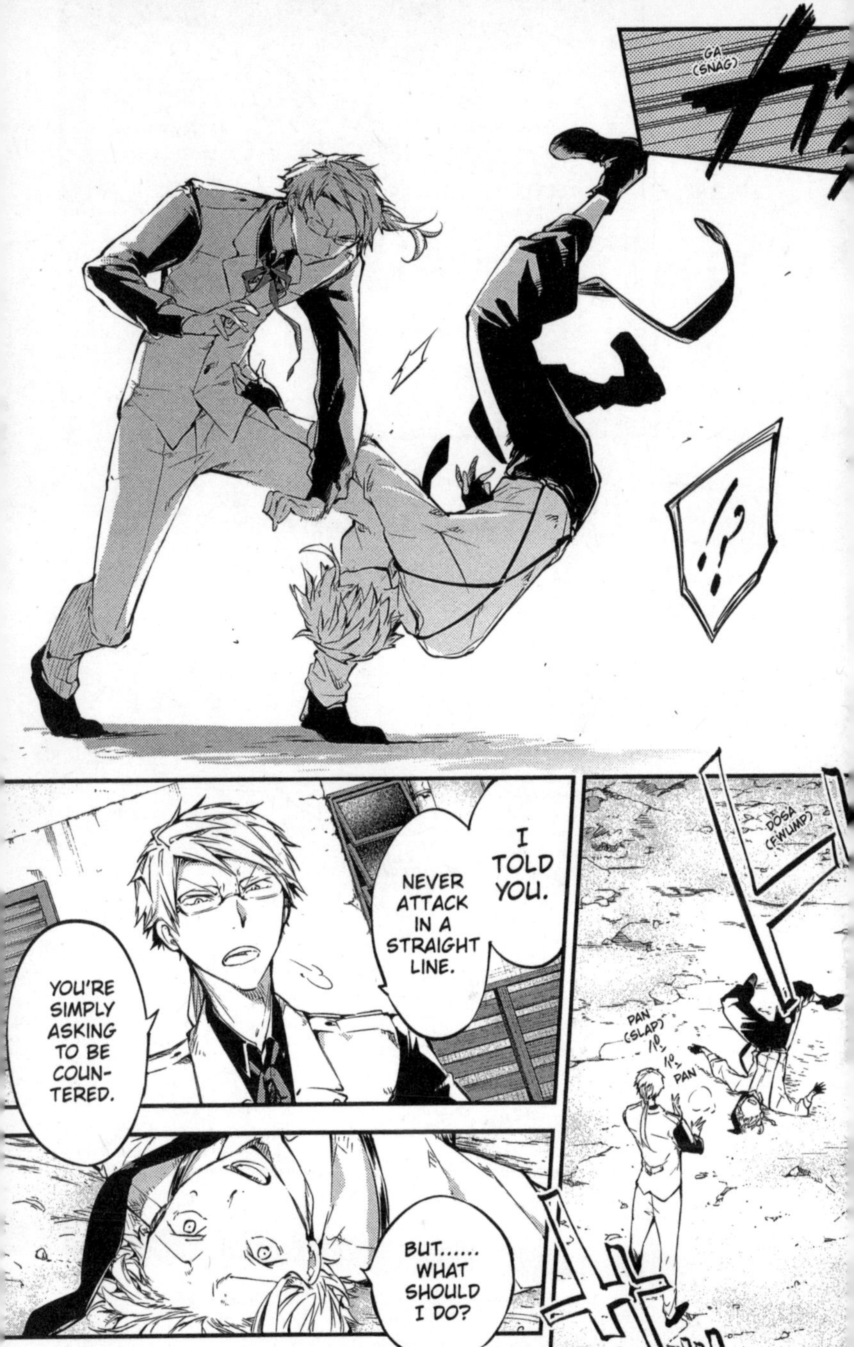
GA (SNAG)
DOSA (FWUMP)
PAN (SLAP)
PAN
I TOLD YOU.
NEVER ATTACK IN A STRAIGHT LINE.
YOU'RE SIMPLY ASKING TO BE COUN-TERED.
BUT...... WHAT SHOULD I DO?

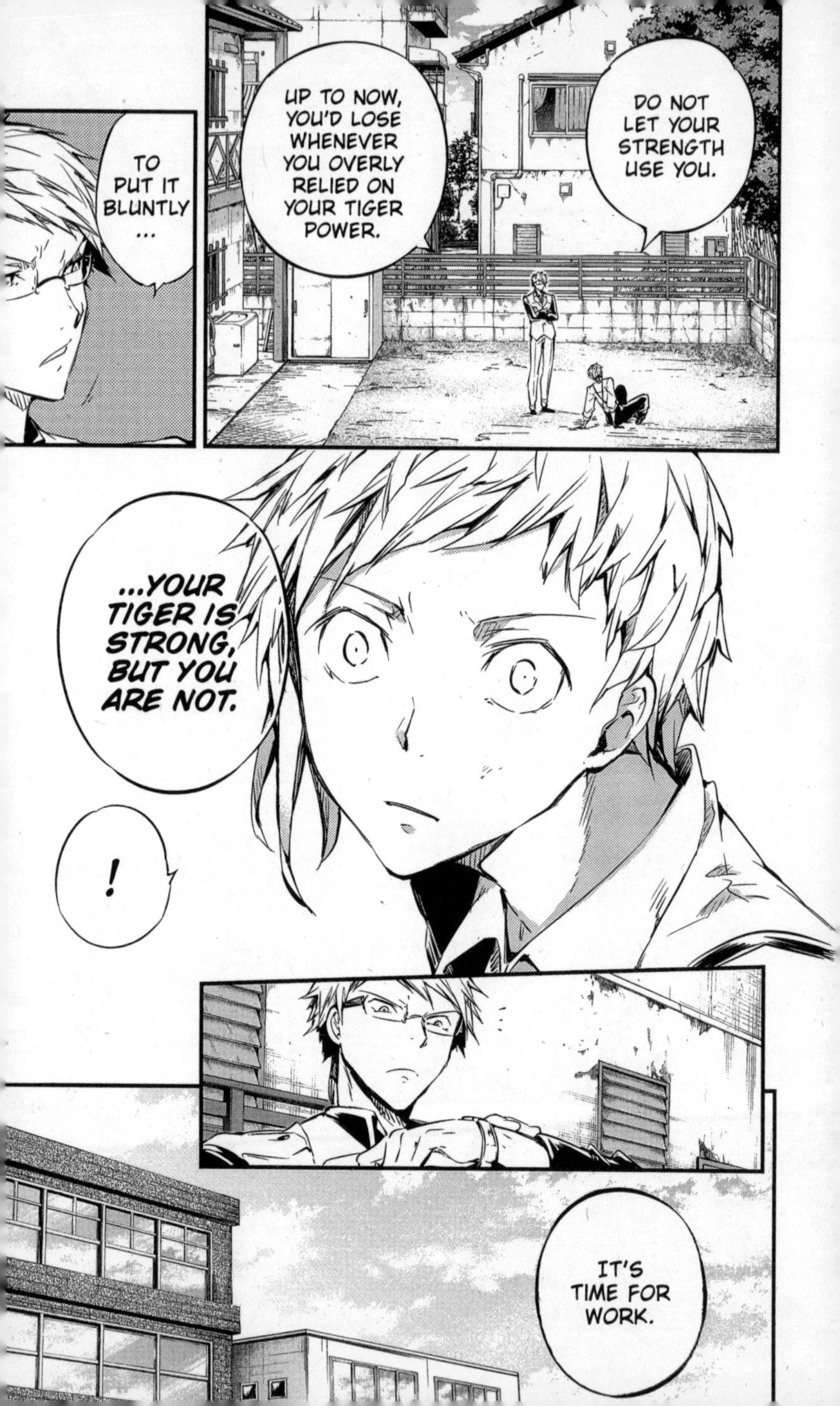
DO NOT LET YOUR STRENGTH USE YOU.
UP TO NOW, YOU'D LOSE WHENEVER YOU OVERLY RELIED ON YOUR TIGER POWER.
TO PUT IT BLUNTLY ...
...YOUR TIGER IS STRONG, BUT YOU ARE NOT.
!
IT'S TIME FOR WORK.

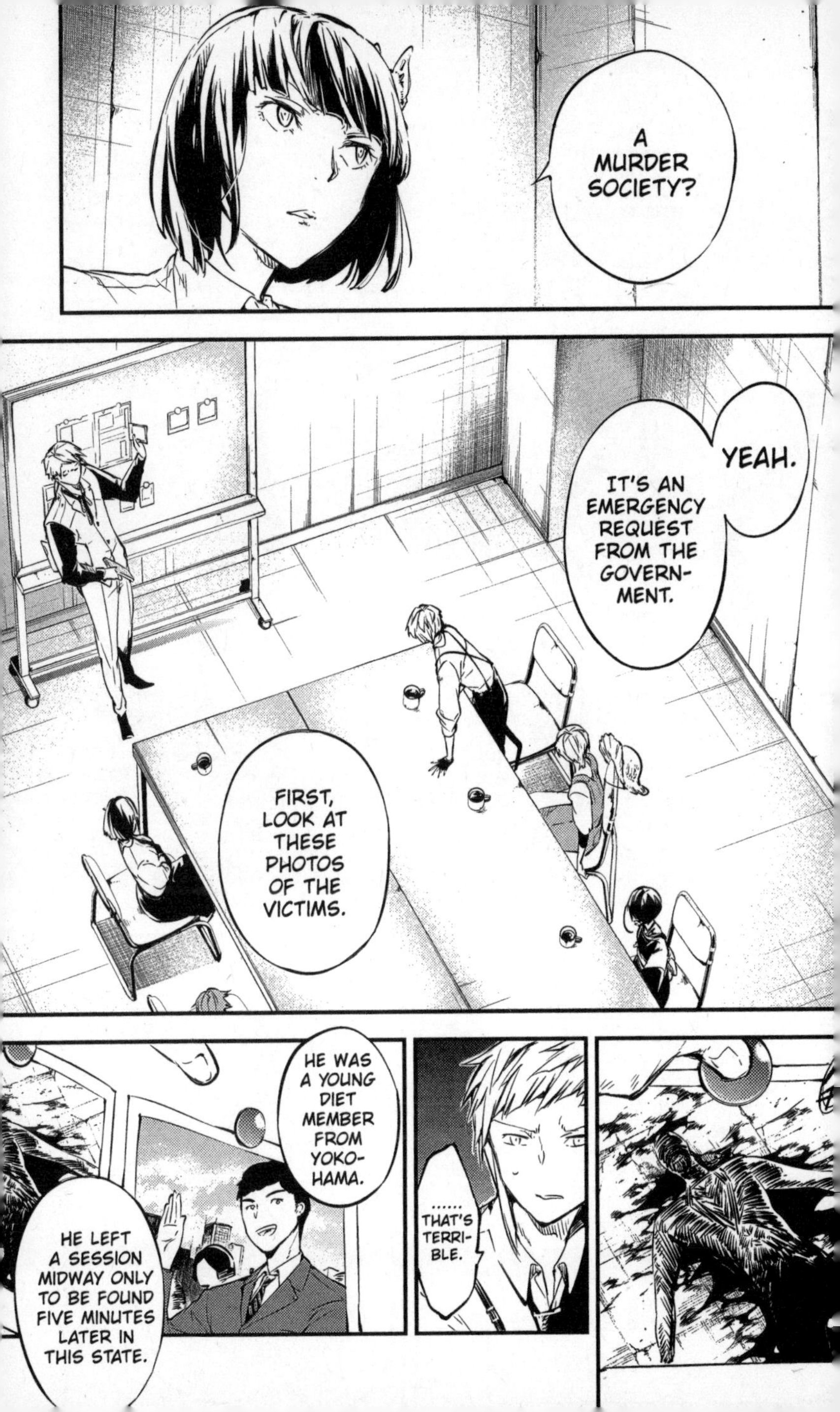
A MURDER SOCIETY?
YEAH.
IT'S AN EMERGENCY REQUEST FROM THE GOVERN-MENT.
FIRST, LOOK AT THESE PHOTOS OF THE VICTIMS.
...... THAT'S TERRI-BLE.
HE WAS A YOUNG DIET MEMBER FROM YOKO-HAMA.
HE LEFT A SESSION MIDWAY ONLY TO BE FOUND FIVE MINUTES LATER IN THIS STATE.

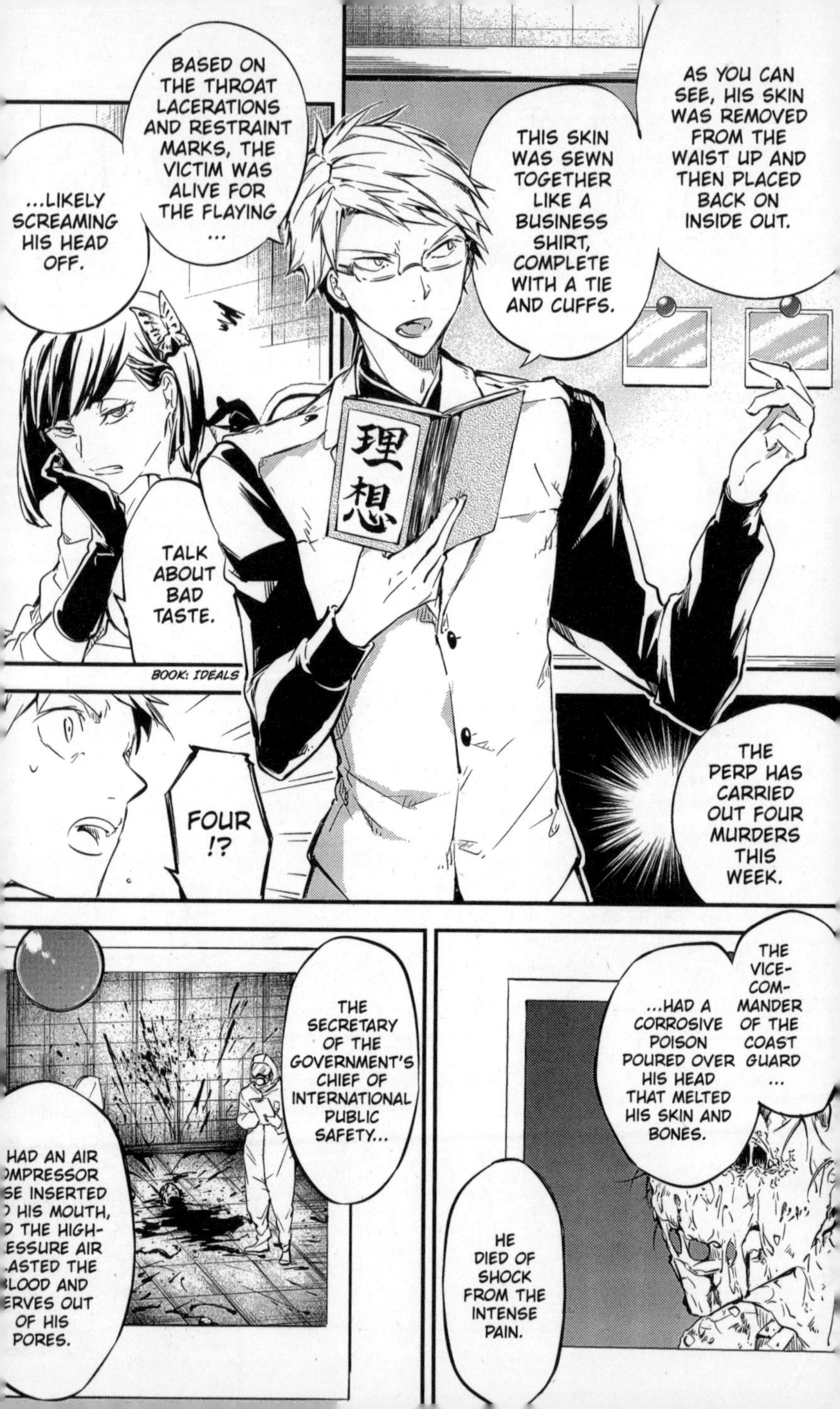
AS YOU CAN SEE, HIS SKIN WAS REMOVED FROM THE WAIST UP AND THEN PLACED BACK ON INSIDE OUT.
THIS SKIN WAS SEWN TOGETHER LIKE A BUSINESS SHIRT, COMPLETE WITH A TIE AND CUFFS.
BASED ON THE THROAT LACERATIONS AND RESTRAINT MARKS, THE VICTIM WAS ALIVE FOR THE FLAYING...
...LIKELY SCREAMING HIS HEAD OFF.
理想
TALK ABOUT BAD TASTE.
BOOK: IDEALS
THE PERP HAS CARRIED OUT FOUR MURDERS THIS WEEK.
FOUR!?
THE VICE-COMMANDER OF THE COAST GUARD...
...HAD A CORROSIVE POISON POURED OVER HIS HEAD THAT MELTED HIS SKIN AND BONES.
HE DIED OF SHOCK FROM THE INTENSE PAIN.
THE SECRETARY OF THE GOVERNMENT'S CHIEF OF INTERNATIONAL PUBLIC SAFETY...
HAD AN AIR OMPRESSOR SE INSERTED D HIS MOUTH, D THE HIGH-ESSURE AIR LASTED THE LOOD AND ERVES OUT OF HIS PORES.

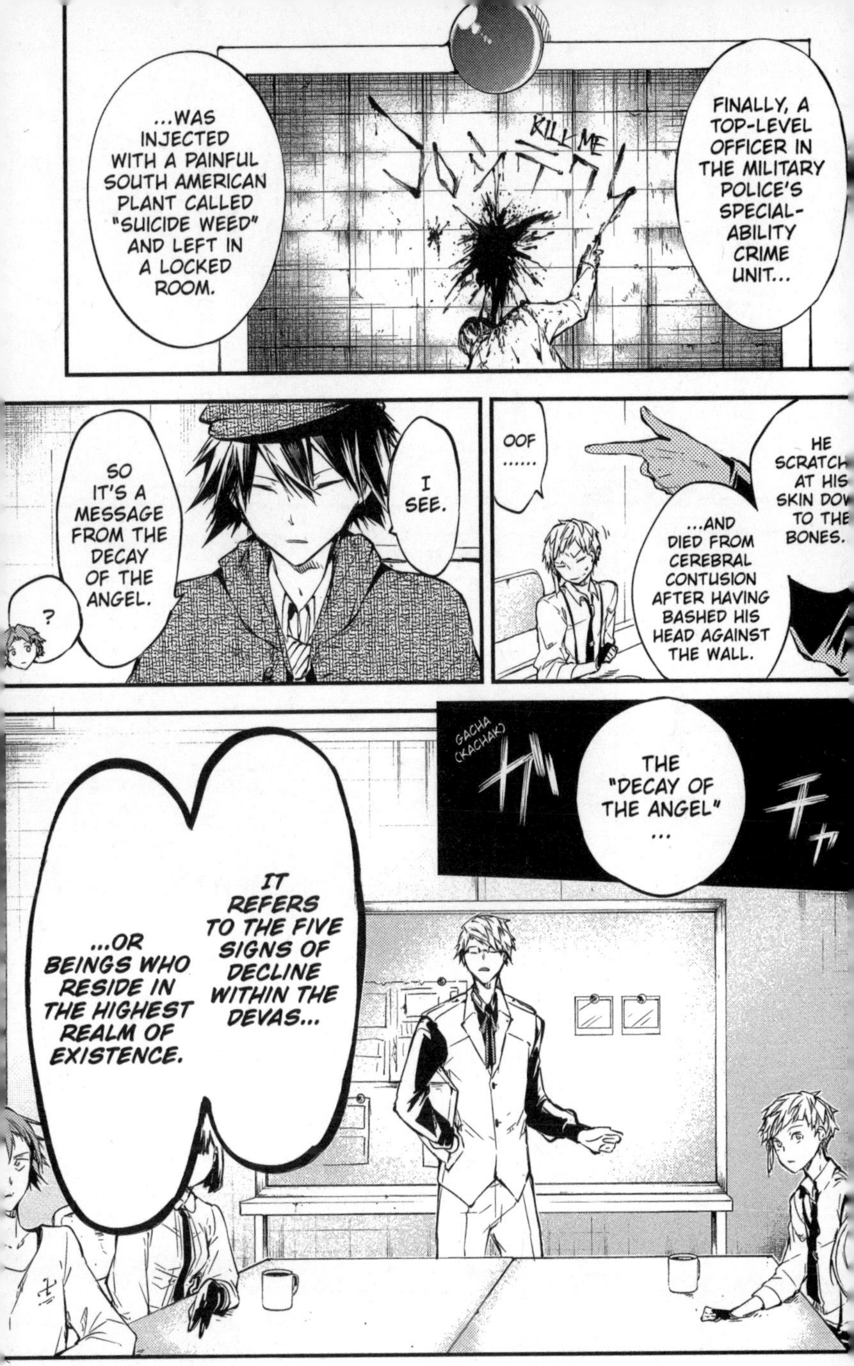

FINALLY, A TOP-LEVEL OFFICER IN THE MILITARY POLICE'S SPECIAL-ABILITY CRIME UNIT...
KILL ME
...WAS INJECTED WITH A PAINFUL SOUTH AMERICAN PLANT CALLED "SUICIDE WEED" AND LEFT IN A LOCKED ROOM.
HE SCRATCH AT HIS SKIN DOW TO THE BONES.
...AND DIED FROM CEREBRAL CONTUSION AFTER HAVING BASHED HIS HEAD AGAINST THE WALL.
OOF ......
I SEE.
SO IT'S A MESSAGE FROM THE DECAY OF THE ANGEL.
?
GACHA (KACHAK)
THE "DECAY OF THE ANGEL" ...
IT REFERS TO THE FIVE SIGNS OF DECLINE WITHIN THE DEVAS...
...OR BEINGS WHO RESIDE IN THE HIGHEST REALM OF EXISTENCE.

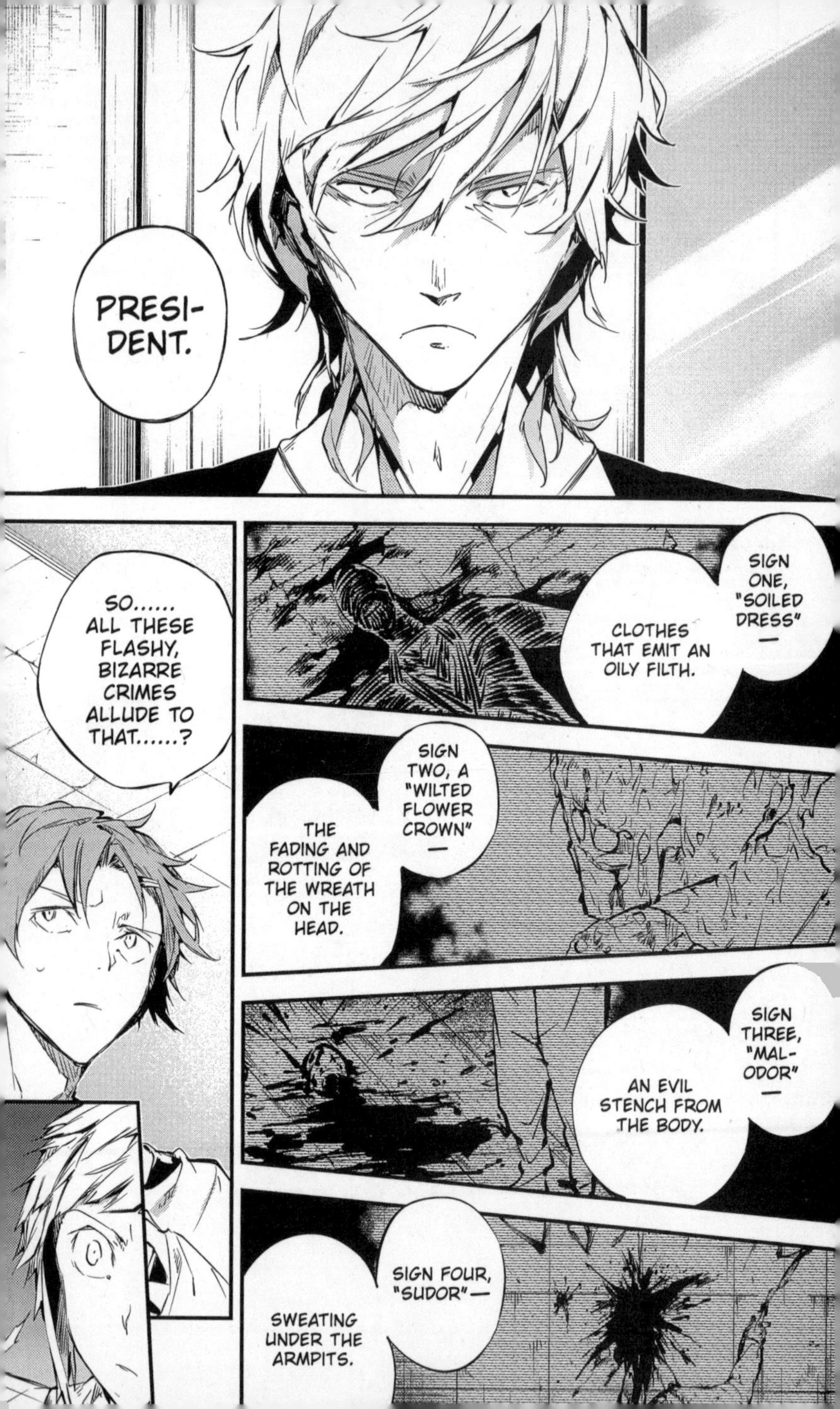

PRESIDENT.
SIGN ONE, "SOILED DRESS" —
CLOTHES THAT EMIT AN OILY FILTH.
SIGN TWO, A "WILTED FLOWER CROWN" —
THE FADING AND ROTTING OF THE WREATH ON THE HEAD.
SIGN THREE, "MALODOR" —
AN EVIL STENCH FROM THE BODY.
SIGN FOUR, "SUDOR"—
SWEATING UNDER THE ARMPITS.
SO...... ALL THESE FLASHY, BIZARRE CRIMES ALLUDE TO THAT......?

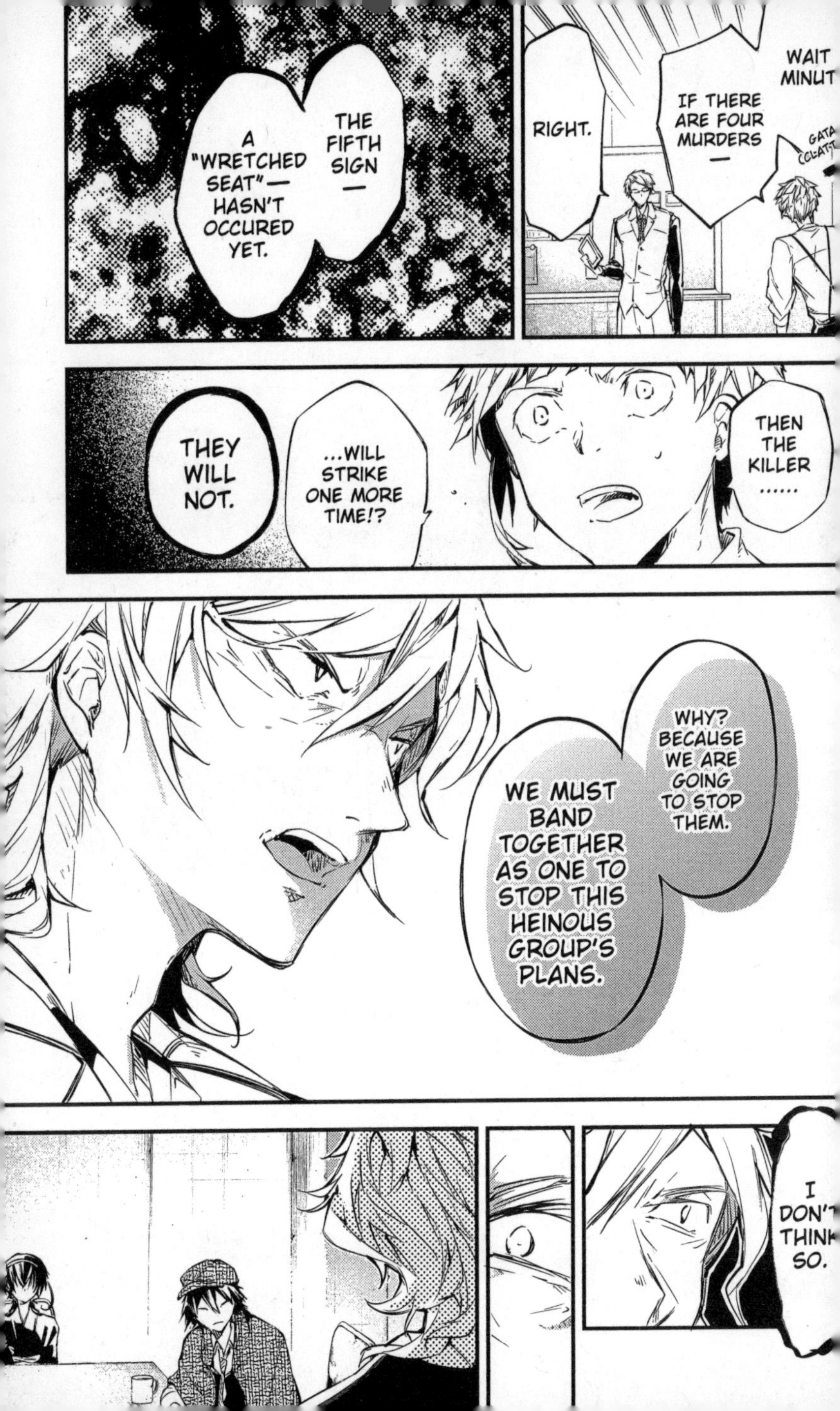
WAIT MINUT
GATA CLATT
IF THERE ARE FOUR MURDERS —
RIGHT.
THE FIFTH SIGN —
A "WRETCHED SEAT"— HASN'T OCCURED YET.
THEN THE KILLER ......
...WILL STRIKE ONE MORE TIME!?
THEY WILL NOT.
WHY? BECAUSE WE ARE GOING TO STOP THEM.
WE MUST BAND TOGETHER AS ONE TO STOP THIS HEINOUS GROUP'S PLANS.
I DON'T THINK SO.

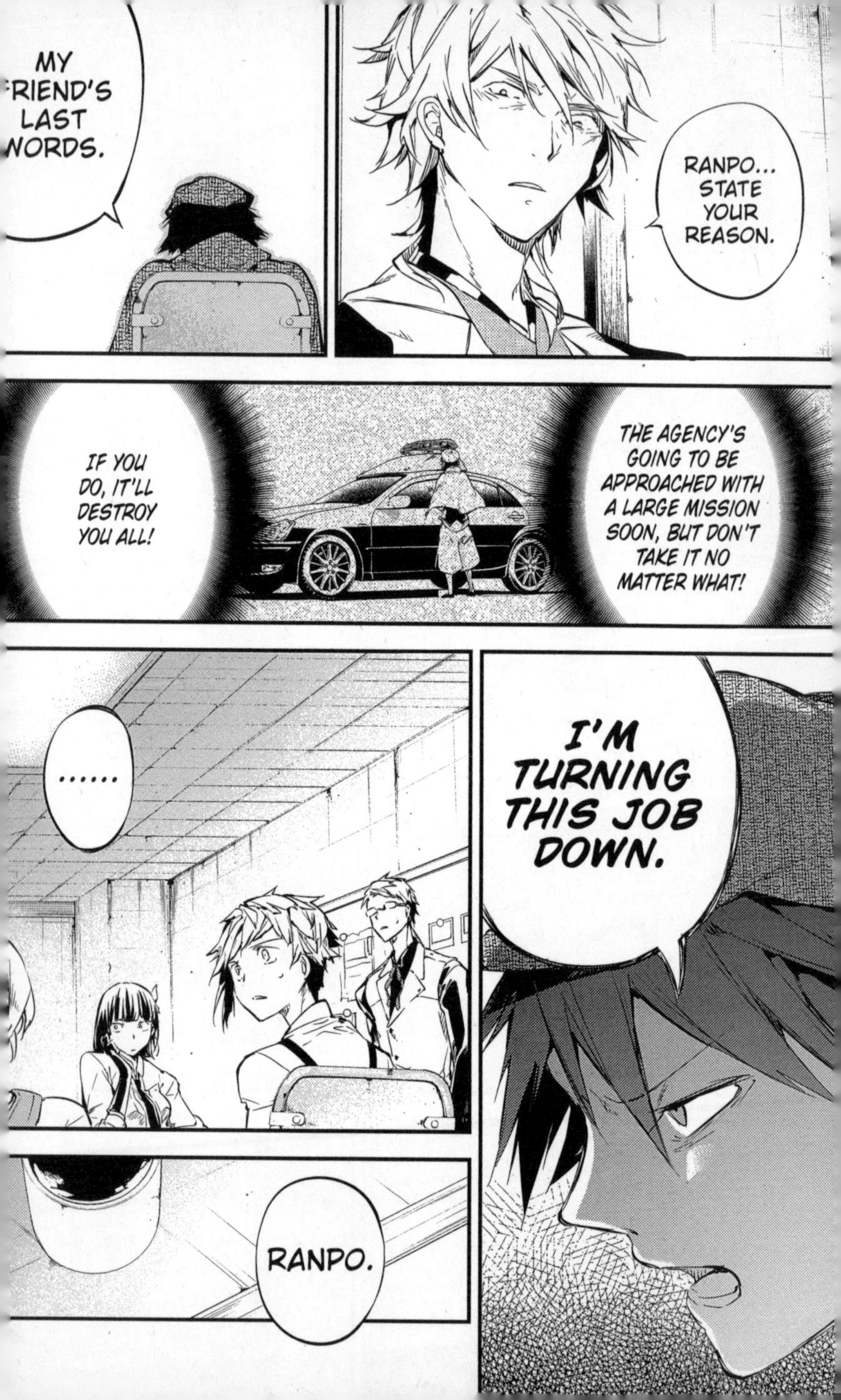
RANPO... STATE YOUR REASON.
MY FRIEND'S LAST WORDS.
THE AGENCY'S GOING TO BE APPROACHED WITH A LARGE MISSION SOON, BUT DON'T TAKE IT NO MATTER WHAT!
IF YOU DO, IT'LL DESTROY YOU ALL!
I'M TURNING THIS JOB DOWN.
......
RANPO.

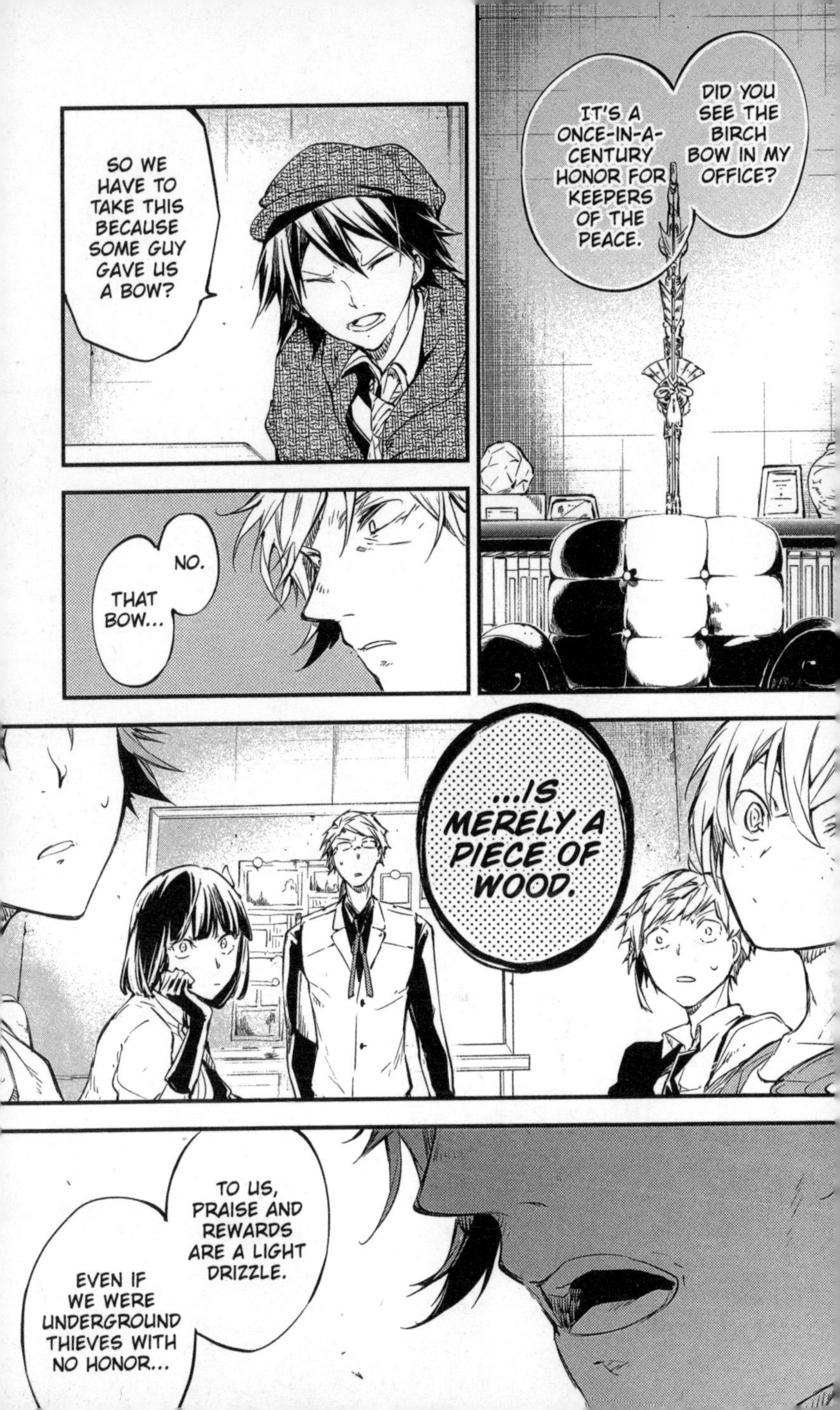
DID YOU SEE THE BIRCH BOW IN MY OFFICE?
IT'S A ONCE-IN-A-CENTURY HONOR FOR KEEPERS OF THE PEACE.
SO WE HAVE TO TAKE THIS BECAUSE SOME GUY GAVE US A BOW?
NO.
THAT BOW...
...IS MERELY A PIECE OF WOOD.
TO US, PRAISE AND REWARDS ARE A LIGHT DRIZZLE.
EVEN IF WE WERE UNDERGROUND THIEVES WITH NO HONOR...

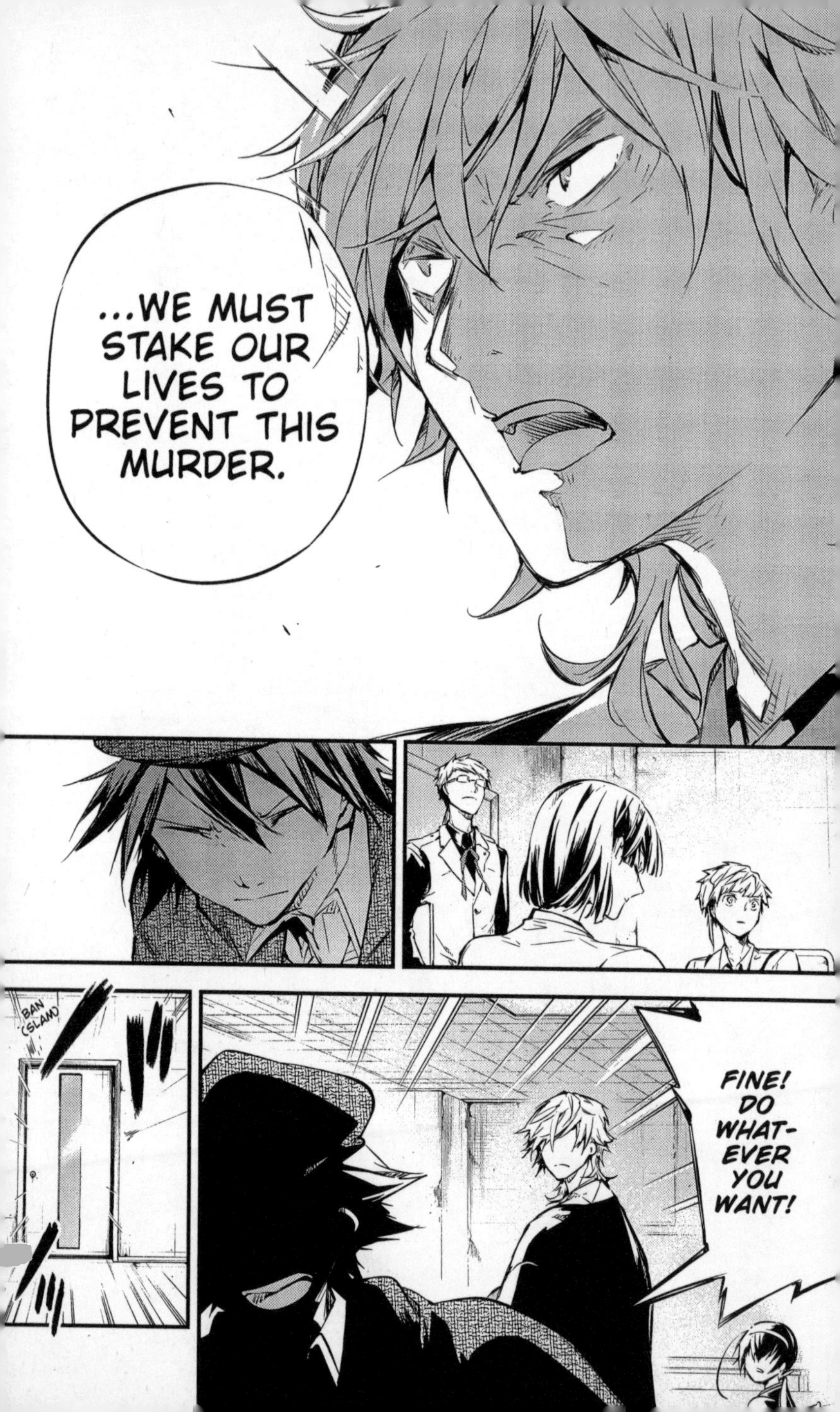
...WE MUST STAKE OUR LIVES TO PREVENT THIS MURDER.
BAN (SLAM)
FINE! DO WHATEVER YOU WANT!

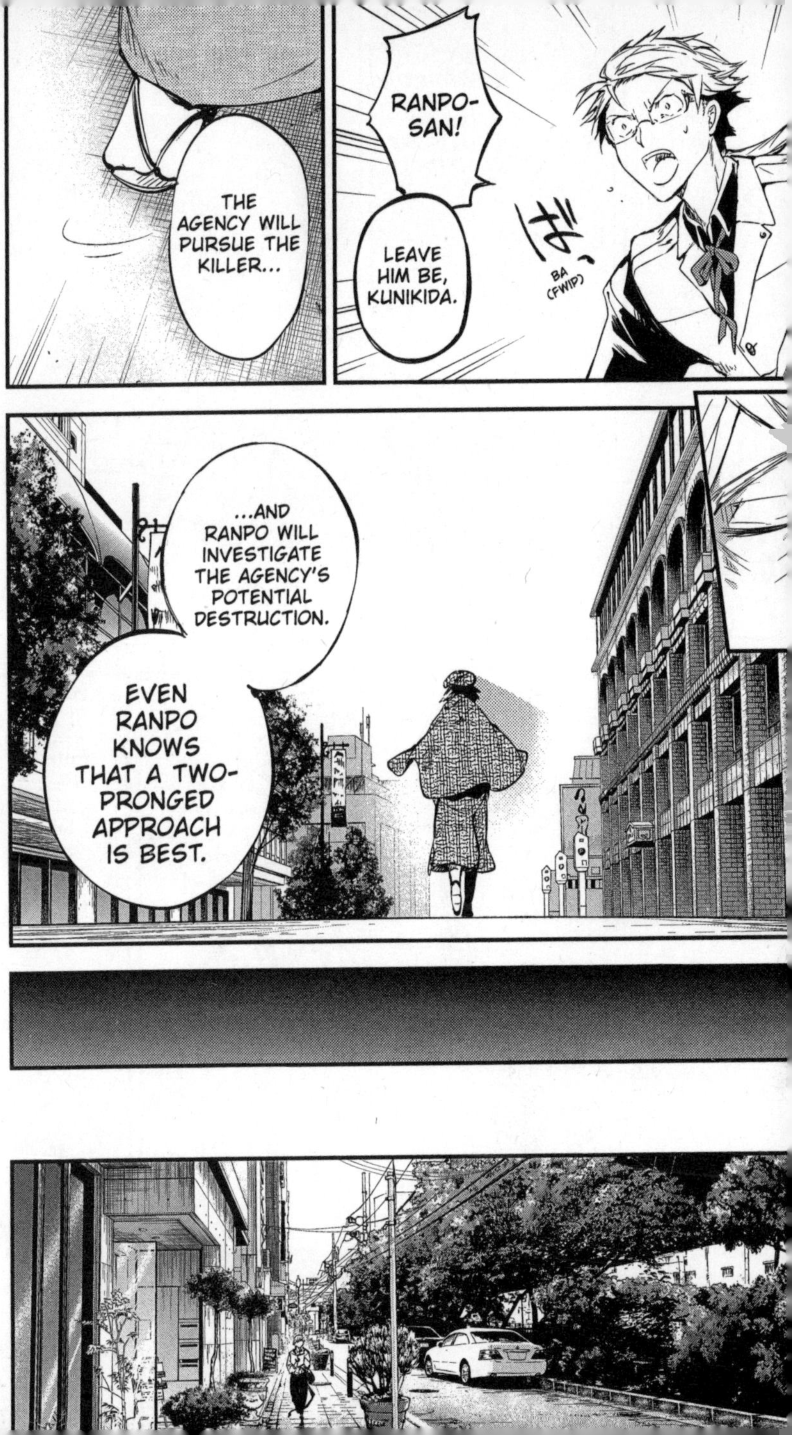
RANPO-SAN!
LEAVE HIM BE, KUNIKIDA.
ばっ
BA (FWIP)
THE AGENCY WILL PURSUE THE KILLER...
...AND RANPO WILL INVESTIGATE THE AGENCY'S POTENTIAL DESTRUCTION.
EVEN RANPO KNOWS THAT A TWO-PRONGED APPROACH IS BEST.

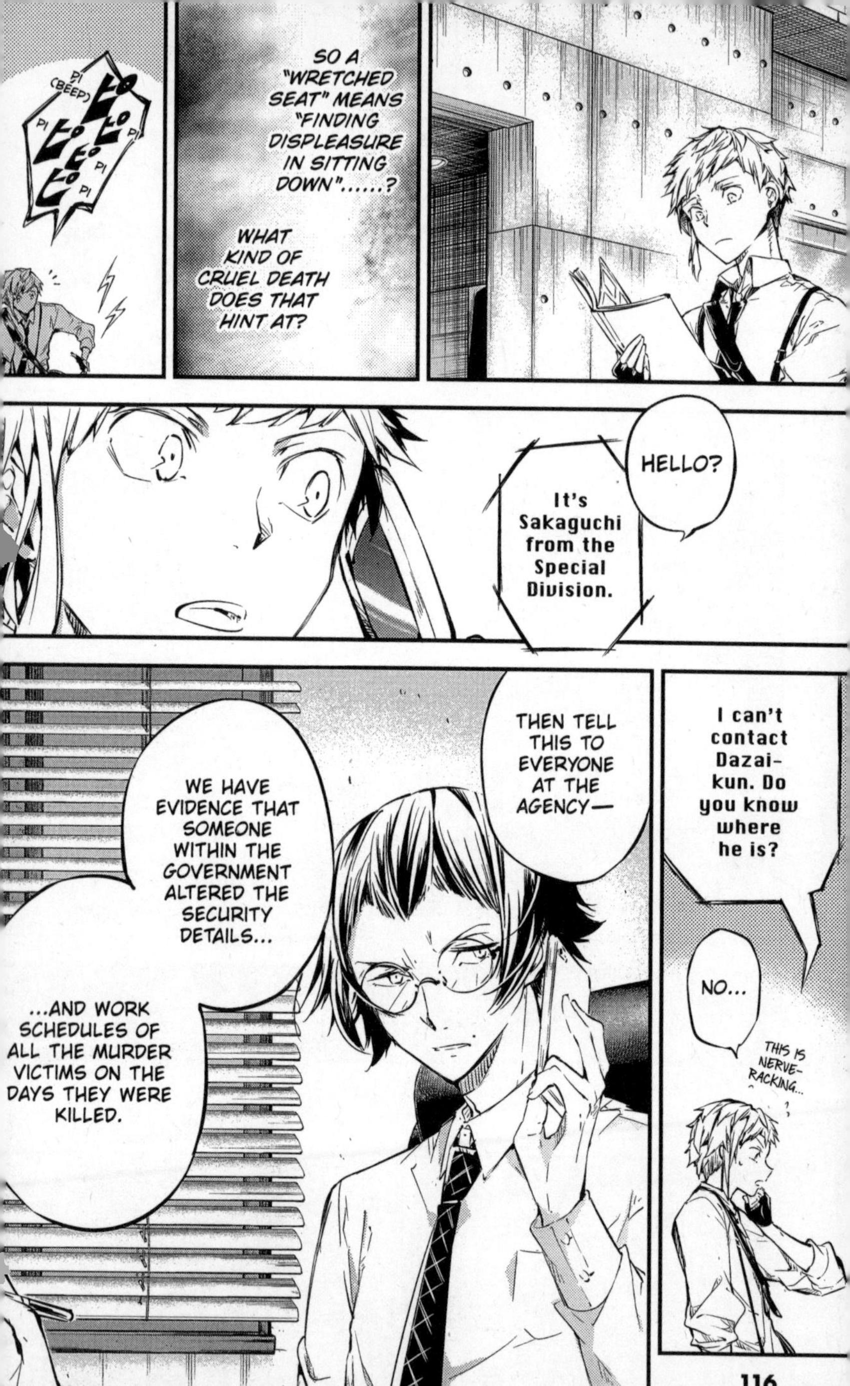
SO A "WRETCHED SEAT" MEANS "FINDING DISPLEASURE IN SITTING DOWN"......?
WHAT KIND OF CRUEL DEATH DOES THAT HINT AT?
PI (BEEP) PI PI PI PI
HELLO?
It's Sakaguchi from the Special Division.
I can't contact Dazai-kun. Do you know where he is?
NO...
THIS IS NERVE-RACKING...
THEN TELL THIS TO EVERYONE AT THE AGENCY—
WE HAVE EVIDENCE THAT SOMEONE WITHIN THE GOVERNMENT ALTERED THE SECURITY DETAILS...
...AND WORK SCHEDULES OF ALL THE MURDER VICTIMS ON THE DAYS THEY WERE KILLED.

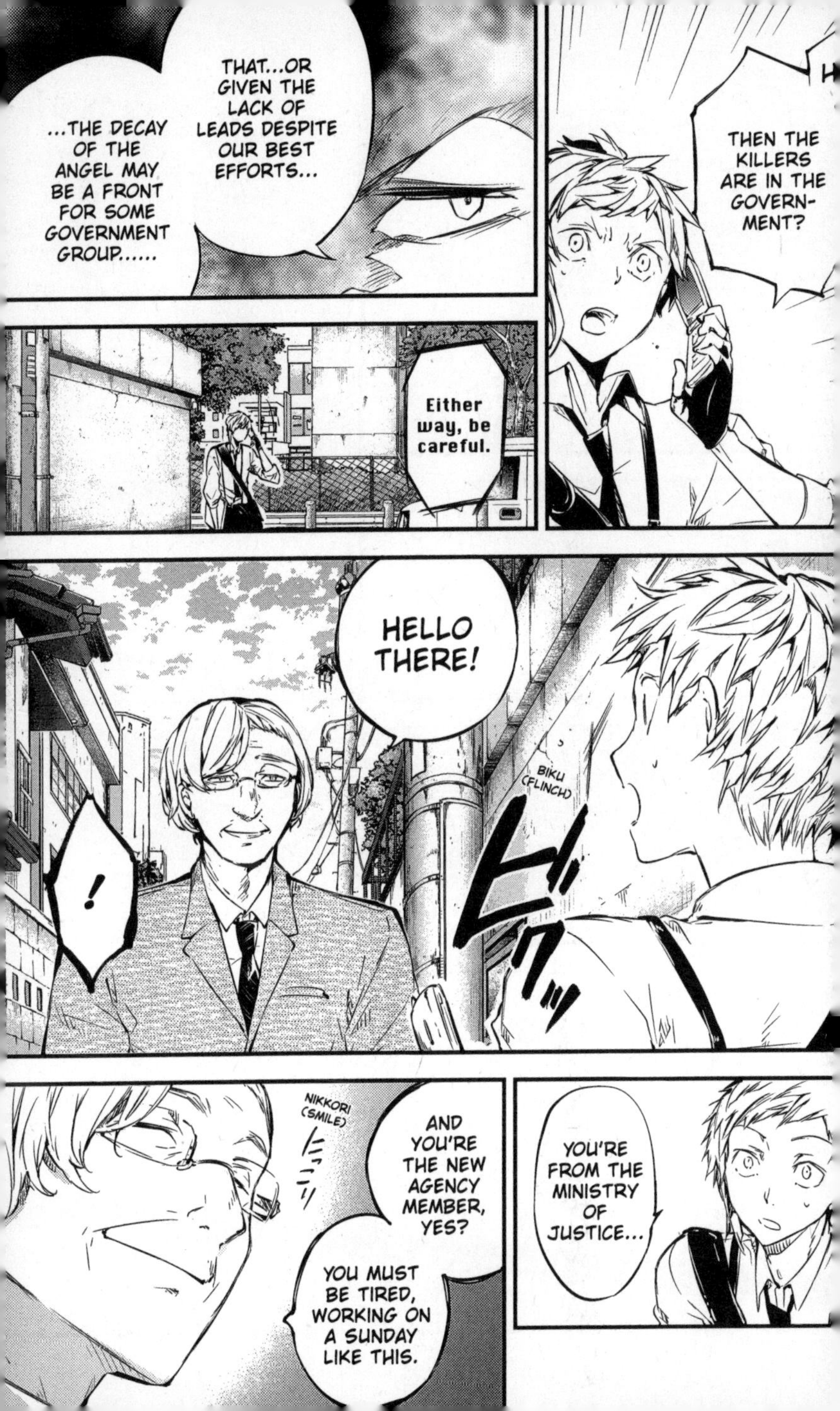
THEN THE KILLERS ARE IN THE GOVERNMENT?
THAT...OR GIVEN THE LACK OF LEADS DESPITE OUR BEST EFFORTS...
...THE DECAY OF THE ANGEL MAY BE A FRONT FOR SOME GOVERNMENT GROUP......
Either way, be careful.
HELLO THERE!
BIKU (FLINCH)
!
YOU'RE FROM THE MINISTRY OF JUSTICE...
NIKKORI (SMILE)
AND YOU'RE THE NEW AGENCY MEMBER, YES?
YOU MUST BE TIRED, WORKING ON A SUNDAY LIKE THIS.

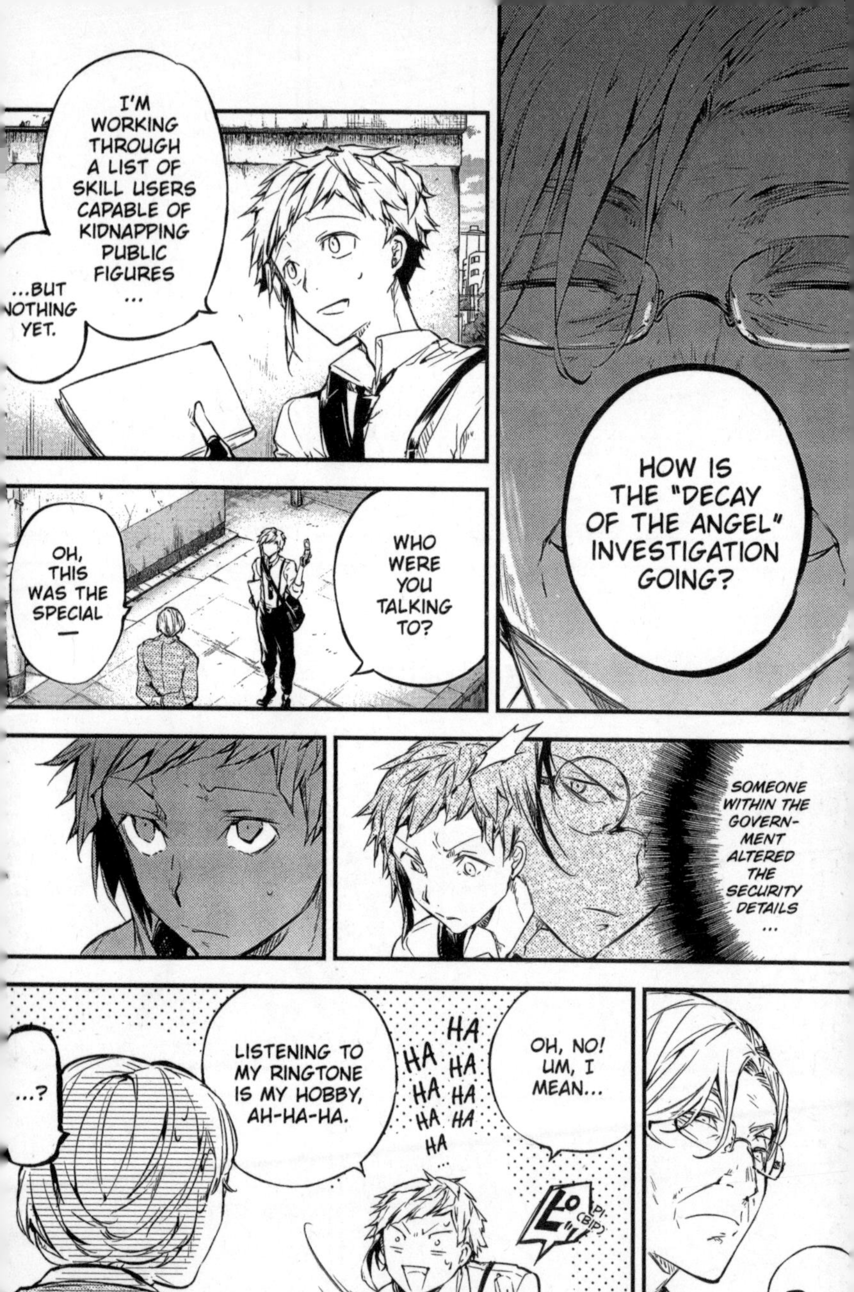
HOW IS THE "DECAY OF THE ANGEL" INVESTIGATION GOING?
I'M WORKING THROUGH A LIST OF SKILL USERS CAPABLE OF KIDNAPPING PUBLIC FIGURES...
...BUT NOTHING YET.
WHO WERE YOU TALKING TO?
OH, THIS WAS THE SPECIAL—
SOMEONE WITHIN THE GOVERNMENT ALTERED THE SECURITY DETAILS...
?
OH, NO! UM, I MEAN...
HA HA HA HA HA HA HA HA HA...
PI (BIP)
LISTENING TO MY RINGTONE IS MY HOBBY, AH-HA-HA.
...?

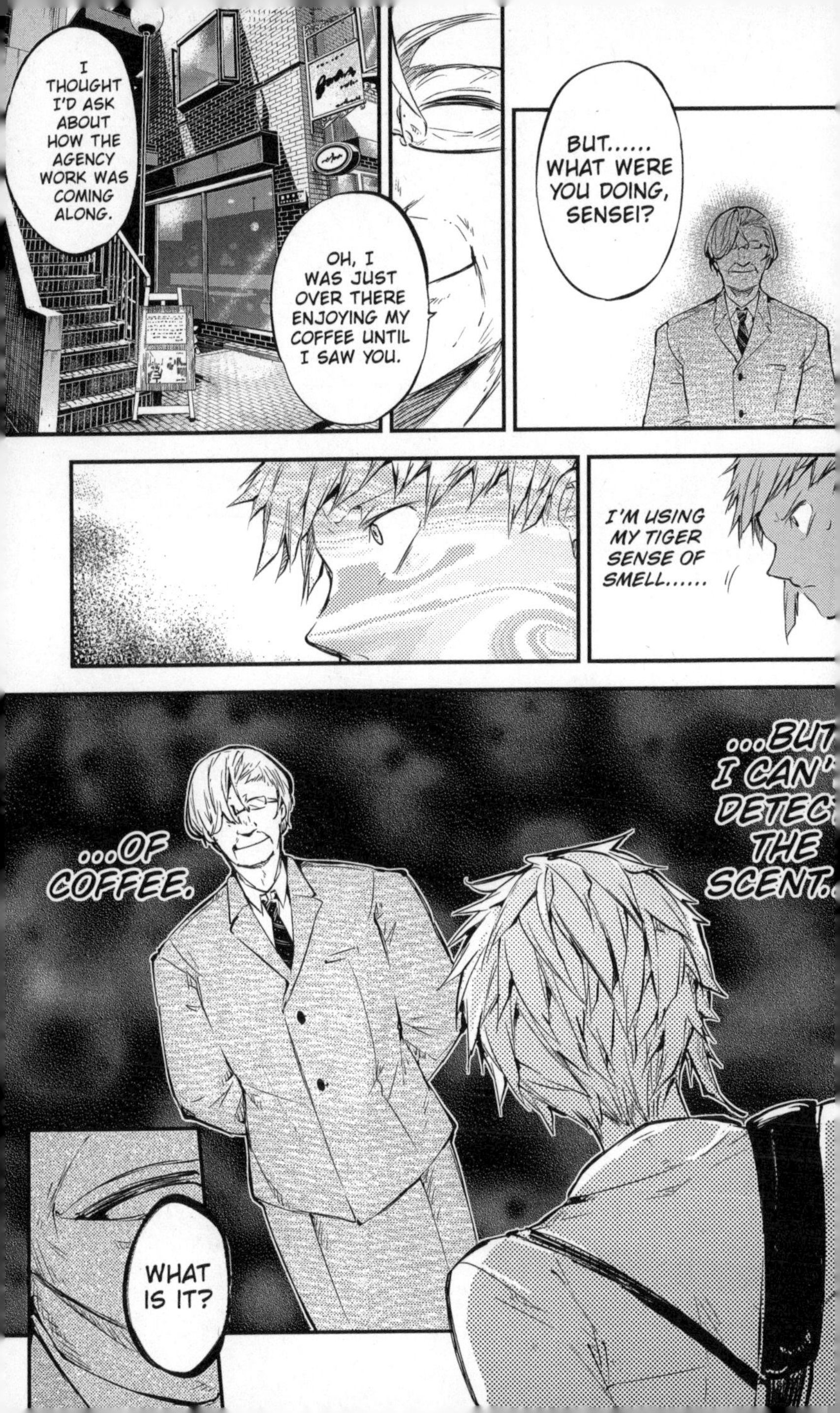
BUT...... WHAT WERE YOU DOING, SENSEI?
OH, I WAS JUST OVER THERE ENJOYING MY COFFEE UNTIL I SAW YOU.
I THOUGHT I'D ASK ABOUT HOW THE AGENCY WORK WAS COMING ALONG.
I'M USING MY TIGER SENSE OF SMELL......
...BUT I CAN' DETEC THE SCENT..
...OF COFFEE.
WHAT IS IT?

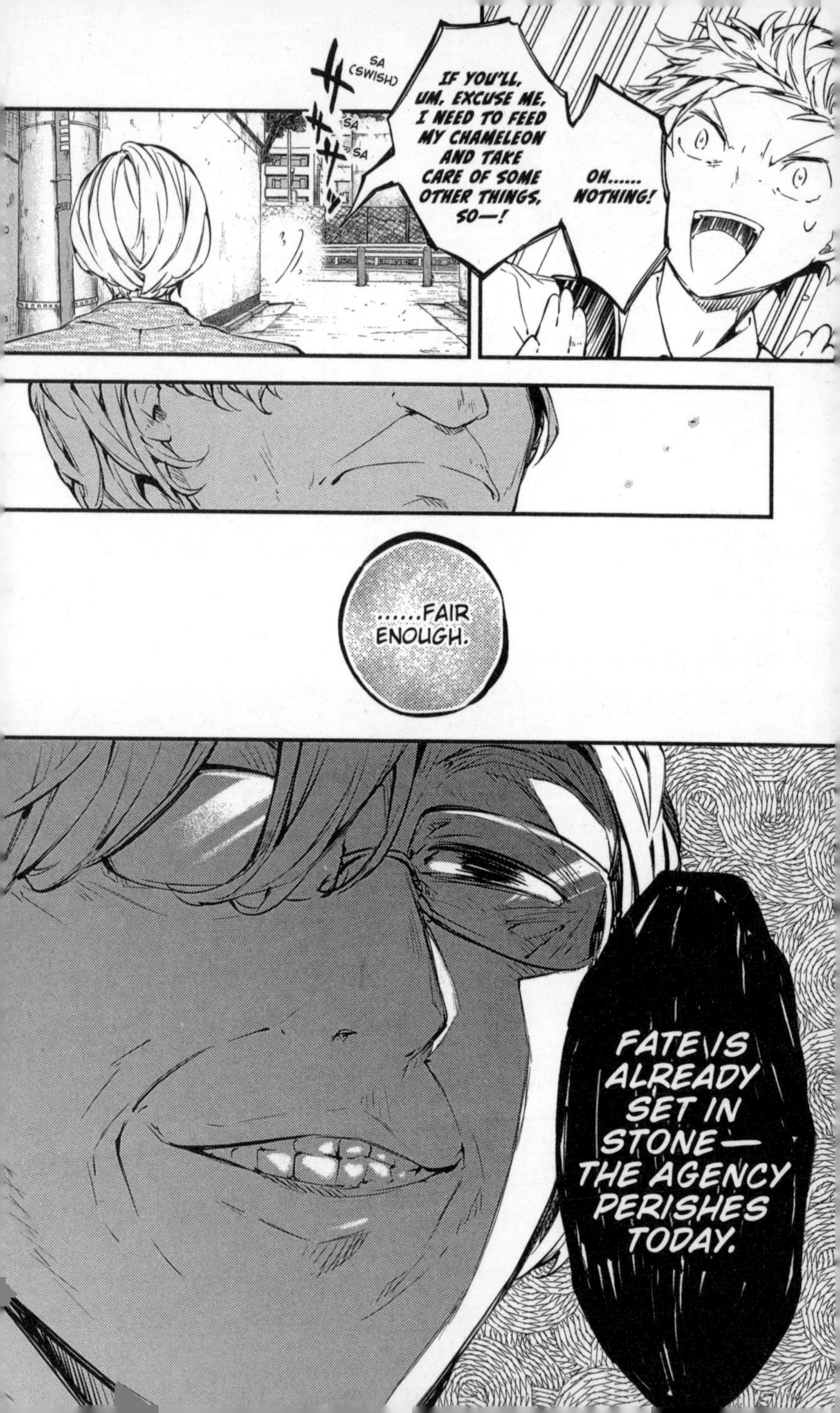
OH...... NOTHING!
IF YOU'LL, UM, EXCUSE ME, I NEED TO FEED MY CHAMELEON AND TAKE CARE OF SOME OTHER THINGS, SO—!
SA (SWISH)
SA
SA
......FAIR ENOUGH.
FATE IS ALREADY SET IN STONE— THE AGENCY PERISHES TODAY.

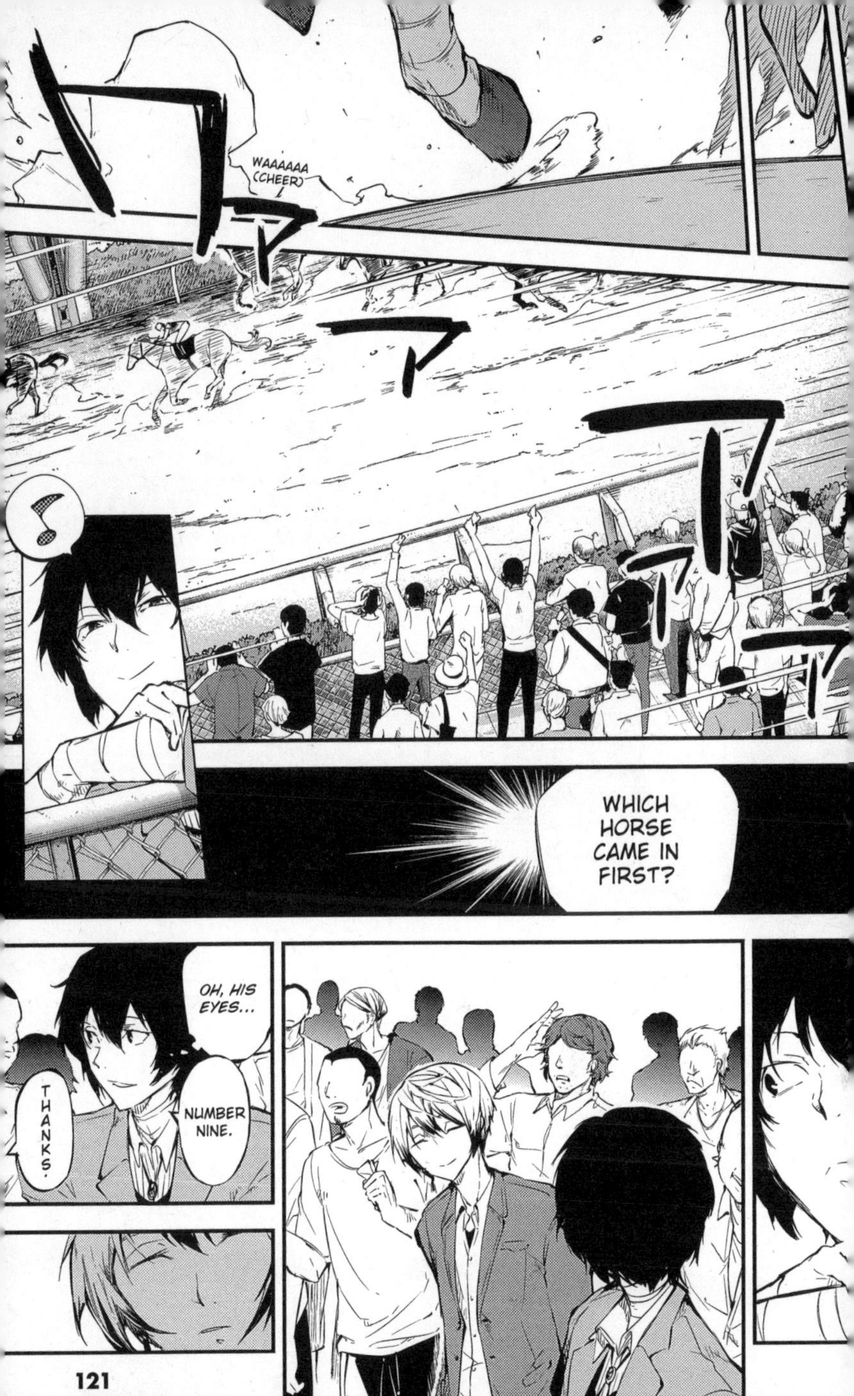

WAAAAAA (CHEER)
ワァァァァ
WHICH HORSE CAME IN FIRST?
OH, HIS EYES...
NUMBER NINE.
THANKS.

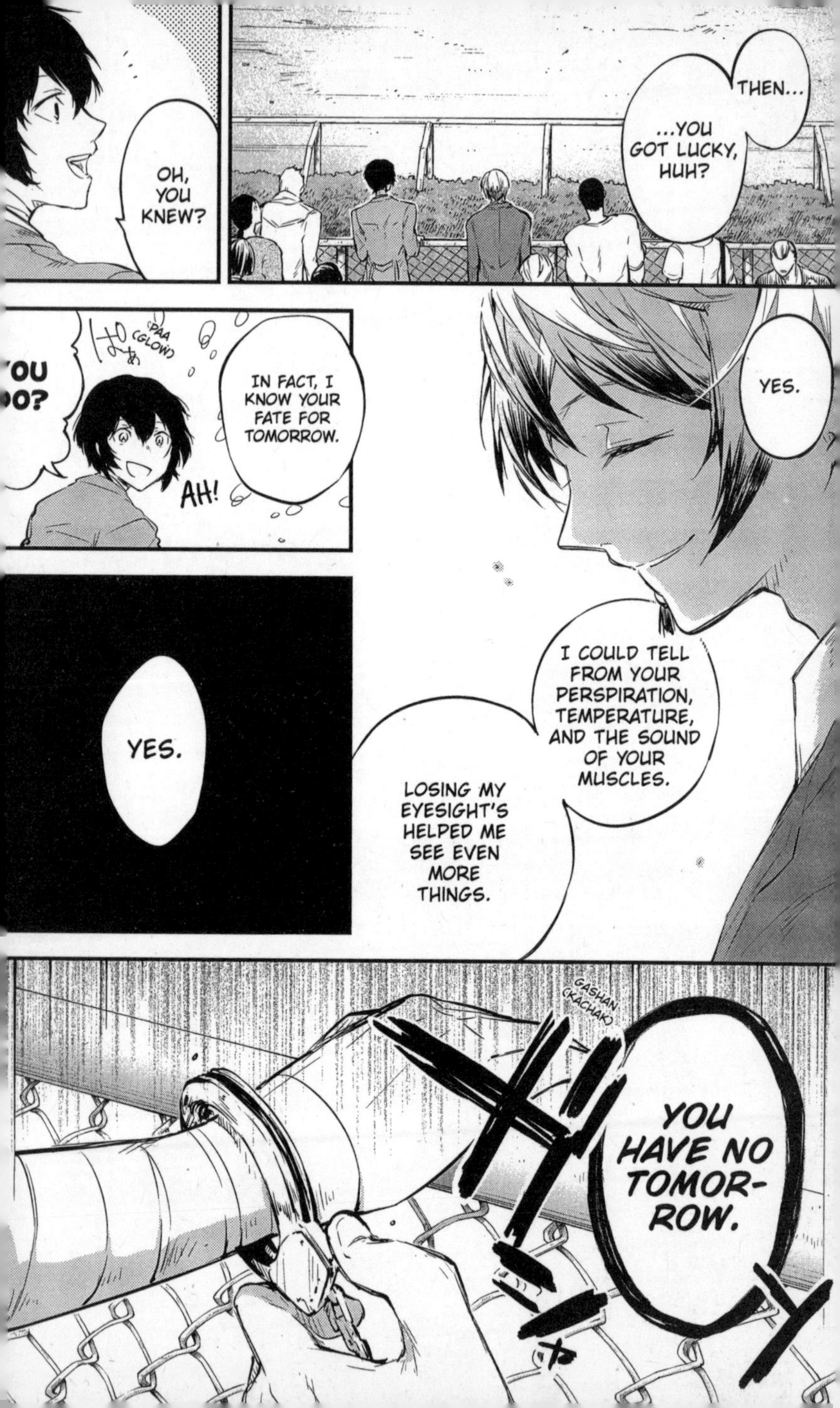
THEN...
...YOU GOT LUCKY, HUH?
OH, YOU KNEW?
YES.
I COULD TELL FROM YOUR PERSPIRATION, TEMPERATURE, AND THE SOUND OF YOUR MUSCLES.
LOSING MY EYESIGHT'S HELPED ME SEE EVEN MORE THINGS.
IN FACT, I KNOW YOUR FATE FOR TOMORROW.
PAA (GLOW)
AH!
YES.
GASHAN (KACHAK)
YOU HAVE NO TOMOR-ROW.

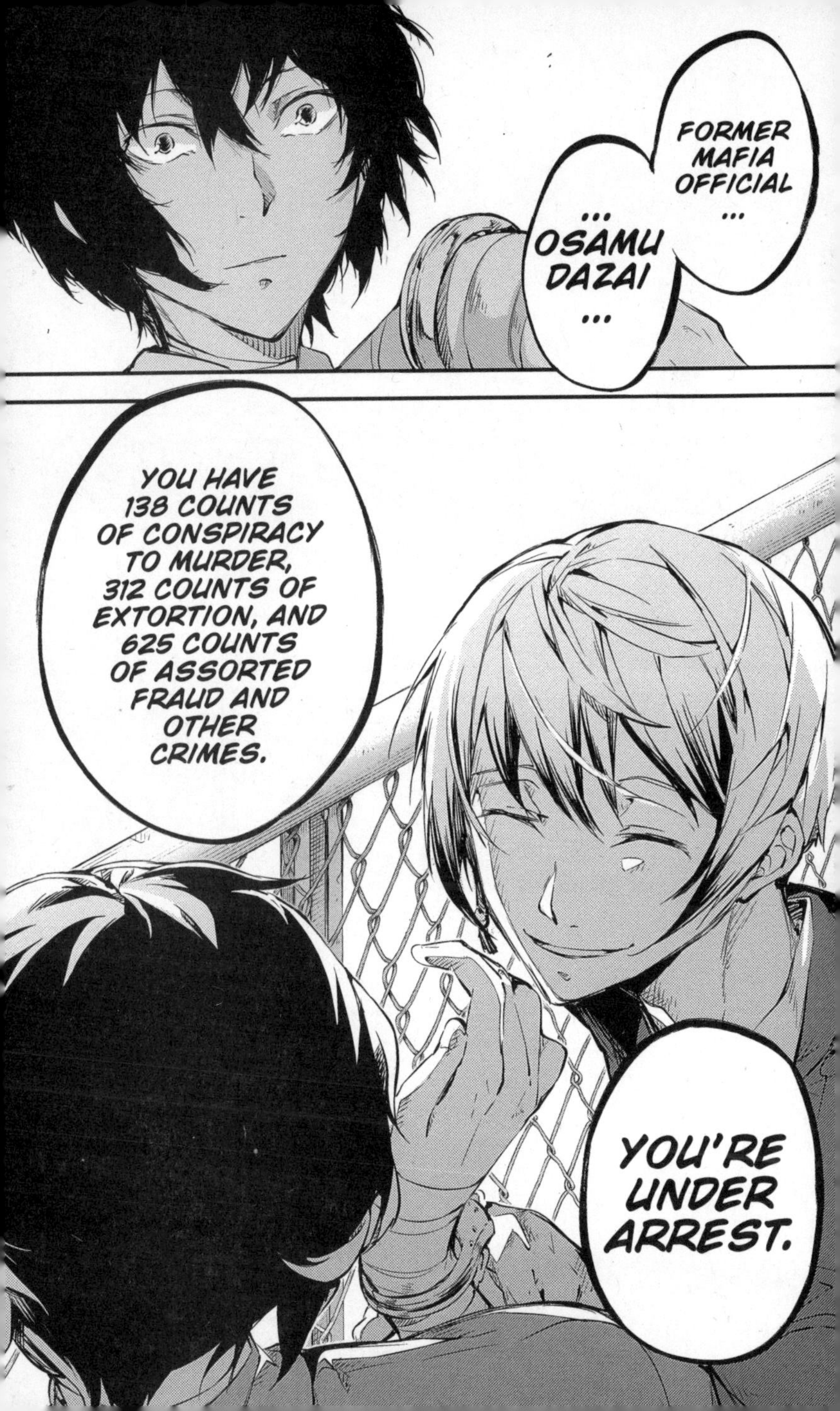
FORMER MAFIA OFFICIAL ...
... OSAMU DAZAI ...
YOU HAVE 138 COUNTS OF CONSPIRACY TO MURDER, 312 COUNTS OF EXTORTION, AND 625 COUNTS OF ASSORTED FRAUD AND OTHER CRIMES.
YOU'RE UNDER ARREST.

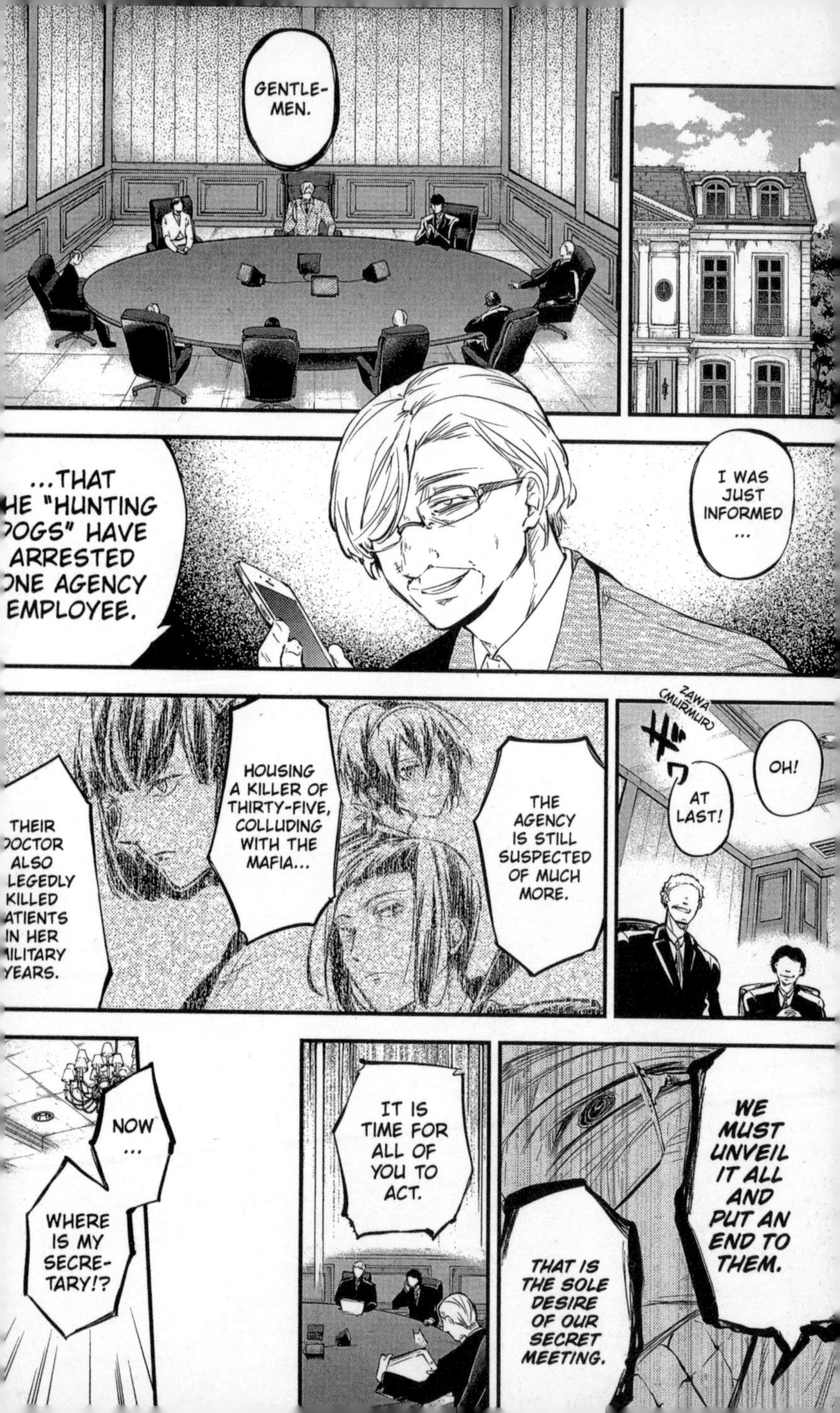
GENTLE-MEN.
I WAS JUST INFORMED...
...THAT HE "HUNTING OGS" HAVE ARRESTED NE AGENCY EMPLOYEE.
ZAWA (MURMUR)
OH!
AT LAST!
THE AGENCY IS STILL SUSPECTED OF MUCH MORE.
HOUSING A KILLER OF THIRTY-FIVE, COLLUDING WITH THE MAFIA...
THEIR OCTOR ALSO LEGEDLY KILLED ATIENTS IN HER ILITARY YEARS.
WE MUST UNVEIL IT ALL AND PUT AN END TO THEM.
THAT IS THE SOLE DESIRE OF OUR SECRET MEETING.
IT IS TIME FOR ALL OF YOU TO ACT.
NOW...
WHERE IS MY SECRETARY!?

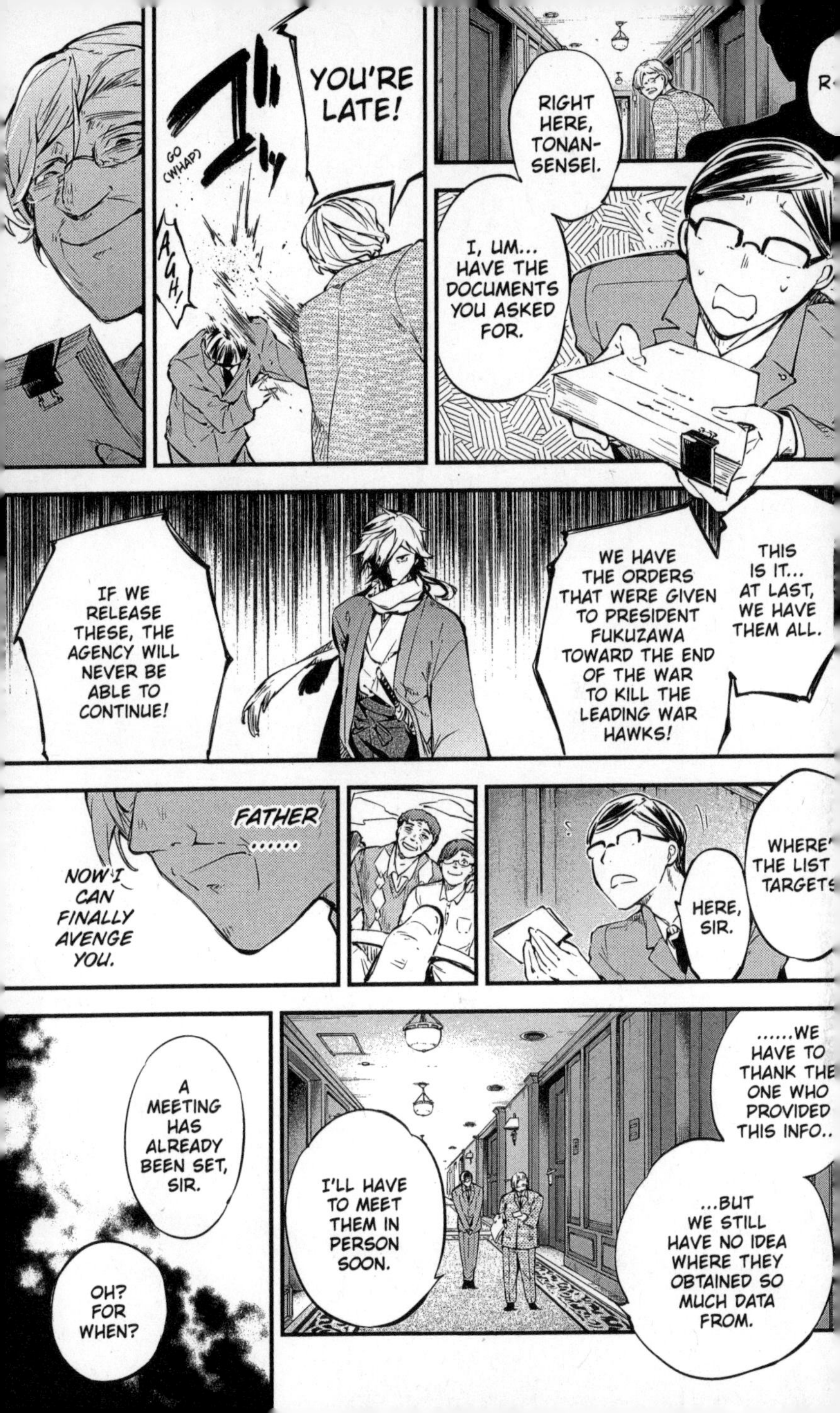
R-
RIGHT HERE, TONAN-SENSEI.
I, UM... HAVE THE DOCUMENTS YOU ASKED FOR.
YOU'RE LATE!
GO (WHAP)
AGH!
THIS IS IT... AT LAST, WE HAVE THEM ALL.
WE HAVE THE ORDERS THAT WERE GIVEN TO PRESIDENT FUKUZAWA TOWARD THE END OF THE WAR TO KILL THE LEADING WAR HAWKS!
IF WE RELEASE THESE, THE AGENCY WILL NEVER BE ABLE TO CONTINUE!
WHERE' THE LIST TARGETS
HERE, SIR.
FATHER ......
NOW I CAN FINALLY AVENGE YOU.
......WE HAVE TO THANK THE ONE WHO PROVIDED THIS INFO..
...BUT WE STILL HAVE NO IDEA WHERE THEY OBTAINED SO MUCH DATA FROM.
I'LL HAVE TO MEET THEM IN PERSON SOON.
A MEETING HAS ALREADY BEEN SET, SIR.
OH? FOR WHEN?

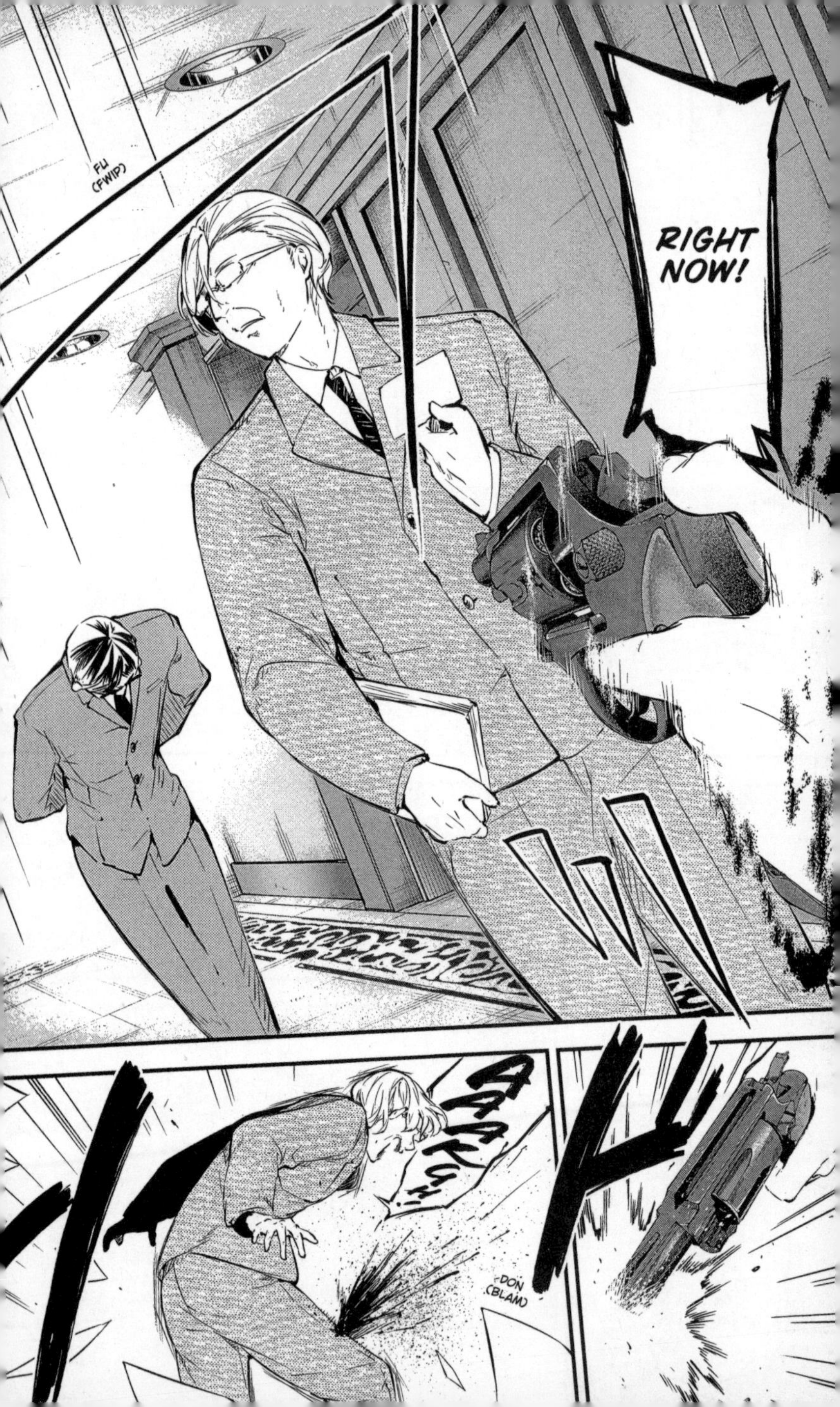

FU (FWIP)
RIGHT NOW!
DON (BLAM)
GAAAKGH!!

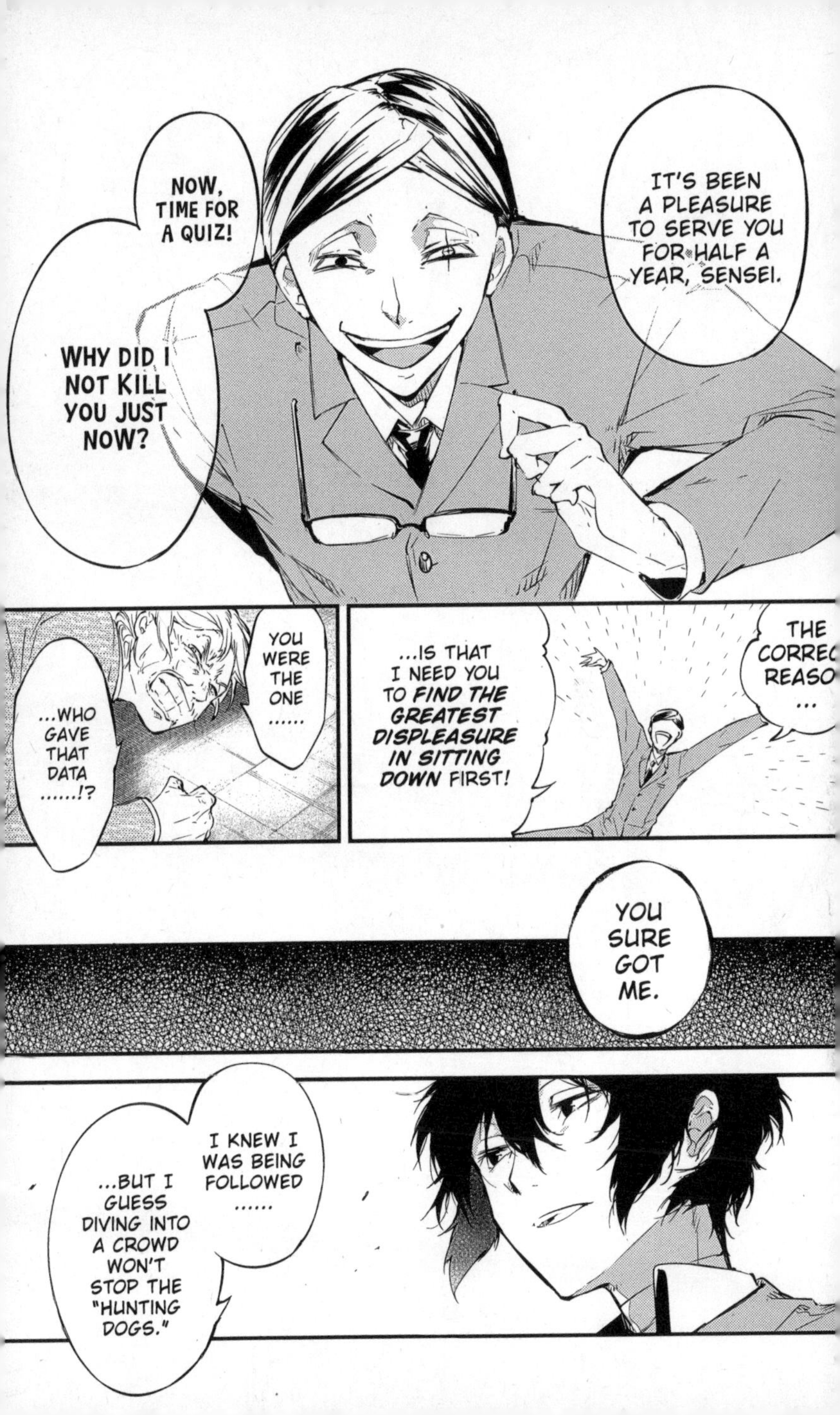

IT'S BEEN A PLEASURE TO SERVE YOU FOR HALF A YEAR, SENSEI.
NOW, TIME FOR A QUIZ!
WHY DID I NOT KILL YOU JUST NOW?
THE CORREC REASO ...
...IS THAT I NEED YOU TO ***FIND THE GREATEST DISPLEASURE IN SITTING DOWN*** FIRST!
YOU WERE THE ONE ......
...WHO GAVE THAT DATA ......!?
YOU SURE GOT ME.
I KNEW I WAS BEING FOLLOWED ......
...BUT I GUESS DIVING INTO A CROWD WON'T STOP THE "HUNTING DOGS."

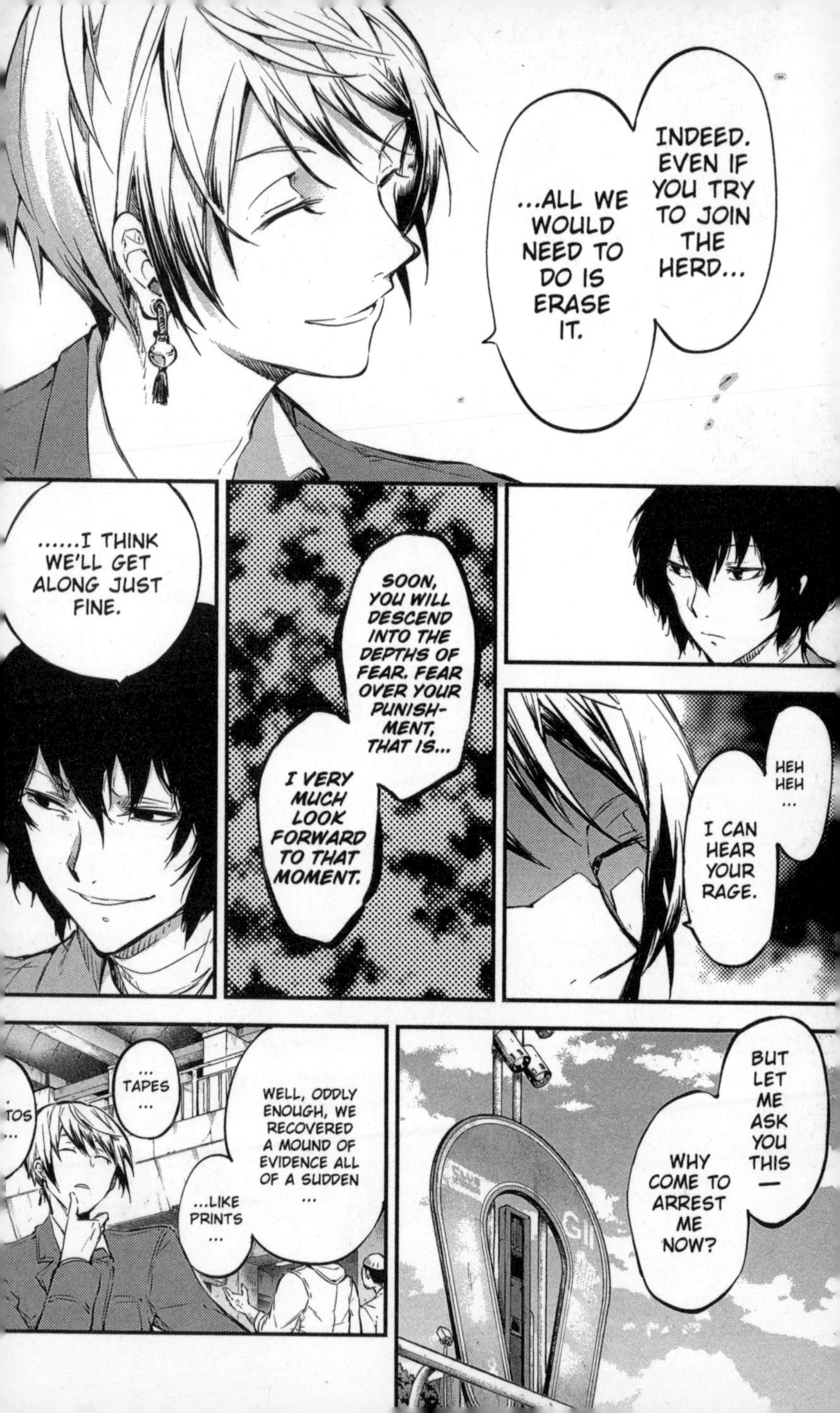
INDEED. EVEN IF YOU TRY TO JOIN THE HERD...
...ALL WE WOULD NEED TO DO IS ERASE IT.
HEH HEH ...
I CAN HEAR YOUR RAGE.
SOON, YOU WILL DESCEND INTO THE DEPTHS OF FEAR. FEAR OVER YOUR PUNISHMENT, THAT IS...
I VERY MUCH LOOK FORWARD TO THAT MOMENT.
......I THINK WE'LL GET ALONG JUST FINE.
BUT LET ME ASK YOU THIS—
WHY COME TO ARREST ME NOW?
WELL, ODDLY ENOUGH, WE RECOVERED A MOUND OF EVIDENCE ALL OF A SUDDEN ...
...TAPES ...
...LIKE PRINTS ...

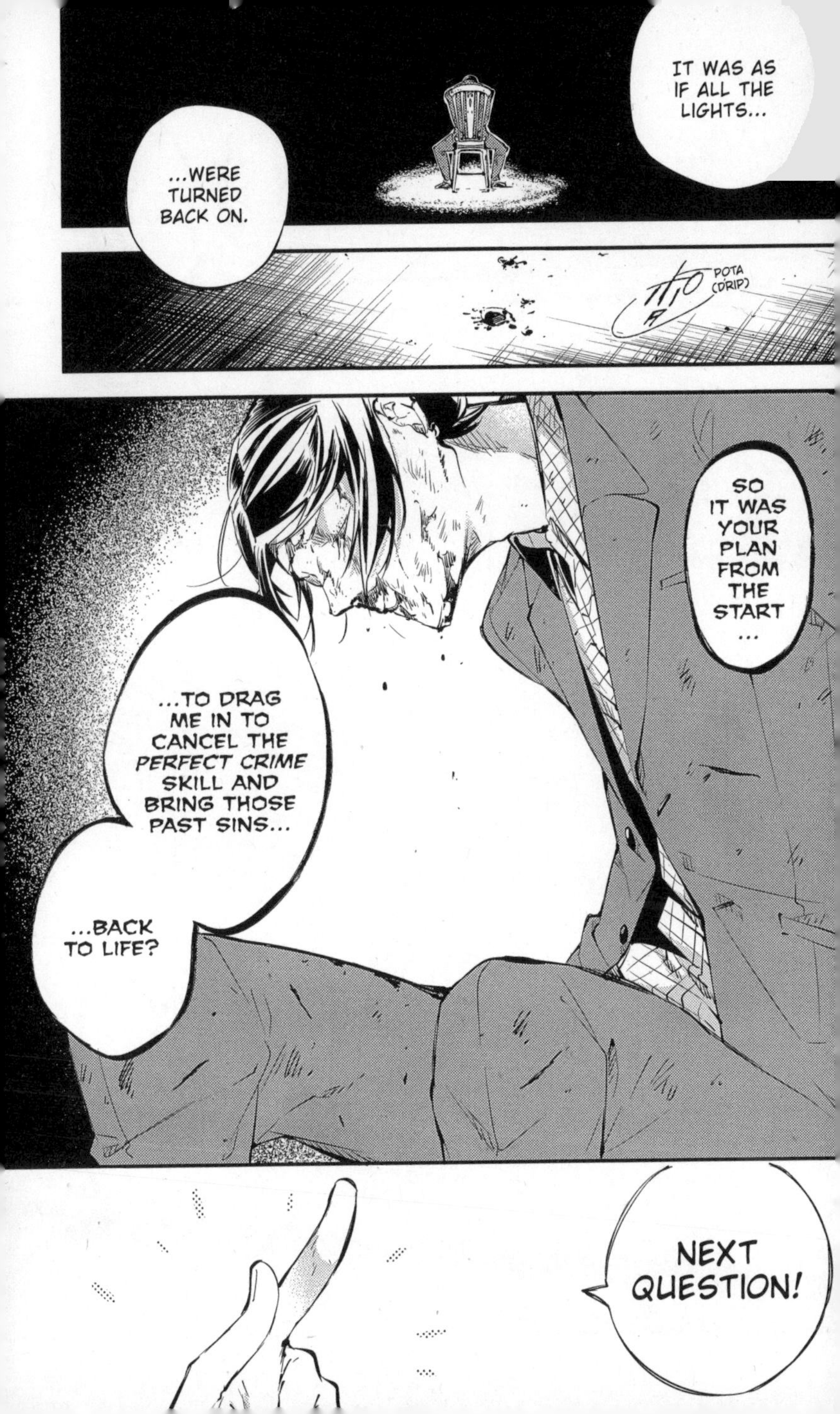
IT WAS AS IF ALL THE LIGHTS...
...WERE TURNED BACK ON.
POTA (DRIP)
SO IT WAS YOUR PLAN FROM THE START...
...TO DRAG ME IN TO CANCEL THE *PERFECT CRIME* SKILL AND BRING THOSE PAST SINS...
...BACK TO LIFE?
NEXT QUESTION!

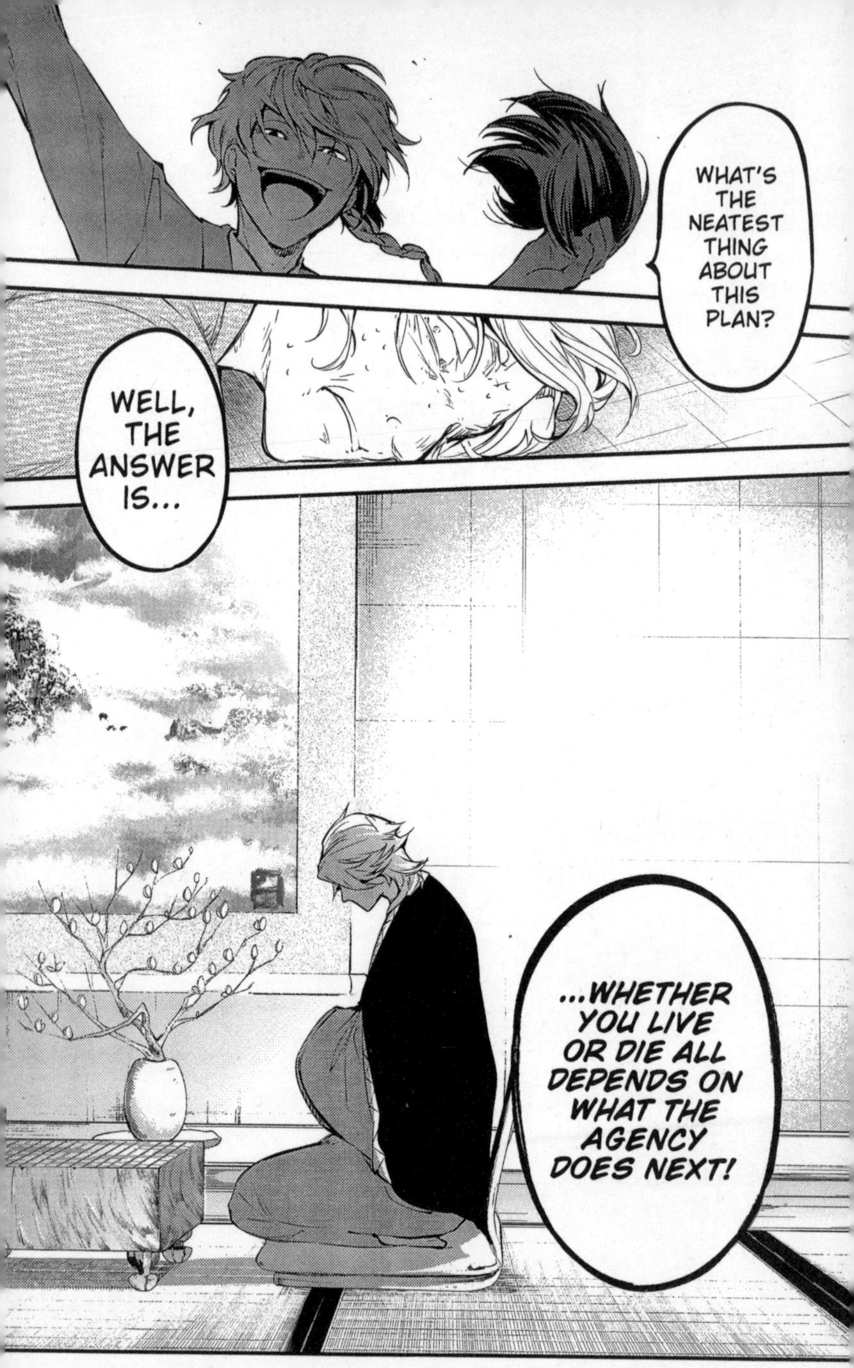
WHAT'S THE NEATEST THING ABOUT THIS PLAN?
WELL, THE ANSWER IS...
...WHETHER YOU LIVE OR DIE ALL DEPENDS ON WHAT THE AGENCY DOES NEXT!

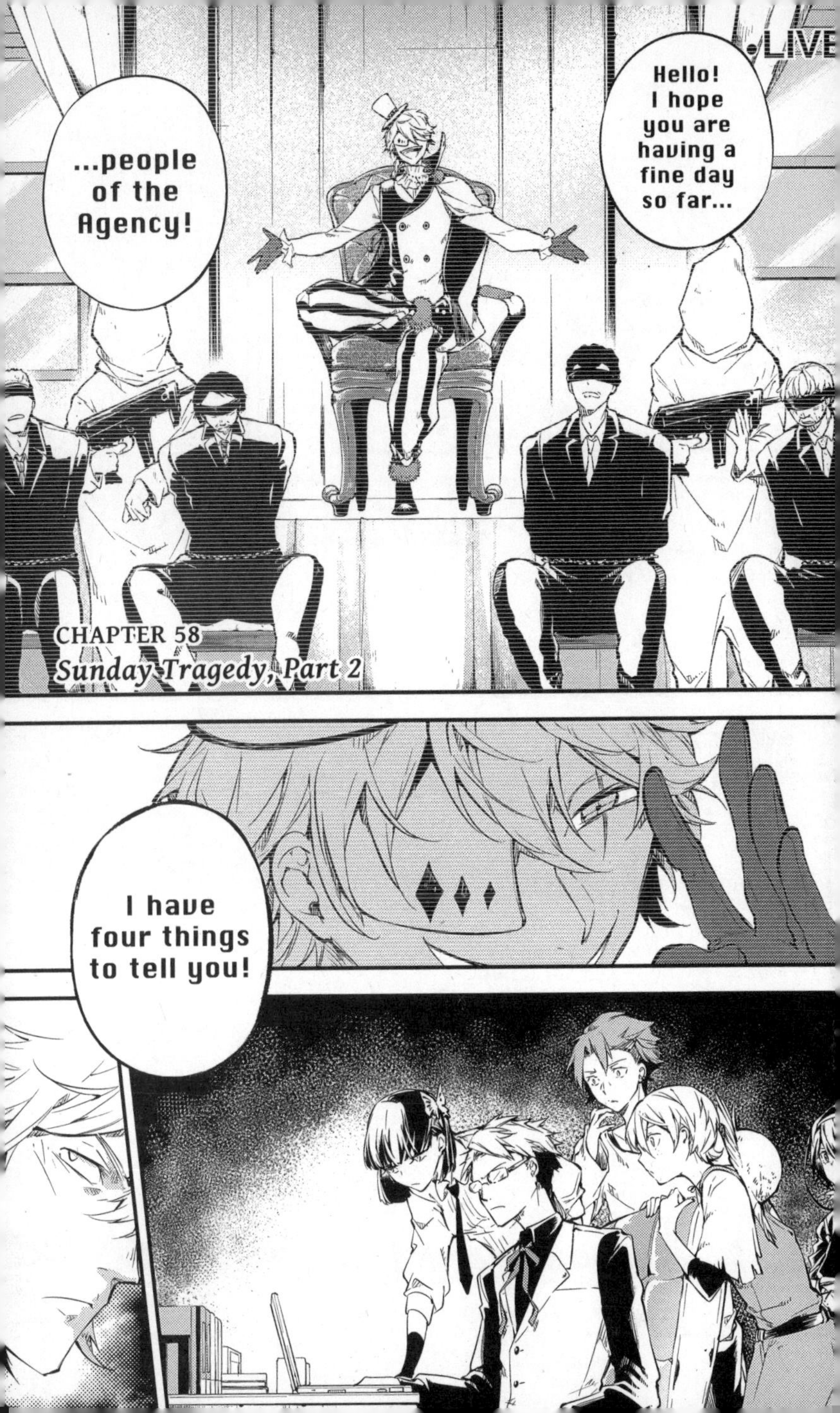
LIVE
Hello! I hope you are having a fine day so far...
...people of the Agency!
CHAPTER 58
Sunday Tragedy, Part 2
I have four things to tell you!

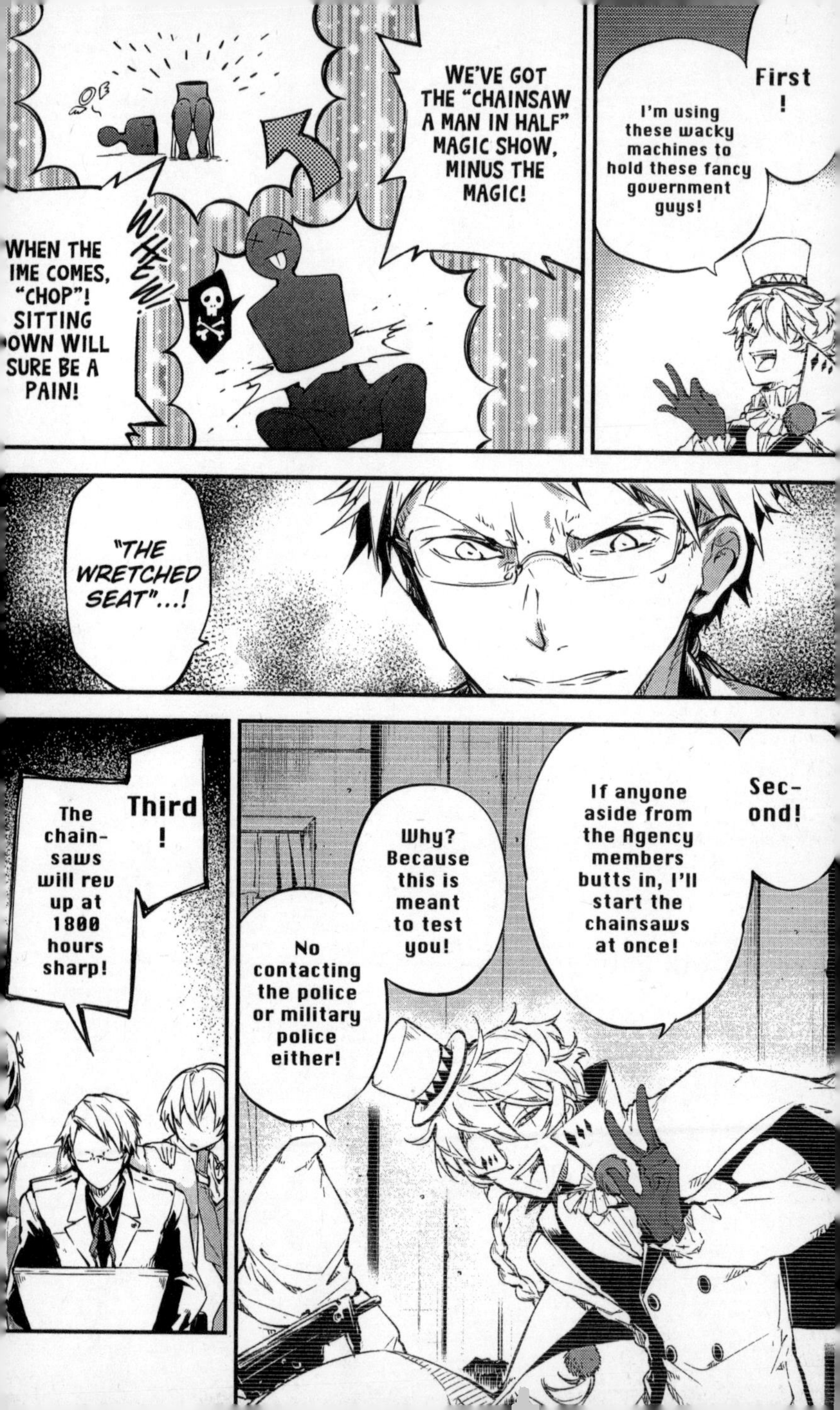
First!
I'm using these wacky machines to hold these fancy government guys!
WE'VE GOT THE "CHAINSAW A MAN IN HALF" MAGIC SHOW, MINUS THE MAGIC!
WHEW!
WHEN THE IME COMES, "CHOP"! SITTING OWN WILL SURE BE A PAIN!
"THE WRETCHED SEAT"...!
Second!
If anyone aside from the Agency members butts in, I'll start the chainsaws at once!
Why? Because this is meant to test you!
No contacting the police or military police either!
Third!
The chainsaws will rev up at 1800 hours sharp!

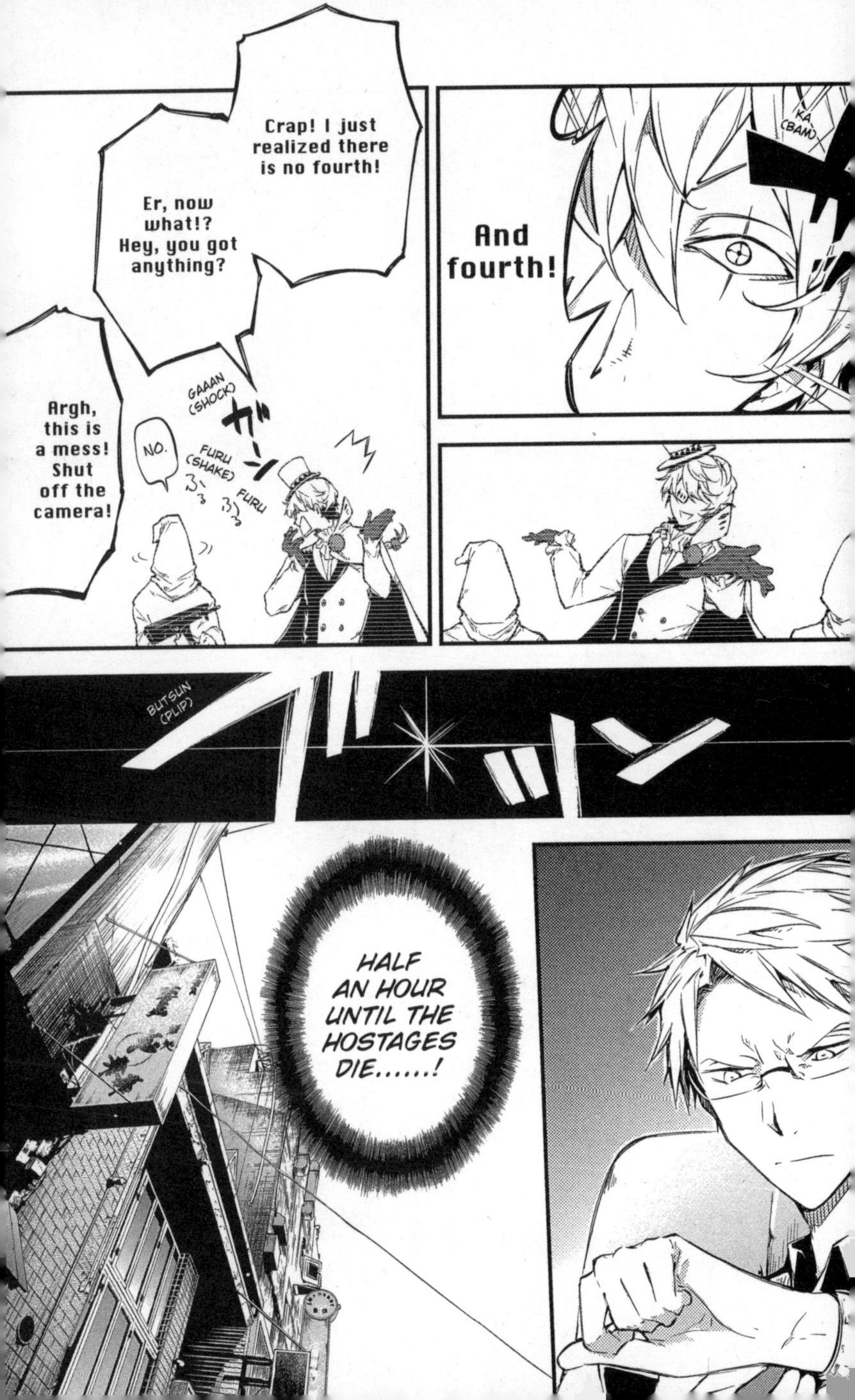

KA (BAM)
And fourth!
Crap! I just realized there is no fourth!
Er, now what!? Hey, you got anything?
GAAAN (SHOCK)
FURU (SHAKE) FURU
NO.
Argh, this is a mess! Shut off the camera!
BUTSUN (PLIP)
HALF AN HOUR UNTIL THE HOSTAGES DIE......!

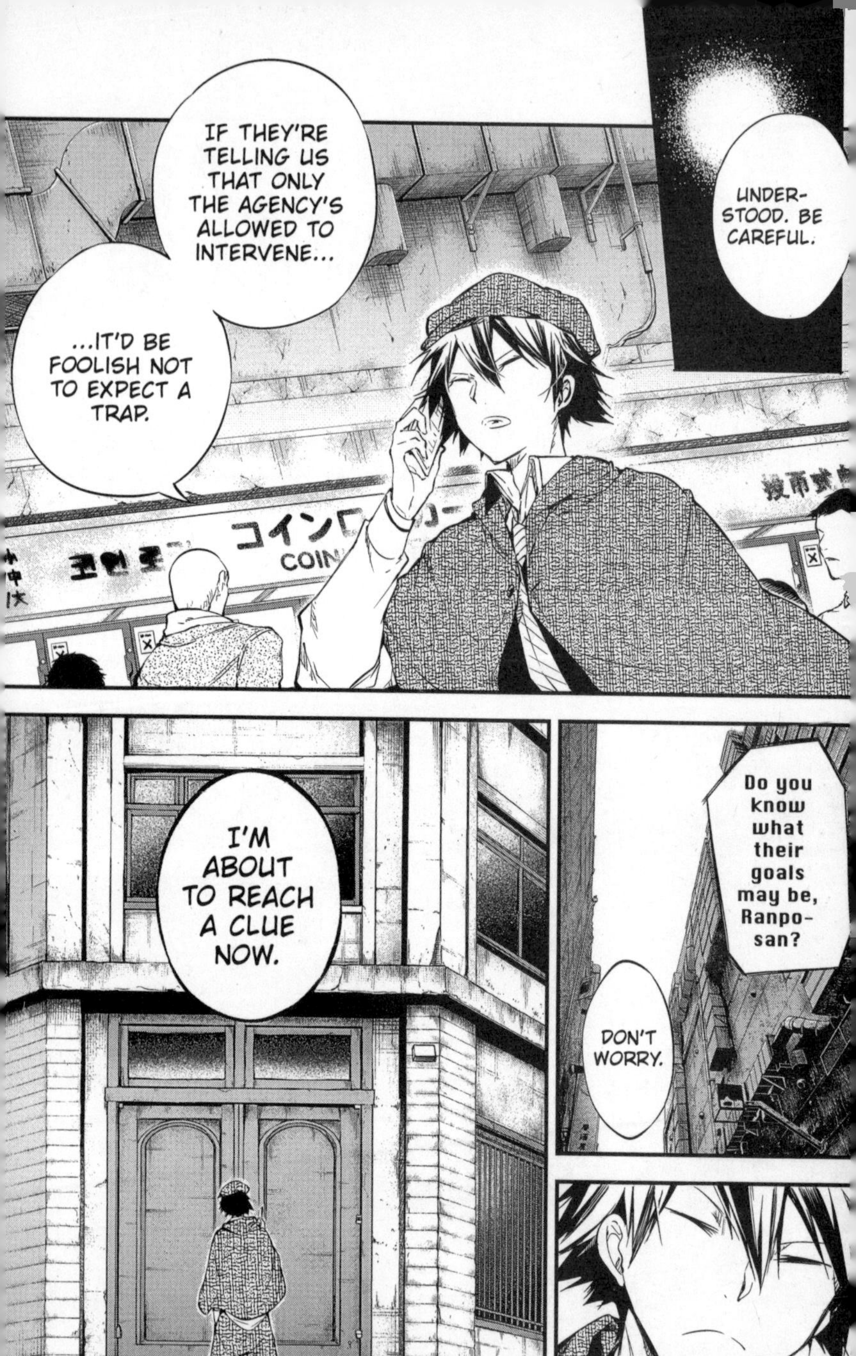
UNDER-STOOD. BE CAREFUL.
IF THEY'RE TELLING US THAT ONLY THE AGENCY'S ALLOWED TO INTERVENE...
...IT'D BE FOOLISH NOT TO EXPECT A TRAP.
Do you know what their goals may be, Ranpo-san?
DON'T WORRY.
I'M ABOUT TO REACH A CLUE NOW.

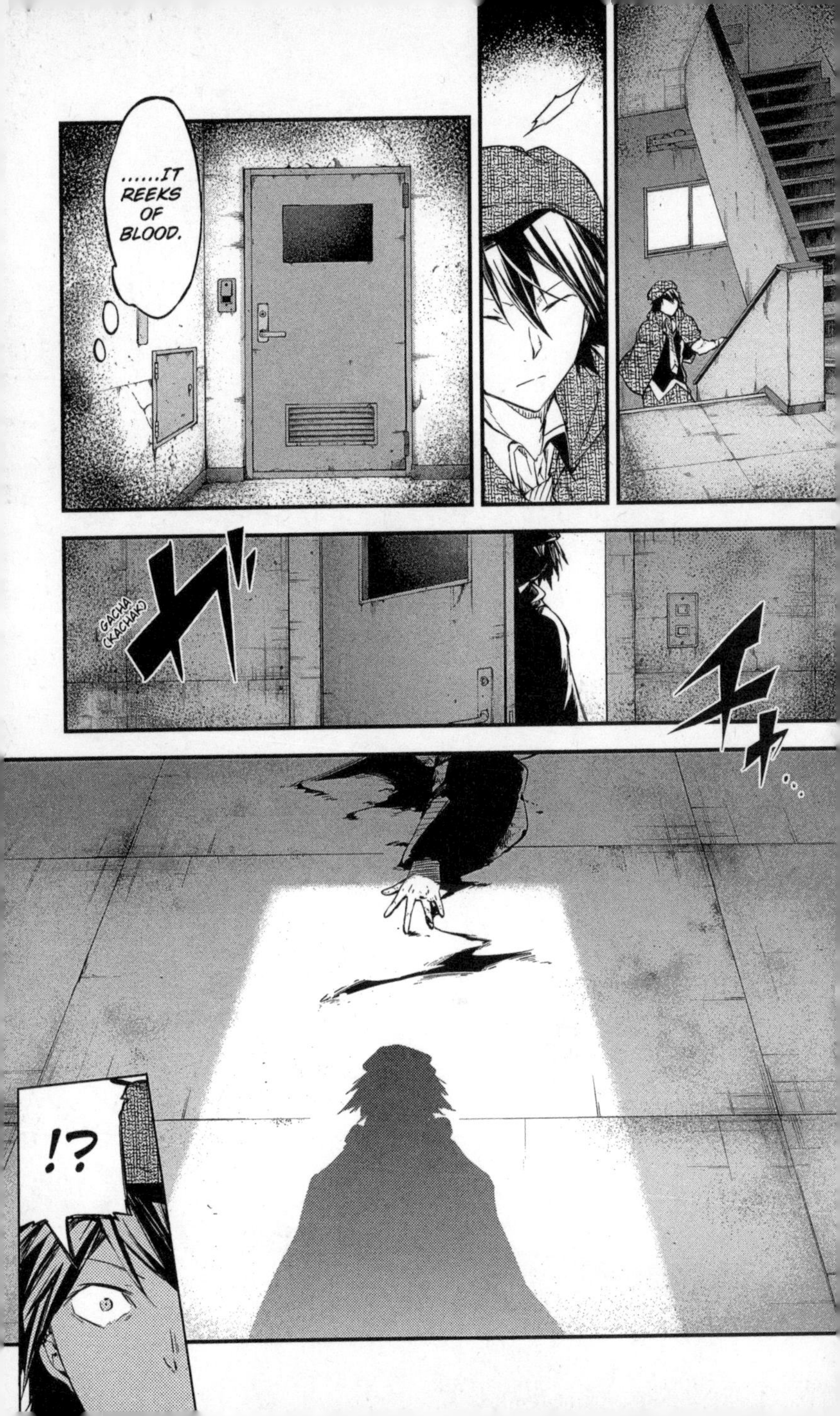
......IT REEKS OF BLOOD.
GACHA (KACHAK)
!?

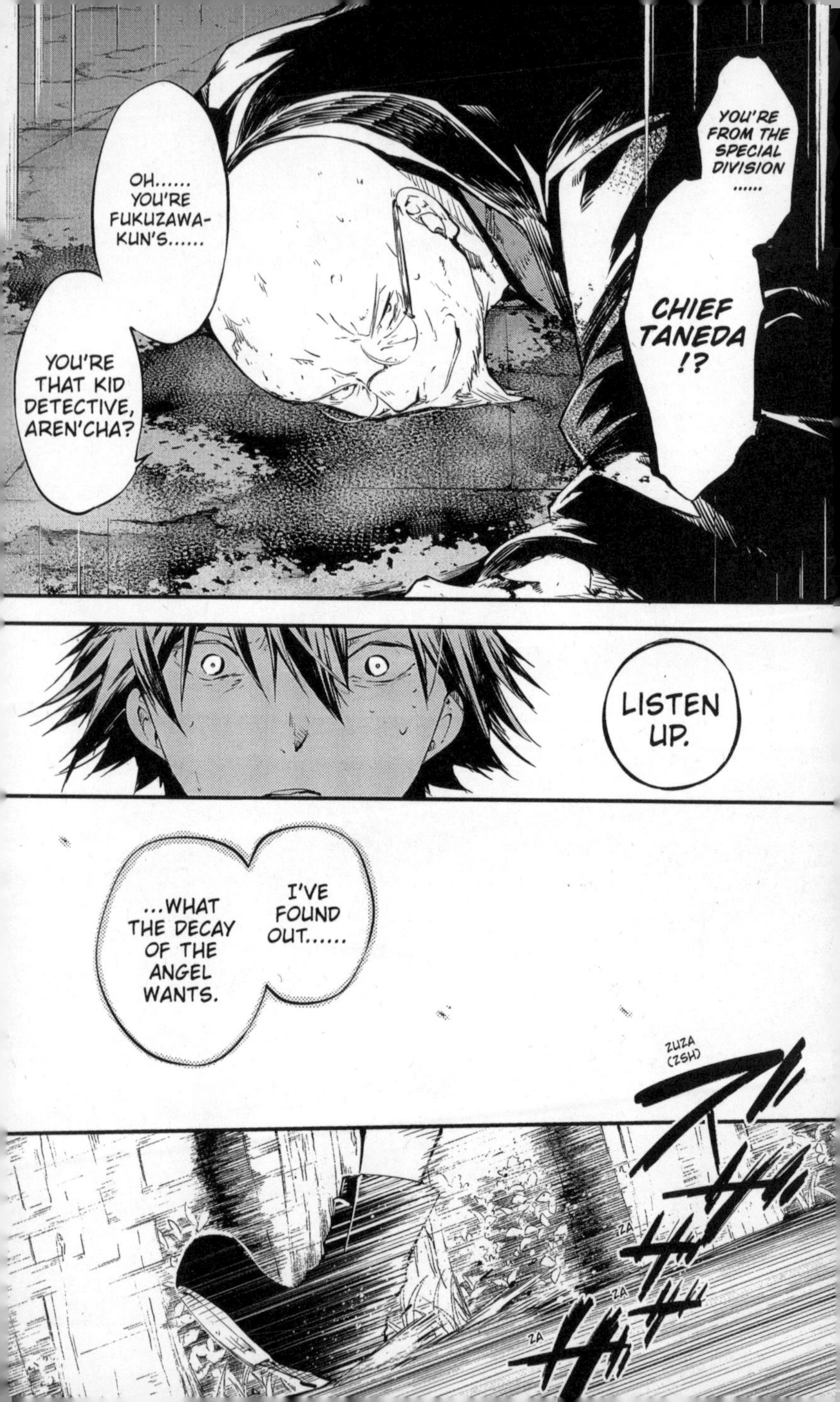
YOU'RE FROM THE SPECIAL DIVISION ......
CHIEF TANEDA !?
OH...... YOU'RE FUKUZAWA-KUN'S......
YOU'RE THAT KID DETECTIVE, AREN'CHA?
LISTEN UP.
I'VE FOUND OUT......
...WHAT THE DECAY OF THE ANGEL WANTS.
ZUZA (ZSH)
ZA
ZA
ZA

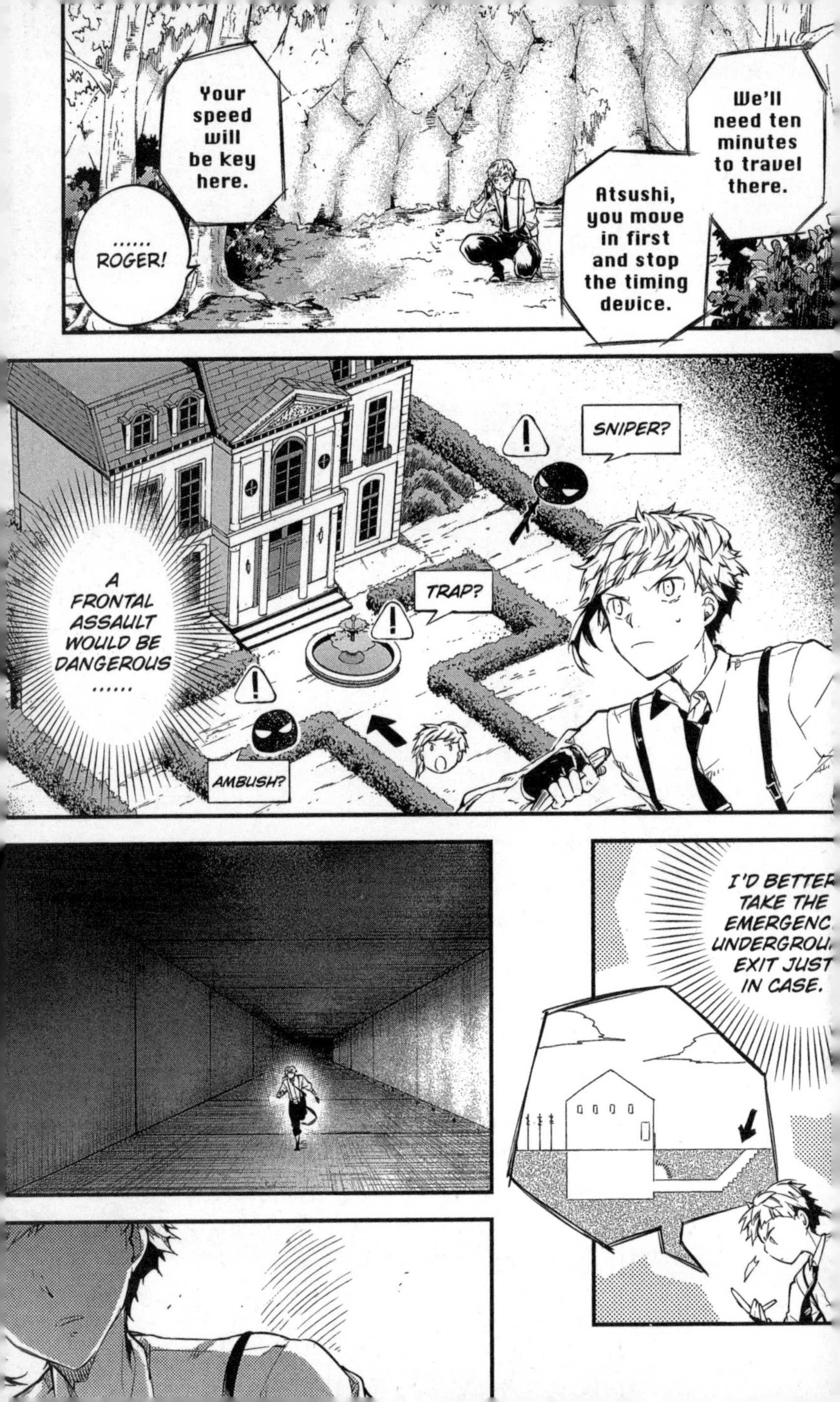
We'll need ten minutes to travel there.
Atsushi, you move in first and stop the timing device.
Your speed will be key here.
......ROGER!
SNIPER?
TRAP?
A FRONTAL ASSAULT WOULD BE DANGEROUS ......
AMBUSH?
I'D BETTER TAKE THE EMERGENC UNDERGROU EXIT JUST IN CASE.

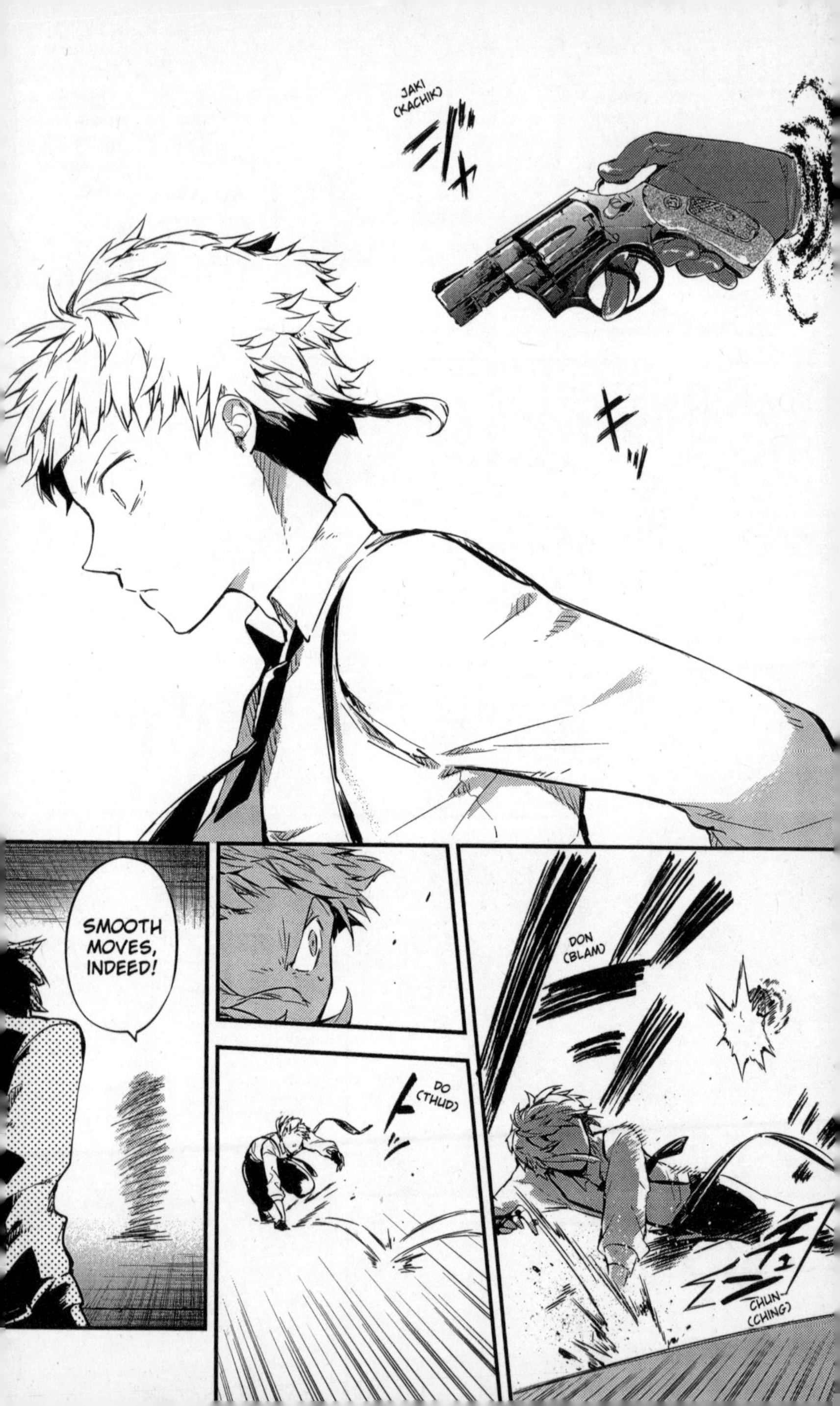
JAKI
(KACHIK)
DON
(BLAM)
CHUN-
(CHING)
DO
(THUD)
SMOOTH MOVES, INDEED!

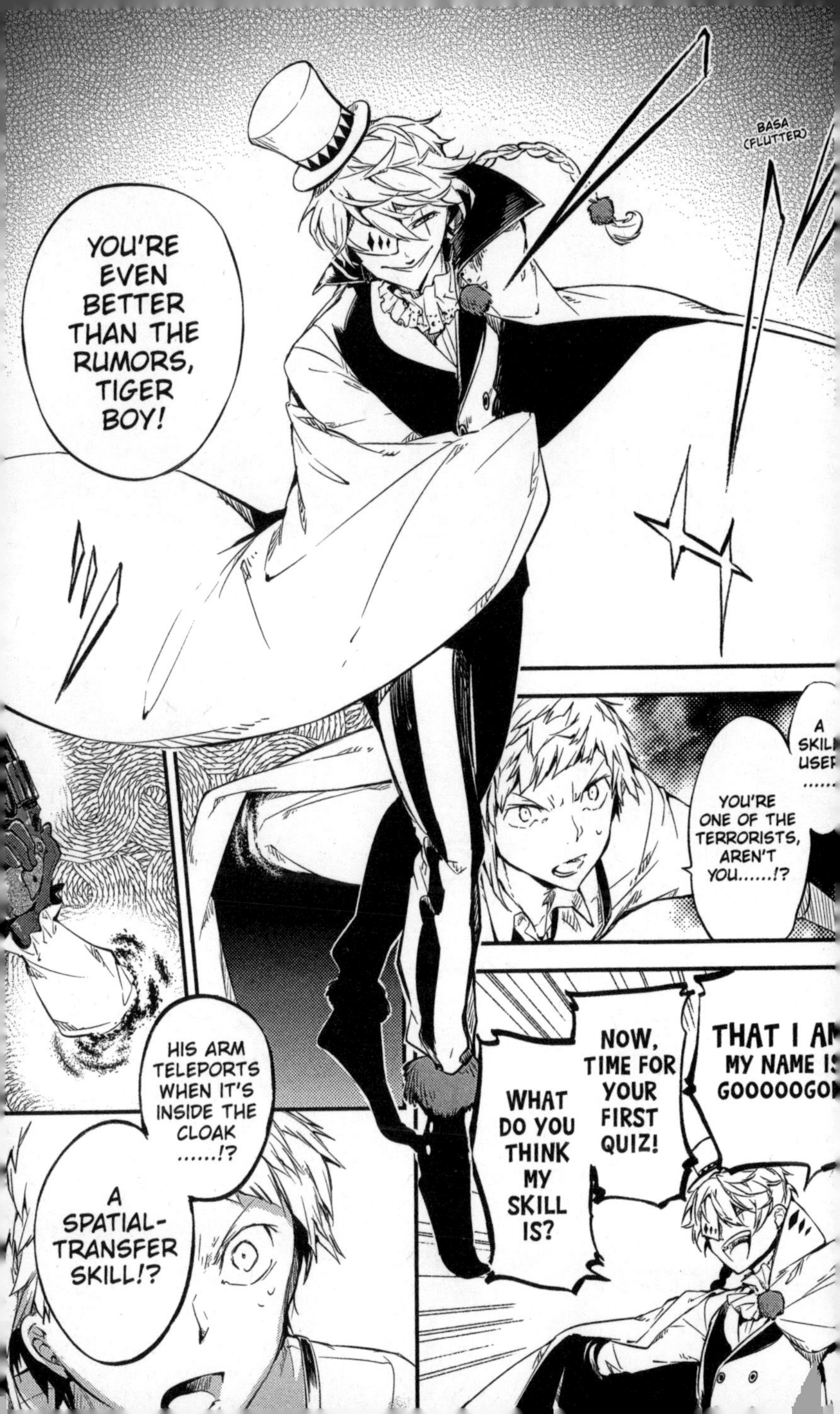

BASA (FLUTTER)
YOU'RE EVEN BETTER THAN THE RUMORS, TIGER BOY!
A SKIL USE ......
YOU'RE ONE OF THE TERRORISTS, AREN'T YOU......!?
THAT I A
MY NAME I GOOOOOGO
NOW, TIME FOR YOUR FIRST QUIZ!
WHAT DO YOU THINK MY SKILL IS?
HIS ARM TELEPORTS WHEN IT'S INSIDE THE CLOAK ......!?
A SPATIAL-TRANSFER SKILL!?

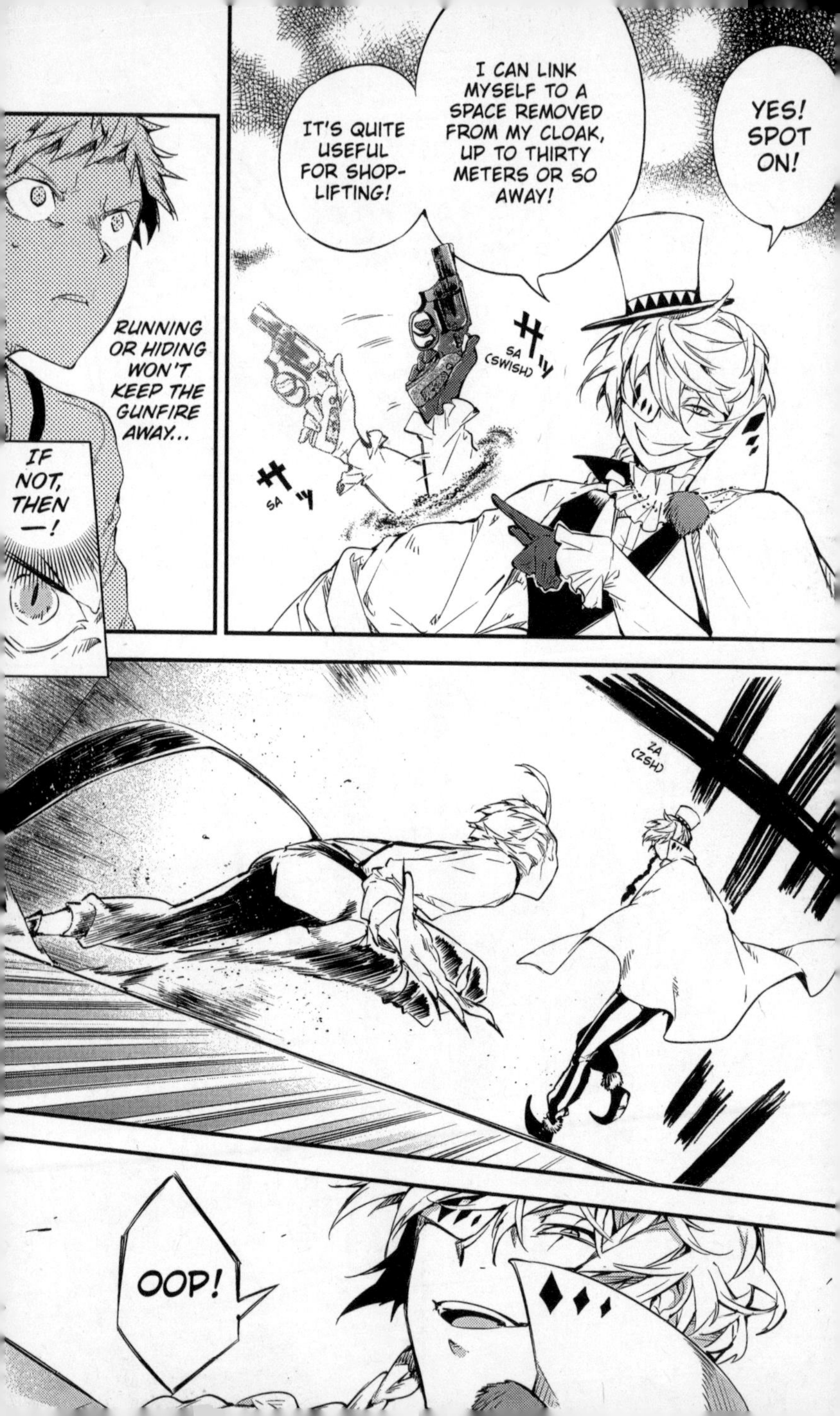
YES! SPOT ON!
I CAN LINK MYSELF TO A SPACE REMOVED FROM MY CLOAK, UP TO THIRTY METERS OR SO AWAY!
IT'S QUITE USEFUL FOR SHOP-LIFTING!
SA (SWISH)
SA
RUNNING OR HIDING WON'T KEEP THE GUNFIRE AWAY...
IF NOT, THEN —!
ZA (ZSH)
OOP!

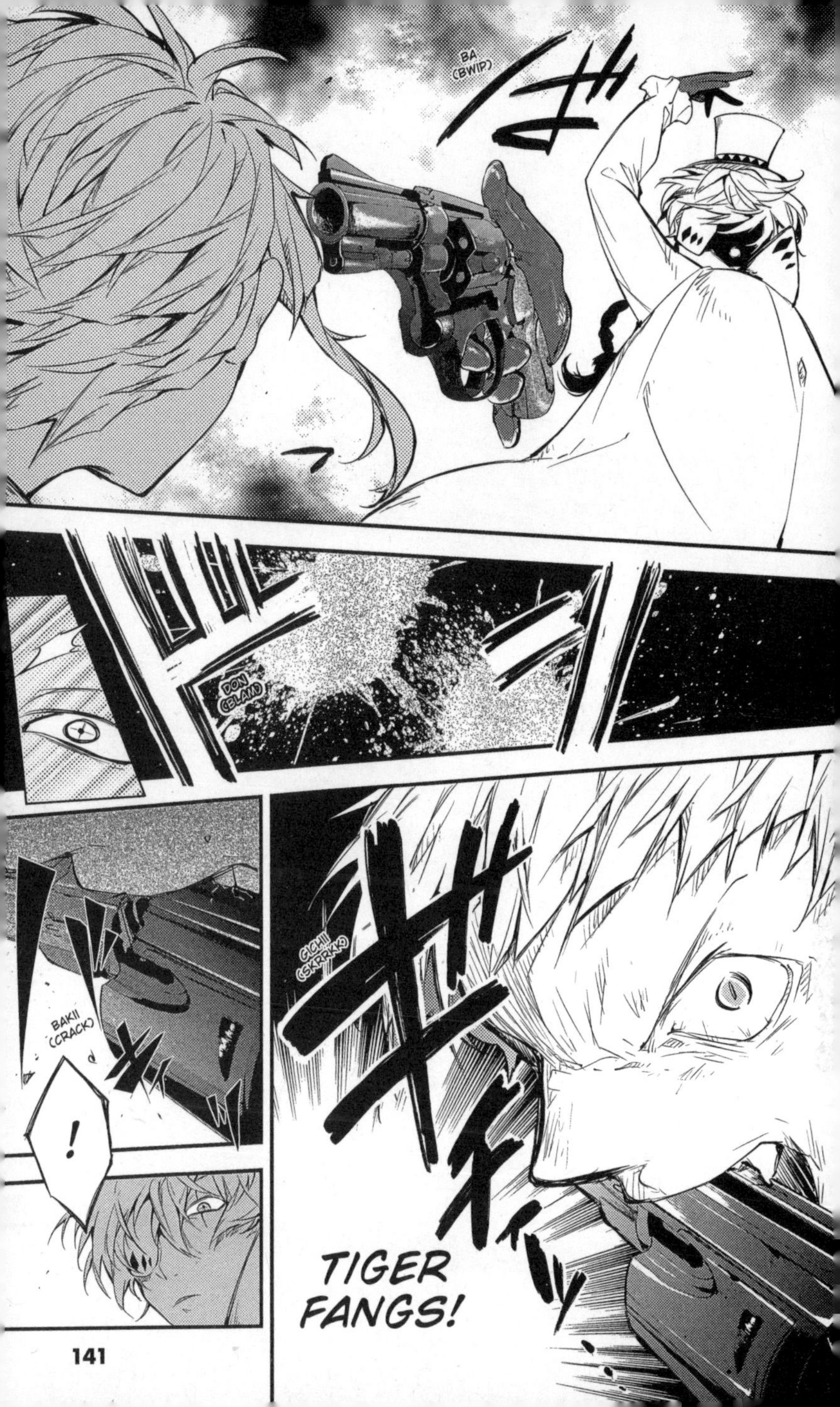
BA (BWIP)
DON (BLAM)
GICHI (SKRRK)
TIGER FANGS!
BAKI (CRACK)
!

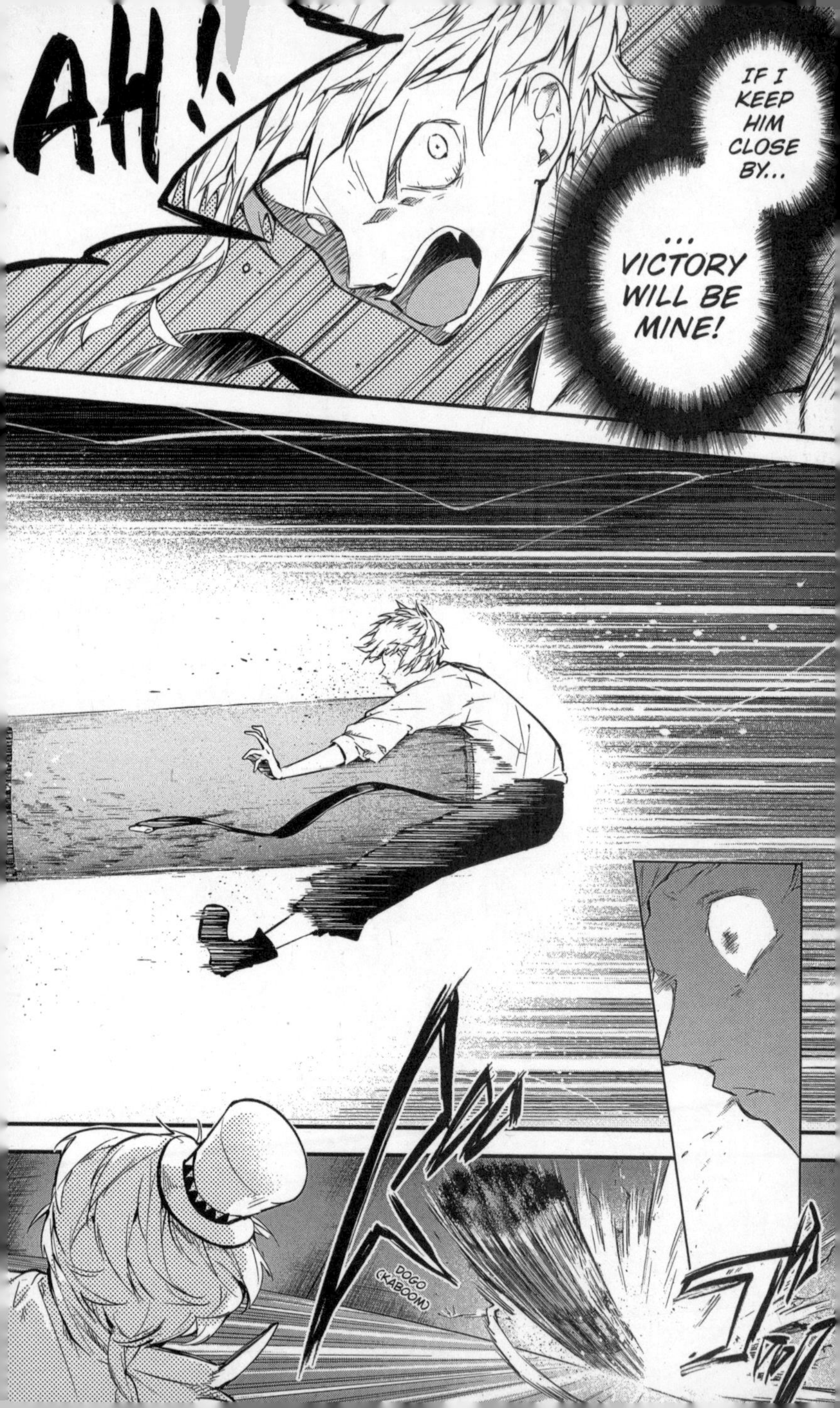
AH!!
IF I KEEP HIM CLOSE BY...
...VICTORY WILL BE MINE!
DOGO (KABOOM)

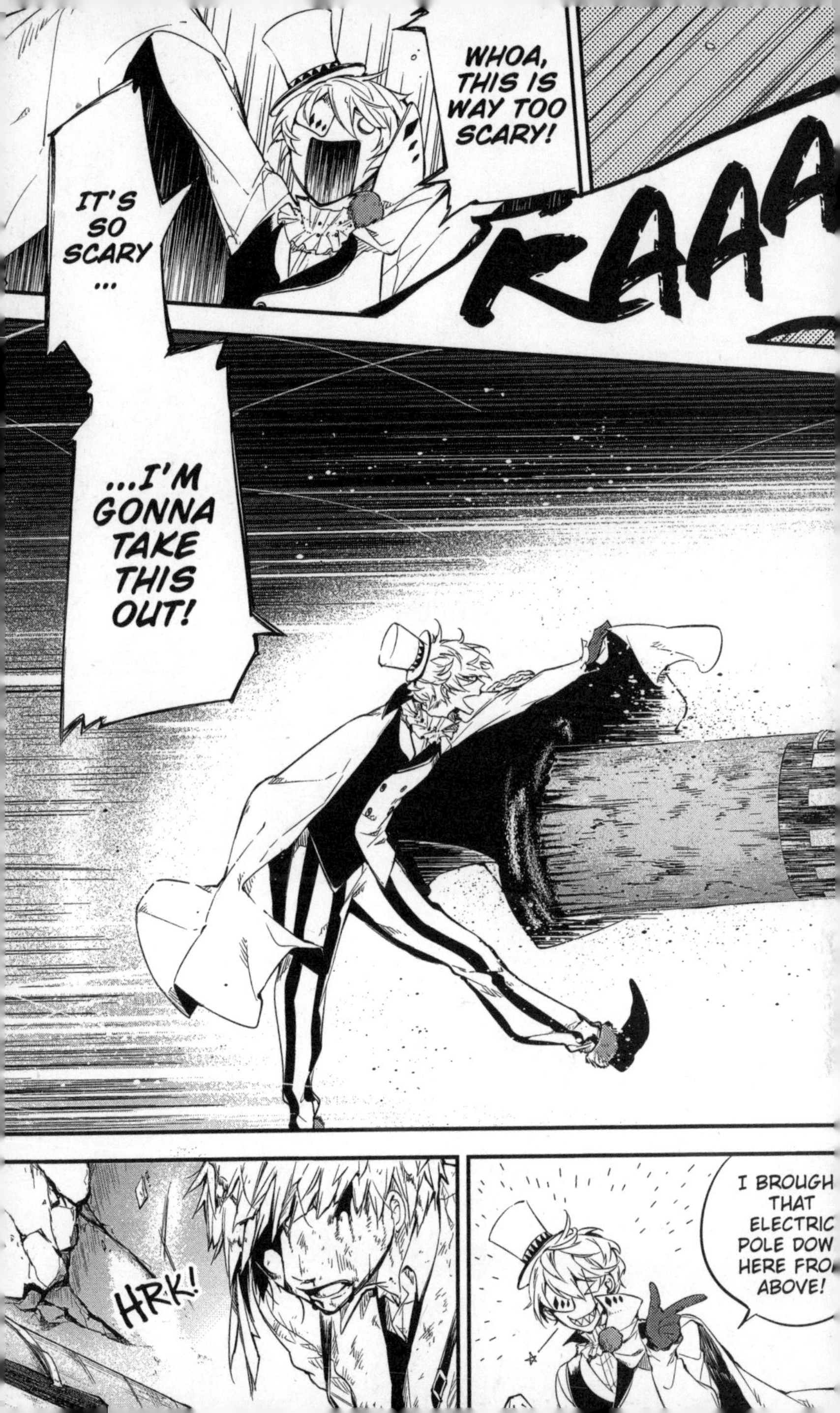
WHOA, THIS IS WAY TOO SCARY!
RAAA
IT'S SO SCARY ...
...I'M GONNA TAKE THIS OUT!
I BROUGH THAT ELECTRIC POLE DOW HERE FRO ABOVE!
HRK!

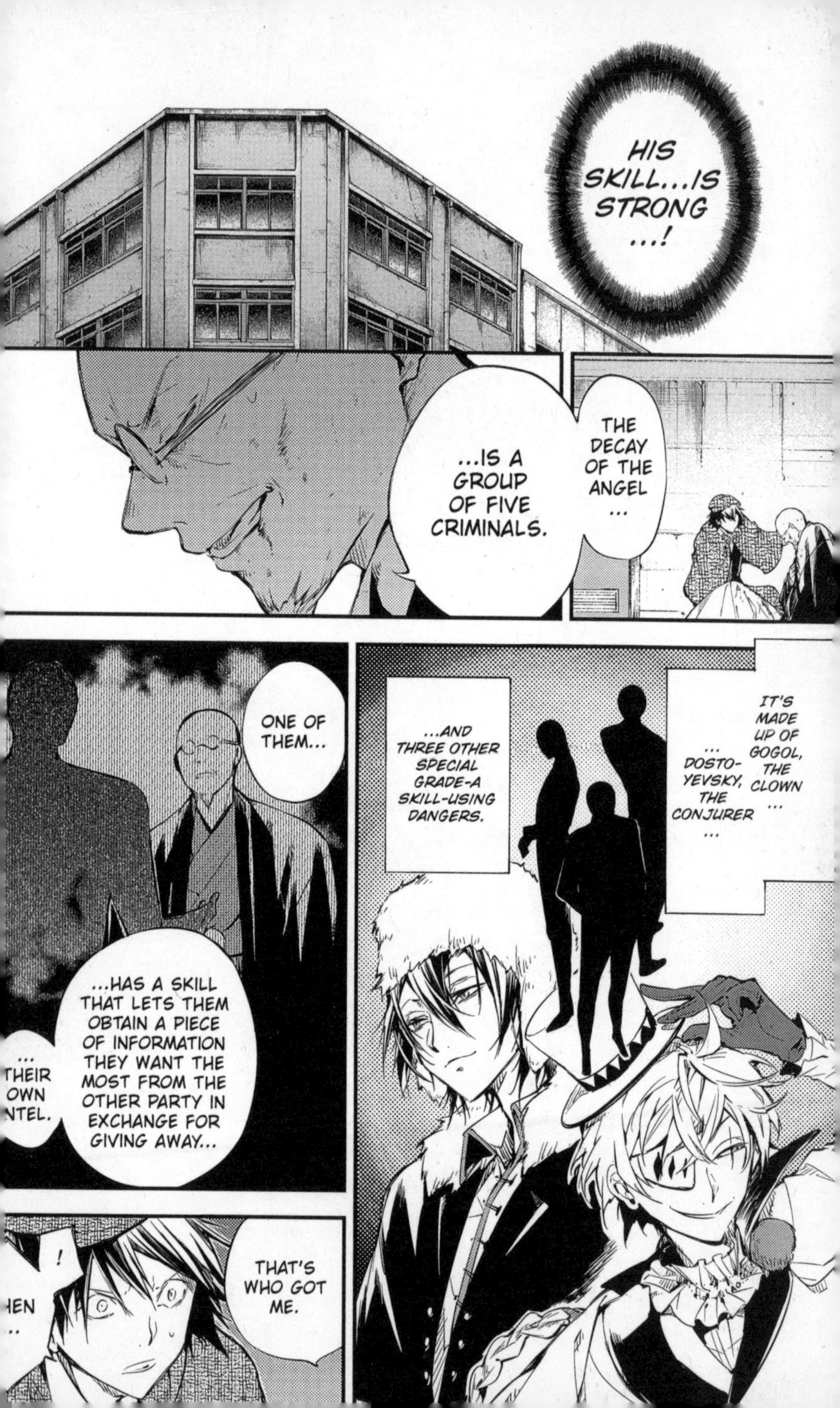
HIS SKILL...IS STRONG ...!
THE DECAY OF THE ANGEL ...
...IS A GROUP OF FIVE CRIMINALS.
IT'S MADE UP OF GOGOL, THE CLOWN ...
... DOSTO-YEVSKY, THE CONJURER ...
...AND THREE OTHER SPECIAL GRADE-A SKILL-USING DANGERS.
ONE OF THEM...
...HAS A SKILL THAT LETS THEM OBTAIN A PIECE OF INFORMATION THEY WANT THE MOST FROM THE OTHER PARTY IN EXCHANGE FOR GIVING AWAY...
... THEIR OWN NTEL.
THAT'S WHO GOT ME.
!
HEN ...

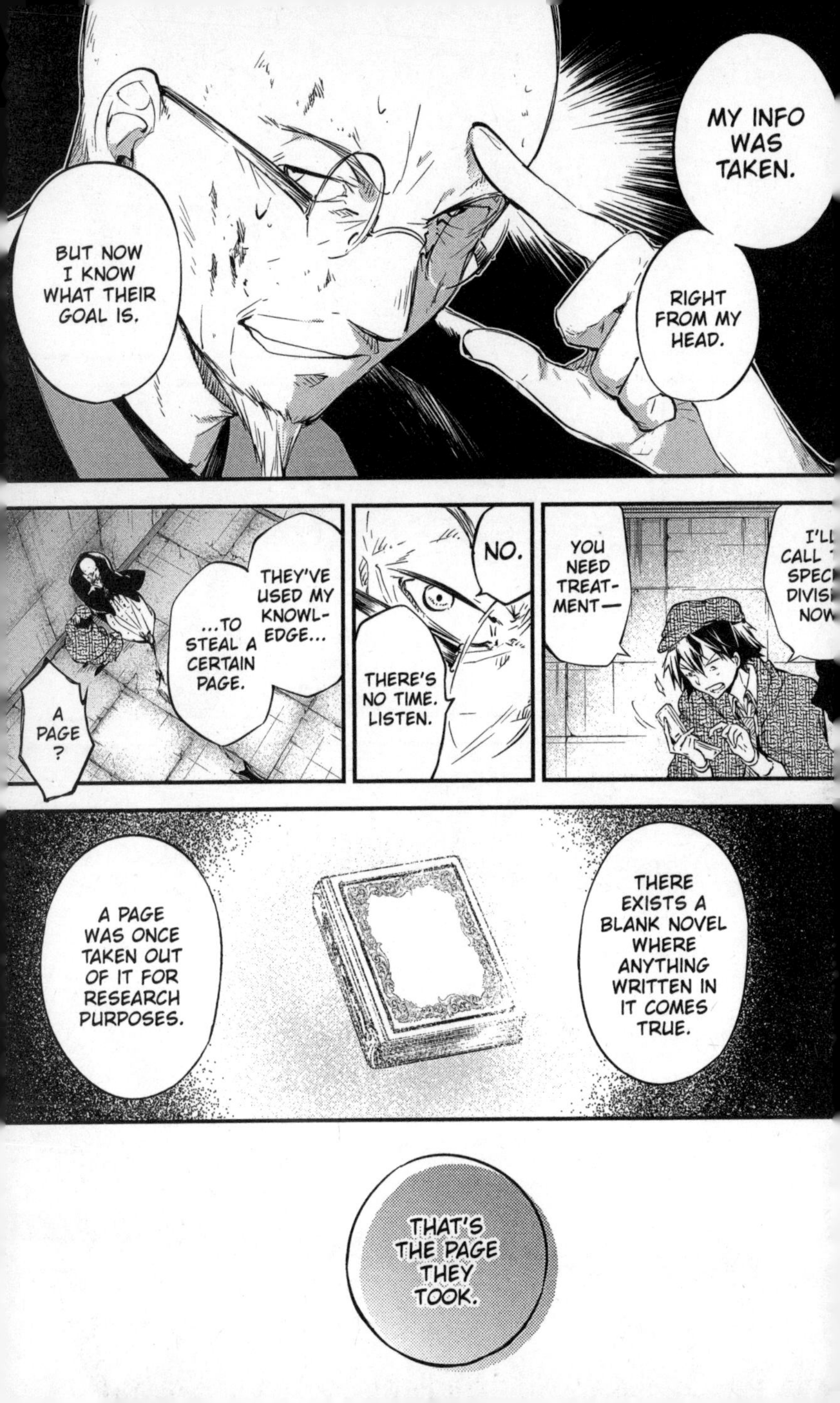
MY INFO WAS TAKEN.
RIGHT FROM MY HEAD.
BUT NOW I KNOW WHAT THEIR GOAL IS.
I'LL CALL
YOU NEED TREATMENT—
NO.
THERE'S NO TIME. LISTEN.
THEY'VE USED MY KNOWLEDGE...
...TO STEAL A CERTAIN PAGE.
A PAGE?
THERE EXISTS A BLANK NOVEL WHERE ANYTHING WRITTEN IN IT COMES TRUE.
A PAGE WAS ONCE TAKEN OUT OF IT FOR RESEARCH PURPOSES.
THAT'S THE PAGE THEY TOOK.

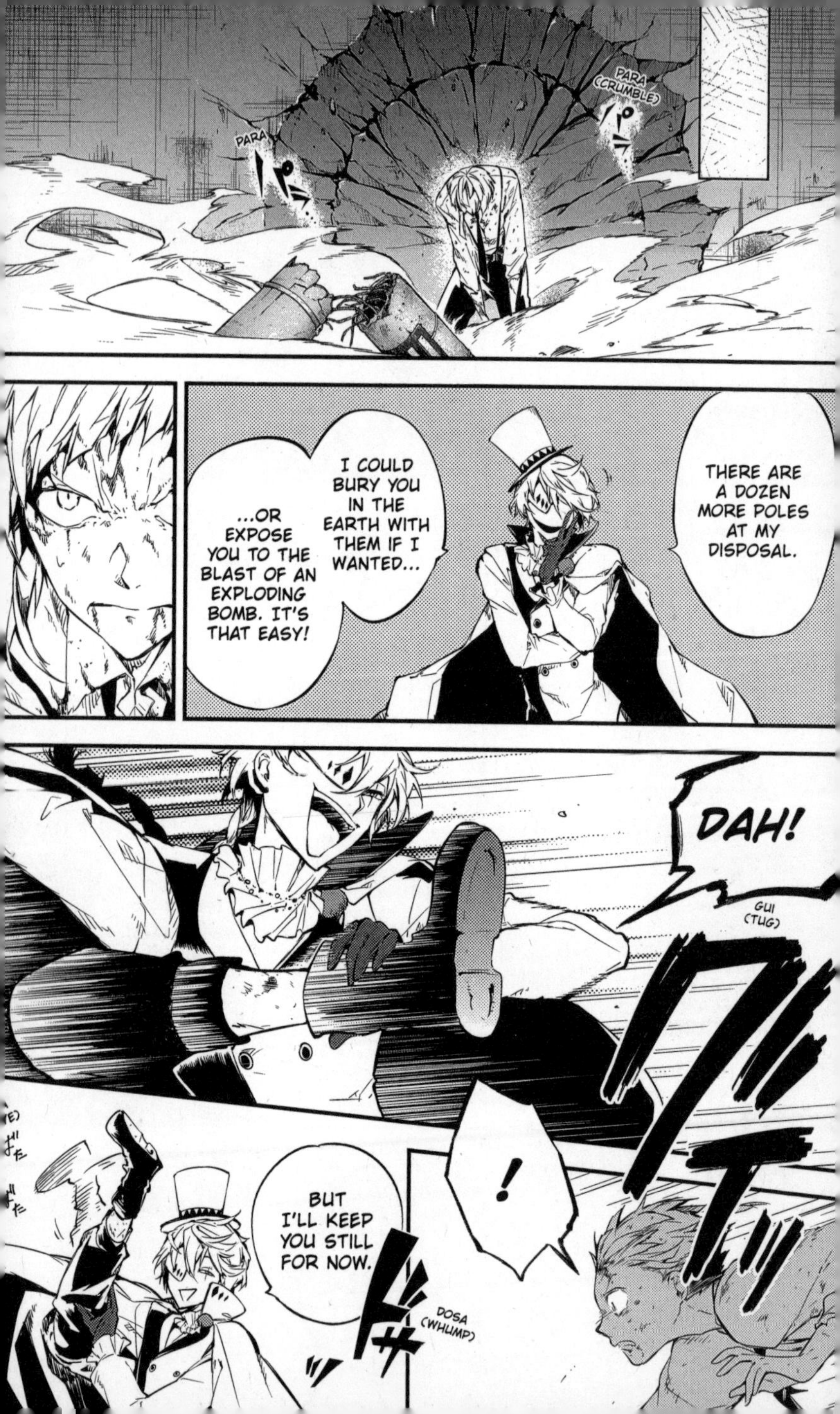
PARA (CRUMBLE)
PARA
THERE ARE A DOZEN MORE POLES AT MY DISPOSAL.
I COULD BURY YOU IN THE EARTH WITH THEM IF I WANTED...
...OR EXPOSE YOU TO THE BLAST OF AN EXPLODING BOMB. IT'S THAT EASY!
DAH!
GUI (TUG)
!
DOSA (WHUMP)
BUT I'LL KEEP YOU STILL FOR NOW.

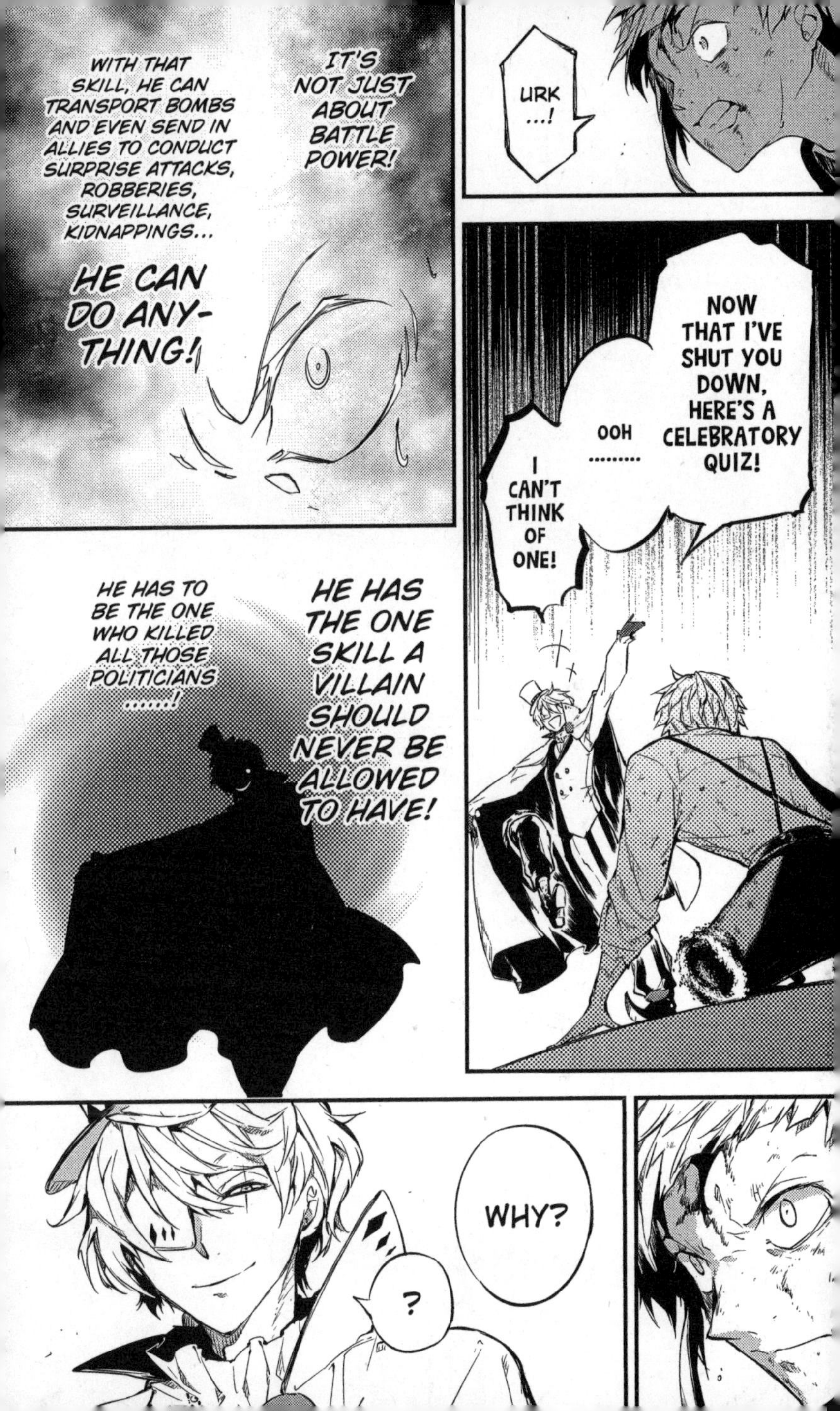
URK ...!
NOW THAT I'VE SHUT YOU DOWN, HERE'S A CELEBRATORY QUIZ!
OOH ....
I CAN'T THINK OF ONE!
IT'S NOT JUST ABOUT BATTLE POWER!
WITH THAT SKILL, HE CAN TRANSPORT BOMBS AND EVEN SEND IN ALLIES TO CONDUCT SURPRISE ATTACKS, ROBBERIES, SURVEILLANCE, KIDNAPPINGS...
HE CAN DO ANY-THING!
HE HAS THE ONE SKILL A VILLAIN SHOULD NEVER BE ALLOWED TO HAVE!
HE HAS TO BE THE ONE WHO KILLED ALL THOSE POLITICIANS ......!
WHY?
?

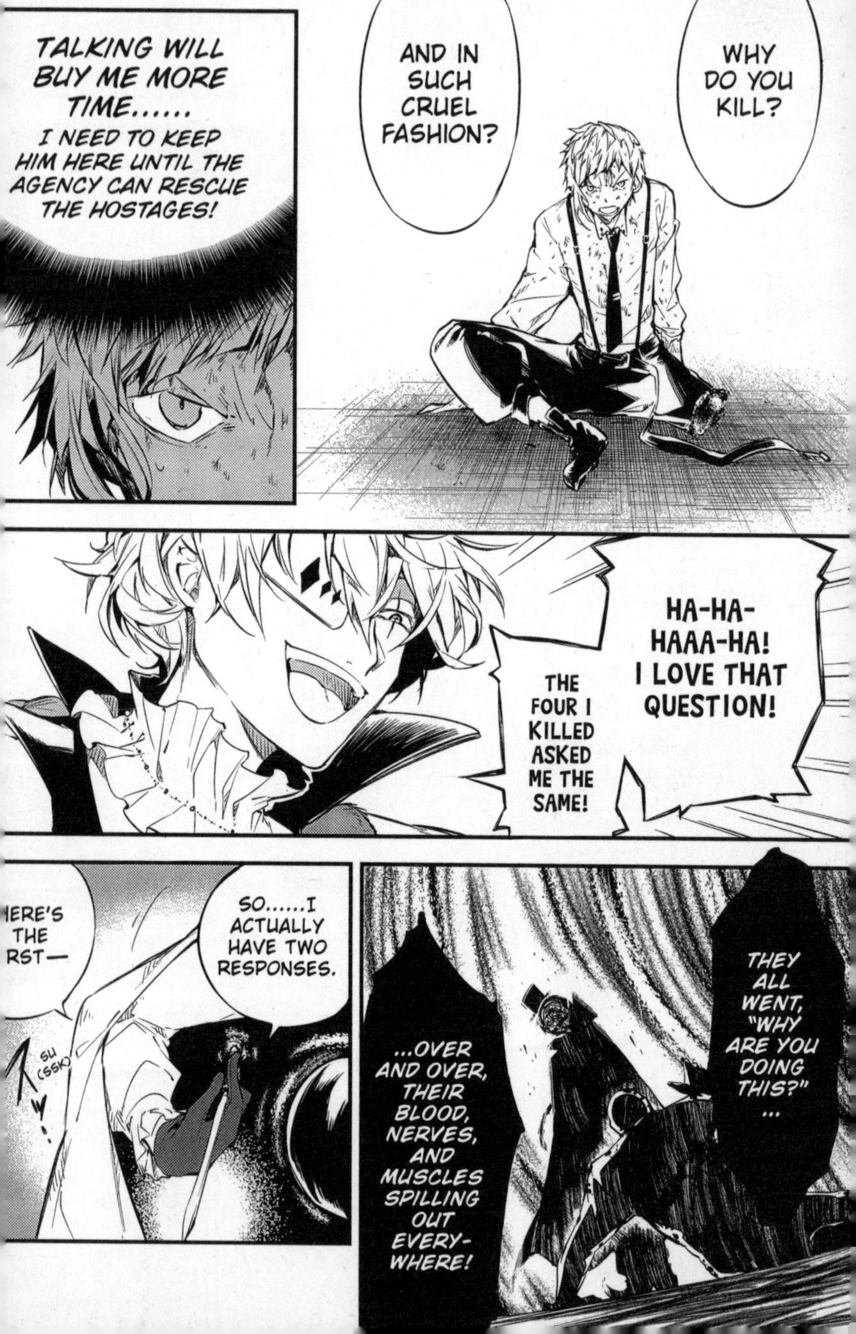
WHY DO YOU KILL?
AND IN SUCH CRUEL FASHION?
TALKING WILL BUY ME MORE TIME...... I NEED TO KEEP HIM HERE UNTIL THE AGENCY CAN RESCUE THE HOSTAGES!
HA-HA-HAAA-HA! I LOVE THAT QUESTION!
THE FOUR I KILLED ASKED ME THE SAME!
THEY ALL WENT, "WHY ARE YOU DOING THIS?" ...
...OVER AND OVER, THEIR BLOOD, NERVES, AND MUSCLES SPILLING OUT EVERYWHERE!
SO......I ACTUALLY HAVE TWO RESPONSES.
HERE'S THE RST—
SU (SSK)

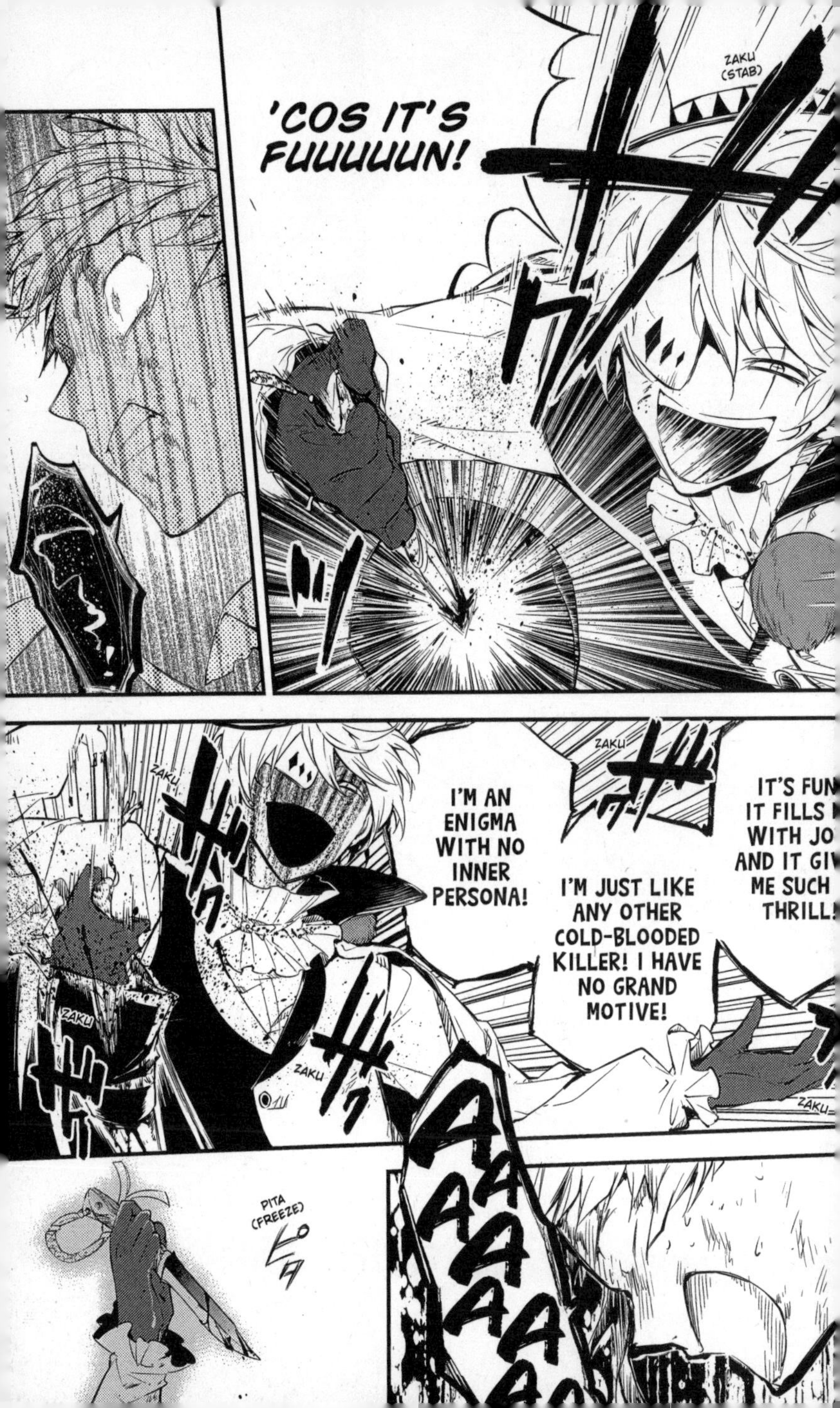
ZAKU
(STAB)
'COS IT'S
FUUUUUN!
IT'S FUN
IT FILLS
WITH JO
AND IT GIV
ME SUCH
THRILL!
ZAKU
I'M JUST LIKE
ANY OTHER
COLD-BLOODED
KILLER! I HAVE
NO GRAND
MOTIVE!
I'M AN
ENIGMA
WITH NO
INNER
PERSONA!
ZAKU
ZAKU
ZAKU
ZAKU
AAAAAAAAA
PITA
(FREEZE)

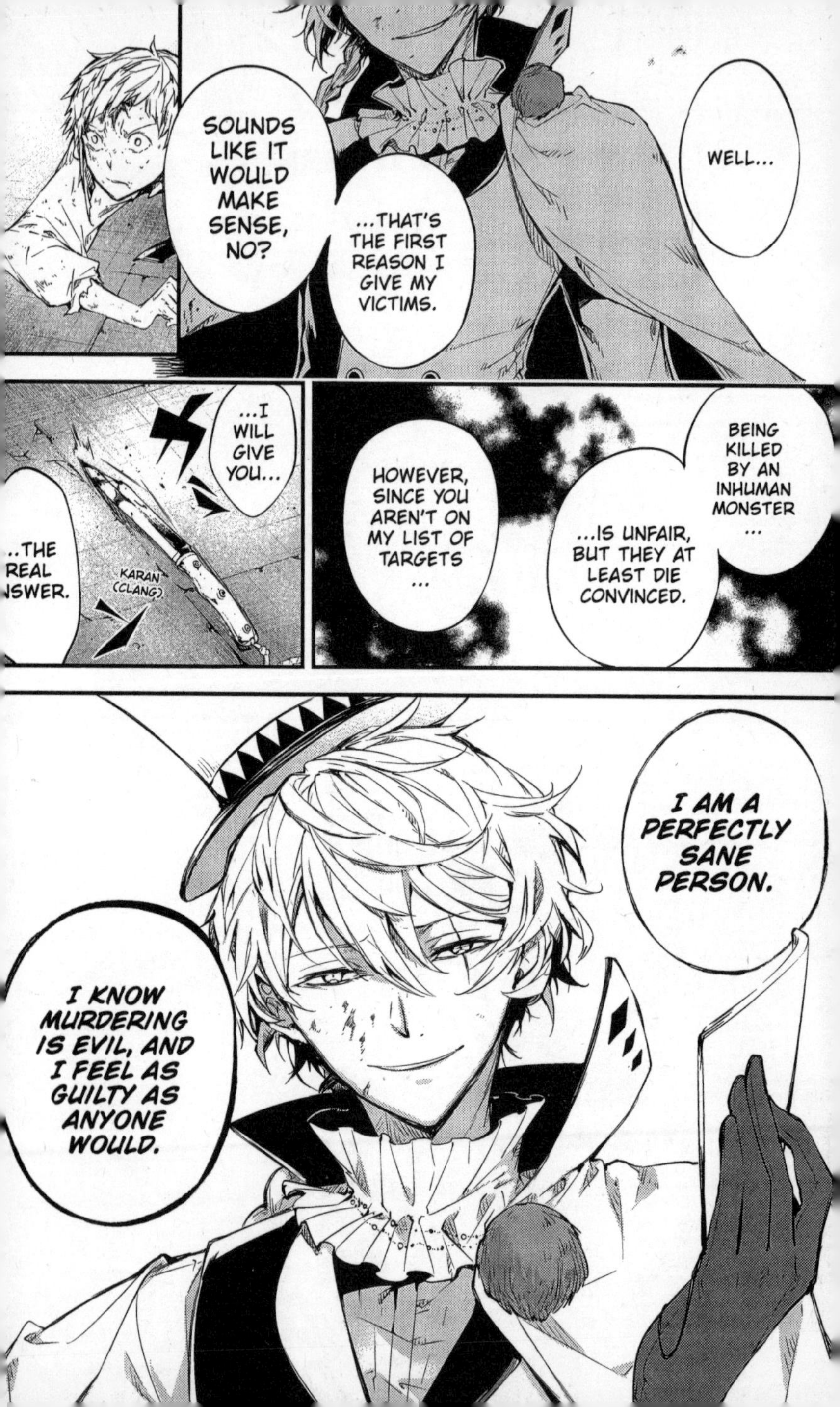
WELL...
SOUNDS LIKE IT WOULD MAKE SENSE, NO?
...THAT'S THE FIRST REASON I GIVE MY VICTIMS.
BEING KILLED BY AN INHUMAN MONSTER ...
...IS UNFAIR, BUT THEY AT LEAST DIE CONVINCED.
HOWEVER, SINCE YOU AREN'T ON MY LIST OF TARGETS ...
...I WILL GIVE YOU...
KARAN (CLANG)
..THE REAL NSWER.
I AM A PERFECTLY SANE PERSON.
I KNOW MURDERING IS EVIL, AND I FEEL AS GUILTY AS ANYONE WOULD.

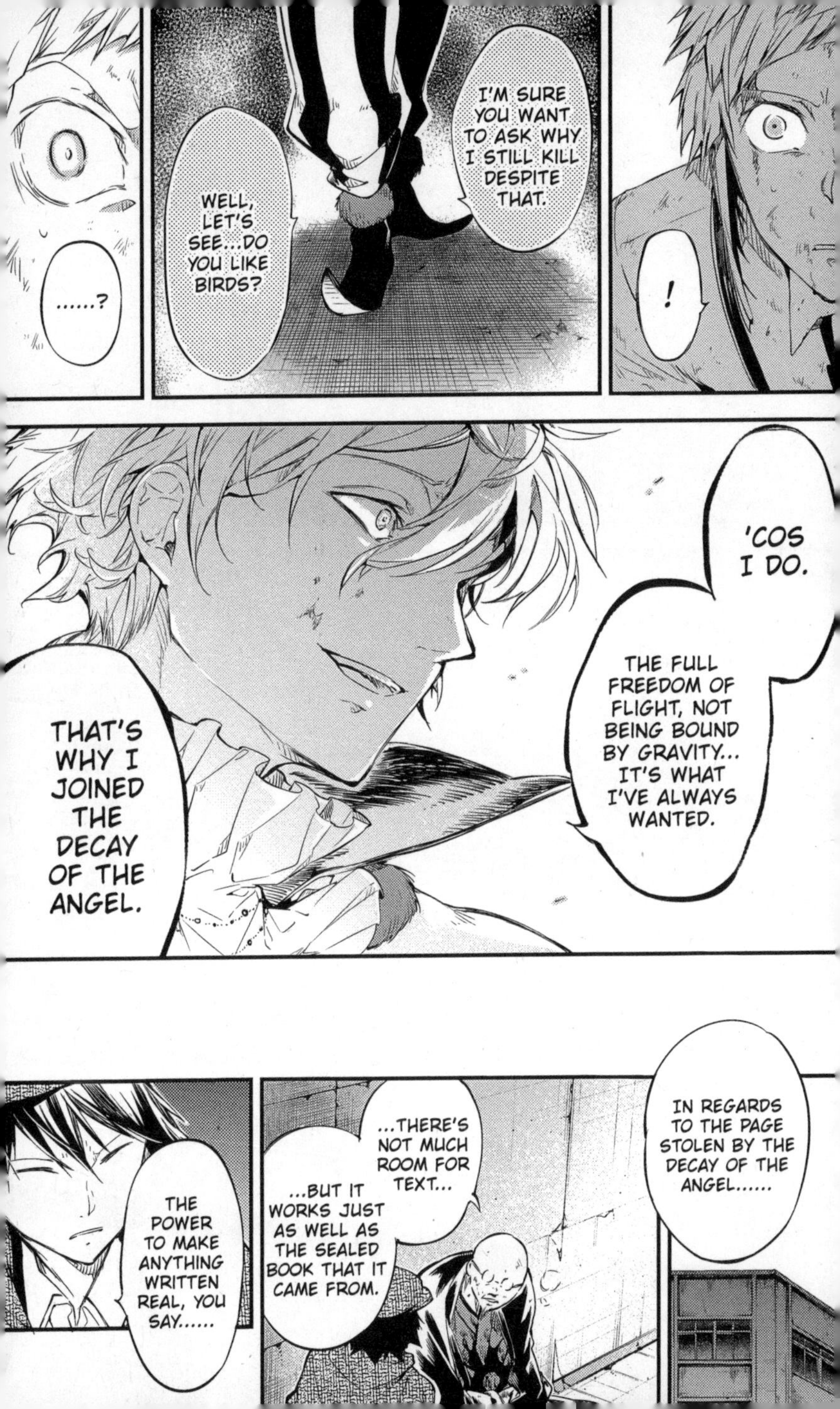
!
I'M SURE YOU WANT TO ASK WHY I STILL KILL DESPITE THAT.
WELL, LET'S SEE...DO YOU LIKE BIRDS?
......?
'COS I DO.
THE FULL FREEDOM OF FLIGHT, NOT BEING BOUND BY GRAVITY... IT'S WHAT I'VE ALWAYS WANTED.
THAT'S WHY I JOINED THE DECAY OF THE ANGEL.
IN REGARDS TO THE PAGE STOLEN BY THE DECAY OF THE ANGEL......
...THERE'S NOT MUCH ROOM FOR TEXT...
...BUT IT WORKS JUST AS WELL AS THE SEALED BOOK THAT IT CAME FROM.
THE POWER TO MAKE ANYTHING WRITTEN REAL, YOU SAY......

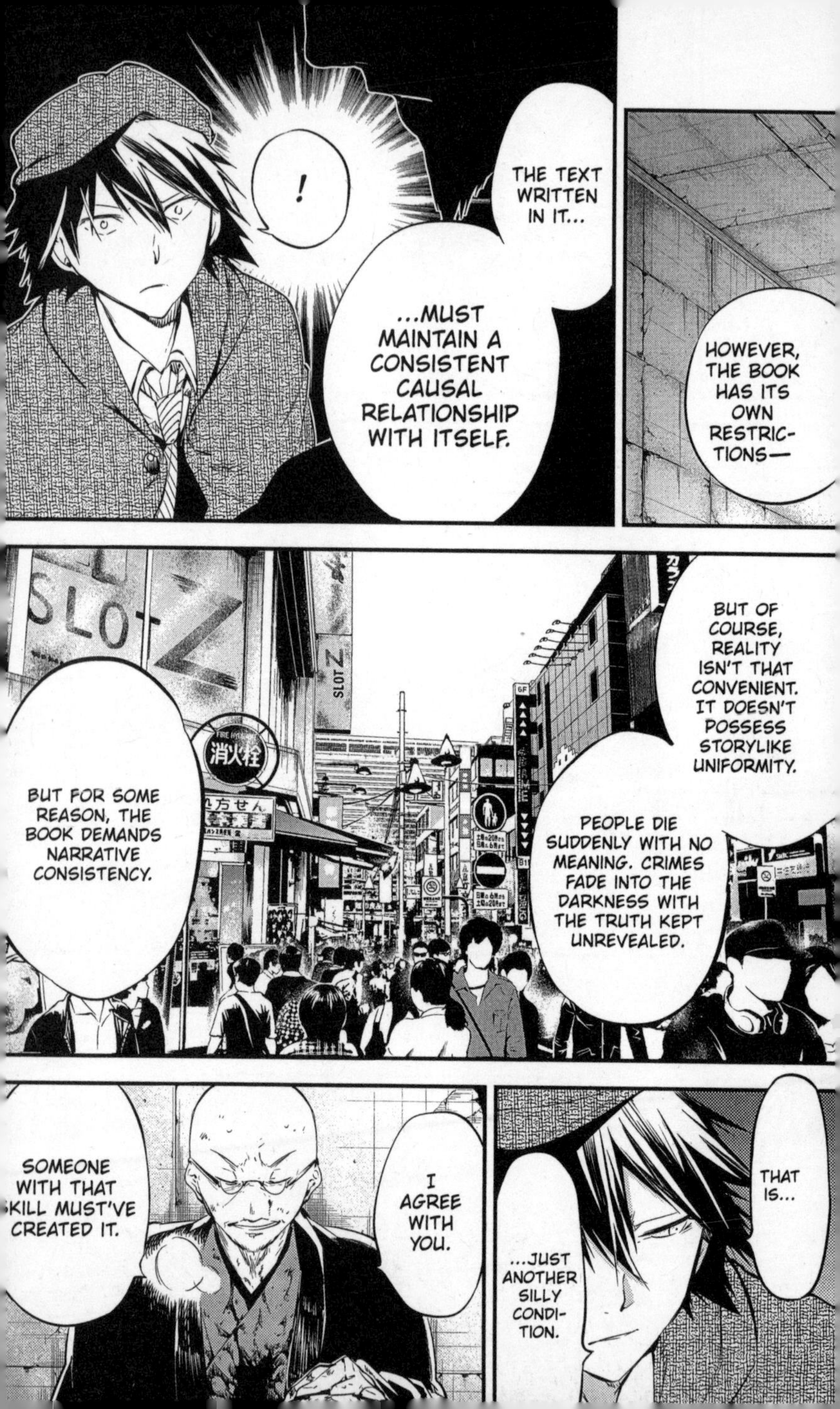
HOWEVER, THE BOOK HAS ITS OWN RESTRIC-TIONS—
THE TEXT WRITTEN IN IT...
!
...MUST MAINTAIN A CONSISTENT CAUSAL RELATIONSHIP WITH ITSELF.
BUT OF COURSE, REALITY ISN'T THAT CONVENIENT. IT DOESN'T POSSESS STORYLIKE UNIFORMITY.
PEOPLE DIE SUDDENLY WITH NO MEANING. CRIMES FADE INTO THE DARKNESS WITH THE TRUTH KEPT UNREVEALED.
BUT FOR SOME REASON, THE BOOK DEMANDS NARRATIVE CONSISTENCY.
SLOT
消火栓
THAT IS...
...JUST ANOTHER SILLY CONDI-TION.
I AGREE WITH YOU.
SOMEONE WITH THAT SKILL MUST'VE CREATED IT.

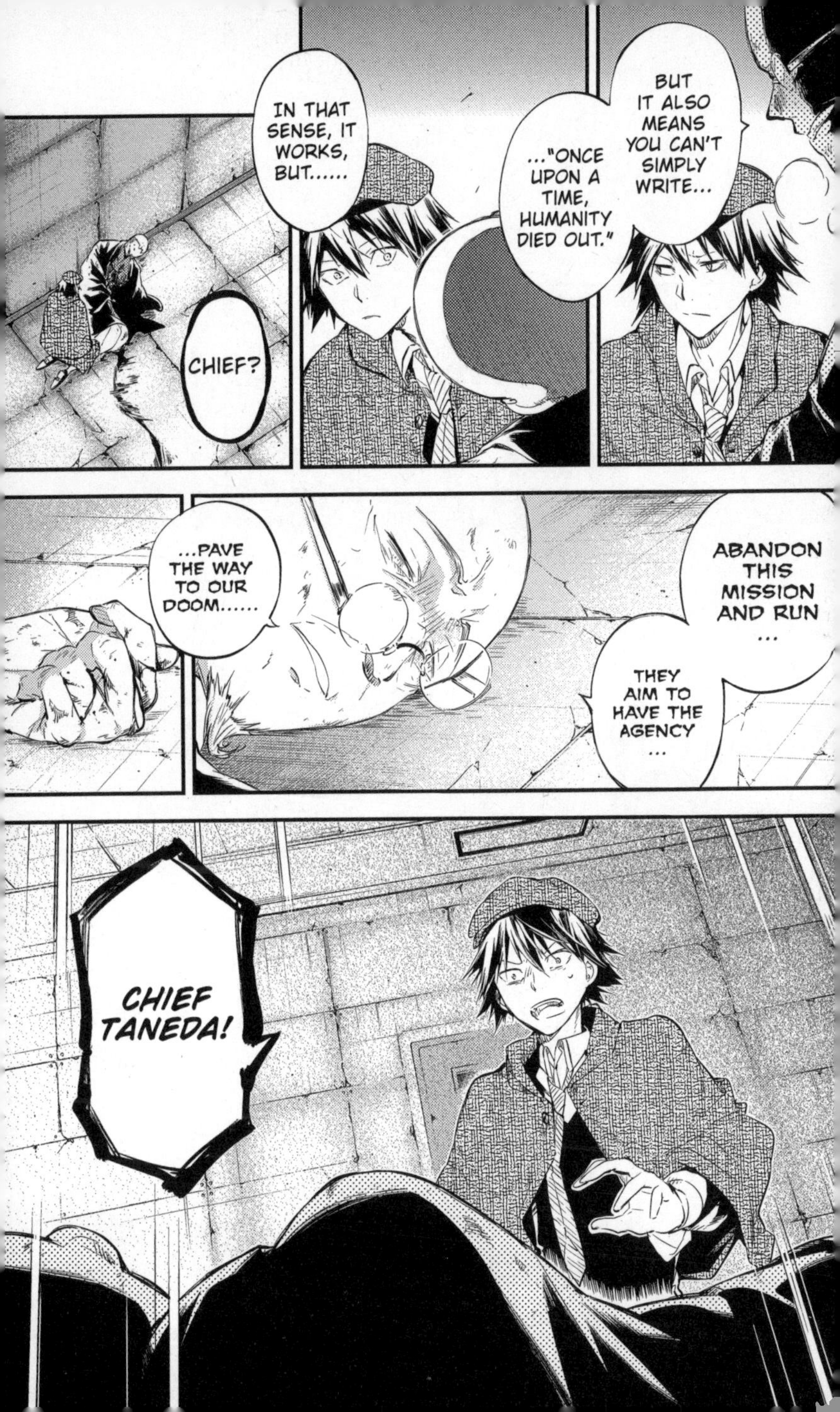
BUT IT ALSO MEANS YOU CAN'T SIMPLY WRITE...
..."ONCE UPON A TIME, HUMANITY DIED OUT."
IN THAT SENSE, IT WORKS, BUT......
CHIEF?
ABANDON THIS MISSION AND RUN ...
THEY AIM TO HAVE THE AGENCY ...
...PAVE THE WAY TO OUR DOOM......
CHIEF TANEDA!

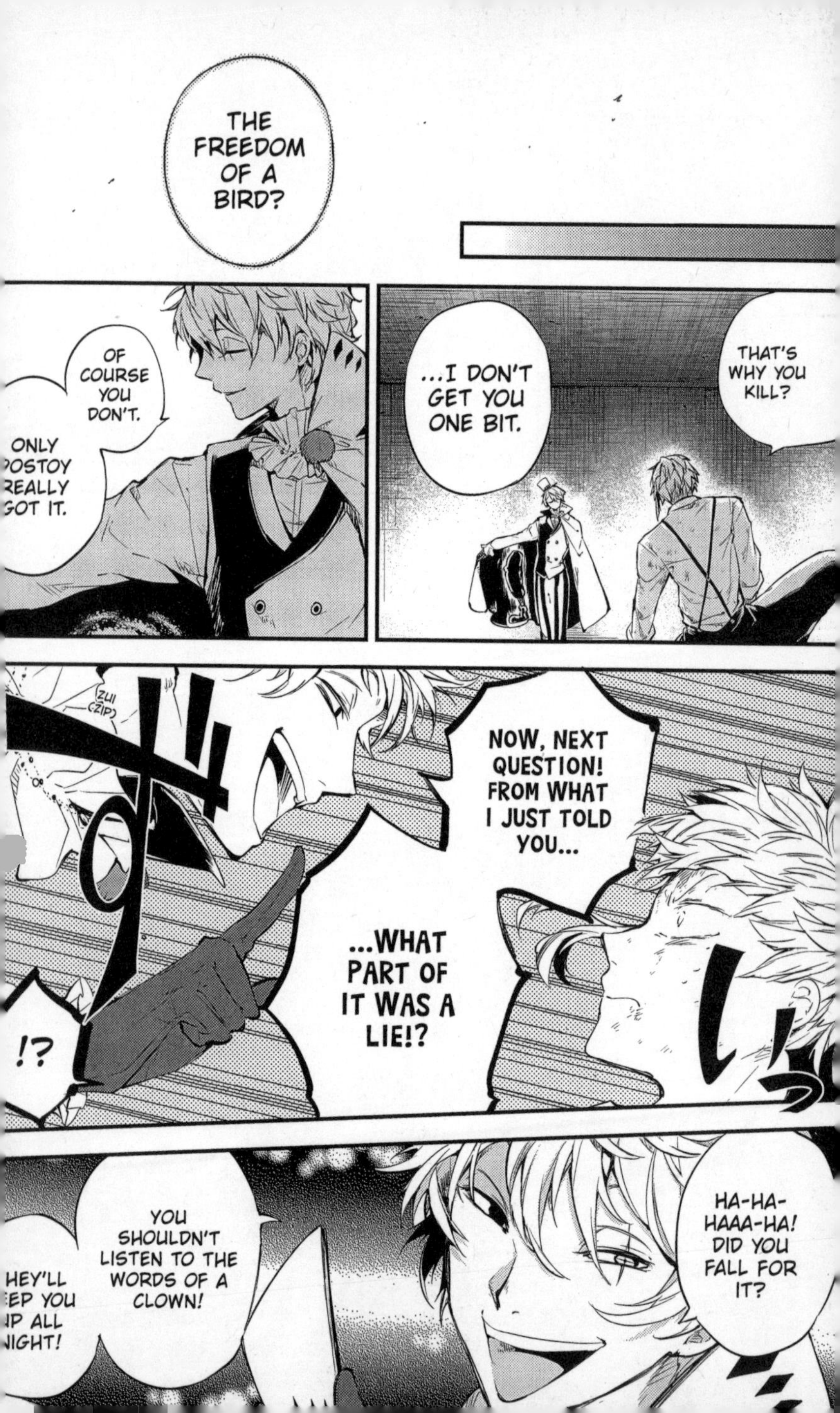
THE FREEDOM OF A BIRD?
THAT'S WHY YOU KILL?
...I DON'T GET YOU ONE BIT.
OF COURSE YOU DON'T.
ONLY OSTOY REALLY GOT IT.
NOW, NEXT QUESTION! FROM WHAT I JUST TOLD YOU...
...WHAT PART OF IT WAS A LIE!?
ZUI (ZIP)
!?
HA-HA-HAAA-HA! DID YOU FALL FOR IT?
YOU SHOULDN'T LISTEN TO THE WORDS OF A CLOWN!
HEY'LL EEP YOU P ALL NIGHT!

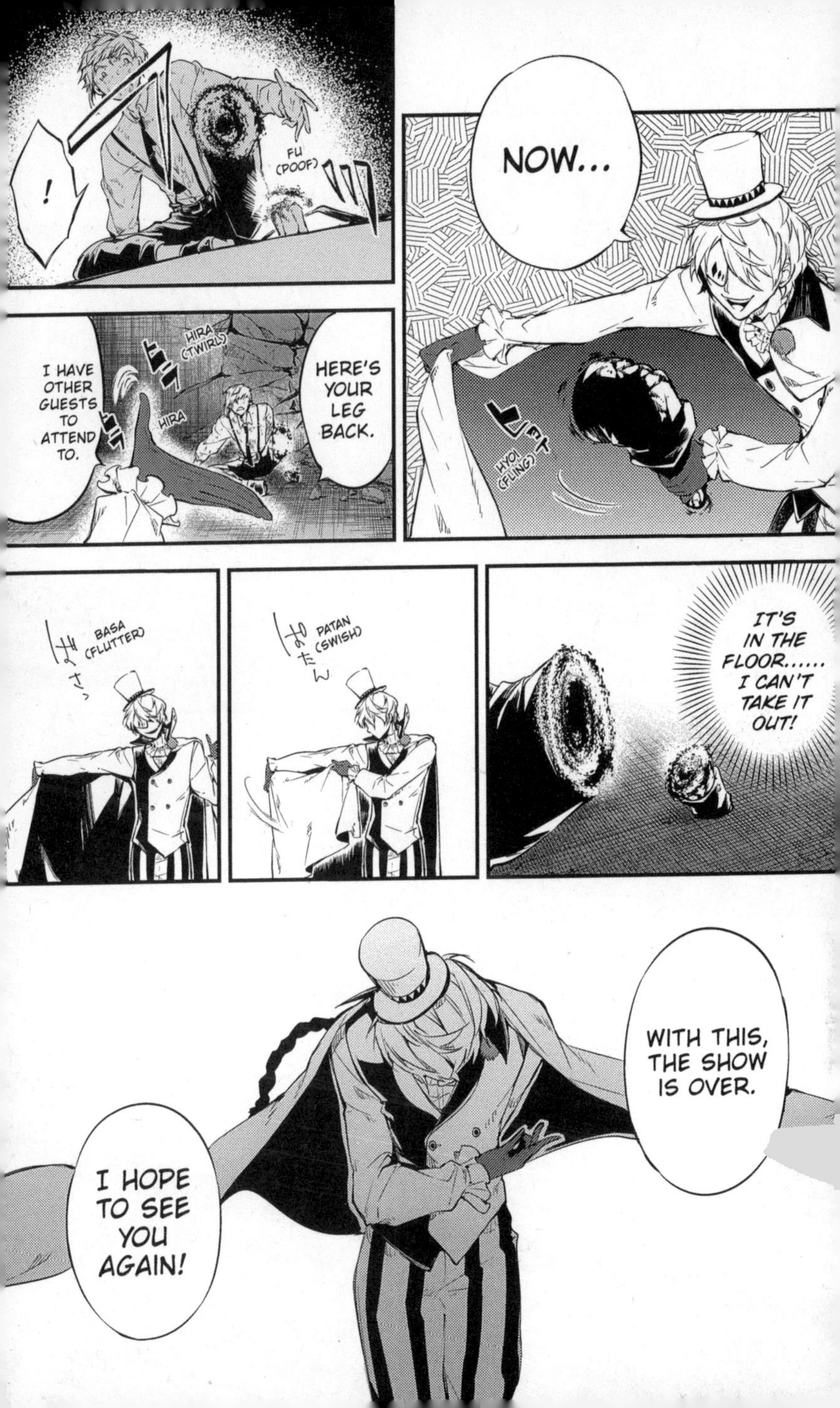
NOW...
HYOI (FLING)
!
FU (POOF)
HERE'S YOUR LEG BACK.
HIRA (TWIRL)
HIRA
I HAVE OTHER GUESTS TO ATTEND TO.
IT'S IN THE FLOOR...... I CAN'T TAKE IT OUT!
ぱたん
PATAN (SWISH)
ぱさっ
BASA (FLUTTER)
WITH THIS, THE SHOW IS OVER.
I HOPE TO SEE YOU AGAIN!

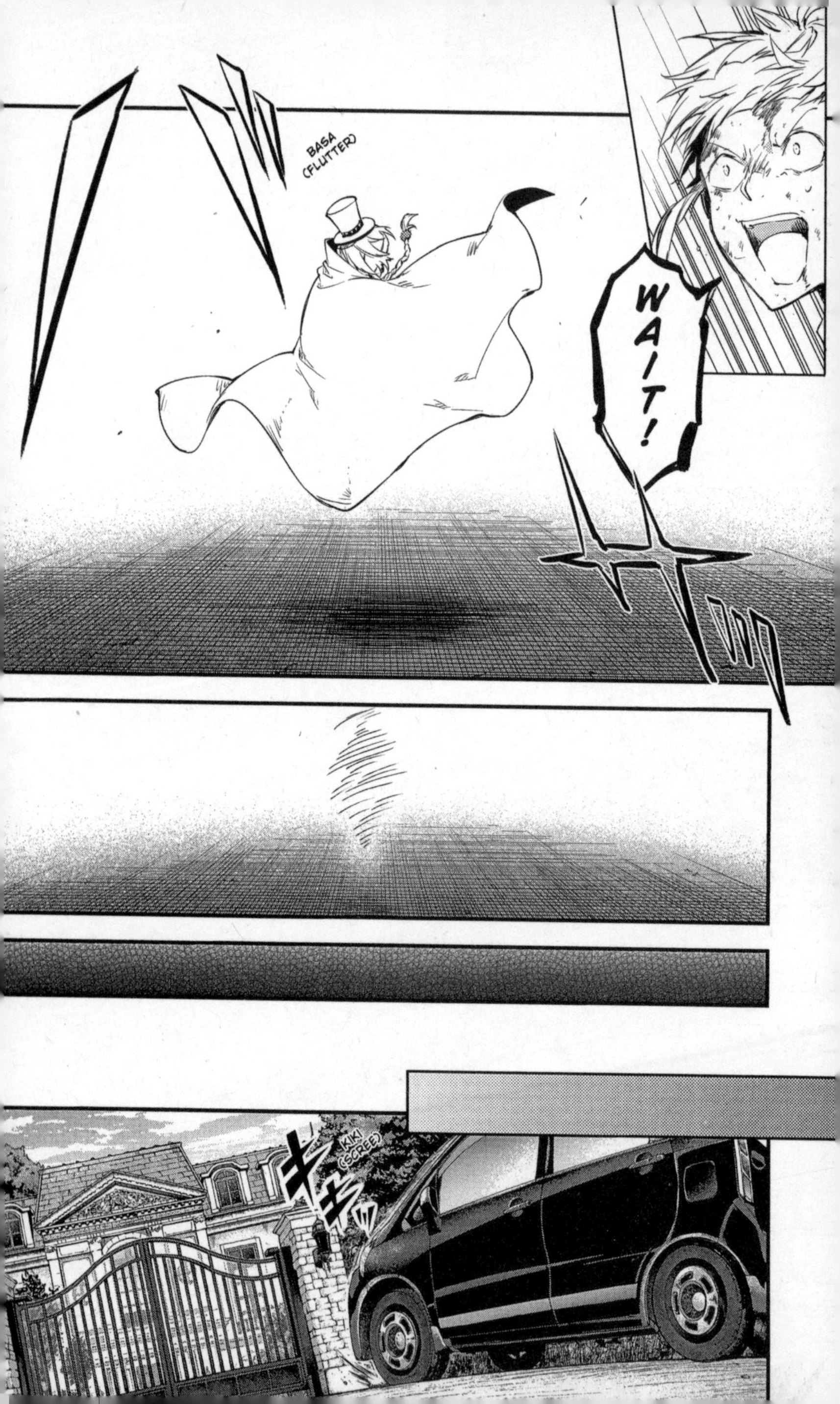
WAIT!
BASA (FLUTTER)
KIKI (SCREE)

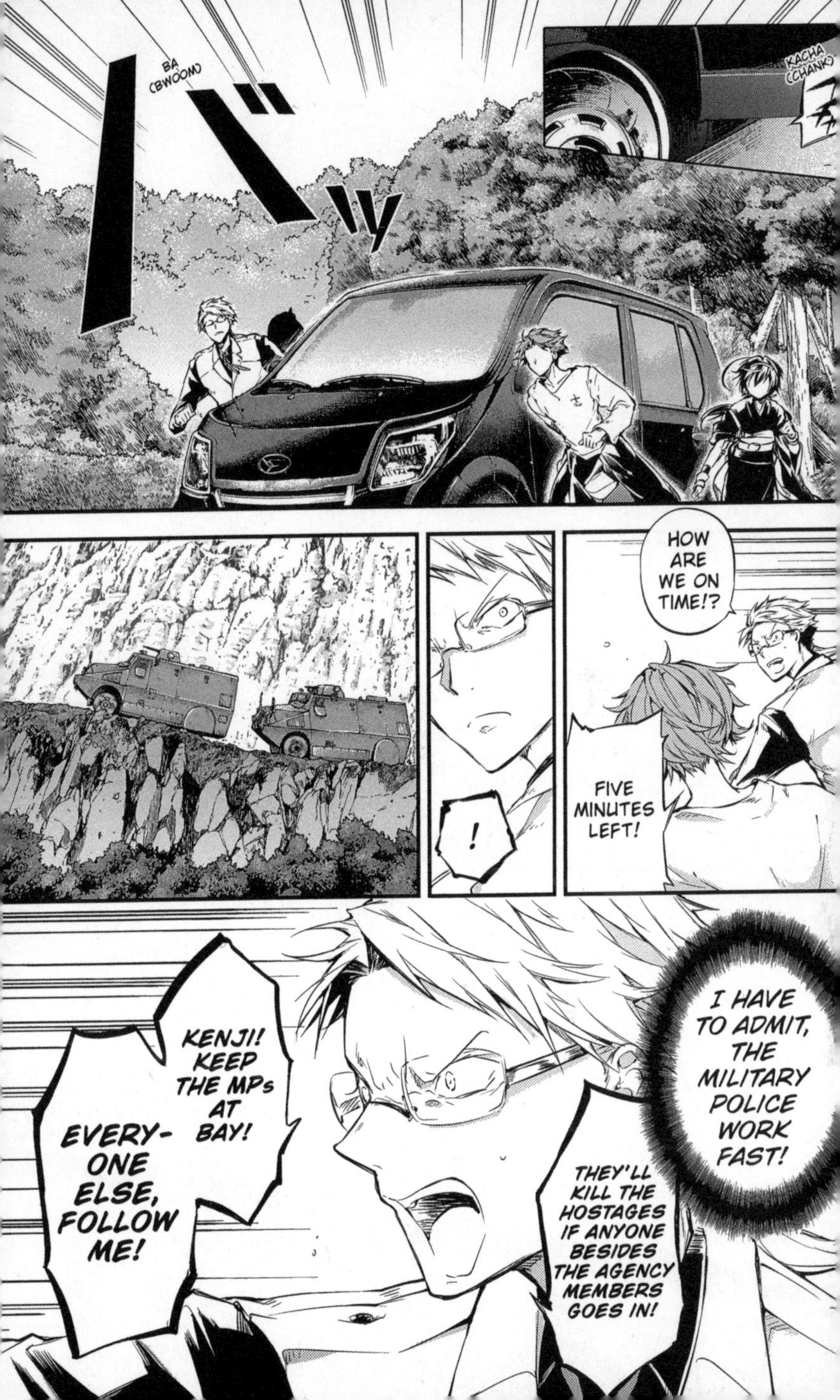
KACHA (CHANK)
BA (BWOOM)
HOW ARE WE ON TIME!?
FIVE MINUTES LEFT!
!
I HAVE TO ADMIT, THE MILITARY POLICE WORK FAST!
THEY'LL KILL THE HOSTAGES IF ANYONE BESIDES THE AGENCY MEMBERS GOES IN!
KENJI! KEEP THE MPs AT BAY!
EVERY-ONE ELSE, FOLLOW ME!

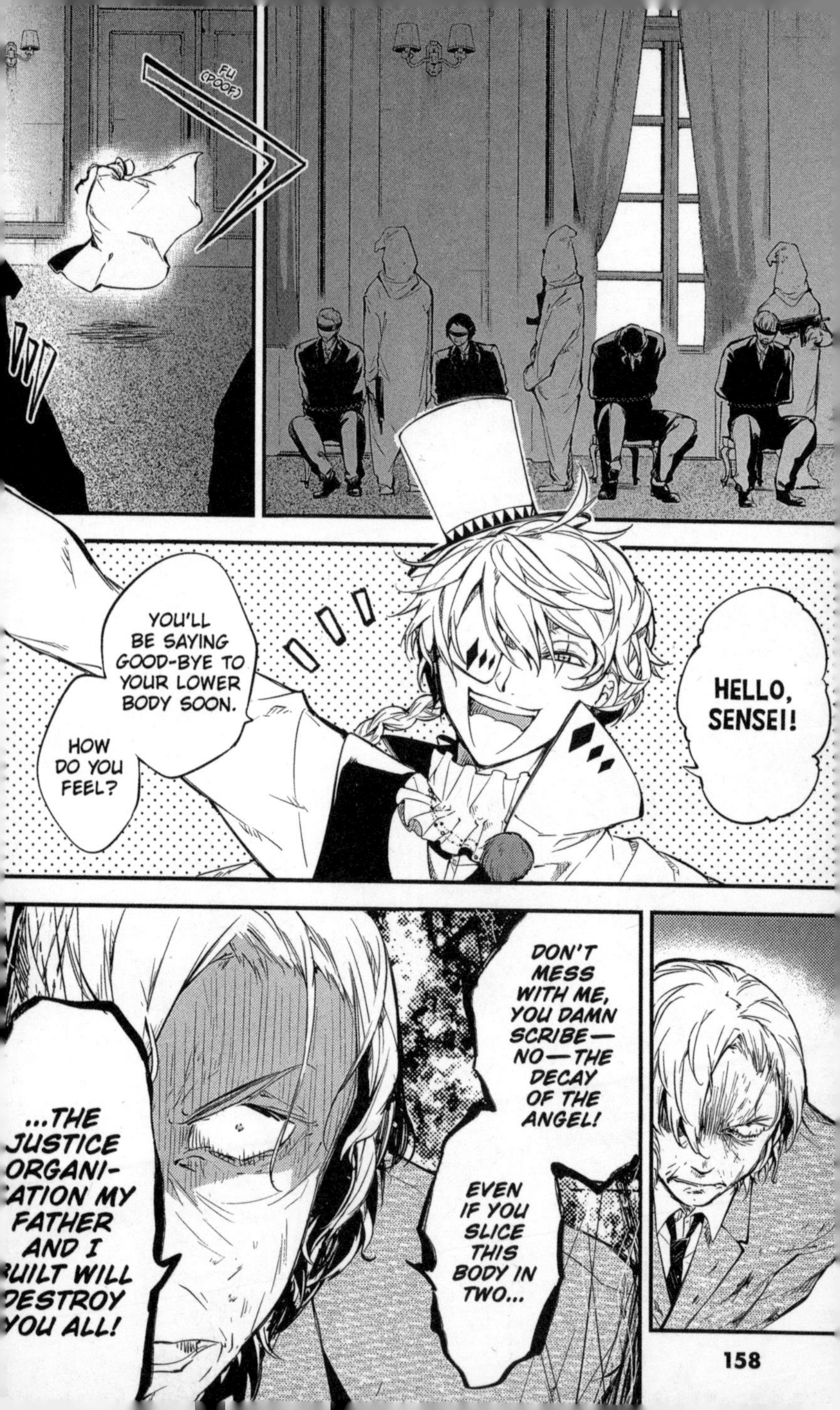
FU (POOF)
HELLO, SENSEI!
YOU'LL BE SAYING GOOD-BYE TO YOUR LOWER BODY SOON.
HOW DO YOU FEEL?
DON'T MESS WITH ME, YOU DAMN SCRIBE—NO—THE DECAY OF THE ANGEL!
EVEN IF YOU SLICE THIS BODY IN TWO...
...THE JUSTICE ORGANI-
ATION MY FATHER AND I
UILT WILL
ESTROY YOU ALL!

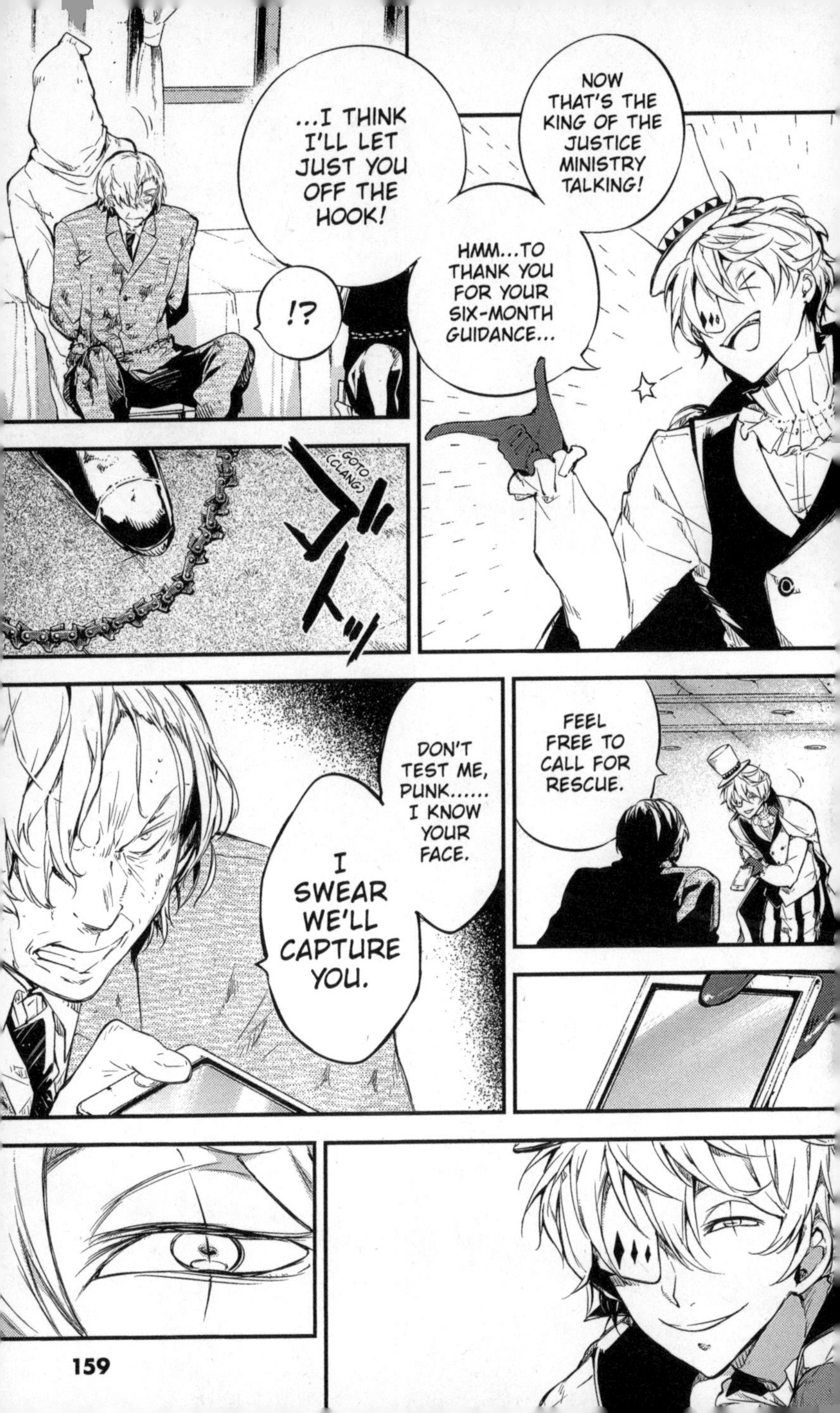
NOW THAT'S THE KING OF THE JUSTICE MINISTRY TALKING!
HMM...TO THANK YOU FOR YOUR SIX-MONTH GUIDANCE...
...I THINK I'LL LET JUST YOU OFF THE HOOK!
!?
ゴトッ
GOTO (CLANG)
FEEL FREE TO CALL FOR RESCUE.
DON'T TEST ME, PUNK...... I KNOW YOUR FACE.
I SWEAR WE'LL CAPTURE YOU.

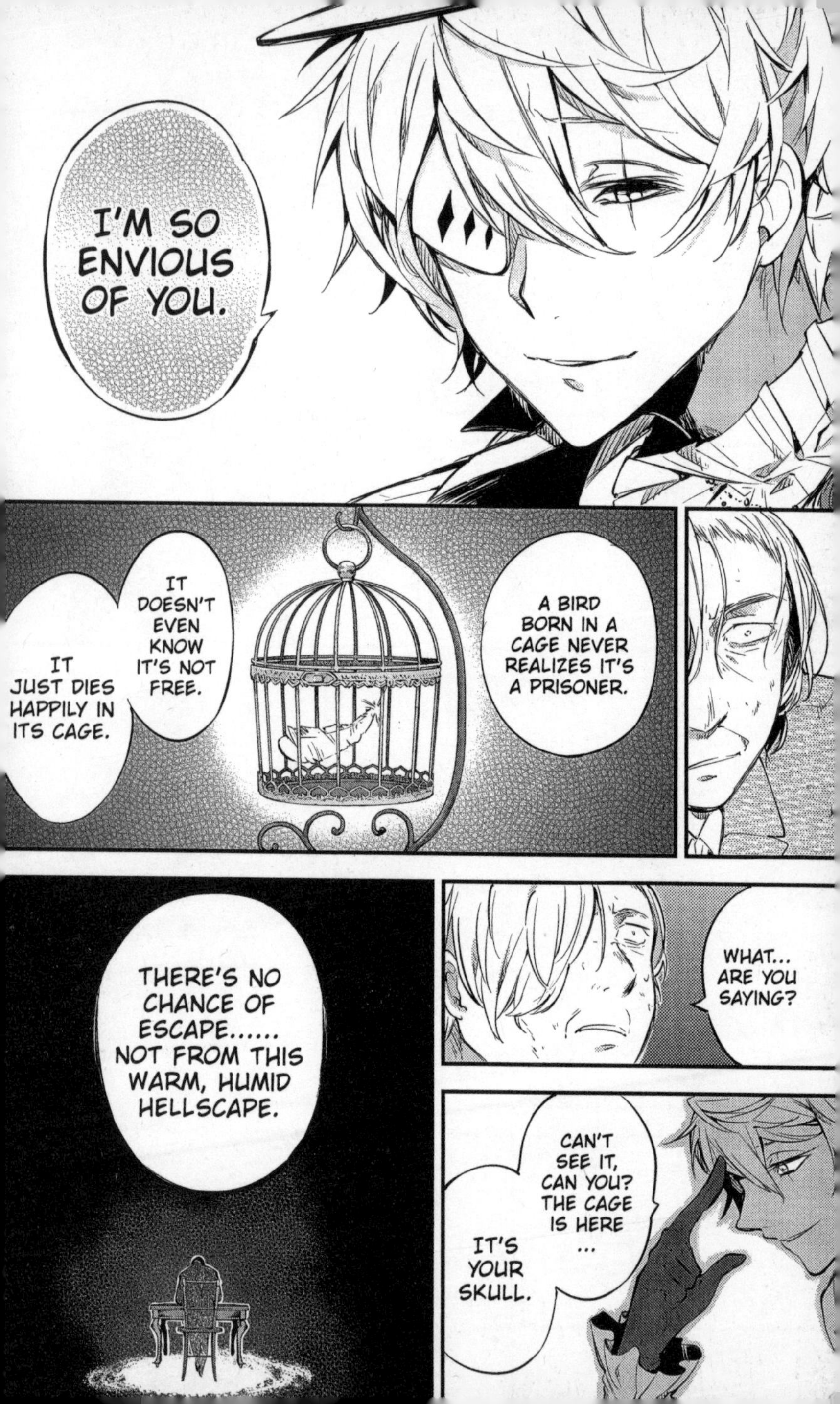
I'M SO ENVIOUS OF YOU.
A BIRD BORN IN A CAGE NEVER REALIZES IT'S A PRISONER.
IT DOESN'T EVEN KNOW IT'S NOT FREE.
IT JUST DIES HAPPILY IN ITS CAGE.
WHAT... ARE YOU SAYING?
CAN'T SEE IT, CAN YOU? THE CAGE IS HERE ...
IT'S YOUR SKULL.
THERE'S NO CHANCE OF ESCAPE...... NOT FROM THIS WARM, HUMID HELLSCAPE.

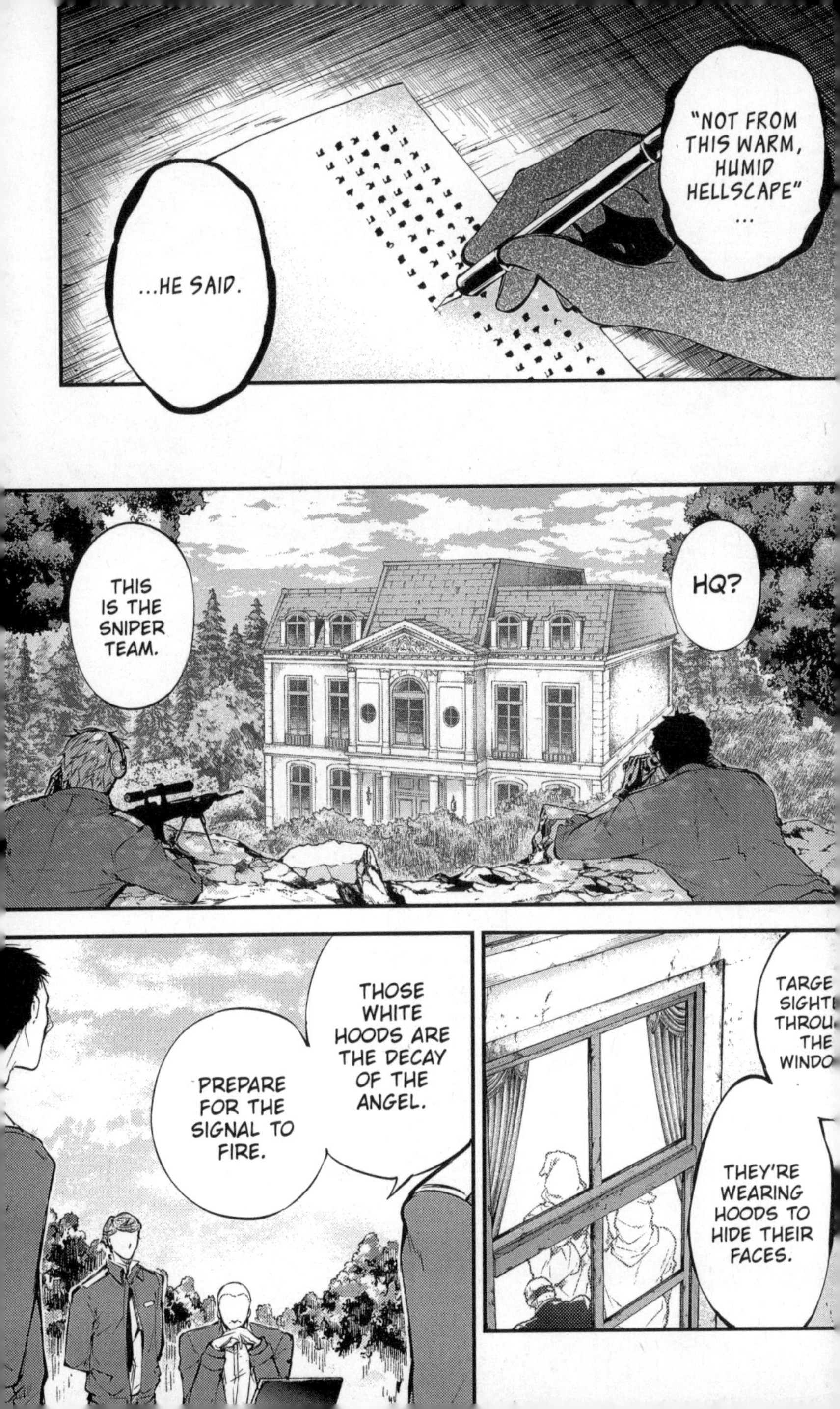
"NOT FROM THIS WARM, HUMID HELLSCAPE"...
...HE SAID.
HQ?
THIS IS THE SNIPER TEAM.
TARGE SIGHT THROU THE WINDO
THEY'RE WEARING HOODS TO HIDE THEIR FACES.
THOSE WHITE HOODS ARE THE DECAY OF THE ANGEL.
PREPARE FOR THE SIGNAL TO FIRE.

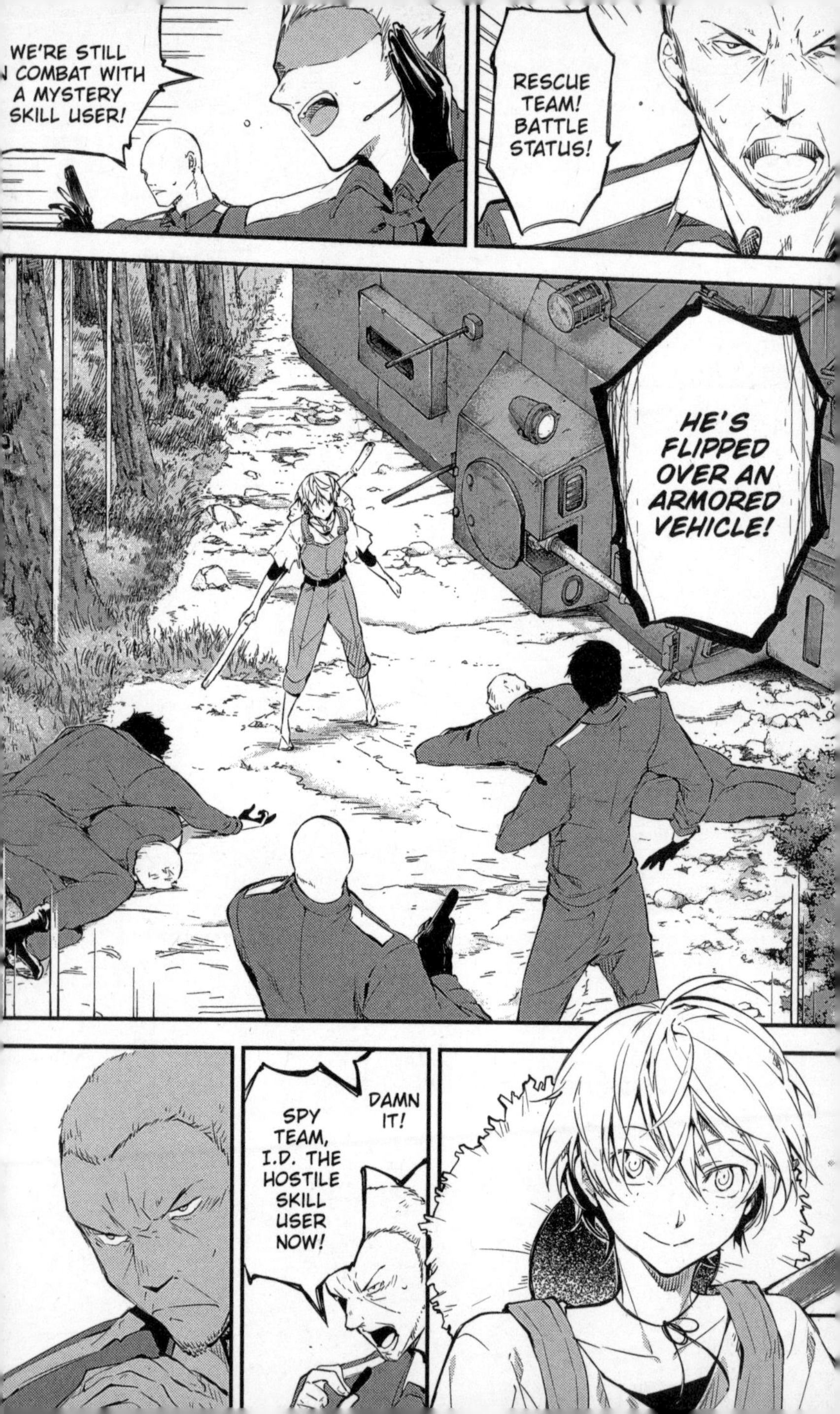
RESCUE TEAM! BATTLE STATUS!
WE'RE STILL IN COMBAT WITH A MYSTERY SKILL USER!
HE'S FLIPPED OVER AN ARMORED VEHICLE!
DAMN IT!
SPY TEAM, I.D. THE HOSTILE SKILL USER NOW!

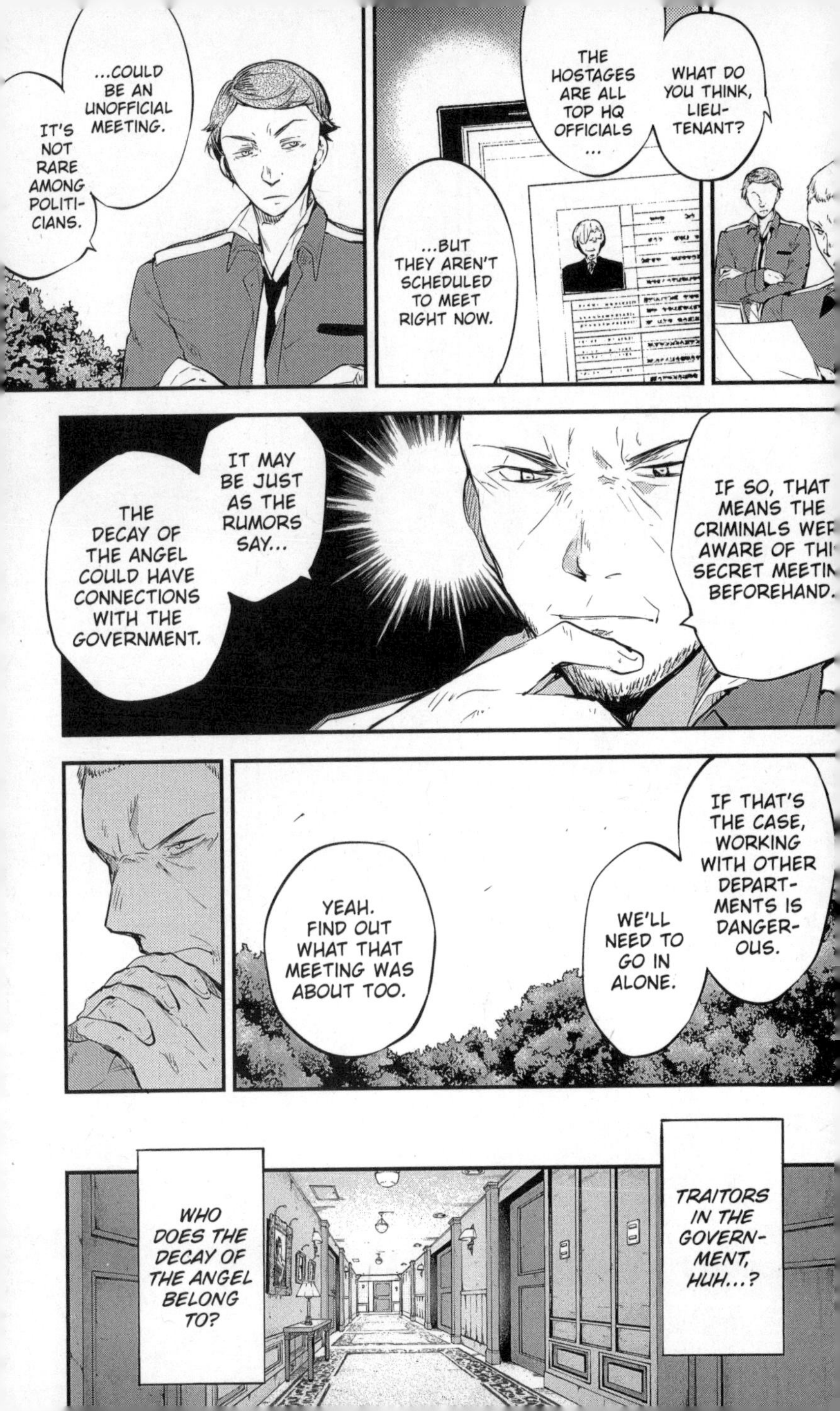
WHAT DO YOU THINK, LIEUTENANT?
THE HOSTAGES ARE ALL TOP HQ OFFICIALS...
...BUT THEY AREN'T SCHEDULED TO MEET RIGHT NOW.
...COULD BE AN UNOFFICIAL MEETING.
IT'S NOT RARE AMONG POLITICIANS.
IF SO, THAT MEANS THE CRIMINALS WER AWARE OF THI SECRET MEETIN BEFOREHAND.
IT MAY BE JUST AS THE RUMORS SAY...
THE DECAY OF THE ANGEL COULD HAVE CONNECTIONS WITH THE GOVERNMENT.
IF THAT'S THE CASE, WORKING WITH OTHER DEPARTMENTS IS DANGEROUS.
WE'LL NEED TO GO IN ALONE.
YEAH. FIND OUT WHAT THAT MEETING WAS ABOUT TOO.
TRAITORS IN THE GOVERNMENT, HUH...?
WHO DOES THE DECAY OF THE ANGEL BELONG TO?

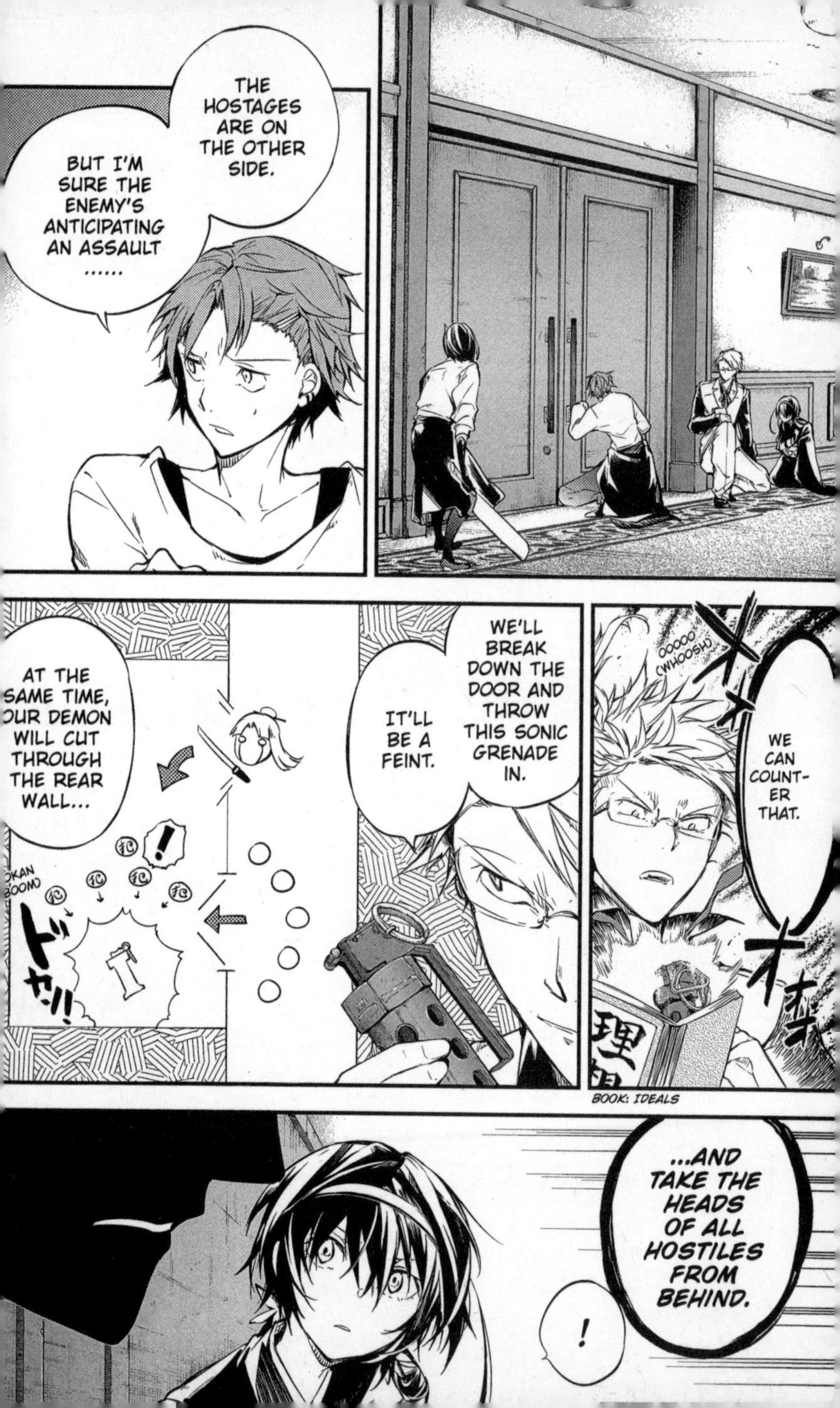
THE HOSTAGES ARE ON THE OTHER SIDE.
BUT I'M SURE THE ENEMY'S ANTICIPATING AN ASSAULT ......
OOOOO (WHOOSH)
WE CAN COUNTER-ER THAT.
BOOK: IDEALS
WE'LL BREAK DOWN THE DOOR AND THROW THIS SONIC GRENADE IN.
IT'LL BE A FEINT.
AT THE SAME TIME, OUR DEMON WILL CUT THROUGH THE REAR WALL...
OKAN
BOOM
...AND TAKE THE HEADS OF ALL HOSTILES FROM BEHIND.
!

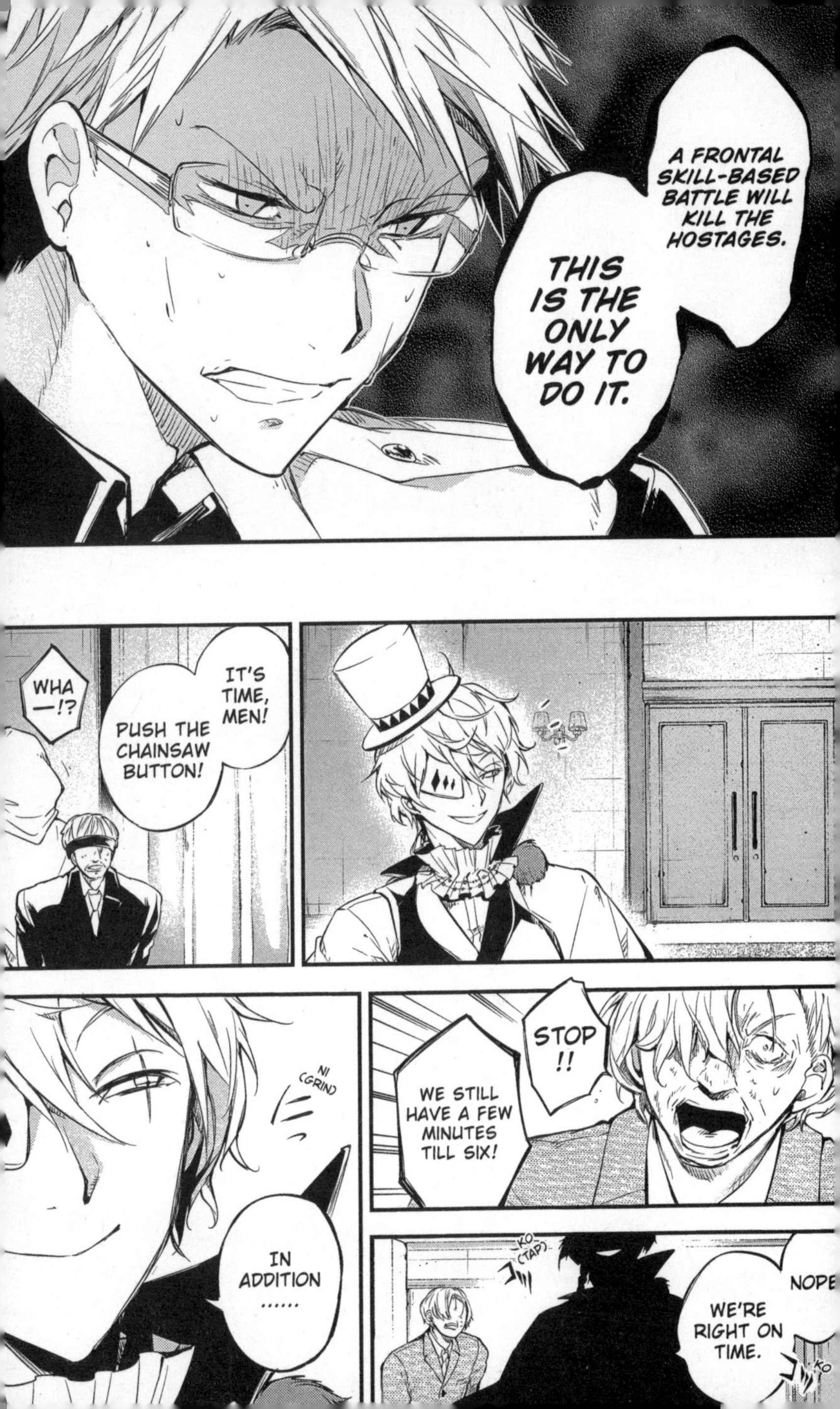
A FRONTAL SKILL-BASED BATTLE WILL KILL THE HOSTAGES.
THIS IS THE ONLY WAY TO DO IT.
IT'S TIME, MEN!
PUSH THE CHAINSAW BUTTON!
WHA—!?
STOP!!
WE STILL HAVE A FEW MINUTES TILL SIX!
KO (TAP)
NOPE
WE'RE RIGHT ON TIME.
KO
NI (GRIN)
IN ADDITION......

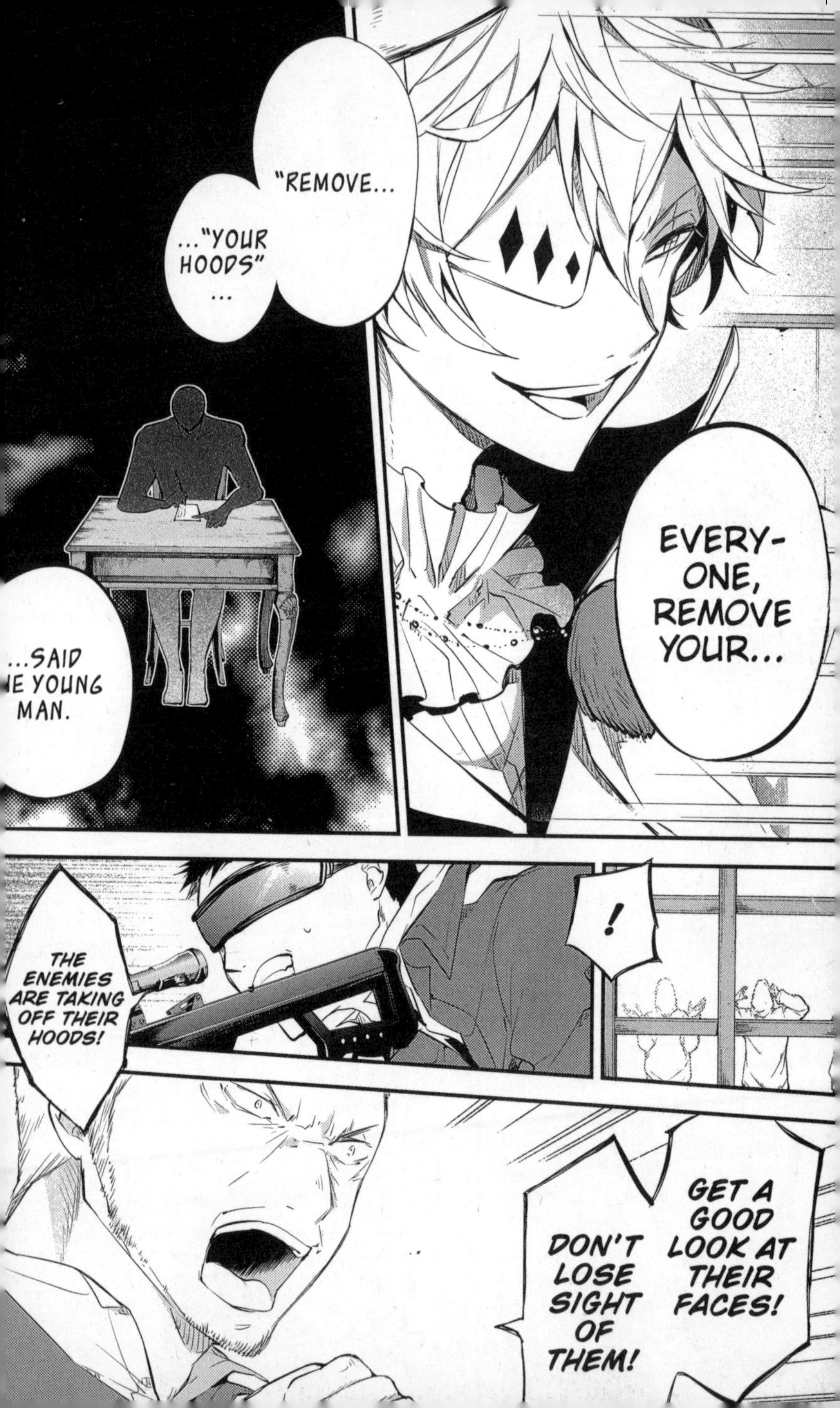
EVERY-ONE, REMOVE YOUR...
"REMOVE...
..."YOUR HOODS" ...
...SAID IE YOUNG MAN.
!
THE ENEMIES ARE TAKING OFF THEIR HOODS!
GET A GOOD LOOK AT THEIR FACES!
DON'T LOSE SIGHT OF THEM!

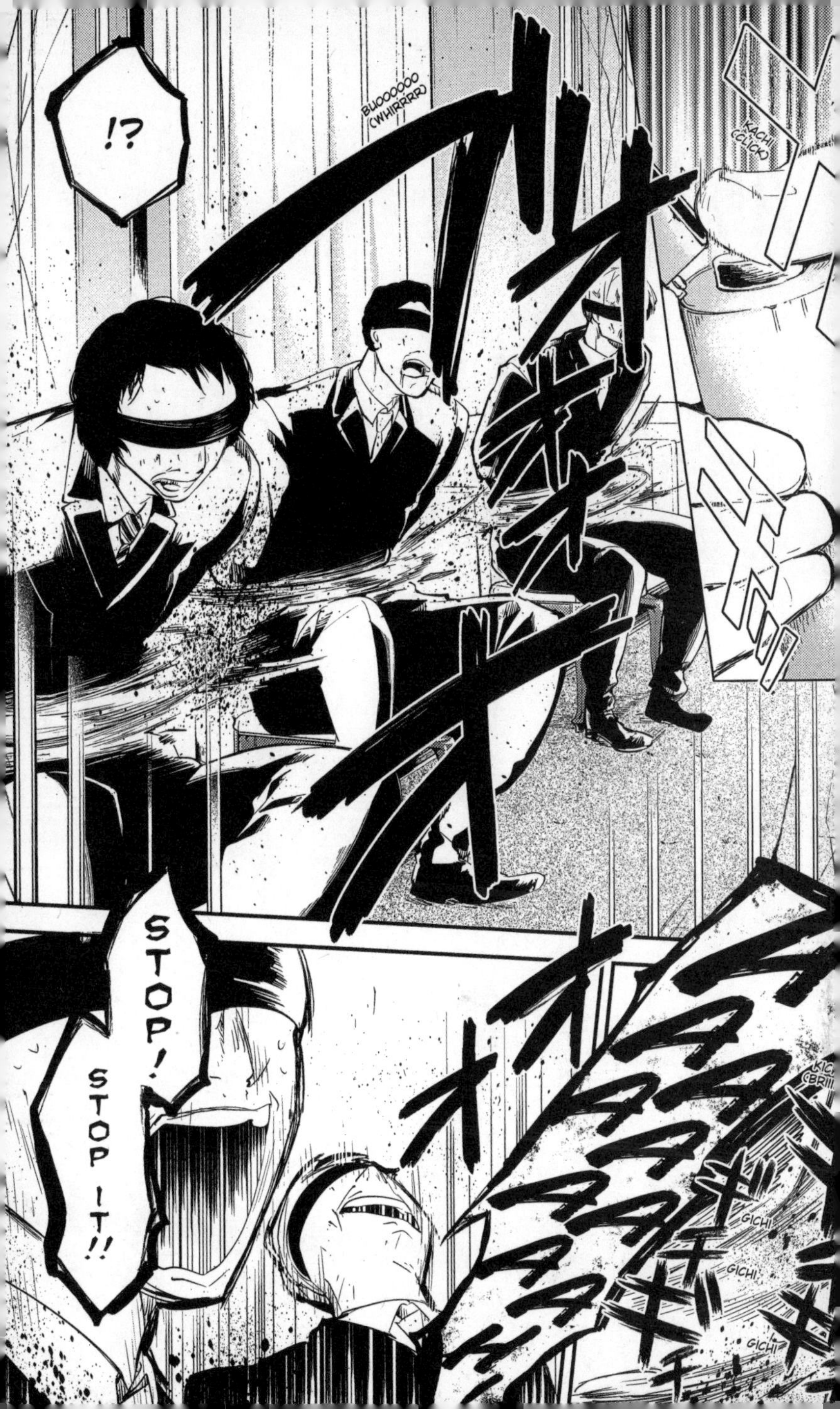
KACHI (CLICK)
BUOOOOOO (WHIRRRR)
!?
GICHI
GICHI
GICHI
STOP! STOP IT!!

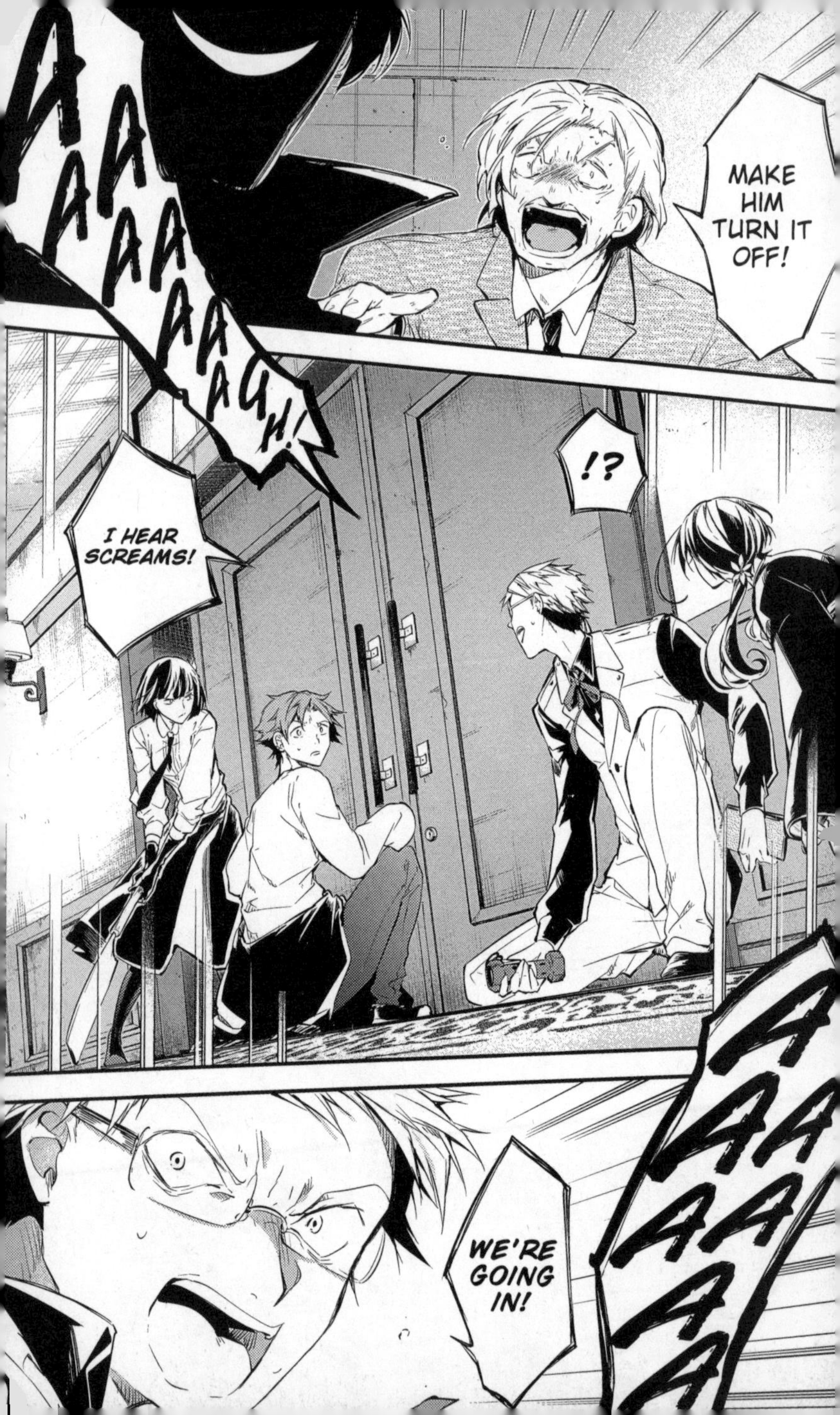
MAKE HIM TURN IT OFF!
AAAAAAAAAAAAGH!
!?
I HEAR SCREAMS!
AAAAAAAAA
WE'RE GOING IN!

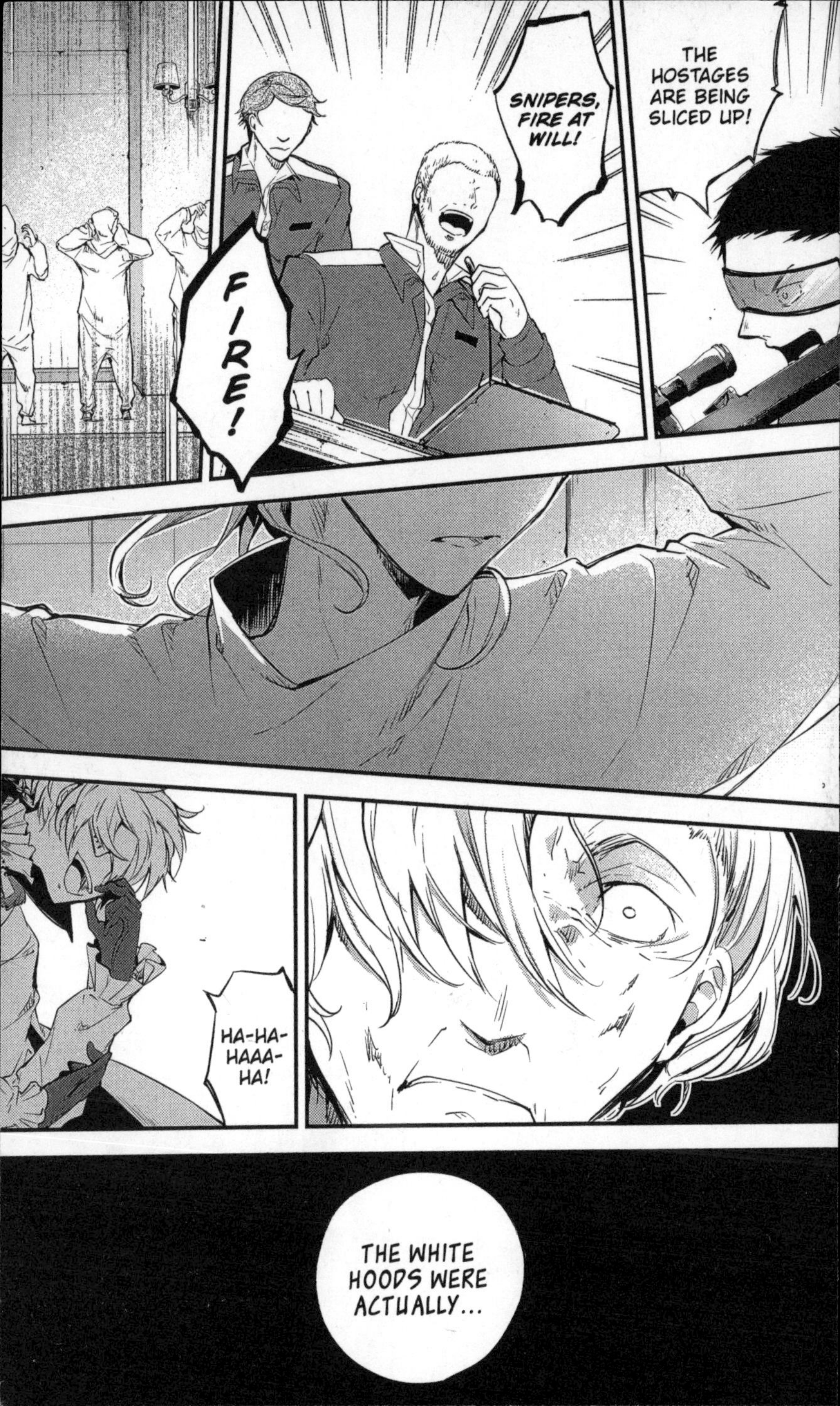
THE HOSTAGES ARE BEING SLICED UP!
SNIPERS, FIRE AT WILL!
FIRE!
HA-HA-HAAA-HA!
THE WHITE HOODS WERE ACTUALLY...

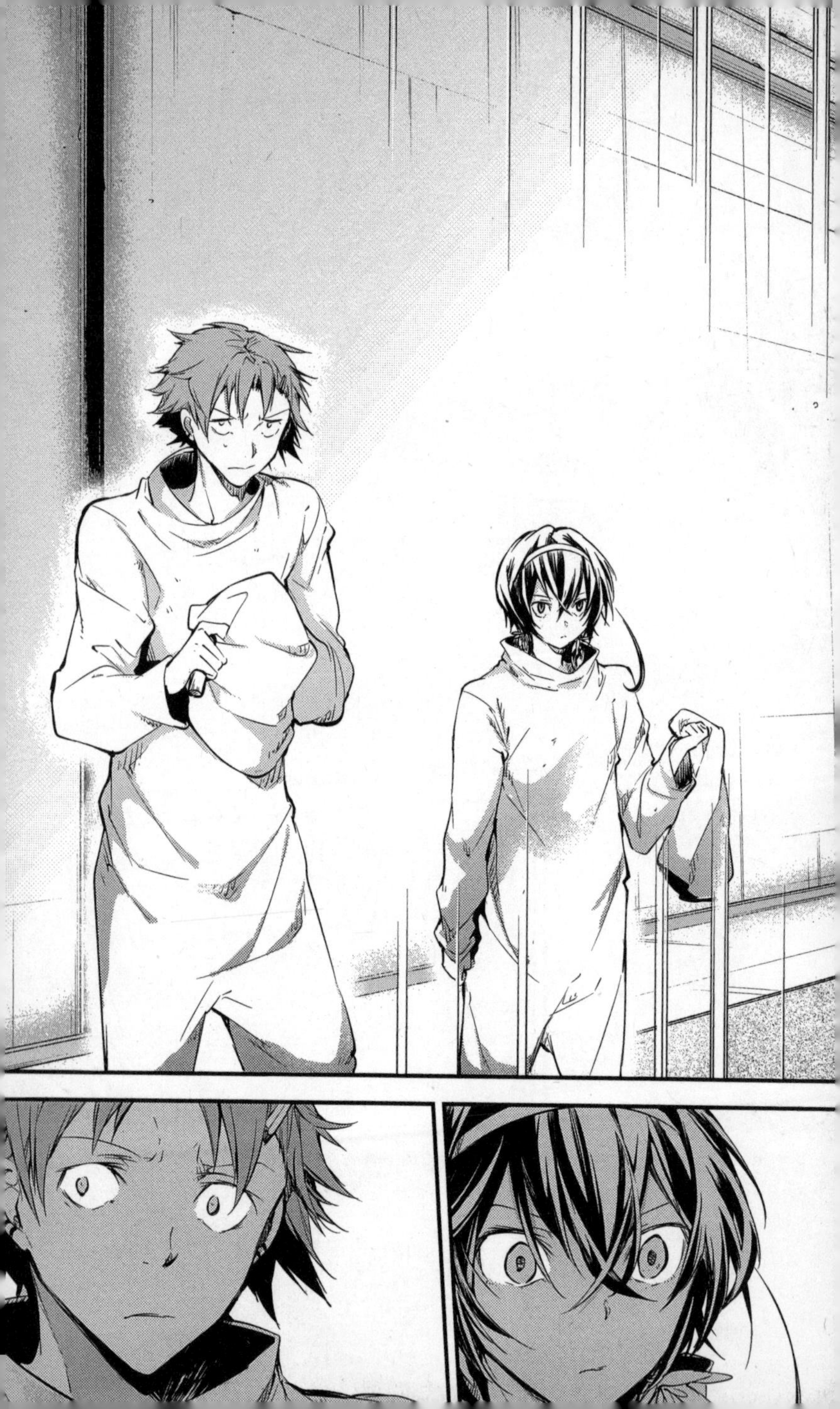

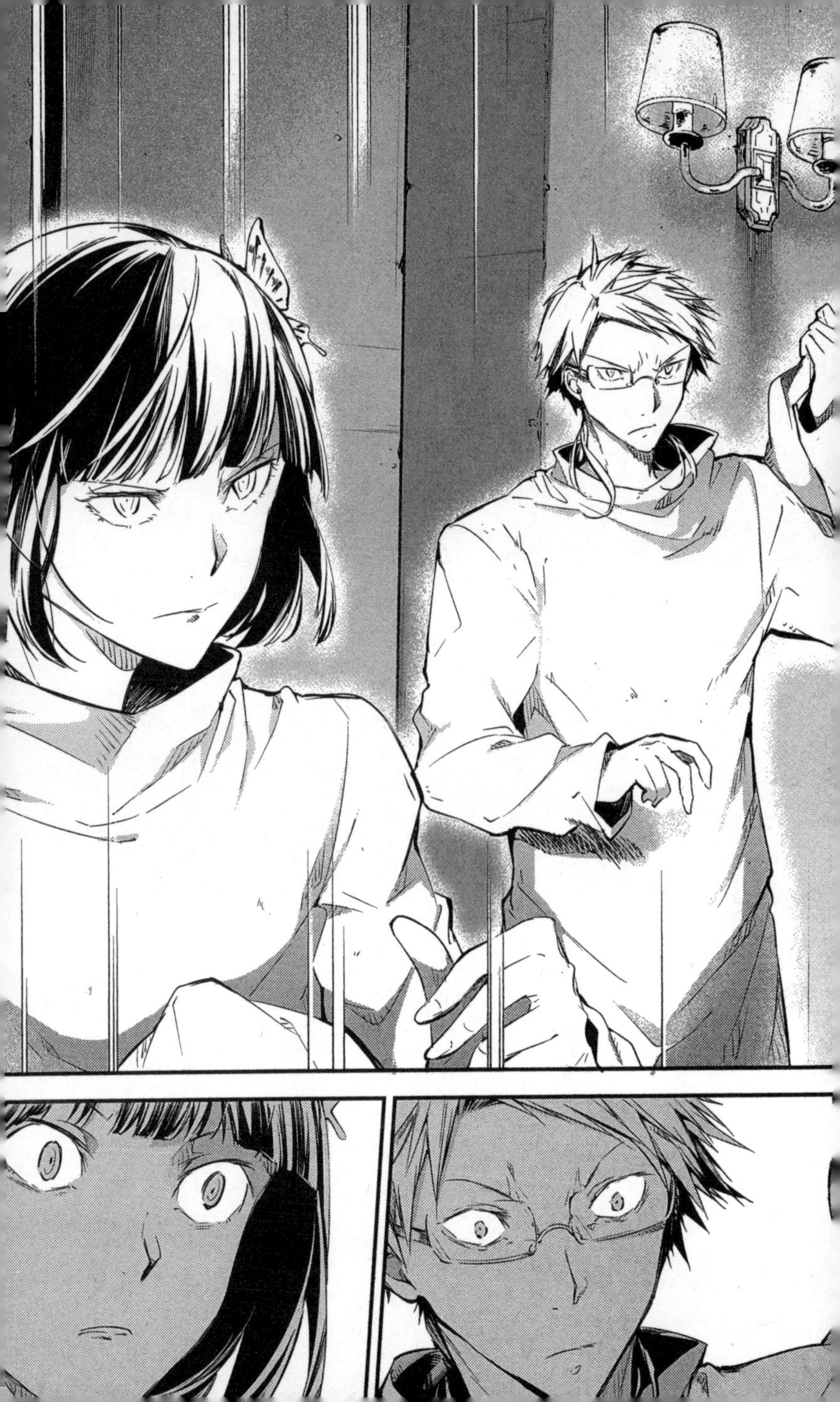

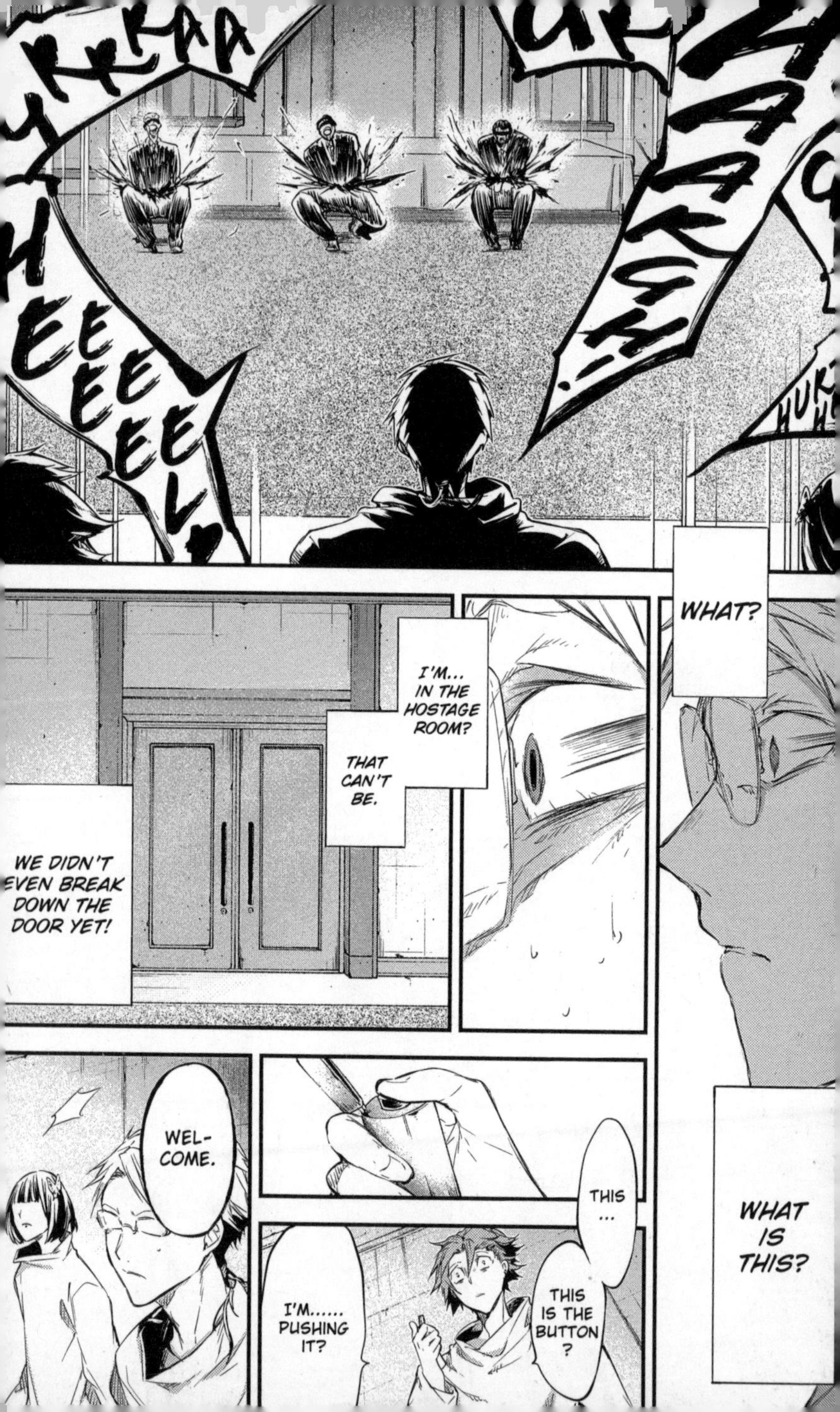
URAAAKGH!!
RRKAA
HEEEEEEL
WHAT?
I'M... IN THE HOSTAGE ROOM?
THAT CAN'T BE.
WE DIDN'T EVEN BREAK DOWN THE DOOR YET!
WHAT IS THIS?
THIS ...
THIS IS THE BUTTON?
I'M...... PUSHING IT?
WEL-COME.

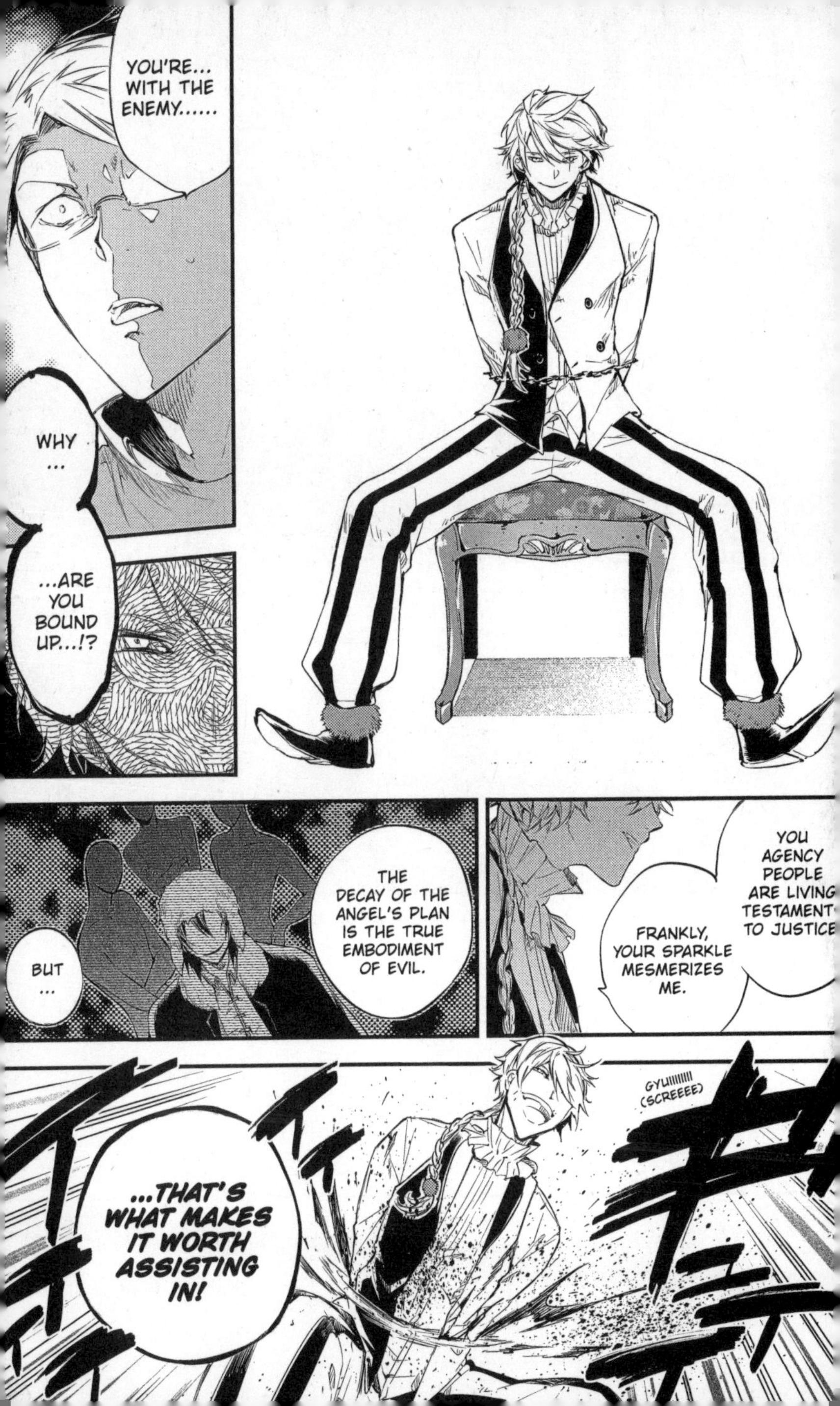
YOU'RE... WITH THE ENEMY......
WHY ...
...ARE YOU BOUND UP...!?
YOU AGENCY PEOPLE ARE LIVING TESTAMENT TO JUSTICE
FRANKLY, YOUR SPARKLE MESMERIZES ME.
THE DECAY OF THE ANGEL'S PLAN IS THE TRUE EMBODIMENT OF EVIL.
BUT ...
GYUIIIIIIIII (SCREEEEE)
...THAT'S WHAT MAKES IT WORTH ASSISTING IN!

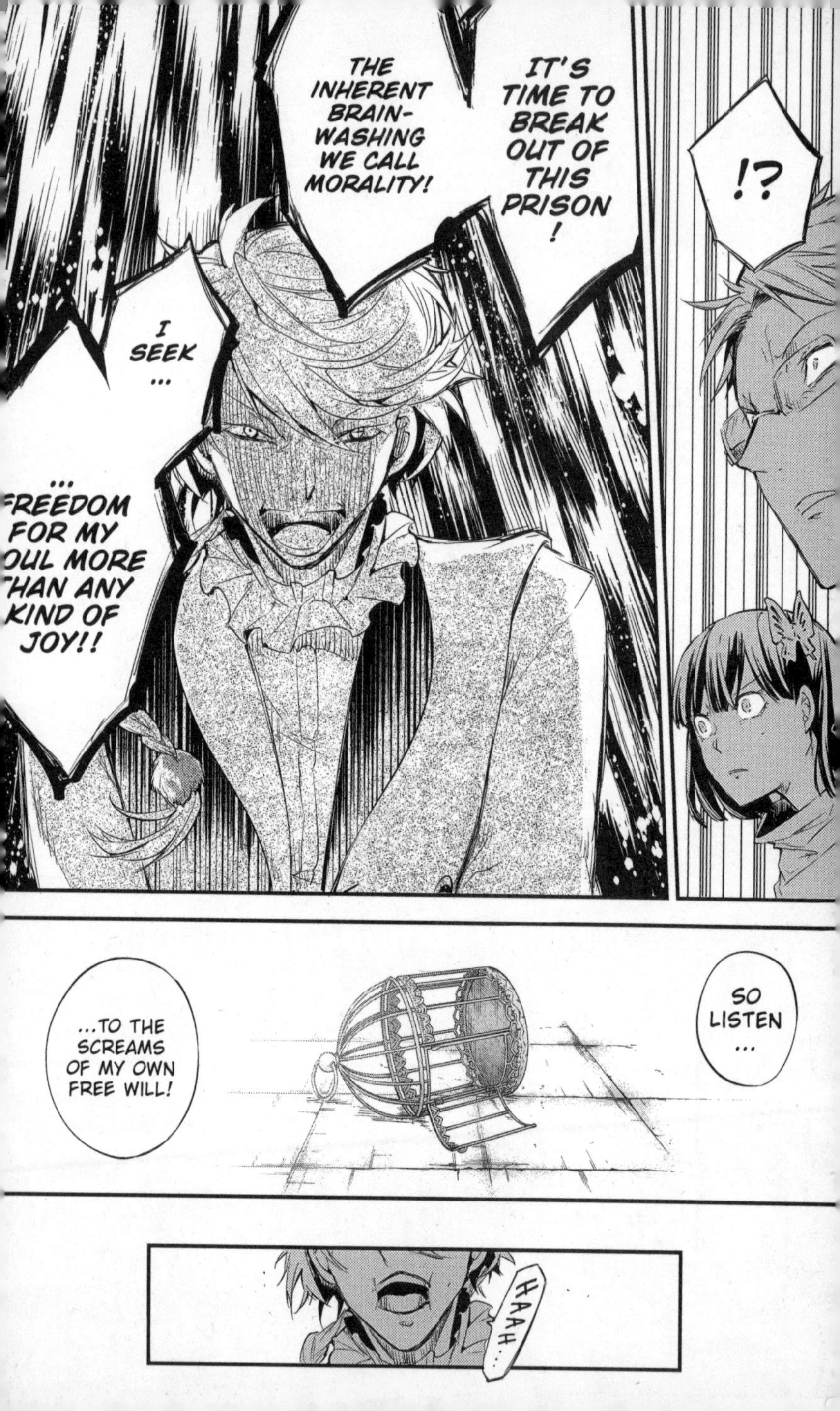
!?
IT'S TIME TO BREAK OUT OF THIS PRISON!
THE INHERENT BRAIN-WASHING WE CALL MORALITY!
I SEEK...
...FREEDOM FOR MY OUL MORE THAN ANY KIND OF JOY!!
SO LISTEN...
...TO THE SCREAMS OF MY OWN FREE WILL!
HAAH...

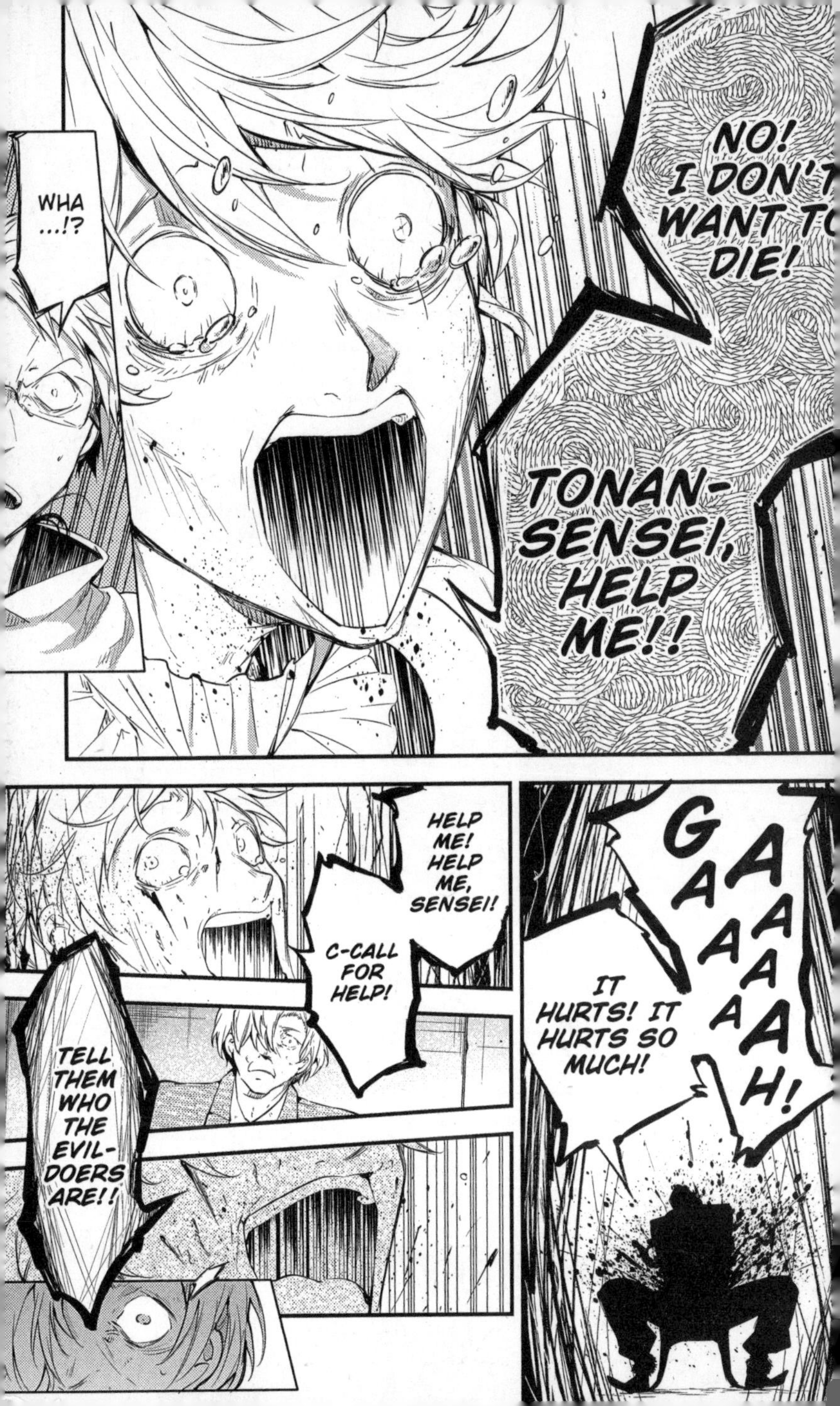
NO! I DON'T WANT TO DIE!
WHA ...!?
TONAN-SENSEI, HELP ME!!
GAAAAAAAAH!
IT HURTS! IT HURTS SO MUCH!
HELP ME! HELP ME, SENSEI!
C-CALL FOR HELP!
TELL THEM WHO THE EVIL-DOERS ARE!!

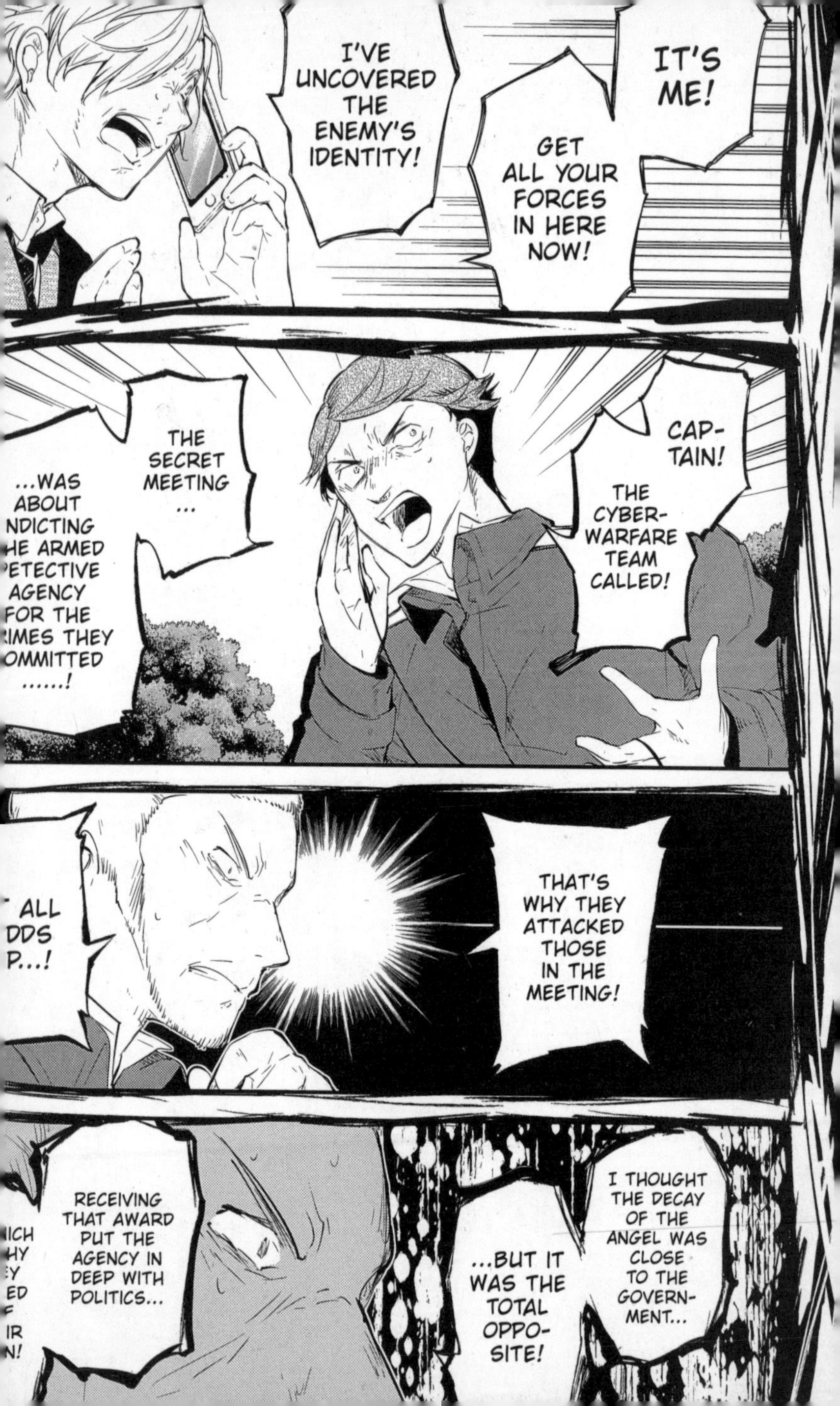
IT'S ME!
I'VE UNCOVERED THE ENEMY'S IDENTITY!
GET ALL YOUR FORCES IN HERE NOW!
CAP-TAIN!
THE CYBER-WARFARE TEAM CALLED!
THE SECRET MEETING ...
...WAS ABOUT NDICTING HE ARMED ETECTIVE AGENCY FOR THE IMES THEY OMMITTED ......!
THAT'S WHY THEY ATTACKED THOSE IN THE MEETING!
T ALL DDS P...!
I THOUGHT THE DECAY OF THE ANGEL WAS CLOSE TO THE GOVERN-MENT...
...BUT IT WAS THE TOTAL OPPO-SITE!
RECEIVING THAT AWARD PUT THE AGENCY IN DEEP WITH POLITICS...
ICH HY Y ED F IR N!

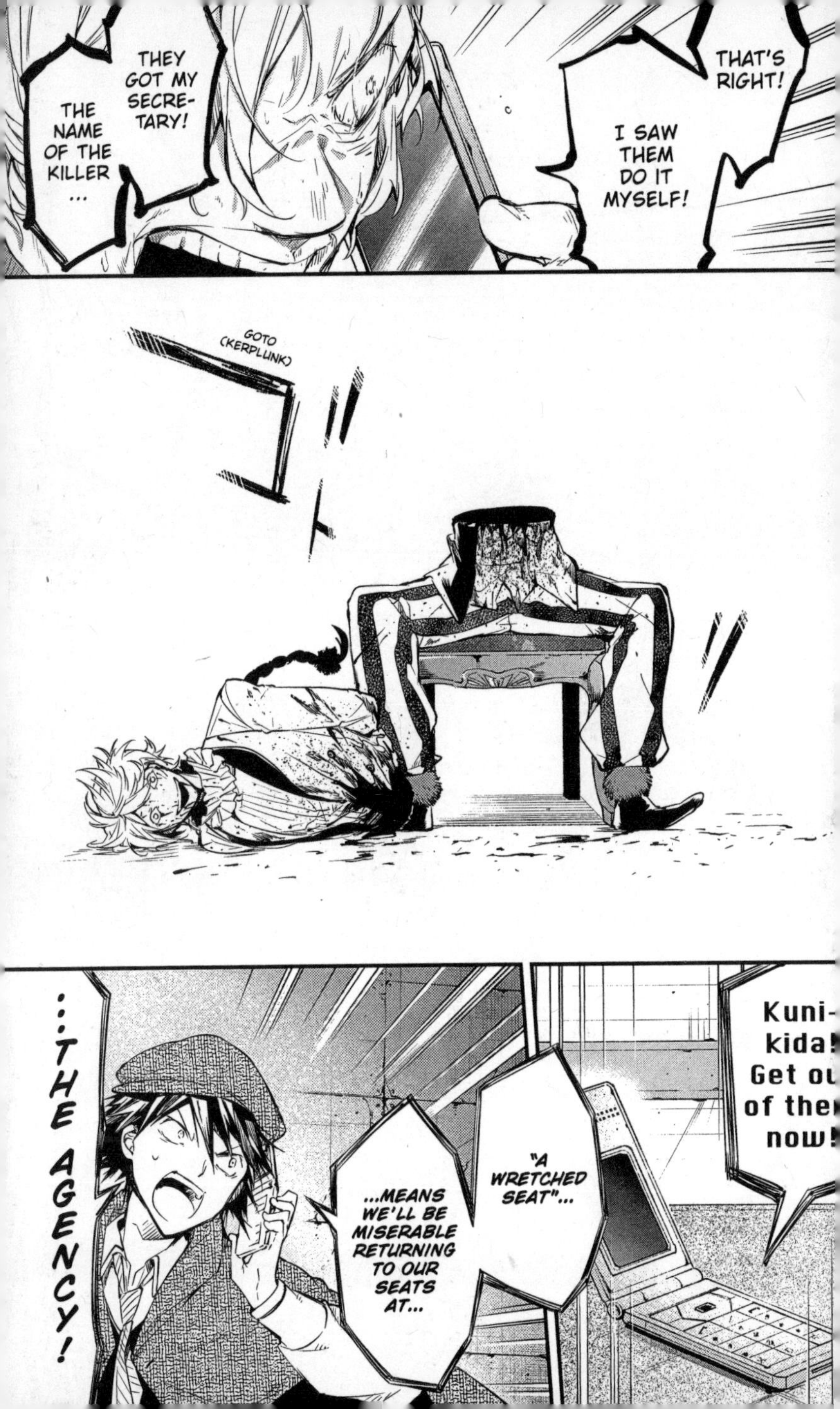
THAT'S RIGHT!
I SAW THEM DO IT MYSELF!
THEY GOT MY SECRE-TARY!
THE NAME OF THE KILLER ...
GOTO (KERPLUNK)
Kuni-kida! Get ou of the now!
"A WRETCHED SEAT"...
...MEANS WE'LL BE MISERABLE RETURNING TO OUR SEATS AT...
...THE AGENCY!

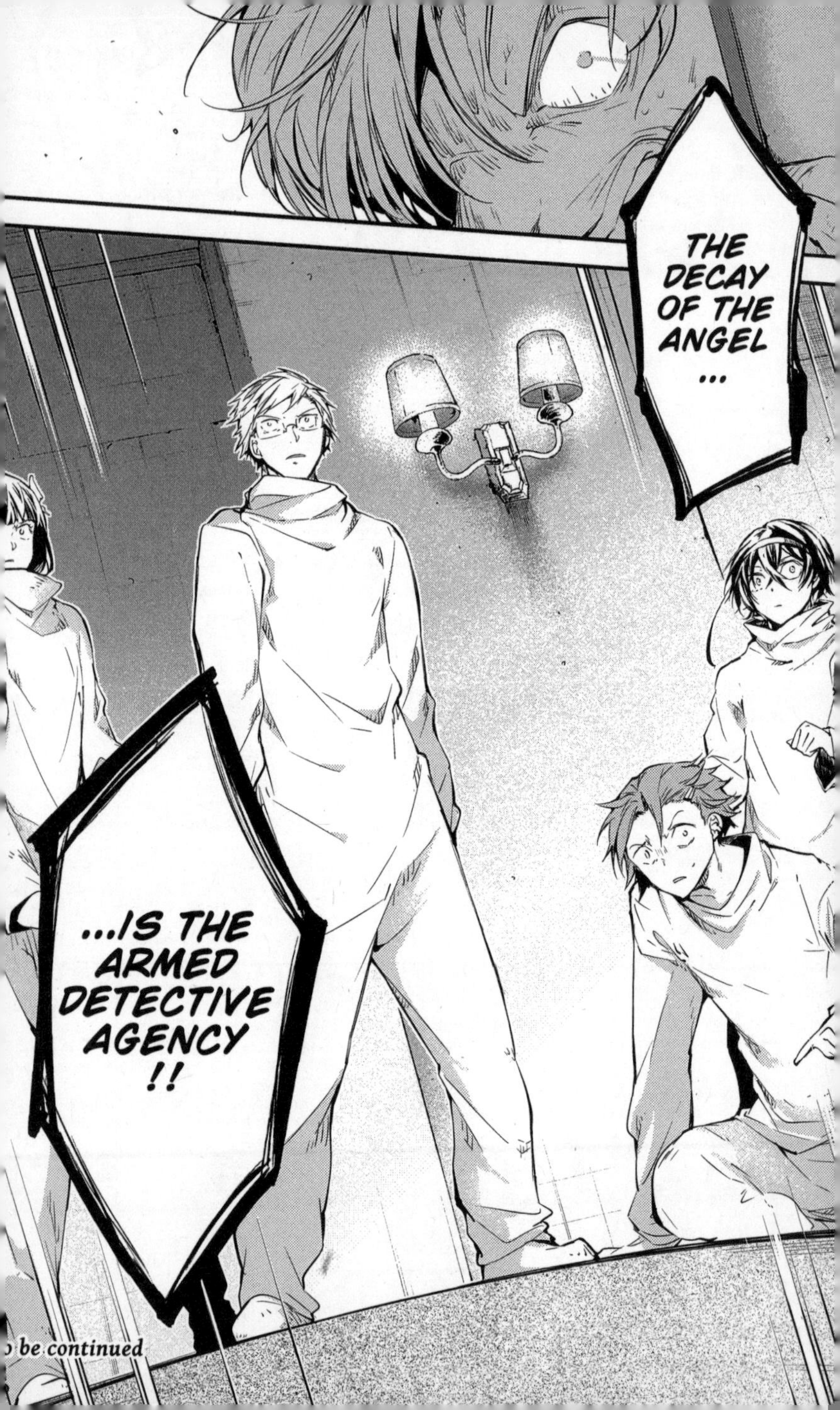
THE DECAY OF THE ANGEL ...
...IS THE ARMED DETECTIVE AGENCY !!
o be continued

Translation Notes

Inside cover
The **"Repeat This Ten Times" quiz** is a well-known Japanese word game where one person makes their companion repeat a word ten times quickly and then asks a question that's subsequently easy to flub the answer to. The classic example, replayed on this page, involves having the target repeat "pizza" ten times, then pointing at your elbow and asking the other player to identify it. Often, the replier will try to answer "elbow" (*hiji*) but end up saying "knee" (*hiza*) instead since their mind is still on "pizza."

Another well-known one is making the other party repeat "chandelier" (*shanderia*) ten times before naming the "fairy-tale character who ate a poison apple." The answer is "Snow White" (*shirayuki-hime*), but it's easy to accidentally say "Cinderella" (*shinderera*) instead.

Page 33
Kindaichi, or Kousuke Kindaichi, is a young fictional detective created by Japan's well-known mystery novelist, Seishi Yokomizo.

Page 96
The Decay of the Angel is the last novel in Yukio Mishima's collection, The Sea of Fertility, which is a series about a man who follows his friend's journey of reincarnation.

The Japanese title of *The Decay of the Angel*—*Tennin Gosui*—means "the five ways a celestial being decays," so the importance of the organization having five members is more readily apparent in Japanese. While some meaning is lost, this translation uses the official English title to make it clear exactly which literary work is being referenced.

BUNGO STRAY DOGS

Story: *Kafka Asagiri*   Art: *Sango Harukawa*

Translation: Kevin Gifford   †   Lettering: Bianca Pistillo

This book is a work of fiction. Names, characters, places, and incidents are the product of the author's imagination or are used fictitiously. Any resemblance to actual events, locales, or persons, living or dead, is coincidental.

BUNGO STRAY DOGS Volume 14
©Kafka Asagiri 2017
©Sango Harukawa 2017
First published in Japan in 2017 by KADOKAWA CORPORATION, Tokyo.
English translation rights arranged with KADOKAWA CORPORATION, Tokyo through TUTTLE-MORI AGENCY, INC., Tokyo.

English translation © 2020 by Yen Press, LLC

Yen Press
150 West 30th Street, 19th Floor
New York, NY 10001

Visit us at yenpress.com
facebook.com/yenpress
twitter.com/yenpress
yenpress.tumblr.com
instagram.com/yenpress

First Yen Press Edition: March 2020

Yen Press is an imprint of Yen Press, LLC.
The Yen Press name and logo are trademarks of Yen Press, LLC.

Library of Congress Control Number: 2016956681

ISBNs: 978-1-9753-0458-4 (paperback)
       978-1-9753-0459-1 (ebook)

10 9 8 7 6 5 4 3 2 1

BVG

Printed in the United States of America